JOURNAL FOR THE STUDY OF THE NEW TESTAMENT
SUPPLEMENT SERIES

259

Editor
Mark Goodacre

Women in Mark's Gospel

Susan Miller

T & T CLARK INTERNATIONAL
A Continuum imprint
LONDON • NEW YORK

Copyright © 2004 T&T Clark International
A Continuum imprint

Published by T&T Clark International
The Tower Building, 11 York Road, London SE1 7NX
15 East 26th Street, Suite 1703, New York, NY 10010

www.tandtclark.com

British Library Cataloguing-in-Publication Data
A catalogue record for this book is available from the British Library

Library of Congress Cataloging-in-Publication Data
A catalogue record for this book is available from the Library of Congress

Typeset by ISB Typesetting, Sheffield
Printed on acid-free paper in Great Britain by Cromwell Press, Trowbridge, Wiltshire

ISBN 0-567-08053-6 (hardback)
       0-567-08063-3 (paperback)

CONTENTS

PREFACE

I have received several scholarships to undertake this research, and I would like to thank the Scottish Awards Agency for the award of a Research Studentship. I would also like to thank Dr Moyna McGlynn for her help in arranging financial support for my studies at Boston University, School of Theology. I am grateful for the award of the May Orr Scholarship given by Hamilton Old Parish Church, and the grant of the Ferguson Bequest Scholarship. I would also like to thank the Church of Scotland for the award of the Kerr Travelling Scholarship.

My family has encouraged me throughout the time I have been writing this book, and I would like to thank my parents, Jean and Harry Miller, and my sister Jane and brother-in-law Brian and their children, Emma and Alice, for their help and support.

My thanks are given to my supervisor, Prof. Joel Marcus, for introducing me to Mark's Gospel, and Prof. John Riches and Prof. John Barclay and the members of the Postgraduate Biblical Studies Seminar at Glasgow University, especially Dr Alistair May and Dr Karen Wenell, for creating a stimulating environment to study the New Testament.

I would also like to thank Joel Marcus for continuing to read drafts of this thesis in Glasgow, Boston and Durham, and his wife, Gloria and daughter, Rachel for welcoming me in Boston and Durham. I am grateful for his careful reading of my work and for his wisdom, encouragement and friendship.

ABBREVIATIONS

AB	Anchor Bible
ABD	David Noel Freedman (ed.), *The Anchor Bible Dictionary* (New York: Doubleday, 1992)
ABR	*Australian Biblical Review*
ABRL	Anchor Bible Reference Library
AJT	*American Journal of Theology*
AnBib	Analecta biblica
BETL	Bibliotheca ephemeridum theologicarum lovaniensium
Bib	*Biblica*
BibInt	*Biblical Interpretation: A Journal of Contemporary Approaches*
BJS	Brown Judaic Studies
BT	*The Bible Translator*
BTB	*Biblical Theology Bulletin*
BZ	*Biblische Zeitschrift*
CBQ	*Catholic Biblical Quarterly*
CGTC	Cambridge Greek Testament Commentary
CP	*Classical Philology*
CrossCurr	*Cross Currents*
DDD	*Dictionary of Deities and Demons in the Bible*, K. van der Toorn, B. Becking and P.W. van der Horst (eds.) (Leiden: E.J. Brill, 1995)
EcumRev	*Ecumenical Review*
EDNT	H. Balz and G. Schneider (eds.), *Exegetical Dictionary of the New Testament* (ET; Grand Rapids: Eerdmans, 1990–93)
EEC	E. Ferguson (ed.), *Encyclopaedia of Early Christianity* (New York: Garland Publishing, 2nd edn, 1990)
EKKNT	Evangelisch-Katholischer Kommentar zum Neuen Testament
EncJud	*Encyclopaedia Judaica*
ExpTim	*Expository Times*
HTKNT	Herders theologischer Kommentar zum Neuen Testament
IBS	*Irish Biblical Studies*
IEJ	*Israel Exploration Journal*
Int	*Interpretation*
JAAR	*Journal of the American Academy of Religion*
JBL	*Journal of Biblical Literature*
JJS	*Journal of Jewish Studies*
JR	*Journal of Religion*
JSNT	*Journal for the Study of the New Testament*
*JSNT*Sup	*Journal for the Study of the New Testament*, Supplement Series
JSOT	*Journal for the Study of the Old Testament*
JTS	*Journal of Theological Studies*
JTSA	*Journal of Theology for Southern Africa*
NCB	New Century Bible
NedTT	*Nederlands theologisch tijdschrift*

Neot	*Neotestamentica*
NICNT	New International Commentary on the New Testament
NovT	*Novum Testamentum*
NTS	*New Testament Studies*
SBL	Society of Biblical Literature
SBLDS	SBL Dissertation Series
SBLSP	SBL Seminar Papers
SBM	Stuttgarter biblische Monographien
SJT	*Scottish Journal of Theology*
SNTSMS	Society for New Testament Studies Monograph Series
SNTW	Studies of the New Testament and its World
TDNT	Gerhard Kittel and Gerhard Friedrich (eds.), *Theological Dictionary of the New Testament* (trans. Geoffrey W. Bromiley; 10 vols.; Grand Rapids: Eerdmans, 1964–)
TynBul	*Tyndale Bulletin*
WBC	Word Biblical Commentary
ZNW	*Zeitschrift für die neutestamentliche Wissenschaft und die Kunde der älteren Kirche*

Chapter 1

INTRODUCTION

1. *Recent Research on Women in Mark*

Feminist scholarship has developed a variety of approaches to the study of the New Testament, both in the recovery of narratives that feature women and in the analysis of the formation of the texts. Feminist interpretation of Mark's Gospel has included a wide range of issues from the historical position of women in the first century,[1] the use of the text to construct gender[2] and the theological examination of Christian doctrines,[3] but there has not yet been an analysis of all the female characters in Mark's Gospel. This study aims to interpret narratives that feature female characters, and to determine the distinctive role of women in Mark's world-view. Later in this chapter and throughout the study our analysis will demonstrate that his world-view is characterized by apocalyptic eschatology.

Previous scholarship has focused on the twelve male disciples in the interpretation of discipleship in Mark.[4] This analysis, however, seeks to examine the role of women who follow Jesus in order to contribute to a deeper understanding of discipleship for both women and men. Mark's portrayal of women will be explored in the context of his understanding of humanity within his expectations of the end-time. It is hoped that an analysis of Mark's presentation of women will lead to further insights into the role of women in his community and within the development of Christianity. An initial study of women within Mark's world-view may also contribute to a feminist analysis of Mark's theology.

Several articles have highlighted the positive portrayal of individual women in the healing narratives such as Peter's mother-in-law (1.29–31), the woman with the

---

1. M. Fander, *Die Stellung der Frau im Markusevangelium. Unter besonderer Berück-sichtigung kultur- und religionsgeschichtlicher Hintergründe* (Münsteraner Theologische Abhand-lungen, 8; Altenberge: Telos, 1989).

2. S.L. Graham, 'Silent Voices: Women in the Gospel of Mark', *Semeia* 54 (1991), 145–58; J. Glancy, 'Unveiling Masculinity: The Construction of Gender in Mark 6.17-29', *BibInt* 2 (1994), 34–50; A. Bach, *Women, Seduction and Betrayal in Biblical Narrative* (Cambridge: Cambridge University Press, 1997), 210–62.

3. J.M. Hopkins, *Towards a Feminist Christology* (London: SPCK, 1995), 37–47; R.N. Brock, *Journeys by Heart: a Christology of Erotic Power* (New York: Crossroad, 1988).

4. K.G. Reploh, *Markus, Lehrer der Gemeinde* (SBM, 9; Stuttgart: Katholisches Bibelwerk, 1969); K. Stock, *Boten aus dem Mit-Ihm-Sein. Das Verhältnis zwischen Jesus und den Zwölf nach Markus* (AnBib 70; Rome: Pontifical Biblical Institute, 1975); E. Best, *Disciples and Discipleship* (Edinburgh: T. & T. Clark, 1986).

flow of blood (5.21–43) and the Syrophoenician woman (7.24–30), and women are interpreted as models of discipleship in the account of the poor widow (12.41–44) and the woman who anoints Jesus (14.3–9). Schmitt[5] and Beavis,[6] for example, regard the women as examples of faith and discipleship, and Kopas[7] and Gill[8] emphasize the sacrificial actions of women. Other scholars, such as Swartley, have taken a literary approach, noting the association of women with key themes in the Gospel including the call to faith (5.24–34), the Gentile mission (7.24–30), true piety (12.41–44) and Jesus' suffering and death (14.3–9).[9]

The positive portrayal of women in these accounts has led some commentators to compare the women favourably to the male disciples, particularly the twelve disciples chosen by Jesus. Schüssler Fiorenza argues that the group of women who are described as being present at the crucifixion (15.40–41) are portrayed as 'true disciples', whereas the twelve male disciples flee at Jesus' arrest (14.50).[10] Similarly, Myers interprets the presence of the women at the cross as an indication of their discipleship, and he proposes that Mark's account of the faithfulness of these women reflects his intention to criticize patriarchal society.[11] He argues that the women who are among the 'last' in society become the 'first' to receive the news of the resurrection.

The negative features of the twelve male disciples are emphasized in Mark's Gospel. The Twelve are criticized for their fear and lack of faith (4.40; 6.50). Although the Twelve are constantly with Jesus, they fail to understand him (6.52; 8.17–21). They argue over which one of them is to be regarded as the greatest (9.33–37), and James and John seek the positions of influence and power next to Jesus in the kingdom of God (10.35–45). Judas, one of the Twelve, betrays Jesus, and the leading disciple, Peter, denies him three times (14.66–72). The male disciples flee at the arrest of Jesus (14.50) and no member of the Twelve is present at the crucifixion of Jesus.

Some scholars have looked for historical reasons behind the negative portrayal of the Twelve. Weeden believes that the Twelve represent a false Christology, since they regard Jesus as a divine man rather than the suffering Messiah.[12] Tyson, moreover, suggests that Mark is writing to discredit the Jerusalem church by using the Twelve to represent the false views of the Jerusalem leadership.[13] On the other hand a narrative reading is given by Tannehill, who proposes that Mark's audience is

5.   J.J. Schmitt, 'Women in Mark's Gospel: An Early Christian View of Woman's Role', *BT* 19 (1981), 231.
6.   M.A. Beavis, 'Women as Models of Faith in Mark', *BTB* 18 (1988), 8.
7.   J. Kopas, 'Jesus and Women in Mark's Gospel', *Review for Religious* 44 (1985), 920.
8.   A. Gill, 'Women Ministers in the Gospel of Mark', *ABR* 35 (1987), 20.
9.   W.M. Swartley, 'The Role of Women in Mark's Gospel: A Narrative Analysis', *BTB* 27 (1997), 20.
10.   E. Schüssler Fiorenza, *In Memory of Her: A Feminist Theological Reconstruction of Christian Origins* (New York: Crossroad, 1985), 320–22.
11.   C. Myers, *Binding the Strong Man: A Political Reading of Mark's Story of Jesus* (Maryknoll, NY: Orbis Books, 1988), 396–97.
12.   T.J. Weeden, 'The Heresy that Necessitated Mark's Gospel', *ZNW* 59 (1968), 145–58.
13.   J.B. Tyson, 'The Blindness of the Disciples in Mark', *JBL* 80 (1961), 261–68.

first intended to identify with the disciples, and then to reject their failures in order to follow the example of Jesus.[14] These studies, however, ignore the positive accounts of the disciples who leave everything to follow Jesus (1.16–20; 10.28–30), and they disregard the desire of Jesus to be reunited with his disciples in Galilee (14.28; 16.7). Best takes a more favourable view of the male disciples, and he is convincing in his argument that Mark writes with a pastoral purpose.[15] As he points out, the failures of the Twelve are used by Jesus as an opportunity to teach the true nature of discipleship (9.35–37; 10.42–45).

Throughout the Gospel Mark focuses on the twelve male disciples who accompany Jesus, and he does not mention the group of women who follow Jesus until the crucifixion (15.40–41). These women have followed and served Jesus in Galilee and travelled with him to Jerusalem. Munro asserts that Mark has intentionally concealed their presence because he is uneasy with the prominence of women in the early church, and he is attempting to downplay their role in Jesus' mission.[16] Mark refers to the women now, only because they serve as witnesses to the events of the crucifixion, burial and resurrection of Jesus. According to Munro, Mark's Gospel suggests that Jesus carried out his mission accompanied by a small group of male disciples, and Jesus meets women only in the private sphere of the home (1.29–31; 5.35–43; 7.24–30; 14.3–9).[17] Munro's analysis highlights the prominent role of the Twelve and the absence of accounts that describe the female followers of Jesus. Dewey, moreover, proposes that the women are employed as foils to the male disciples.[18] In her view Mark uses stories that feature women only as they are required by the plot and as examples of teaching addressed to men. The distinctive role of women, however, may be lost by concentrating on a comparison between the women and the Twelve.

There have been three full-length monographs written on the role of women in Mark's Gospel. Fander aims to interpret the portrayal of women in Mark's Gospel as a contribution to the historical assessment of the role of women within early Christianity.[19] She interprets the role of women in the context of Theissen's theories of the division of the early Christian communities into wandering charismatics and settled supporters, arguing that women are not missionaries, but primarily representatives of the communities who support the male disciples.[20] Kinukawa also explores the role of women within their social and historical setting, writing from a Japanese feminist perspective, and aiming to relate the accounts of women in Mark

---

14. R.C. Tannehill, 'The Disciples in Mark: The Function of a Narrative Role', *JR* 57 (1977), 386–405.

15. E. Best, 'The Role of the Disciples in Mark', *NTS* 23 (1977), 399.

16. W. Munro, 'Women Disciples in Mark?', *CBQ* 44 (1982), 234–36.

17. Munro, 'Women Disciples', 227–29.

18. J. Dewey, 'The Gospel of Mark', in E. Schüssler Fiorenza (ed.), *Searching the Scriptures*, 2 (New York: Crossroad, 1994), 508.

19. Fander, *Stellung*, 9–10.

20. Fander, *Stellung*, 320–22. For an analysis of Theissen's interpretation of the Jesus movement see G. Theissen, *The First Followers of Jesus: a Sociological Analysis of the Earliest Christianity* (London: SCM Press, 1978) and *Social Reality and the Early Christians. Theology, Ethics, and the World of the New Testament* (Edinburgh: T. & T. Clark, 1993), 33–93.

to the experiences of women in present-day society in Japan.[21] Kinukawa differentiates between Jesus' acceptance of women and Mark's androcentric perspective, and she proposes that Mark concludes with the silence of the women because he wishes to avoid offending the male members of his audience by portraying the women more favourably than the male disciples.[22]

The third monograph is by Mitchell, who takes a feminist-literary approach to the account of the fear and silence of the women at the empty tomb.[23] She interprets the women's fear positively as religious awe suggesting that their silence is a literary device intended to encourage the second generation of Christians who form Mark's audience to cross the 'threshold of faith'. Other scholars, such as Malbon, have also developed a literary interpretation of the Gospel, but she argues that the women are not presented as the true disciples in comparison with the men.[24] The male disciples flee at the arrest of Jesus (14.50), but the women stand at a distance at the crucifixion and they are described as fearful at the tomb. Malbon proposes that both women and men are 'fallible followers' of Jesus, and the female characters are intended to complement the portrayal of the male disciples. Tolbert interprets Mark in the context of the parable of the sower (4.1–20).[25] In her view, the male disciples and the group of women at the crucifixion all fail as disciples, but the women and the men in the healing accounts who respond to Jesus in faith are among those who represent the seed sown on good ground.

The literary approaches of Mitchell, Malbon and Tolbert are helpful in their aim to interpret the role of women in the context of the narrative unity of the Gospel. They fail in their analysis of the role of women, however, as they do not take into account Mark's understanding of humanity. Robinson[26] and Kee[27] point to the apocalyptic context of the Gospel in which human beings are caught up in the intensification of the conflict between God and evil as the earth moves towards the end-time. In his analysis of Mark's apocalyptic eschatology, Marcus argues that Jesus, the Son of God, comes to liberate human beings from evil and inaugurate the new age.[28] Through the death of Jesus the new creation begins, and will be fully realized at the parousia.

Mark's portrayal of the disciples, moreover, is influenced by his apocalyptic world-view. Freyne compares the disciples to the *maskilim* in Daniel who are given

---

21. H. Kinukawa, *Women and Jesus in Mark: a Japanese Feminist Perspective* (Maryknoll, NY: Orbis Books, 1994), 1.

22. Kinukawa, *Women*, 142.

23. J.L. Mitchell, *Beyond Fear and Silence: A Feminist-Literary Reading of Mark* (London: Continuum, 2001).

24. E.S. Malbon, 'Fallible Followers: Women and Men in the Gospel of Mark', *Semeia* 28 (1983), 29–48.

25. M.A. Tolbert, *Sowing the Gospel: Mark's World in Literary-Historical Perspective* (Minneapolis: Fortress Press, 1989), 181.

26. J.M. Robinson, *The Problem of History in Mark* (London: SCM Press, 1957), 28.

27. H.C. Kee, *Community of the New Age* (London: SCM Press, 1977), 176.

28. J. Marcus, *Mark 1–8: A New Translation with Introduction and Commentary* (AB 27; New York: Doubleday, 2000), 71–73.

special instructions about the meaning of the end-time.[29] In Daniel and Mark revelation is given by God, and the struggle to believe is part of the cosmic struggle against evil. In Mark the misunderstanding of the disciples arises through their unwillingness to follow Jesus on the way to the cross. No human being is able to understand the identity of Jesus until his death on the cross, when the Roman centurion recognizes him as the Son of God (15.39). Freyne's analysis offers insights into the ways in which the portrayal of the Twelve has been influenced by Mark's apocalyptic world-view. His work may be applied to the role of women because they are also caught up in the misunderstanding of the present age. Mark, however, describes the flight of the male disciples at the time of Jesus' arrest, whereas the women run away after the news of the resurrection (16.8). The misunderstanding of the followers of Jesus thus continues into the period between the resurrection and the parousia.

Our analysis of previous research on women in Mark has produced conflicting interpretations of Mark's attitude to women. Schüssler Fiorenza and Myers argue that Mark portrays the women as the 'true disciples'. Munro and Kinukawa believe that Mark writes from an androcentric perspective which downplays the historical role of female disciples in early Christianity. Other scholars, such as Malbon and Tolbert, highlight the positive portrayal of women in individual narratives. They raise the issue of whether the women are regarded as models of discipleship or as disciples in their own right. These commentators, however, have not examined the role of women within Mark's belief that his community is living at the turning point of the ages, which is a time of increasing evil as they await the parousia. The portrayal of women, and their relation to discipleship, therefore, will be explored in connection with Mark's expectations of the new age.

2. *Methodology*

This study aims to interpret Mark's portrayal of women in relation to his definition of discipleship and his understanding of the new creation. The historical-critical method will be adopted in order to examine Mark's intentions behind his presentation of women within his apocalyptic world-view. The narratives that feature female characters will be examined in order to discern the distinctive role of women within Mark's Gospel. These accounts will also be analysed in the context of the Gospel as a narrative unity in order to determine the ways in which Mark's presentation of women develops throughout the Gospel.

Each account will be interpreted in relation to three sub-headings:

1. The portrayal of women will be examined in their social and historical setting. This sub-heading will assess the ways in which women are introduced and described, the use of names and references to family relationships. The work of women, their financial autonomy and their role in society will be

29. S. Freyne, 'The Disciples in Mark and the *Maskilim* in Daniel. A Comparison', *JSNT* 16 (1982), 7–23.

analysed, and we will also explore the role of women in relation to the Law
and to the religious and political authorities.

2.   The role of women will be examined in the context of Mark's understanding
     of discipleship. The relationship of women to the Twelve and Mark's distinc-
     tive presentation of the discipleship of women will be explored.

3.   A final sub-heading will analyse the ways in which narratives that feature
     women are integrated into Mark's apocalyptic world-view. The role of
     women will be explored in connection with Mark's account of Jesus as a
     male Messiah and Son of God. The portrayal of women will also be exam-
     ined in relation to Mark's concept of redemption and of new creation.
     Mark's attitude to patriarchy will be analysed in the context of his under-
     standing of the new age.

A Feminist Reading of Mark

Feminist interpretation involves a wide range of approaches and methodologies in
the analysis of the New Testament.[30] Some scholars examine positive and negative
representations of women within the texts, and other critics aim to reconstruct the
historical role of women in the development of early Christianity. Feminist interpreters explore the ways in which the texts construct gender and assess the theology
of the Gospels from a feminist perspective. Womanist theologians have widened
the scope of feminist interpretation by highlighting the interrelationship between
gender, race and social context.[31] Feminist critics also raise the issue of the ethics
of biblical interpretation both in connection with the methodology employed and in
the social context of scholarship. They highlight the ways in which biblical texts
are rhetorical discourses, which may be used to support current values in society or
to effect change. [32]

Although feminist interpretation is varied, one common focus is the desire to
oppose structures within society which oppress women and to support the empowerment of women. Feminist theology has a liberationist perspective seeking to trans-
form society and to move beyond patriarchy. The present study takes a feminist
approach in that the purpose of the analysis of women in Mark's Gospel is to assess
the extent to which Mark's portrayal of discipleship is inclusive and the ways in
which his understanding of the new creation is liberating for women and men.
Previous scholarship has focused on the male disciples, and Mark's concept of discipleship has been examined primarily with reference to his portrayal of the Twelve.
This thesis seeks to recover the distinctive role of women in the Gospel and to

---

30.   For an analysis of feminist scholarship, see Y. Sherwood, 'Feminist Scholarship', in *The
Oxford Illustrated History of the Bible* (Oxford: Oxford University Press, 2001), 296–315.

31.   For a range of articles by women from the Two-Thirds World, see P.A Bird, K.D. Sakenfeld
and S.H. Ringe (eds.), *Reading the Bible as Women: Perspectives from Africa, Asia, and Latin
America* (Semeia 78; Atlanta: SBL, 1997).

32.   E. Schüssler Fiorenza, 'Defending the Center, Trivialising the Margins', in H. Räisänen
(ed.), *Reading the Bible in the Global Village* (Atlanta: Scholars Press, 2000), 29–48. See also E.
Schüssler Fiorenza, 'The Ethics of Biblical Interpretation: Decentering Biblical Scholarship', *JBL*
107 (1988), 3–17.

examine discipleship from the perspective of Mark's portrayal of female characters. The extent to which a focus on women contributes to a deeper understanding of Mark's presentation of discipleship and new creation will be explored.

Feminist scholars have noted the androcentric features of the New Testament texts. The women in Mark are portrayed from the perspective of a male author who is responsible for both the selection and presentation of the material in the Gospel. Mark's text is also androcentric in that the male is considered to be the norm, and androcentric language is used as in the use of masculine plural terms which may conceal the presence of women. For these reasons it is necessary to examine the text carefully in order to determine where women are present. Scholars, such as Schüssler Fiorenza, have developed a 'hermeneutics of suspicion' aiming to read behind the text to discover the historical role of women in the Jesus movement.[33] She argues that women are directly cited only when they are exceptional or their actions are problematic, and she proposes that we should assume women are present unless the text explicitly excludes them. This strategy, however, risks distorting the portrayal of women by including their presence in accounts where it is not intended by the author.

Our analysis, moreover, does not aim to reconstruct the role of the women who followed the historical Jesus as Schüssler Fiorenza's does. This study focuses on the level of Mark's portrayal of women examining whether or not Mark intends to include women within masculine inclusive terms such as μαθηταὶ 'disciples'. We will explore the extent to which Mark's presentation of discipleship is inclusive of women and also the degree to which his portrayal of women is liberating in the context of the patriarchal society of the first century. This study will examine Mark's definition of liberation within the text, and seek to discern the ways in which first-century women in Mark's audience would respond to the gospel.

The work of feminist scholars raises the issue of the authority of the biblical writings. Schüssler Fiorenza gives priority to the historical Jesus and his first followers and reads the texts in order to find evidence of the egalitarian nature of the first Christians.[34] Kinukawa also wishes to recover traditions describing the positive interactions between women and Jesus because she believes that Mark has begun to downplay the role of women in the context of the repatriarchalization of the gospel.[35] Other critics have adopted a 'liberationist approach' searching for traces within the texts which challenge the androcentric nature of the writing. Dewey, for example, writes with the aim of exposing the 'androcentrism of the text' and of highlighting the 'liberating egalitarian vision of the gospel'.[36] She argues that Mark's portrayal of women does not support his egalitarian view of community, since women only appear as models of discipleship for men or as they are required by the plot.[37] Dewey raises the question of the relationship between Mark's portrayal of

33. Schüssler Fiorenza, *In Memory*, 41–60.
34. Schüssler Fiorenza, *In Memory*, 41.
35. Kinukawa, *Women*, 142.
36. Dewey, 'Mark', 470–509.
37. Dewey, 'Mark', 508.

women and his presentation of the gospel and we will explore this issue in our study.

The purpose of our analysis is to take a feminist approach to the interpretation of the Gospel and to examine the role of women within Mark's theology. Kitzberger, however, notes the tension between feminist interpretation and theology in her work on the Gospel of John.[38] As she observes, feminist interpretation involves a critical stance towards the text requiring a distancing from the text. On the other hand a theological analysis reflects a desire to empathize with the text. Theological interpretation involves reading the text as a 'document of faith' which reveals insights into the nature of God. Furthermore, we will return to the issue of the relationship between feminist interpretation and theology after our examination of the exegesis of Mark at the end of our analysis.

This study will employ the historical-critical method, but with the awareness that all interpreters are influenced by their presuppositions and there is no such thing as a completely objective examination of a text.[39] All scholars approach texts with questions, and these concerns form the impetus for research, and may lead to an increased engagement with the text.[40] The questions themselves influence the direction of the research, but they should not prejudice the results. The historical-critical method, moreover, enables presuppositions to be challenged or even over-turned. An understanding of Mark's social and historical context is required for our assessment of Mark's attitude to the patriarchal society of the first century. The his-torical-critical method is therefore helpful in highlighting the differences between Mark's portrayal of women in their social and historical context, and the lives of women in present-day society. The historical-critical method is employed in order to prevent reading current situations into Mark's text, and to avoid an uncritical application of Mark's Gospel to present-day society.

The analysis of the role of women in the New Testament also encounters the dif-ficulty of assessing the relationship between Jesus and Judaism. Scholars, such as Plaskow, warn of the danger of denigrating the position of first-century Jewish women in order to highlight the liberating practice of Jesus.[41] She notes that some scholars, such as Swidler, have attempted to reconstruct the lives of Jewish women in the first century by using evidence from the Mishnah.[42] Although the Mishnah may contain some early traditions, it is difficult to assess the dates of these tradi-tions. The Mishnah, moreover, is written from the perspective of male scholars, and Wegner points out that it may reflect male ideals of women rather than giving

---

38. I.R. Kitzberger, ' "How Can This Be?" (John 3:9): A Feminist Theological Re-Reading of the Gospel of John', in F.F. Segovia (ed.), *'What is John?'*, 2 (Atlanta: Scholars Press, 1998), 19–41.

39. E. Schüssler Fiorenza, *Bread not Stone: the Challenge of Feminist Biblical Interpretation* (Boston: Beacon Press, 1984), 93–115.

40. R. Bultmann, 'Is Exegesis Without Presuppositions Possible?', in *New Testament and Mythology and Other Basic Writings* (London: SCM Press, 1985), 145–53.

41. J. Plaskow, 'Anti-Judaism in Feminist Christian Interpretation', in E. Schüssler Fiorenza (ed.), *Searching the Scriptures*, 1 (New York: Crossroad, 1993), 119–20.

42. L. Swidler, *Biblical Affirmations of Woman* (Philadelphia: Westminster Press, 1979).

an accurate picture of women's lives.[43] As she observes, in the Mishnah the autonomy and the dependency of a woman is defined by whether or not a man has
control of her biological function.[44]

Furthermore, Levine points out that Jesus and the women who followed him
were ethnically and culturally Jewish.[45] Levine challenges the portrayal of Second
Temple Judaism as monolithically restrictive for the lives of women.[46] As Ilan
records, moreover, the lives of women during the Second Temple period were
diverse. She notes that Jewish society was varied, and that different groups adhered
to different interpretations of the Law.[47] Many of the sources advocating the seclu-
sion of women originate in the upper classes of society (cf. Sir. 42.11–12; 2 Macc.
3.19; Philo, *Spec. Leg.* 3.169; *Flacc.* 89). These regulations are more likely to have
been followed by the wealthy who could afford houses with separate living quarters
for women. On the other hand the majority of poorer women, female servants and
slaves may have been required to work outside the household.

The research of these scholars indicates the problems in examining the portrayal
of women in the written sources from the Greco-Roman world. As Pomeroy observes, the focus of history has been upon the military and political action of men
and on their intellectual history and the everyday lives of a large proportion of the
population have not been recorded.[48] Most extant formal literature is written by
men and there are only fragments of lyric poetry by women.[49] In addition Plaskow
notes that one of the difficulties in developing Jewish feminist theology is the
absence of accounts of women within the tradition.[50] There is little written evidence of the daily lives of women who are not part of the higher social groups. In
fact the Gospel texts are one of the few sources which portray the lives of women
who inhabited the villages and towns of first-century Galilee.

The Jesus movement arose during the occupation of Palestine by the Romans,
and Mark's Gospel is written around the time of the Jewish War (66–72 CE). This
historical context leads Schottroff to argue that the Jesus movement should not be
regarded as a renewal movement within Judaism, since this description implies that
the Jesus movement aimed to liberate human beings from unjust situations within
Judaism. She prefers to focus on the liberation of the Jewish people from the

43. J.R. Wegner, *Chattel or Person? The Status of Women in the Mishnah* (Oxford: Oxford
University Press, 1988), 4.

44. Wegner (*Chattel or Person?*, 14–17) divides her study of women in the Mishnah into an
analysis of three categories of autonomous women (the unmarried woman over the age of twelve
and a half, the divorcee and the widow) and three categories of dependent women (the minor
daughter, the wife and the Levirate widow).

45. A.-J. Levine, 'Second Temple Judaism, Jesus, and Women: Yeast of Eden', *BibInt* 2
(1994), 12–13.

46. Levine, 'Second Temple Judaism', 12–13.

47. T. Ilan, *Jewish Women in Greco-Roman Palestine* (Peabody, MA: Hendrickson, 1996), 228.

48. S.B. Pomeroy, *Goddesses, Whores, Wives and Slaves: Women in Classical Antiquity*
(London: Halle, 1976), ix.

49. Pomeroy, *Goddesses*, x.

50. J. Plaskow, *Standing at Sinai: Judaism from a Feminist Perspective* (San Francisco:
Harpers, 1991), 1.

political and economic oppression of the Romans.[51] In her view the starting point of the struggle for liberation is the suffering of the majority of the people, both women and men. Schottroff, moreover, wishes to avoid the possibility of idealizing the role of women in early Christian communities instead of examining their struggles for justice within a patriarchal society.[52] Schottroff's work raises the issue of which features of the Jesus movement particularly attracted women. In our analysis, therefore, we will examine Mark's portrayal of women in relation to their hopes and expectations of the kingdom of God.

A Literary Approach to Mark's Gospel
This study will interpret passages that feature women in the context of the narrative unity of the Gospel. In the past scholars believed that Mark's style of writing was unsophisticated on account of the simple vocabulary and sentence structure, the frequent use of parataxis and of the cognate accusative. These features, however, reflect a semitic influence and are reminiscent of the literary style within the Old Testament and the Septuagint. Mark, moreover, was not writing freely, but was working with the traditions he received. Mark's sources may include a pre-Markan passion narrative, and it is possible that he has also worked with collections of parables, controversy stories and miracle accounts.[53]

Mark's Gospel is a skilfully crafted narrative with a clear structure describing Jesus' mission in Galilee and the surrounding area, his journey to Jerusalem and the events of the Passion Narrative. Mark's creativity in the construction of his narrative has led Dewey to describe the Gospel as an 'interwoven tapestry'.[54] Mark employs identifiable literary techniques such as repetition, chiastic literary structures and intercalation which suggest that the Gospel is intended to be read aloud as a complete text. The Gospel could be read in the context of worship and some scholars have suggested that it was intended to be read at an Easter vigil service when new members were baptized.[55] The bleak ending of the Gospel with the fear and silence of the women suggests that Mark is not intended to be a missionary document. It appears more likely that the Gospel is written for a Christian audience rather than as material to evangelize others.

In Mark, Jesus teaches in parables which encourage his audience to approach him to discover their meaning (4.10–12). Mark's Gospel may be compared to a parable which relates the significance of Jesus' identity through the story of his mission, death and resurrection. Kermode interprets the experience of reading Mark's Gospel in relation to the parable theory (4.10–12), but according to his analysis the

---

51. L. Schottroff, *Lydia's Impatient Sisters: A Feminist Social History of Early Christianity* (Louisville: Westminster John Knox Press, 1995), 8.

52. Schottroff, *Lydia's Impatient Sisters*, 15.

53. Marcus, *Mark*, 57–59.

54. J. Dewey, 'Mark as Interwoven Tapestry: Forecasts and Echoes for a Listening Audience', *CBQ* 53 (1991), 221–36.

55. B. Standaert, *L'Évangile selon Marc. Composition et Genre Littéraire* (Nijmegen: Stichting Studentenpers, 1978).

reader remains outside the text unable to discern Mark's meaning.[56] Kermode, however, does not take account of the purpose of parables within Mark's apocalyptic world-view. Parables are prominent in apocalyptic texts and are associated with the revelation of God in *1 Enoch* 37–71 and *4 Ezra*. The parables have an eschatological focus, since they reveal God's purposes in the events of the end-time. In Mark parables function as part of Jesus' struggle against evil. They reveal the true reality of God's rule which is obscured by the rule of Satan on earth. Mark's text may be compared to a parable because it serves as a revelation of Jesus' identity as the Son of God and his inauguration of the new age. His writing is also parabolic, since we are drawn into the text in order to seek the deeper meaning of the gospel.

The Markan Community
This study will take a literary approach to the interpretation of the role of women in Mark, but not in such a way that the historical setting of the Gospel is ignored. The presentation of women in the Gospel, for example, may reflect the role of women in Mark's community. This issue is open to further analysis since Schierling[57] suggests that the positive portrayals of women imply that women have a leadership role in Mark's community, whereas other scholars, such as Gill,[58] believe that Mark aims to promote the role of women because the status of women is diminishing in his community. We will, therefore, seek to determine the historical situation of Mark's community in order to gain a deeper understanding of the role of women within it.

Commentators, such as Reploh, argue that Mark's Gospel may be interpreted as a two-level narrative in which we have an initial account of the earthly life of Jesus, and a second level which reflects the later concerns of Mark's community.[59] Dahl[60] and Juel[61] propose that Mark is writing for a complacent community to remind them of the demands of the gospel. As van Iersel notes, however, there are several indications that the community may be threatened with persecution (4.17; 10.29–30; 10.38–39), and additional passages suggest specific situations of persecution, in which a Christian may be threatened with death for the sake of Jesus and the gospel (3.28–29; 8.34–9.1; 9.42–48; 13.9–13).[62] These passages, therefore, lead van Iersel to believe that Mark's Gospel is written in view of persecutions which severely test the community's faith. This theory is supported by the frequent references to fear and faith in the healing accounts (5.33–34, 36; 9.23–24), and in the experiences of the Twelve on the boat journeys (4.40–41; 6.50). The struggle

---

56. F. Kermode, *The Genesis of Secrecy: On the Interpretation of Narrative* (Cambridge, MA: Harvard University Press, 1979), 23–47.

57. M.J. Schierling, 'Women as Leaders in the Marcan Communities', *Listening* 15 (1980), 250–56.

58. Gill, 'Women Ministers', 19.

59. Reploh, *Markus*, 228.

60. N.A. Dahl, 'The Purpose of Mark's Gospel', in C.M. Tuckett (ed.), *The Messianic Secret* (Philadelphia: Fortress Press, 1983), 32–33.

61. D.H. Juel, *A Master of Surprise: Mark Interpreted* (Minneapolis: Fortress Press, 1994), 88.

62. B.M.F. van Iersel, 'The Gospel according to St. Mark – Written for a Persecuted Community?', *NedTT* 34 (1980), 35.

between faith and fear is developed throughout the Gospel and culminates in the description of the terror of the women at the end of the Gospel (16.8). Barton thus notes the 'dark strenuous spirituality' of Mark, which does not avoid the experience of abandonment, and the sense of the absence of God.[63]

Scholars, such as Hengel, have argued that the location of Mark's community is Rome, partly on account of Papias' reference to Mark as the interpreter of Peter in Eusebius' *Hist. eccl.* 3.39.15 since Peter died in Rome, and also because of the persecutions of Christians under Nero at Rome in 64 CE.[64] Kee, however, suggests the location of Syria during the Jewish Revolt.[65] As Marcus points out, the events of chapter 13 which describe the claims of Messianic pretenders and the desolation of the Temple correspond to the events of the Jewish War (66–72 CE).[66] Mark may, then, be addressed to a marginalized community caught up in the midst of the struggle of the Jewish revolutionaries for freedom, and the retaliation of the Roman authorities. The women and men in the community read the events which are taking place around them as signs of the end-time struggle with evil (cf. 13.4–23).

Recently, however, Bauckham has argued that the Gospels, unlike Paul's letters, are not written for particular communities.[67] Paul's letters are addressed to distant communities, whereas the evangelists could respond to the concerns of their communities without writing.[68] According to Bauckham, the early Christian movement did not consist of isolated communities, but there was a strong network of communication with one another.[69] Bauckham's analysis downplays the differences between the Gospels, whereas Brown has identified a range of perspectives within Jewish Christianity and Gentile Christianity.[70] Brown's interpretation is supported by the differences between Mark and the other Synoptic Gospels. Mark, for example, is the only Gospel in which Jesus declares all food to be clean (7.19). Matthew omits this saying, and Luke does not include Mark (6.45–8.21) which relates the healing of the Gentile SyroPhoenician woman's daughter (7.24–30) and the feeding of the four thousand in Gentile land (8.1–10). Best, moreover, notes that Simon of Cyrene is identified by a reference to his sons, Alexander and Rufus (15.21).[71] As Best proposes, there is no need for Mark to mention these names unless they were known to Mark's community and both Matthew and Luke omit any reference to them. It is also possible that James and Joses, the sons of Mary, were known to Mark's community (15.40), since it is more usual for a woman to be identified by citing her husband's name or her father's name.

63. S.C. Barton, *The Spirituality of the Gospels* (London: SPCK, 1992), 63.

64. M. Hengel, *Studies in the Gospel of Mark* (Philadelphia: Fortress Press, 1985), 1–30.

65. Kee, *Community*, 100–105.

66. J. Marcus, 'The Jewish War and the *Sitz im Leben* of Mark', *JBL* 111 (1992), 446–48.

67. R. Bauckham, 'For Whom Were Gospels Written?', in R. Bauckham (ed.), *The Gospels for All Christians: Rethinking the Gospel Audiences* (Edinburgh: T. & T. Clark, 1998), 9–48.

68. Bauckham, 'For Whom', 28–29.

69. Bauckham, 'For Whom', 30.

70. R.E. Brown, 'Not Jewish Christianity and Gentile Christianity But Types of Jewish/Gentile Christianity', *CBQ* 45 (1983), 74–79.

71. E. Best, 'Mark's Readers: A Profile', in F. Van Segbroeck *et al.* (eds.), *The Four Gospels 1992: Festschrift Frans Neirynck* (BETL, 100; Leuven: Leuven University Press, 1992), II, 857.

In chapter 13 Jesus prophesies that the present generation will witness the end of the world (13.30). He teaches that the purpose of the disciples in the period between the resurrection and the parousia is to proclaim the gospel to all nations (13.10). Just as Jesus encountered opposition and rejection, the Markan community will also be persecuted (13.9), and Mark writes to strengthen the women and men in his community in the context of the persecution of the end-time in which there is an intensification of the struggle against evil. In the course of this study we will examine the role of women in relation to the Markan community's experience of opposition and persecution on account of their faith.

Mark's Understanding of New Creation
The portrayal of women in Mark will be examined within the context of Mark's apocalyptic world-view. Scholars, such as Rowland, argue that the apocalyptic movement may be defined by the focus on the 'direct revelation' of the mysteries of God to human beings.[72] As Collins points out, however, there is a distinction between the literary genre of the apocalypse, apocalypticism as a social ideology and apocalyptic eschatology as a range of concepts and motifs.[73] Collins suggests that Mark, the other Gospels and Paul contain apocalyptic eschatology.[74] Mark interprets the world in terms of two ages (10.30), which may be seen in other apocalyptic texts such as *4 Ezra* (6.7–10; 8.52).

Apocalyptic texts frequently compare the end-time to the beginning. The prophecies of Isaiah point forward to a new creation (Isa. 65.17; 66.22) and this concept is developed in apocalyptic texts and may also be seen in the writings of Paul (2 Cor. 5.17; Gal. 6.15) and in later texts such as *Barn.* 6. Russell observes that apocalyptic writings depict the world under the rule of Satan, and God will redeem not only human beings but the whole of creation.[75] The opening verse of Mark 'The beginning of the gospel of Jesus Christ' (Ἀρχὴ τοῦ εὐαγγελίου Ἰησοῦ Χριστοῦ, 1.1) recalls the opening of Genesis 'In the beginning' (Ἐν ἀρχῇ, Gen. 1.1 LXX). In chapter 13 Jesus describes the events of the end-time as the beginning of the birth pangs (ἀρχὴ ὠδίνων ταῦτα, 13.8), a standard apocalyptic term for the onset of the new age (Isa. 26.17; *1 Enoch* 62.4; *4 Ezra* 4.42; Rev. 12.2). As Kee points out, the culmination of history is in accordance with the purpose of God in creation.[76] The present suffering is such as has not been witnessed since the beginning of creation until now (ἀπ᾽ ἀρχῆς κτίσεως ἣν ἔκτισεν ὁ θεὸς ἕως τοῦ νῦν, 13.19). Mark's community thus believe themselves to be living at the turn of the ages. Jesus has overcome evil through his death on the cross, and they await his imminent return (9.1; 13.30).

---

72. C. Rowland, *The Open Heaven: A Study of Apocalyptic in Judaism and Early Christianity* (New York: Crossroad, 1982), 14.

73. J.J. Collins, *The Apocalyptic Imagination: An Introduction to the Jewish Matrix of Christianity* (New York: Crossroad, 1984), 2.

74. Collins, *Apocalyptic Imagination*, 9.

75. D.S. Russell, *The Method and Message of Jewish Apocalyptic 200 B.C.-A.D. 100* (London: SCM Press, 1964), 280–84.

76. Kee, *Community*, 66.

3. *The Prologue*

The apocalyptic context of the Gospel is illustrated in the prologue when the heavens are torn apart as the Spirit descends upon Jesus at his baptism, and a voice from heaven declares him to be the beloved Son of God (1.9–11). The Spirit is the eschatological gift of the new age which heralds the end-time (Joel 2.28–29; Isa. 44.3; Ezek. 36.26–27), and it serves as the driving force of the Gospel. After the baptism of Jesus, the Spirit immediately casts him into the desert, where he is tested by Satan for forty days. During this time he is described as being among the wild animals and served by angels (1.13).

The prologue inaugurates the cosmic struggle between Jesus and Satan. Some scholars, such as Best, argue that Jesus overcomes the testing of Satan in the prologue (1.12) and that the exorcisms may be regarded as 'mopping up operations'.[77] Similarly, Gibson, proposes that the description of Jesus with the wild animals implies that Jesus has overcome their hostility.[78] He compares our passage to Ps. 91.11–13; *T. Iss.* 7.7; *T. Benj.* 5.2 and *T. Naph.* 8.4, and he points out that obedience to the commandments of God prompts the flight of the devil and the fear of the wild animals in the *Testaments of the Twelve Patriarchs*. Gibson thus suggests that the obedience of Jesus to the will of God overcomes the enmity of the wild animals in our passage. The interpretations of Best and Gibson, however, fail to take into account the significance of the remainder of Mark's Gospel which culminates in the crucifixion. In the prologue of Mark the omission of the outcome to the conflict encourages us to seek a resolution in the remainder of the Gospel.

The events of the prologue depict the starting point of Jesus' mission, and Matera rightly observes that the prologue is the key to the interpretation of Mark's Gospel. We are told Jesus' identity as Son of God, but the significance of his identity may only be understood in the light of the remainder of the Gospel.[79] Robinson points out, moreover, that the conflict between Jesus and Satan in the prologue is dramatized in the course of the Gospel in the battle between Jesus and the demoniacs and Jesus and his human opponents.[80] Jesus is tested by his human enemies (8.11; 10.2; 12.15) and he warns the disciples that they will also be tested (14.38). Those possessed by demons are described in language associated with wild animals (5.3–4; 9.18), and the enemies of Jesus, the scribes, are described as those who devour widows' houses (12.40). On the other hand, the service of Simon's mother-in-law to Jesus and his companions (1.31) and the service of the women that is described in the crucifixion scene (15.41) correspond to the service of the angels to Jesus in the temptation narrative (1.13). As Marcus notes, almost the whole of the Gospel takes place between two references to women who serve

---

77. E. Best, *The Temptation and the Passion: The Markan Soteriology* (SNTSMS, 2; Cambridge: Cambridge University Press, 2nd edn, 1980 [1965]), 15.

78. J.B. Gibson, 'Jesus' Wilderness Temptation according to Mark', *JSNT* 53 (1994), 21–32.

79. F.J. Matera, 'The Prologue as the Interpretative Key to Mark's Gospel', *JSNT* 34 (1988), 3–4.

80. Robinson, *Problem*, 34–35.

Jesus 1.31; 15.41).[81] These correspondences suggest that there is a particular relationship between the women and service in Mark.

In the prologue the service of the angels is not defined, but it is likely that they bring him food. Beyer interprets the concrete meaning of the verb διακονέω as 'to wait at table'.[82] In Matthew's Gospel Jesus fasts for forty days and is served by angels at the end of his testing, which may imply that they bring him food (Mt. 4.4). The interpretation of the service of the angels as bringing food is also supported by the account of Elijah's sojourn for forty days in the desert, in which he is brought food by an angel (1 Kgs 19.5–8).

Some scholars, such as Guelich, compare the testing of Jesus in the desert to the testing of the Israelites for forty years in the desert before they entered the promised land (Exod. 34.28).[83] In Exodus the Israelites are given manna during their testing in the desert, and manna is described as the food of angels (Ps. 78.25; Wis. 16.20; *4 Ezra* 1.19). Drury draws correspondences between the account of all the country of Judea and all the people of Jerusalem who approach John the Baptist for baptism in the Jordan (1.5) and the passage of the Israelites through the Jordan to receive the promises of God.[84] The account of the baptism and temptation of Jesus recapitulates the history of Israel and presents Jesus as the one who will bring history to fulfilment.

Marcus, moreover, notes that the testing of Jesus may primarily correspond to the testing of Adam by the snake in Genesis.[85] Adam lives peacefully among the wild animals (Gen. 2.19–20) and he is fed by angels in Jewish legends (*LAE* 4; *b. Sanh.* 59b). The account of the testing of Jesus thus looks forward to the end-time expectation that human beings will recover the status of the pre-Fall Adam and live at peace with wild animals in the new creation (Isa. 11.6–9; 65.17–25; Hos. 2.18; *2 Bar.* 73.6). Furthermore, Marcus observes that the verb διακονέω corresponds to the Hebrew verb עבד and may have the additional meaning of 'to worship' (cf. Josephus, *Ant.* 7.365).[86] This interpretation is supported by the description of the angelic worship of God in response to his works of creation in *Jubilees* (2.3).

In these Old Testament allusions the service of the angels may primarily be interpreted as the serving of food. Collins, however, disputes Beyer's basic definition of διακονέω by arguing that 'to serve at table' is only one application of a verb which has the wider meaning of 'to act as a go between' or 'to carry out actions on behalf of another'.[87] This definition of διακονέω suggests that the angels act as go-betweens sent by God to aid Jesus in his struggle against evil. Cranfield, moreover, proposes that the angels may have the role of witnesses to the

81. Marcus, *Mark*, 196.
82. H. Beyer, 'διακονέω, διακονία, κτλ', *TDNT*, II, 81–93.
83. R.A. Guelich, *Mark 1-8:26* (WBC 34; Dallas: Word Books, 1989), 38.
84. J. Drury, 'Mark 1:1–15. An Interpretation', in A.E. Harvey (ed.), *Alternative Approaches to New Testament Study* (London: SPCK, 1985), 25–36.
85. Marcus, *Mark*, 169.
86. Marcus, *Mark*, 168.
87. J.N. Collins, *Diakonia: Re-interpreting the Ancient Sources* (Oxford: Oxford University Press, 1990), 194.

encounter between Jesus and Satan if they are present throughout the testing of Jesus.[88] The combination of testing, the presence of the wild animals and the angels may be found in Ps. 91.11–13 and in *T. Naph.* 8.4. In these texts the angels have the role of protectors which may indicate that the angels in the prologue are sent by God to protect Jesus in his struggle against Satan.

The prologue thus introduces the apocalyptic conflict between Jesus and Satan which will be played out on a human level in the course of the Gospel. The service of the angels foreshadows the service of women (1.31; 15.41). The concrete meaning of the verb διακονέω is 'to wait at table', which implies that the angels bring Jesus food, but the additional connotations of the verb suggest that they also protect Jesus and worship him. These associations of the verb διακονέω with women and service (1.31; 15.41) will be explored in our analysis of the role of women. The first chapter will examine the portrayal of Simon's mother-in-law, who is the first woman to serve Jesus (1.31). We will then interpret the passages that feature women in Mark's Gospel in relation to discipleship, and examine the ways in which the portrayal of women relates to the struggle of Jesus against evil, and his inauguration of the new creation.

---

88. C.E.B. Cranfield, *The Gospel according to St. Mark* (CGTC; Cambridge: Cambridge University Press, rev. edn, 1974 [1959]), 60.

Chapter 2

THE HEALING OF SIMON'S MOTHER-IN-LAW (1.29–31)

1. *Introduction*

The healing of Simon's mother-in-law (1.29–31) is the first account of the healing of a woman by Jesus in Mark, and this passage has a key position describing the final action of Jesus at the close of the first day of his mission in Capernaum (1.21–31). An exorcism of a man in the public setting of the synagogue (1.21–28) is followed by the healing of a woman in the private setting of a house (1.29–31). Jesus enters the house of Simon and Andrew, his first disciples, and heals Simon's mother-in-law from her fever. The account illustrates the scope of Jesus' power to heal, and the woman's service of a meal closes the first day of Jesus' mission on a note of fulfilment (1.31).

The link with Simon encourages Gnilka to believe that the passage is preserved on account of its connection with Simon Peter.[1] Fander associates the story with a tradition concerning the foundation of a Christian community in Capernaum, but she points out that Peter is only a peripheral figure in the story.[2] She prefers to focus on the role of the woman, who serves Jesus in response to her healing. Scholars debate the interpretation of the woman's service: Schweizer, for example, represents the traditional view that her service may be seen as the preparation of a meal.[3] Some feminist scholars, such as Dewey, also emphasize the link between the account of this woman and the sphere of the home associated with women.[4] In Fander's view, however, the healing account records the way in which Simon's mother-in-law becomes a disciple, and her service is interpreted as a model of discipleship.[5] As Fander notes, it is significant that our passage concludes with the service of a woman, and we will explore the association of Simon's mother-in-law with discipleship in the course of this chapter.

2. *The Portrayal of the Woman*

The woman is anonymous, and is introduced by her relationship to Simon as his mother-in-law (1.29). Her anonymity is characteristic of the portrayal of women in

---

1. J. Gnilka, *Das Evangelium nach Markus* (2 vols.; EKKNT; Zurich: Benziger, 1978–79), 1.84–85.
2. Fander, *Stellung*, 28.
3. E. Schweizer, *The Good News according to Mark* (London: SPCK, 1971), 53.
4. Dewey, 'Mark', 477.
5. Fander, *Stellung*, 318–19.

the healing accounts of Mark (5.21–43; 7.24–30). This situation reflects the androcentric bias of the first century, in which male names are recorded more frequently
than the names of women.[6] For example, we are told the name of Jairus, the president of the synagogue, but not the name of his daughter (5.21–43), and the names
of Jesus' brothers are listed, but not those of his sisters (6.3). This characteristic,
however, does not indicate that Mark has deliberately excluded the name of Simon's
mother-in-law, since it may have been missing from the pre-Markan source. Women
are often defined in terms of male relations, and we will see another instance of this
feature in the portrayal of the women who are present at the crucifixion and the
burial of Jesus (15.40, 47; 16.1).

There is no reference to the woman's husband, which may imply that she is a
widow, since women were characteristically identified by their husbands' names.
Widows were regarded as amongst the most vulnerable groups in society, and the
concern for widows along with orphans is a frequent commandment in the Old
Testament (Exod. 22.22; Deut. 24.17; Isa. 10.2).[7] As the house belongs to Simon
and Andrew (1.29), she appears to live with them as part of an extended family.[8]
The description of Simon and Andrew as fishermen, and the reference to the hired
men who work alongside James and John, suggest that they are not poverty-stricken
(1.20). Our account thus depicts a positive view of family compared to the later
conflict of Jesus with his own family (3.31–35) and Jesus' prophecy of family disruption (13.12).

The reference to Simon may be significant as the account of the healing of this
woman occurs in a section of the Gospel particularly associated with the name of

6.   Ilan examines the references to the names of Jewish women in Palestine from the Second
Temple and Mishnaic periods (330 BCE–200 CE). She finds the names of 247 women compared to
2040 men in her sources, which include the writings of Josephus, the New Testament (the Gospels
and the chapters of Acts relating to Palestine), rabbinic literature, funerary inscriptions and papyri
and ostraca from the Judean desert. See 'Notes on the Distribution of Women's Names in Palestine
in the Second Temple and Mishnaic Periods', *JJS* 40 (1989), 186–200.

7.   For an analysis of the lives of widows in the first century see Ilan (*Jewish Women*, 147–51).

8.   Ilan (*Jewish Women*, 167–72) notes the difficulties women faced in inheriting property.
According to biblical law (Num. 27.8) a woman cannot inherit from her father unless she has no
brothers. Ilan also cites the later text of the Mishnah which states 'A woman bequeaths property to
her sons, a wife to her husband and maternal uncles, but they do not inherit from them' (*m. B.B.*
8.1). Ilan, however, does record examples of wealthy women who owned property such as Queen
Berenice (Josephus, *Life* 119) and Herodias (Josephus, *Ant.* 18.253). In addition, Ilan mentions the
mother of John Mark who is described as the owner of a house in Jerusalem (Acts 12.12). Ilan
notes that a woman cannot inherit from her husband unless this is stipulated in her *ketubbah* (marriage contract). In the Mishnah a woman may stay in the house of her late husband and be main-
tained there as long as she remains a widow (*m. Ket.* 4.12). This law is accepted in Galilee and
Jerusalem, but the Judeans add the provision that the woman is required to be supported until her
ketubbah is paid. It is difficult to determine the extent to which these laws were observed in the
first century, but the Babatha archive has given evidence of the finances of one second-century
woman. Babatha's *ketubbah* dates from around 125 CE and it states that in the event of her husband's death she was entitled to remain as a widow in the house of her late husband and be supported by his heirs until her *ketubbah* is paid. For an analysis of this material see Y. Yadin, J.C.
Greenfield and A. Yardeni, 'Babatha's *Ketubba*', *IEJ* 44 (1994), 75–101; M.A. Friedmann,
'Babatha's *Ketubba*: Some Preliminary Observations', *IEJ* 46 (1996), 55–76.

Simon, the leading disciple in Mark. Simon is mentioned throughout the events of the first day of Jesus' mission in Capernaum (1.16, 29, 30), later initiating the search for Jesus the following morning (1.35–39). At this point in the narrative, Jesus has not chosen his twelve disciples, and Simon has not yet been given the name of Peter (3.16). The use of the name of Simon stresses that the timing of the passage occurs at the initial stages of Jesus' mission, taking place before the first of his conflicts with the religious and political authorities (2.1–3.6) and before the call of the Twelve (3.13–19).

There is no mention of the woman's daughter, Peter's wife, in the account, although she is mentioned by Paul as accompanying Peter on his missionary journeys (1 Cor. 9.5), and Clement of Alexandria records that Peter had children (*Strom.* 3.52). Peter's wife may be present in the house, and other women may also be included within the anonymous group who tell Jesus about the woman's illness (1.30). In Mark the presence of women may be concealed by the use of masculine plural grammatical terms. As Schüssler Fiorenza notes, androcentric terminology may include women without directly referring to them.[9] Feminine terms are used only when there are no men present, or the presence of women is exceptional. Similarly, collective masculine nouns such as the crowd (ὁ ὄχλος) may also include women without directly mentioning their presence. In chapter 5, for example, the woman with the flow of blood emerges from a crowd to touch Jesus' clothes (5.24–34), and Jesus refers to the women who sit around him, listening to his teaching, as his sister and mother (3.35).

The unnamed woman who is the focus of this healing account contrasts with the four male named disciples and Jesus. In this passage the disciples act as witnesses to the healing of the woman. The anonymity of the woman, moreover, enables her to act as a representative of all who seek healing from Jesus. Jesus' actions of exorcism and healing not only bring release to individuals, they are also paradigms of the salvation of all human beings in a world enslaved by evil.

3. *The Account of the Healing*

The account of the healing follows the pattern of Hellenistic miracle stories noted by Theissen in his analysis of the form of miracles of the early Christian tradition.[10] We are told of the arrival of the miracle worker, then given a description of the ill person, and the accounts conclude with a reference to a character other than the miracle worker. Fander, however, notes a discrepancy from the usual pattern of healing accounts, since Jesus does not visit the house with the purpose of healing the woman.[11] He only learns of her illness once he has entered the house (1.30). This situation is similar to the portrayal of the exorcism in the synagogue, in which Jesus goes to the synagogue in order to teach but his teaching prompts the demoniac

---

9. Schüssler Fiorenza, *In Memory*, 45.

10. G. Theissen, *The Miracle Stories of the Early Christian Tradition* (SNTW; Edinburgh: T. & T. Clark, 1983), 46.

11. Fander, *Stellung*, 26.

to cry out (1.23–24).[12] The presence of Jesus himself causes situations of evil and of disease to be revealed, and in this way the incompatibility of Jesus with the force of evil is stressed.

In Mark, the healing of the woman is depicted as a conflict between Jesus and the power of evil. Initially, the woman is characterized by her illness, and she is described as lying down burning with a fever (κατέκειτο πυρέσσουσα, 1.30). As Guelich notes, in the first century a fever was not seen as a symptom of an illness but was regarded as an illness itself,[13] and it was believed to be a serious and life-threatening condition. The fever was relentless in its attack on the suffering person. The term fever derives from πῦρ (fire) and Gnilka quotes a baraita that defines a fever as 'a fire, which drinks and does not eat' (*b. Yom.* 21b).[14] In some texts fevers are linked to unclean spirits, and Davies and Allison point out the association of fevers with demons in *T. Sol.* 7.5–7.[15] In the account of the exorcism of the boy possessed by a deaf and mute spirit, the unclean spirit attempts to destroy the boy by throwing him into a fire (9.22).

The description of the woman's fever, moreover, may have eschatological connotations, since fire is associated with the torments of the end-time (Isa. 66.24; Zech. 13.9). In a later Markan passage fire is linked with judgement and cleansing (9.48–49). The description of the woman lying down burning with a fever (1.30) suggests a deteriorating condition, which corresponds to the increasing evil in the end-time. Jesus warns his disciples that the end-time is a time of such evil that has never been experienced before (13.19), and unless God cuts short this time, no human being may be saved (13.20). In the healing of Simon's mother-in-law we see Jesus intervene to pull the woman from the clutches of death.

The account contrasts with many miracle stories in its lack of reference to invocation and prayers. Instead, there is a focus on the power of Jesus' touch as the source of healing, and the participle προσελθών (having approached, 1.31) suggests that Jesus pulls the woman towards him. Jesus heals the woman by seizing her hand, and raising her to life (προσελθὼν ἤγειρεν αὐτὴν κρατήσας τῆς χειρός, 1.31). The central verb ἤγειρεν (he raised) gains significance through its position between two participles. The verb ἐγείρω will occur in future healing accounts, where it is used as a command of Jesus 'rise' (ἔγειρε, 2.9, 11; 3.3; 5.41). It is also used of the resurrection of Jesus in his prophecy at the Mount of Olives (τὸ ἐγερθῆναί, 14.28) and in the message of the young man at the tomb (ἠγέρθη, 16.6). In the last two examples the use of the divine passive emphasizes that it is God's action that raises Jesus. As Marcus points out, the use of this verb in the healing accounts suggests that the power through which Jesus heals human beings is the same power which raises Jesus from death.[16]

12. Marcus, *Mark*, 195.

13. Guelich, *Mark*, 62.

14. Gnilka, *Evangelium*, 1.84.

15. W.D. Davies and D.C. Allison, *A Critical and Exegetical Commentary on the Gospel according to Saint Matthew* (Edinburgh: T. & T. Clark, 1991), 2.35.

16. Marcus, *Mark*, 199.

An impression of conflict is suggested by the violent connotations of the verb κρατέω which may be used with the meaning 'to seize' or 'to arrest'. This verb is used of the arrest of John the Baptist (6.17), and of Jesus (14.1, 44, 46, 49). The use of the verb κρατέω in our passage contrasts with the portrayal of Jesus' action of healing in Matthew, where he is described as touching the woman's hand (ἥψατο τῆς χειρὸς αὐτῆς, Mt. 8.15), rather than seizing her by the hand. In Luke, there is no mention of Jesus touching the woman, and he focuses on the power of Jesus' word to cast out disease. Luke associates the fever with demon possession, and the healing is depicted as an exorcism. Jesus rebukes the fever (ἐπετίμησεν τῷ πυρετῷ, 4.39), with the verb ἐπιτιμάω, which Kee defines as a technical term for casting out demons.[17]

In Mark, the power of Jesus' touch is so great that the woman's disease departs from her immediately, as is indicated by the phrase 'the fever left her' (ἀφῆκεν αὐτὴν ὁ πυρετός, 1.31). The fever is portrayed as a personal force, and its departure is reminiscent of the unclean spirit which leaves the demoniac in the synagogue (ἐξῆλθεν ἐξ αὐτοῦ, 1.26). Sabin points out that the verb ἀφίημι has the additional meaning of 'to release', which suggests that disease is a power that binds humanity.[18] Jesus heals human beings by releasing them from the power of evil. He does so by the power of the Holy Spirit, which has come upon him at his baptism (1.10). These connotations are later seen in the parable of the strong man (3.27). Human beings are depicted as stolen goods secured in the house of a strong man. Jesus, however, is portrayed as the stronger one, who comes to release humanity from the power of evil. Sabin also notes that ἀφίημι may be interpreted as 'to forgive' (2.5; 3.28), and forgiveness may be seen as a release of the hold of evil upon human beings. The association of healing and forgiveness is also evident in the account of the healing of the paralysed man in which Jesus forgives the man's sins and also restores his health (2.1–12). Jesus' actions of healing and forgiving are both ways in which the new age breaks into the world.

In Mark, the use of the verbs κρατέω and ἀφίημι convey the concept of healing as a struggle against the force of evil. Disease is the power of Satan to torment and destroy human beings. Just as the unclean spirit torments the man in the synagogue (1.21–28), this woman is depicted as suffering from a burning fever. Mark distinguishes this account from an exorcism. Exorcisms are depicted as actions that break the power of evil, whereas healings focus on the restoration of human beings. In Mark, exorcisms are depicted first, then healings, and together these actions illustrate the power of God to break the bonds that enslave human beings and restore them to health (1.21–28, 29–31; 5.1–20, 21–43; 6.13).

The brief account of the healing of Simon's mother-in-law includes key elements, which form the basis of future healing accounts. The healing of Jairus' daughter (5.21–43) and the exorcism of the boy with a deaf and mute spirit (9.14–29) follow a pattern similar to that in our passage, as in all three narratives Jesus seizes human

17. H.C. Kee, 'The Terminology of Mark's Exorcism Stories', *NTS* 14 (1967), 232–46.
18. M. Sabin, 'Women Transformed: The Ending of Mark is the Beginning of Wisdom', *CrosCurr* 48 (1998), 151.

beings by the hand and raises them to life. The correspondences in the accounts are stressed by the verbal similarities (κρατήσας τῆς χειρός, 1.31; 5.41; 9.27). It is also significant that the three passages are associated with death. Jairus' daughter dies in the course of the story, and the boy with the deaf and mute spirit is described as lying down as if he were dead (ἐγένετο ὡσεὶ νεκρός, 9.26). In this way, the healing of Simon's mother-in-law forms a paradigm of Jesus' power to raise humanity. Jesus not only liberates human beings from disease but has the power to raise them from death.

4. *Discipleship*

A woman who formerly has been powerless is now completely transformed through the healing power of Jesus, and she becomes active in serving others. In other passages Jesus praises the faith of those who seek healing (5.34; 10.52) or he responds to the faith of the friends who intercede for a sick person (2.5). This story, however, is not about the faith of the woman, since she is not depicted as someone who has heard of Jesus or of his teaching as in the account of the woman with the flow of blood, who hears of Jesus and then seeks healing from him (5.27). At the beginning of our account, Simon's mother-in-law is completely powerless, and she relies on others to inform Jesus of her illness (λέγουσιν αὐτῷ περὶ αὐτῆς, 1.30).

In response to her healing, we are told, the woman serves 'them' (διηκόνει αὐτοῖς, 1.31). Some commentators, such as Schweizer, associate the service of the woman with domestic care, which was traditionally regarded as the role of women, and think that her service consists of the meal she prepares for her guests.[19] Taylor suggests that the service of the women is a sign which confirms her healing.[20] Theissen, moreover, observes that miracles are characteristically demonstrated by a new act, particularly one which illustrates the receipt of a new physical power.[21] He notes additional examples in Mark, including the healed man who carries his bed (2.12) and Jairus' daughter who walks (5.42). Theissen observes that the instruction that Jairus' daughter should be given something to eat is also a demonstration of her cure (5.43). Fander, however, suggests that the account of the woman's service goes beyond the requirements characteristic of Hellenistic miracle stories.[22] As she points out, it is more usual for the healed person to eat than for the miracle worker to do so.

The woman's act of service is also unusual, since it is the only narrative in which a human being responds to Jesus' healing with service (διηκόνει αὐτοῖς, 1.31). In other narratives those healed are praised for their faith (5.34; 10.52) but are instructed by Jesus to go (ὕπαγε, 5.19, 34; 7.29; 10.52). Even the healed demoniac, who wishes to stay with Jesus, is sent away to proclaim his healing (5.19). Fander argues that Mark portrays Simon's mother-in-law as a disciple, but the woman only

19. Schweizer, *Mark*, 53.
20. V. Taylor, *The Gospel according to St. Mark* (London: Macmillan, 1952), 180.
21. Theissen, *Miracle Stories*, 66.
22. Fander, *Stellung*, 28.

appears in this narrative, and there is no indication that she leaves her home to accompany Jesus. Instead, Jesus returns to the house in Capernaum at a later stage (2.1).

On this occasion the woman's service more likely consists of the preparation of a meal. Krause argues that the portrayal of Simon's mother-in-law' table-service conforms to the expectations of the role of women within patriarchal households.[23] She proposes that feminist interpretations of our passage which associate the women's service with discipleship reflect a desire to read feminist liberation principles into the text. She believes that the women's service should be interpreted within the immediate context of the passage rather than by relating it to the later description of the service of the female disciples which is not mentioned until the crucifixion of Jesus (15.40–41).

We have, however, noted that Mark has placed references to service at key places within the Gospel. The angels serve Jesus in the prologue (1.13) and Jesus' mission is framed by two references to the service of women (1.31; 15.41).[24] Fander is thus correct in emphasizing that διακονέω is a discipleship term, closely connected with Jesus' own mission (10.45). As we have observed, moreover, apart from its reference to Jesus in 10.45, this verb is used only of women in Mark, and it recurs in the description of the women who remain at the crucifixion. They have followed and served Jesus in Galilee before accompanying him to Jerusalem (15.40–41). These references suggest that the table-service of Simon's mother-in-law is related to Mark's concept of discipleship.

The portrayal of Simon's mother-in-law, moreover, does convey insights into Mark's understanding of discipleship. Although Fander implies that the woman serves Jesus alone, Mark writes that the woman serves a wider anonymous group of people (αὐτοῖς, 1.31). Taylor, however, points out that Matthew replaces αὐτοῖς with the singular αὐτῷ (8.15).[25] As Davies and Allison show, Matthew employs three verbs with Jesus as the subject (ἐλθών, εἶδεν, 8.14; ἥψατο, 8.15), followed by three verbs associated with the woman (ἀφῆκεν, ἠγέρθη, διηκόνει, 8.15).[26] The symmetrical structure of the account draws attention to the power of Jesus and the results of his action. In Matthew, the woman does serve Jesus alone (διηκόνει αὐτῷ, 8.15), and as Davies and Allison point out, the Matthean Jesus is always the subject or the object of the verb διακονέω.[27]

Mark, however, begins with a wider group who inform Jesus of the woman's condition and ends with the service of the woman towards Jesus and the wider group. The use of the wider undefined group in Mark conveys the sense of reciprocity in the healing; the woman not only responds to Jesus' action of healing her by serving him, but she also serves other people present in the house, who may even include

---

23. D. Krause, 'Simon Peter's Mother-in-Law – Disciple or Domestic Servant? Feminist Biblical Hermeneutics and the Interpretation of Mark 1.29-31', in A.-J. Levine (ed.), *A Feminist Companion to Mark* (Sheffield: Sheffield Academic Press, 2001), 37–53.

24. Marcus, *Mark*, 196.

25. Taylor, *St. Mark*, 180.

26. Davies and Allison, *Matthew*, 2.32.

27. Davies and Allison, *Matthew*, 2.35.

those who have interceded with Jesus for her health. The woman who receives healing, now acts to sustain others.

The woman's response of service illustrates the reciprocity of the gospel, since her healing enables her to serve her community. The concept of reciprocity may also be seen in the prologue, as Jesus first receives the Holy Spirit (1.10), then casts out demons and heals human beings in the power of the Spirit. Jesus' mission leads to his death, since he gives his life in his service to others (10.45). The self-giving of Jesus, however, goes beyond concepts of exchange because the giving of his life leads to the abundance of the kingdom of God. In a similar way, the healing of a single woman enables her to serve all of those present. The woman is not only restored to health, she is now able to act in a way that supports others, and her service foreshadows the abundance of the kingdom of God. The woman's healing points to the interdependency of human beings. The suffering of one person is related to the suffering of all people. Healing does not only involve the sick person, but also includes the restoration of that person to the community. In this way the healing of one person may be seen as a paradigm for the restoration of the whole community.

5. *Excursus: The Use of the Verb* διακονέω

In his analysis of the verb διακονέω, Beyer notes that the basic concrete meaning of this verb is 'to wait at table'.[28] An additional meaning of διακονέω as 'to provide or care for' is particularly associated with women. According to the Greek worldview this work is regarded as the role of a servant or slave, and is seen as unfitting for free men. In the Old Testament, however, the hospitality offered to guests is viewed positively. Abraham and Sarah, for example, serve strangers who turn out to be angels (Gen. 18.1–8). This form of hospitality is also associated with women who serve prophets. The widow of Zarephath serves food to Elijah (1 Kgs 17.8–16), and the Shunamite woman prepares meals for Elisha (2 Kgs 4.8). Both women are rewarded for their service by the prophets' acts of healing their sons.

In the New Testament the verb διακονέω is also used with the meaning 'to serve at table'. As Collins notes, the cognate noun διάκονος is used of the servants in the parable of the wedding feast (Mt. 22.13) and in the account of the wedding at Cana (Jn 2.5, 9).[29] In John's Gospel, Martha is depicted as serving at the table, while her brother Lazarus joins Jesus at the dinner (12.2). Similarly, Beyer regards the response of Peter's mother-in-law as serving food.[30]

In Mark, however, Jesus uses the verb διακονέω in the definition of his own mission. Jesus comes not to be served, but to serve, and his service is identified as the giving of his life (10.45). This verse reveals the paradox that the loss of Jesus' life brings life to others. The giving of Jesus' life on the cross is the turning point in the Gospel as Jesus' death brings salvation to human beings. The reciprocity of

28. Beyer, *TDNT*, II, 82.
29. Collins, *Diakonia*, 245.
30. Beyer, *TDNT*, II, 85.

serving, giving and receiving expresses the mutuality involved in Mark's under-standing of redemption. Jesus teaches his disciples that they should be servants (9.35; 10.43–44). The woman in our story takes the role of a servant, and her service acts as an example for the disciples to follow. The associations of women with service thus connect them to the portrayal of Jesus' own mission as one of service.

As we have noted, the verb διακονέω is also used of the angels who serve Jesus in the prologue (1.13). The service of the angels, moreover, foreshadows the service of women (1.31; 15.41). They offer positive support to Jesus in the midst of the opposition he experiences. The service of Simon's mother-in-law is described as a continuing action (διηκόνει, imperfect tense, 1.31), and likewise, the service of the angels is presented in the imperfect tense (διηκόνουν, 1.13). In Mark, the angels support Jesus during his testing, which suggests that women may also have the role of sustaining Jesus throughout his mission.

6. *The Discipleship Setting of the Healing Account*

In the course of his day's mission in Capernaum, Jesus moves from the synagogue to the private setting of the house of his first disciples, Simon and Andrew. Even in the first chapter of the Gospel, we see the house replacing the synagogue as the safe place of Jesus' mission. In the synagogue there are signs of the future conflict between Jesus and the religious authorities, as Mark stresses his superiority over the scribes who lack his authority (1.22) and as those present debate with one another over the significance of his teaching (ἐθαμβήθησαν ἅπαντες ὥστε συζητεῖν, 1.27). The verb συζητέω (to discuss, question) has negative connotations, since it is later used in connection with the opposition of Jesus' enemies (8.11; 9.14). In this passage the debate among the witnesses thus conveys their lack of under-standing of Jesus' mission and the distance between Jesus and human beings, who fear to approach him directly.

The male demoniac is healed in the public setting of the synagogue, whereas the woman in our passage is healed in her own home. Dewey interprets the location of the house as reflective of the association of women with the private sphere of the home, whereas men are portrayed in public settings.[31] In Mark, however, the house becomes the main location associated with the discipleship group. The house at Capernaum may function as the initial base for Jesus' mission, since he returns there in 2.1, and at a later stage he is depicted in a house in Capernaum (9.33–37). In addi-tion, 'the house' becomes the setting in which Jesus teaches his disciples (7.17; 9.28, 33; 10.10).[32] Frequently there is a movement from the public teaching of the crowds to the private teaching of Jesus' disciples within the setting of a house (7.1–16 → 7.17–23; 9.14–27 → 9.28–29; 10.1–9 → 10.10–11). These references to the house as a place of gathering and teaching may reflect the setting of the house as a base for early Christian communities (cf. Rom. 16.5; 1 Cor. 16.19; Phm. 2).

---

31. Dewey, 'Mark', 477.
32. Gnilka, *Evangelium*, 1.84.

The healing of Simon's mother-in-law in a house associates it with private instruction of the disciples. Fander suggests that the reference to the four disciples at the beginning of the passage depicts the healing account as an episode of teaching for the disciples, in which the woman acts as a model of discipleship.[33] The disciples witness a healing, which in some ways foreshadows the resurrection of Jesus. As we have seen, the woman's healing has similarities with other healing accounts such as the raising of Jairus' daughter (5.21–43). Jesus selects three of his disciples to witness this event, which takes place in the girl's room apart from the public mourners. The secrecy of the miracle is stressed, since Jesus commands those present to tell no one about the raising of the girl (5.43). The healing of Simon's mother-in-law is similar to a resurrection narrative, and the healing of Jairus' daughter is an account of the raising of the girl from the dead. These healings, then, are significant in that they foreshadow Jesus' own death and resurrection. In this way they serve as teaching for the disciples.

It is striking that both accounts are preceded by exorcism stories (1.21–28; 5.1–20). The exorcisms depict the battle of Jesus against evil, and they are followed by miracles associated with the restoration of human beings from the power of death. Jesus overcomes evil on earth, and the power of death itself. The significance of these healings, however, is concealed from outsiders. Simon's mother-in-law is healed in the privacy of her home, away from the crowds. Similarly, Jairus' daughter is healed with only her parents and the inner circle of disciples present. The healings, which follow the pattern of Jesus' death and resurrection, reveal his identity as the Son of God to Mark's audience. Jesus is declared the beloved Son by a voice from heaven at his baptism (1.11) and the transfiguration (9.7), but no human being recognizes his identity until his death on the cross (15.39). The knowledge of Jesus' identity is to be concealed until he is raised from the dead (9.9). At this stage in the narrative these healings are shown to the disciples alone, out of sight of the crowds.

The house becomes the boundary between the community and the world. At the close of the day, the sick and demon-possessed gather at the door of the house, seeking help from Jesus (1.32–34). The extent of human suffering becomes apparent in the numbers of people who are present. Gnilka notes that the healing of Simon's mother-in-law is the only healing that takes place directly within the setting of the discipleship community.[34] The news of Jesus' mission, nevertheless, radiates outwards from the discipleship setting of the house in Galilee, attracting the attention of crowds from many other places (3.7–8).

7. New Creation

In Mark, the healing of Simon's mother-in-law takes place on the Sabbath, and her act of service ends the first day of Jesus' mission on a note of fulfilment (1.31). The timing of the Sabbath recalls the account of creation in Gen. 1.1–2.3. God rests on

---

33. Fander, *Stellung*, 34.
34. Gnilka, *Evangelium*, 1.83.

the Sabbath after six days of creation, and he blesses and makes the Sabbath holy (2.2–3). In this way the Sabbath represents the culmination of creation. In Mark, Simon's mother-in-law serves Jesus and his companions a meal (1.31). Similarly, in *Jubilees* the Sabbath is associated with a meal since it is intended to be kept as a sign in which human beings may 'eat and drink and bless the one who created all things' (2.21).

In our passage Jesus takes the woman by the hand and seizes her from the clutches of her disease. His action banishes her fever, and she is restored to health. Her healing thus becomes a sign of new creation. The pattern of conflict and resolution may be seen in the accounts of creation in the Old Testament in which God struggles against enemies to bring about creation. Levenson compares these accounts of creation to the combat myths of the creation accounts in ancient Near Eastern texts.[35] In the *Enuma elish* Marduk creates the world from the body of the sea goddess, Tiamat, after a battle amongst the gods. Allusions to this concept in which God fights sea monsters may also be seen in the Old Testament (for example Ps. 74.12–17 and Isa. 51.9–11). Levenson explores the portrayal of creation in Genesis, and he argues that God does not create *ex nihilio* but separates creation from chaos.[36] He notes that creation is depicted as a struggle against a threatening chaos, in order that God may create conditions in which the earth may flourish. In Genesis there is less focus on an active opposition to God, but the threat of chaos remains.

Levenson suggests that the desire of God for rest is the impetus behind his acts of creation, and creation is depicted as a victory, an act of liberation from evil.[37] In this way the Sabbath represents the rest of God after the struggle involved in creation (cf. Heb. 4.4, 9–10). In texts such as *LAE* 51.2 the Sabbath is associated with the resurrection, as a sign of the new creation, 'The seventh day is a sign of the resurrection, the rest of the coming age, and on the seventh day the Lord rested from all his works'. This interpretation may also be seen in the Mekilta to Exod. 31.17 'The world to come is characterised by the kind of holiness possessed by the Sabbath in this world... The Sabbath possesses a holiness like that of the world to come.'[38]

The commandment to keep the Sabbath occurs in the Decalogue (Exod. 20.8–11; Deut. 5.12–15). Exodus records a cosmological purpose behind the Sabbath command; the Israelites are instructed to rest because God rested on the Sabbath after creating the world in six days (Gen. 2.2). In Deuteronomy, the commandment to rest has a historical focus; it looks back to God's action of liberating the Israelites by leading them by the hand from slavery in Egypt. As Levenson points out, the cosmological and historical features of the Sabbath commandment complement one another.[39] The Exodus account alludes to the rest of God after his battle with

---

35. J.D. Levenson, *Creation and the Persistence of Evil* (San Francisco: Harper & Row, 1988), 3–13.

36. Levenson, *Creation*, 47.

37. Levenson, *Creation*, 101.

38. Cf. A.J. Heschel, *The Sabbath: Its Meaning for Modern Man* (New York: Noonday Press/ Farrar, Straus & Young, 1975 [1951]), 73.

39. Levenson, *Creation*, 82.

the forces of evil, and the Deuteronomic passage refers to the relief of the Israelites after the overcoming of their human enemies.

These associations of the Sabbath commandment are similar to the dimensions of the Markan healing of Simon's mother-in-law. In Genesis, God separates creation from chaos so that human beings may thrive, whereas in Mark, Jesus liberates Simon's mother-in-law from the evil of disease, enabling her to serve others. In Genesis, God's desire for rest is the impetus behind the struggle of creation. In Mark, Jesus responds to the news of the illness of Simon's mother-in-law, and he does not rest until she has been healed. In Deut. 5.15, God takes his people by the hand and saves them from slavery, whereas in the healing of Simon's mother-in-law Jesus seizes the woman by the hand, and releases her from her oppressive fever.

The healings of Jesus on the Sabbath depict the kingdom of God breaking into the world and are proleptic of the new creation. At his baptism the Holy Spirit descends upon Jesus (1.10), and he is declared to be the beloved Son of God (1.11). The presence of the Holy Spirit corresponds to the holiness of the Sabbath. In the prologue the Spirit casts Jesus into the desert to be tested by Satan (1.12). The Spirit, then, becomes the driving force in his mission and the power through which Jesus casts out evil and heals human beings. In this way Jesus' miracles foreshadow the Sabbath rest of the new creation.

In the apocalyptic world-view of Mark's Gospel, creation is enslaved under the power of Satan. Jesus, the Son of God, comes to cast out evil and liberate humanity, inaugurating the new creation. Forsyth notes that in the combat myths the one who conquers his enemies becomes king, and these myths thus support the institution of kingship in the ancient world.[40] In Mark, Jesus' ability to cast out demons and disease points to his identity as Messiah and king.

In the course of the Gospel, the healing of Jesus on the Sabbath forms one of the main issues of contention between Jesus and the religious authorities. The disciples are accused of plucking corn on the Sabbath (2.23–28), and later the religious authorities watch to see if Jesus will heal on the Sabbath (3.1–6). The opposition of Jesus' enemies to his miracles on the Sabbath reflects their rejection of his identity as Son of God. As van Iersel notes, on the first day of Jesus' mission on the Sabbath there are no objections to his exorcism or his healing on the Sabbath.[41] This healing takes place in the privacy of a house with no hostile observers. There is, however, a contrast between Jesus who heals on the Sabbath and the crowds who wait until the Sabbath is over before travelling to Jesus (1.32). The news of Jesus' healing spreads among the people during the Sabbath. The crowds, however, are depicted as law-observant, avoiding journeys on the Sabbath.

The word, the message of Jesus' healing, transcends these boundaries during the Sabbath, and the whole town gathers at the door of the house after the day ends. The crowd wait until darkness falls, which Marcus notes is a numinous time,

---

40. N. Forsyth, *The Old Enemy: Satan and the Combat Myth* (Princeton: Princeton University Press, 1987), 45.

41. B.M.F. van Iersel, *Mark: A Reader Response Commentary* (trans. W.H. Bisscheroux; *JSNT*Sup, 164; Sheffield: Sheffield Academic Press), 138–39.

associated with the conflict with demonical powers.[42] The alternation of day and night relates also to the creation account of Genesis, in which God separates light from darkness. Levenson notes that in the creation account the Sabbath is the only day without an evening (Gen. 2.1–3), which he relates to the absence of evil powers on the Sabbath.[43]

The healing of this woman on the Sabbath, then, foreshadows the new creation, which Jesus inaugurates as Son of God. As we have observed, her healing is depicted as a conflict with evil, and her condition is associated with the eschatological torments of the end-time. She represents human beings facing the destructive powers of evil at the close of the age, whereas Jesus has the power to liberate humanity. The woman responds to her healing by serving a meal, which sustains Jesus and those with him. Her action is reminiscent of the conclusion of the raising of Jairus' daughter, in which Jesus tells her parents to give the girl something to eat (5.43). A similar association of healing with eating occurs in the exorcism of the Syrophoenician woman's daughter, in which the request of the woman for healing is depicted in terms of asking for bread (7.27).

Jesus describes his mission as a time of feasting (2.18–20), and his miracles of healing and his feedings of the crowds (6.30–44; 8.1–9) are signs of the kingdom of God breaking into the world. In Exodus, similarly, God's action of liberating his people from slavery is associated with meals; the Israelites celebrate the Passover meal before their journey to the promised land, and they are fed with manna while they travel in the wilderness (Exod. 16). As Smith observes, the creation accounts associate the celebration of victory with a banquet (for example *Enuma elish* 6.68–94), and he observes that there are similar descriptions in the Old Testament (e.g. Isa. 34.5–7 and Zech. 9.15).[44] A victory banquet of David may also be seen in 1 Chron. 12.38–40. Josephus records an account of a victory celebration of the Romans after the siege of Jerusalem in which a vast number of oxen are sacrificed and distributed to the army for a banquet (*War* 7.16–17).

In apocalyptic texts, the victory over evil is celebrated with the messianic feast (Isa. 25.6–8; *1 Enoch* 62.12–14; *2 Baruch* 29.5–8). As Smith notes, some texts make reference to the presence of the Son of Man (*1 Enoch* 62.12–14) or of the Messiah at the banquet (1QSa 2.11–22).[45] Levenson, moreover, argues that the apocalypse in Isa. 24–27 portrays the messianic feast as a victory banquet, which takes place after a struggle against evil.[46] He points out that the defeat of evil becomes the defeat of death in texts such as Isa. 26.19. As Levenson observes, apocalyptic texts project the victory over evil into the imminent future, a hope which serves as a contrast to the present experience of suffering. In Mark, similarly, Jesus battles against evil in healing the woman, and her service of a meal is proleptic of the victory banquet of the new creation. The account of her being raised from her fever also foreshadows

42. Marcus (*Mark*, 200) refers to the Havdalah service at the end of the Sabbath in *b. Pesaḥ* 53b–54a and *Gen. R.* 11.2.
43. Levenson, *Creation*, 123.
44. D.E. Smith, 'Messianic Banquet', *ABD*, IV, 788–91.
45. Smith, *ABD*, IV, 789–90.
46. Levenson, *Creation*, 29–32.

Jesus' own resurrection and the defeat of death. The role of Simon's mother-in-law in serving this meal shows the integral role of women as active participants within the new creation.

8. *Conclusion*

The healing of Simon's mother-in-law is depicted as a battle between Jesus and the force of evil. Jesus raises the woman, seizing her by the hand, and the fever releases her. In response she serves a meal to Jesus and the others present. This action may be regarded as paradigmatic of Jesus' healing of humanity. His action reveals the kingdom of God breaking into the world and inaugurating the new creation. Simon's mother-in-law, moreover, is the only person who serves Jesus in response to her healing. Jesus usually instructs those who have been healed to return to their homes (5.19, 34; 7.29; 10.52) and Bartimaeus alone follows Jesus on the way (10.52). This woman's service is thus the most positive response given by a human being to Jesus' act of healing. Her action is a sustaining power in the midst of the evil of the end-time, and she foreshadows Jesus' own service in his mission to redeem humanity.

Chapter 3

JESUS' BREAK WITH HIS FAMILY (3.20–35)

1. *Introduction*

In the opening chapters of Mark, Jesus begins a successful mission in Galilee, teaching, casting out demons and healing the sick. In our passage, however, those who might be expected to be closest to him, his own family, fail to understand him. His relatives, including his mother and sisters, set out to take him from his mission, believing that he is mad (3.21). The account of the break between Jesus and his family is framed around the dispute between Jesus and the scribes from Jerusalem (3.22–30).[1] The literary technique of intercalation aligns the misunderstanding of Jesus' family with the opposition of the scribes who accuse him of being possessed by Beelzebul (3.22). In response, Jesus redefines his family as those who do the will of God, and his brothers, sisters and mother as those who sit around him listening to his teaching (3.35).

Mark's negative presentation of Jesus' mother, sisters and brothers contrasts with their favourable portrayal in Matthew, Luke and John. Unlike Matthew and Luke, Mark does not have genealogies (Mt. 1.1–17; Lk. 3.23–38) or birth narratives describing the positive roles of Mary and Joseph (Mt. 1.18–25; Lk. 1.26–2.20). In John's Gospel, moreover, Mary is present at the wedding at Cana (Jn 2.1–11) and at the crucifixion where Jesus shows concern that she will be cared for after his death (Jn 19.25–27). Jesus' family is depicted as his followers in Acts, since Mary is described with Jesus' brothers and the first disciples in Jerusalem (Acts 1.14). In addition, Eusebius, mentions that after the martyrdom of James, Simeon a cousin of Jesus, takes over the leadership of the Jerusalem church (*Hist. eccl.* 3.11).

The negative portrayal of Jesus' family in our passage is toned down in Matthew (12.46–50) and Luke (8.19–21), who both omit the verse 'for they said, "He has gone out of his mind"' (ἔλεγον γὰρ ὅτι ἐξέστη, 3.21). Mark records that Jesus' family send word to him calling him (3.31), whereas in Matthew Jesus' relatives request to speak to him (εἰστήκεισαν ἔξω ζητοῦντες αὐτῷ λαλῆσαι, 12.46). In Luke, moreover, the family attempt to reach him but are prevented from doing so by the crowd (8.19). Mark's account compares Jesus' relatives unfavourably to the crowd, whereas Luke's Gospel does not exclude Jesus' family from among those who hear and do the word of God (8.21).

---

1. J.R. Edwards, 'Markan Sandwiches: The Significance of Interpolations in Markan Narratives', *NovT* 31 (1989), 209–10.

There does, however, appear to be a historical basis for the conflict between Jesus and his family because John's Gospel also reports that Jesus' brothers did not believe him (Jn 7.5). James is later recorded as a prominent figure in the early church (Acts 12.17; 15.13; 21.18), and he is associated with a law-observant mission in Gal. 2.11–14. This situation encourages Tyson to link the portrayal of Jesus' family to a dispute between Mark's community and the Jerusalem church.[2] Crossan supports Tyson's view by arguing that Jesus' family represent the Jerusalem hierarchy.[3] Other scholars, such as Barton, reject this interpretation because James does not have a prominent role in Mark and he was already dead by the time Mark was writing.[4] Mark's community, however, does not adhere to the teaching associated with James, since they have abandoned the food laws (7.19). Although Mark does not associate Jesus' family with a law-observant party, his omission of any direct reference to James may indicate a desire to distance his community from the law-observant teaching of James.

Other scholars place more emphasis on the interpretation of our passage as teaching on discipleship. Lambrecht compares the opposition of Jesus' family to that of the religious authorities, the Herodians and even the disciples.[5] According to Lambrecht, the tensions between Jesus and his family are intended to prepare disciples for the opposition they may experience on account of their faith. Best believes that disciples may also experience conflicts within their families.[6] He takes a more positive view of the breakup of Jesus' family, since he suggests that Mark's audience would be aware that Jesus' brothers later became church leaders. The implied restoration of Jesus' family, therefore, may encourage members of Mark's community rejected by their families to hope for a future reconciliation.

Whatever the exact significance of the Markan picture of Jesus' family, our passage thus gives a negative portrayal of women in the description of Mary and Jesus' sisters. Nevertheless, there are positive views of women in the reference to the women who sit around Jesus listening to his teaching. These women are incorporated into the new family of Jesus, and they are described as his mothers and sisters (3.35). According to Barton, Jesus does not reject the concept of family, but redefines family as the new eschatological community around Jesus who are related to him through their desire to do the will of God.[7] The new community is still structured as a family, and members of the group are linked together through fictive kinship ties.

There are, however, differences between birth families and the new eschatological community. As Schüssler Fiorenza observes, there is no reference to father in the new community.[8] She argues that this omission depicts the new family of Jesus as

2.   Tyson, 'Blindness', 40–42.
3.   J.D. Crossan, 'Mark and the Relatives of Jesus', *NovT* 15 (1973), 111–13.
4.   S.C. Barton, *Discipleship and Family Ties in Mark and Matthew* (Cambridge: Cambridge University Press, 1994), 84.
5.   J. Lambrecht, 'The Relatives of Jesus in Mark', *NovT* 16 (1974), 255–56.
6.   E. Best, 'Mark III.20, 21, 31–35', *NTS* 22 (1976), 317–18.
7.   Barton, *Discipleship*, 122–23.
8.   Schüssler Fiorenza, *In Memory*, 147.

an alternative to the male domination of the patriarchal family. Schüssler Fiorenza's analysis highlights the equality of women and men within the community, but Mark still retains the portrayal of God as father (8.38; 11.25; 13.32; 14.36). In addition, the male Jesus has a central role; those who do the will of God sit in a circle around Jesus listening to his teaching. Members of the community, moreover, relate to one another primarily through their relationship to Jesus; they are defined as his brother, sister and mother (3.35). Our passage thus raises the question of the role of women within Mark's apocalyptic world-view, a question that will be examined later in this chapter.

2. *The Portrayal of Jesus' Mother and Sisters*

Jesus' mother is not named in our passage, although Jesus is later described as 'son of Mary' in his hometown (6.3). The omission of Mary's name emphasizes her position as Jesus' mother. Similarly, the names of Jesus' brothers do not appear in this account, whereas they are recorded in 6.3. The omission of individual names reflects the focus of our passage on generic family relationships rather than on individual ones, and allows a direct comparison between Jesus' birth family and his new family of brothers, sisters and mothers (3.35).

We are told Mary's name in chapter 6 when Jesus is described as the 'son of Mary', which is unusual since according to Jewish custom human beings are normally identified by their father's name (cf. Mk 1.19; 2.14; 10.46). Some scholars suggest that this description may simply be used by the people of Jesus' hometown because they know that Joseph has already died.[9] The absence of a father's name, however, may have connotations of illegitimacy, and the description may be used by the townspeople as an insult (cf. Judg. 11.1). As Cranfield observes, the charge of illegitimacy is also made against Jesus in John 8.41 and 9.29, and in the later text Origen, *Cels.* 1.28–32.[10]

Nevertheless, there are a few instances in which a matronymic may be a positive description. Ilan notes that there are cases of men who are known by the names of their mothers, and she argues that 'son of Mary' does not necessarily have negative connotations. The examples she cites, however, characteristically occur if the man's mother comes from a priestly or royal family.[11] In these cases the use of a matronymic is a sign of social status rather than a derogatory term. This analysis does not apply to Mark's Gospel, since there is no indication that Mary came from a prominent family, and indeed Jesus is described as a carpenter (6.3).

Other scholars have also attempted to interpret 'son of Mary' in a positive way. Bauckham proposes that Mark refers to Jesus as the 'son of Mary' in order to dis-

---

9.   R.E. Brown *et al.*, *Mary in the New Testament: A Collaborative Assessment by Protestant and Roman Catholic Scholars* (London: Chapman, 1978), 64.

10.   Cranfield, *St. Mark*, 195.

11.   T. Ilan, ' "Man Born of Woman…" (Job 14.1) The Phenomenon of Men Bearing Matronymes at the Time of Jesus', *NovT* 34 (1992): 23–45.

tinguish Jesus from his half-brothers who have a different mother.[12] Mark does not suggest that Jesus and his brothers and sisters have different mothers. There are several other references to the brothers and sisters of Jesus in the New Testament (Mt. 12.46; 13.55–56; Lk. 8.19–20; Jn 2.12; 7.3, 5, 10; Acts 1.14; 1 Cor. 9.5; Gal. 1.19) and at no point is there a sign that the term brother or sister is not to be taken literally. The theory that Jesus' brothers and sisters are children from a previous marriage is not attested in the New Testament and first appears in the second-century text *Prot. Jas.* 9.2; 17.1–18.1. This belief, moreover, appears to lead to the later doctrine of the perpetual virginity of Mary.[13]

It is probable that the description 'son of Mary' is intended to be derogatory, since the townspeople do not believe that Jesus is a prophet because of his background. His work as a carpenter and the description 'son of Mary' are both used to denigrate his prophetic claims. The other Gospels, moreover, avoid this description. Matthew refers to Jesus as the 'son of the carpenter' (13.55), while Luke and John describe him as the 'son of Joseph' (Lk. 4.22; Jn 1.45; 6.42). One manuscript (P^{45}) even changes the description 'son of Mary' to 'son of the carpenter and Mary'. In the literary context of Mark, however, the omission of any reference to Joseph has the theological effect of stressing both the sonship of Jesus (1.11; 9.7; 15.39), and the role of God as the father of Jesus (11.25; 14.36).

The names of the sisters of Jesus are unrecorded in our passage, and they are not listed in chapter 6. The omission of the sisters' names may reflect Mark's sources, since first-century texts characteristically name more men than women, and this feature occurs in all the Gospels.[14] Mark includes the names of Jesus' brothers in 6.3, but they do not appear again in Mark's narrative. Similarly, all twelve male disciples are recorded, despite the fact that they do not all act individually. Mark may thus employ the list of both the Twelve and Jesus' brothers because they have been preserved from an early stage in the tradition. It may also reflect the prominence of Jesus' brothers in the early church. As we have seen, James becomes a leader of the church (Acts 12.17; 15.13; 21.18; Gal. 2.11–14), and we have New Testament letters attributed to James and to another brother of Jesus, Jude.

The names of Jesus' four brothers give a greater sense of their individuality (6.3), whereas his sisters are defined as a group. We know the number of Jesus' brothers, but not that of his sisters. The townspeople say that the sisters are 'here' with them, which suggests that the women still live in their hometown (οὐκ εἰσὶν αἱ ἀδελφαὶ αὐτοῦ ὧδε πρὸς ἡμᾶς, 6.3). Women traditionally joined the families of their husbands.[15] It is possible that Jesus' sisters are more closely associated with the townspeople because they have married men from the town.

---

12. R. Bauckham, 'The Brothers and Sisters of Jesus: An Epiphanian Response to John P. Meier', *CBQ* 56 (1994), 686–700.

13. Some of the Church Fathers held the doctrine of the perpetual virginity of Mary. Epiphanius (*Pan.*) believed that Jesus' brothers were sons of Joseph by an earlier wife, and Jerome (*Helv.*) argued that they were sons of Mary's sister who was also called Mary, and who was married to Clopas. Jesus' brothers are thus cousins of Jesus.

14. See Ilan, 'Notes', 186–200.

15. Wegner, *Chattel or Person?* 40–45.

Our passage and its synoptic parallels is the only account which refers directly to the presence of Jesus' sisters in the New Testament (cf. Mt. 12.46–50; Lk. 8.19–21). His sisters are mentioned by the inhabitants of his hometown in Mark 6.3 and Matthew 13.56. The reference to Jesus' sisters (καὶ αἱ ἀδελφαί σου, 3.32), however, appears in manuscripts A and D, but does not occur in the earliest manuscripts. Taylor argues that the phrase is a scribal addition influenced by 3.34 and 6.3, and he finds no evidence that Jesus' sisters are present.[16] Other scholars, such as Marcus, accept this verse as authentic, and he points out that it is more likely that this part of the verse was omitted from these manuscripts in order to correspond to 3.33 or on account of their homoeoarcton and homoeoteleuton (καὶ οἱ ἀδελφοί σου καὶ αἱ ἀδελφαί σου).[17] Scribes, moreover, tend to omit references to women rather than to add them, particularly when the term οἱ ἀδελφοί (brothers, 3.31, 33, 34) is a masculine plural noun which may be used inclusively to refer to Jesus' brothers and sisters.

The use of οἱ ἀδελφοί in our account thus provides an example of the ways in which androcentric language may act to conceal the presence of women, leading scholars such as Taylor to assume that Jesus' sisters are not present. The question of the crowd, which directly refers to Jesus' sisters (3.32), adds to the contrast between the behaviour of his family and the actions of the women and men who listen to his teaching (3.35). In this way all the members of Jesus' birth family, both male and female, oppose his mission.

The negative portrayal of Jesus' relatives is continued in chapter 6, where Jesus teaches that a prophet is not honoured in his country, by his kin, and in his house (ἐν τῇ πατρίδι αὐτοῦ καὶ ἐν τοῖς συγγενεῦσιν αὐτοῦ καὶ ἐν τῇ οἰκίᾳ αὐτοῦ, 6.4). As Barton points out, the threefold list of terms is unique to Mark, since Luke (4.24) and John (4.44) only refer to country, and Matthew (13.57) has country and house.[18] Barton suggests that the reference to kin appears to be an example of Markan redaction which continues the theme of family breakup. It is possible, however, that Matthew and Luke omit the reference to kin in their desire to distance themselves from Mark's negative portrayal of Jesus' family.

Our passage begins with the determination of οἱ παρ᾽ αὐτοῦ (3.21) to set out to take hold of him because they believe that he is mad. The description οἱ παρ᾽ αὐτοῦ is a general term with the literal meaning 'those from beside him'. Taylor notes that in classical Greek the phrase refers to 'envoys' or 'ambassadors', and in the LXX it occurs with the meaning 'adherents' or 'followers' (1 Macc. 9.44; 11.73; 12.27; 2 Macc 11.20), but may also signify 'parents' and other 'relatives' (Prov. 31.21; Sus 33; Josephus, *Ant.* 1.193).[19] According to Painter οἱ παρ᾽ αὐτοῦ refers to the disciples, since our passage immediately follows the call of the Twelve (3.13–19).[20] He believes that the disciples wish to restrain Jesus because the crowd

16. Taylor, *St. Mark*, 246.
17. Marcus, *Mark*, 276–77.
18. Barton, *Discipleship*, 90.
19. Taylor, *St. Mark*, 236.
20. J. Painter, 'When is a House not Home? Disciples and Family in Mark 3.13-35', *NTS* 45 (1999), 501–509.

say that he is mad. It is more likely that οἱ παρ' αὐτοῦ (3.21) refers to Jesus' relatives, since our passage is constructed in the form of Mark's characteristic technique
of intercalation. In this way the relatives (3.31) may be identified with Jesus' mother,
sisters and brothers (3.31, 32, 33). The literary technique of intercalation thus
allows a lapse of time between the departure and arrival of Jesus' family.

The family of Jesus is depicted as a unity who act together under the leadership
of Jesus' mother, who is mentioned first (3.31, 32, 33, 34; 6.3). This portrayal of
Mary is reminiscent of that in the account of the wedding at Cana in John's Gospel,
in which Mary takes control of the situation and asks Jesus to help (Jn 2.1–11). The
leading role of Mary in these accounts challenges the assumption that first-century
women did not act independently of their husbands and sons. Mary's determination
and initiative foreshadow that of other women in Mark, such as the woman with the
flow of blood who approaches Jesus for healing (5.24–34) and the Syrophoenician
woman who seeks help for her daughter (7.24–30).

These women, however, respond positively to Jesus, whereas his mother, brothers
and sisters set out to take him from his mission. In Fander's view Jesus' relatives
plan to interrupt his mission because they believe he is damaging their reputation.[21]
She compares the reaction of Jesus' family to the opposition of the people of his
hometown (6.1–6). The people of Nazareth cannot believe that Jesus is a prophet
because he is a carpenter, and they know his family (6.3). According to Fander
both groups reject Jesus because he acts outwith the norms of his community. In
addition, May interprets the passage in relation to social scientific studies of honour
and shame, suggesting that Jesus' relatives are afraid that Jesus' behaviour will
bring dishonour to his family.[22] These interpretations are questionable, since there
is no reference in the passage to the family's concern for their damaged reputation
or honour. Instead, the crowds appear to acclaim Jesus, which implies that so far he
has a positive reputation. In his analysis, Myers emphasizes the threat to Jesus from
the religious authorities and suggests that Jesus' family seek to protect him from the
danger his mission is creating.[23] There is no indication, however, that Jesus' family
are aware of the opposition from the scribes. Jesus' family come from Nazareth in
Galilee, whereas the scribes travel from Jerusalem, and there is no meeting between
the two groups.

Both Fander and Myers fail to interpret the action of Jesus' family in the immediate context of the surrounding narrative, which states that the pressure of the crowd
is so great that Jesus and his disciples do not have time to eat (3.20). This introduction is followed by the phrase ἀκούσαντες οἱ παρ' αὐτοῦ (when his relatives
heard, 3.21), and Lane rightly points out that the action of Jesus' family is a response
to hearing that he has not eaten.[24] The opening verse thus implies that the demands
of the crowd and the inability of Jesus and his disciples to find time to eat lead
Jesus' relatives to believe that he is mad. This interpretation is supported by the
associations of madness with lack of food or fasting. The charge that John the

21. Fander, *Stellung*, 326–27.
22. D.M. May, 'Mark 3.20-35 From the Perspective of Shame/ Honor', *BTB* 17 (1987), 85.
23. Myers, *Binding*, 168.
24. W.L. Lane, *The Gospel of Mark* (NICNT; Grand Rapids: Eerdmans, 1974), 139.

Baptist is possessed by a demon, for example, is linked to the portrayal of him as someone who does not eat bread or drink wine (Mt. 11.18; Lk. 7.33). Jesus' relatives, therefore, set out to seize him in an attempt to protect him from the crowds.

Other scholars, such as Crossan, reject the view that Jesus' relatives act out of concern for him. Crossan argues that 3.20 is the concluding verse to the previous pericope and that 3.21 is the beginning of our passage.[25] As evidence he points to a pattern of the call of disciples followed by a description of a meal with Jesus. The call of the first four disciples concludes with a meal in the house of Simon (1.31), the call of Levi is also followed by an account of a meal (2.15), and Crossan regards the desire to eat as the conclusion to the call of the Twelve (3.13–19). Crossan is right to note the Markan emphasis on the role of meals to indicate the conclusion of a day's events, but on this occasion Jesus and the disciples are unable to have a meal. Crossan, moreover, ignores the progression of the text since Mark's audience would hear the two verses read one after the other, and this juxtaposition implies that Jesus' relatives are motivated by the news that Jesus' mission is preventing him from eating.

The inability to eat points to the personal cost of Jesus' mission, and the threat of the crowd to Jesus' well-being may be seen in other passages. Jesus asks his disciples to prepare a boat for him lest the crowd crush him (3.9), and when a large crowd gathers he sits in the boat on the sea (4.1). In our passage the demands of the crowd prevent Jesus and his disciples from eating, and this situation is repeated after the mission of the Twelve when Jesus and his disciples have no opportunity to eat (6.31).

The family of Jesus are portrayed as concerned for his welfare, but they fail to understand his mission. They react by attempting to take hold of him, and the vehemence of their intention is indicated by the use of the verb κρατέω (seize, 3.21). The violent connotations of the verb κρατέω may be seen in the account of the arrest of John the Baptist (6.17) and of Jesus (14.1, 44, 46, 49). The desire of Jesus' mother, sisters and brothers to seize him thus foreshadows the plot of his enemies to arrest him in the Passion Narrative. Through their aim to stop the mission of Jesus, the relatives of Jesus are aligned with those who wish to stop the work of God.

The response of Jesus' family is reminiscent of the reaction of the people of Gerasa, who attempt to control the demoniac who lives in their midst (5.1–20). They illustrate the human response of attempting to control and domesticate those they cannot understand. The townspeople of Gerasa try to tame the demoniac, treating him as if he were a wild animal (αὐτὸν δαμάσαι, 5.4). When Jesus casts out the demons and liberates the man from his affliction, the townspeople ask Jesus to leave their land. Jesus seizes human beings in order to save them from the forces of disease and death (1.31; 5.41; 9.27). The desire of Jesus' family to take hold of him, on the other hand, is an action that restricts Jesus' freedom and aligns them with the controlling force of Satan.

25. Crossan, 'Mark', 83–87.

The relatives of Jesus perceive that Jesus' mission is causing him harm, and they thus interpret the personal cost to Jesus as a sign of madness. As Edwards suggests, their view foreshadows that of Peter, who attempts to dissuade Jesus from his mission of suffering and death.[26] In response to Peter's protestations, Jesus calls Peter 'Satan' and makes a distinction between the human sphere and God's sphere: Peter does not think the things of God, but the things of human beings (οὐ φρονεῖς τὰ τοῦ θεοῦ ἀλλὰ τὰ τῶν ἀνθρώπων, 8.33). In the same way, Jesus' family illustrates a human rather than a divine response, and they stand outside the house in contrast to those inside who do the will of God (3.35). In this passage, however, the family of Jesus do not succeed in their plan, and they are left standing outside the house. The family do not reappear in Mark's narrative, and the group of disciples become the primary human relationships of Jesus.

3. *The Intercalation of Mark 3.20–35*

Scholars identify the literary technique of intercalation as a characteristic of Mark's Gospel (5.21–43; 11.12–25; 14.1–11) that is designed to enable two stories to reflect and comment on one another.[27] In Mark, the attempt of Jesus' family to restrain him is juxtaposed to the accusations of the scribes from Jerusalem, which heightens the harsh portrait of Jesus' relatives by comparing them to Jesus' enemies. The comparison between Jesus' relatives and the scribes is further indicated by the verbal correspondences in their accusations:

> ἔλεγον γὰρ ὅτι ἐξέστη (3.21),
> ἔλεγον ὅτι Βεελζεβοὺλ ἔχει καὶ ὅτι ἐν τῷ ἄρχοντι τῶν δαιμονίων
> ἐκβάλλει τὰ δαιμόνια (3.22).
> for they said, 'He has gone out of his mind.'
> for they said, 'He has Beelzebul, and by the ruler of the demons he casts
> out demons.'

The inner section of our passage concludes with the saying about the sin against the Holy Spirit (3.28–29). Edwards rightly observes that the middle section of the Markan sandwiches provides the key to the interpretation of the outer sections.[28] His article raises the question of the culpability of Jesus' relatives. Are they as guilty as the scribes in Mark's eyes? Crossan, for example, thinks so, arguing that the saying about the sin against the Holy Spirit (3.28–29) is placed at the conclusion of Jesus' teaching in order to show that both Jesus' relatives and the scribes are guilty of this sin.[29]

The inner section of the intercalation focuses on the dispute between Jesus and the scribes over the source of his power to cast out demons. The scribes argue that Jesus is possessed by Beelzebul and casts out demons through the power of demons (3.22). The accusation of demon possession is related to the charge of sorcery

---

26. Edwards, 'Markan Sandwiches', 210.
27. See, e.g., Edwards, 'Markan Sandwiches', 193–216.
28. Edwards, 'Markan Sandwiches', 196.
29. Crossan, 'Mark', 96.

which is associated with Jesus in the writings of the church fathers (Justin, *Dial.* 69; Origen, *Cels.* 1.6; 8.9) and in the Talmud (*b. Sanh.* 43a; 107b). Marcus, moreover, observes that the charge of sorcery may be related to the attempt to encourage human beings to disregard the Law and in this case could carry the death penalty (cf. Deut. 18.19–20; cf. Philo, *Spec. Leg.* 4.50–52).[30] The accusations of the scribes, therefore, may reflect their desire to condemn Jesus to death.

Jesus responds to his opponents in parables by asking if Satan can cast out Satan. If this were true, Jesus' exorcisms would show that Satan's house was divided and at an end. The fact that Satan's reign is not over implies that Jesus does not carry out exorcisms through the power of Satan. The following parable of the strong man (3.27) suggests that the reign of Satan is being broken by Jesus' miracles and exorcisms. Satan is described as the strong man (ὁ ἰσχυρός, 3.27), who must first be bound so that his house may be plundered. Jesus, however, is described by John the Baptist as the stronger one (ὁ ἰσχυρότερος, 1.7). As Hooker observes, Satan's kingdom is being threatened by Jesus from the outside rather than by internal division.[31] In the apocalyptic context of the Gospel Satan has temporarily taken over the world, but Jesus the Son of God has come to inaugurate the new creation and liberate humanity. The binding of evil powers has an eschatological dimension (Isa. 24.22; Rev. 20.2–3; *T. Levi* 18.12). Jesus' exorcisms are signs of the kingdom of God breaking into the world (1.25), and they are proleptic of the end-time when evil will be fully overthrown.

Jesus concludes with the saying about the sin against the Holy Spirit (3.28–29). The Spirit is the creative power of God and the eschatological gift of the new age (Isa. 44.3; Ezek. 36.26–27; Joel 2.28–29). In Mark, Jesus has been baptized in the Holy Spirit (1.9–11), and he carries out his miracles in the power of the Spirit (cf. 1.24). Blasphemy against the Holy Spirit, therefore, corresponds to blasphemy against Jesus. The charge of blasphemy is the key charge against Jesus during his trial before the Sanhedrin. Jesus is convicted of blasphemy when he confesses his identity as the Messiah, the Son of the Blessed (14.61–64). Jesus warns the scribes of the danger of being guilty of an eternal sin (ἔνοχός ἐστιν αἰωνίου ἁμαρτήμα-τος, 3.29), yet Jesus himself is pronounced guilty by them among others (ἔνοχον εἶναι θανάτου, 14.64). There is a verbal similarity between the account of Satan rising up against himself (ὁ σατανᾶς ἀνέστη ἐφ᾽ ἑαυτὸν, 3.26) and the description of the chief priest who rises up against Jesus (ἀναστὰς ὁ ἀρχιερεὺς, 14.60). Behind the accusations of the chief priest, then, is the figure of Satan who desires to put Jesus to death. Jesus is condemned, but paradoxically the religious authorities condemn themselves.

As we have seen, the intercalation raises the question of whether or not Mark equates the charge of Jesus' relatives with the accusations of the scribes. There is a link between the belief of Jesus' family that he is mad and the charge of the scribes that Jesus is possessed by a demon. Scholars, such as Nineham, observe that the

---

30. Marcus, *Mark*, 281.
31. M.D. Hooker, *A Commentary on the Gospel according to St. Mark* (Black's New Testament Commentaries; London: A. & C. Black, 1991), 116.

charge of madness is associated with demon possession in Jn 10.20–21; 7.20; 8.48, 52.[32] Lambrecht, however, is convincing when he points out that the accusation ἐξέστη (He has gone out of his mind, 3.21) is not as strong as the accusation of blasphemy.[33] Although madness may be associated with demon possession, the latter belief is not explicitly stated by Jesus' relatives.

The parables of the inner section of the intercalation, moreover, are addressed particularly to the scribes. Jesus calls the scribes together in response to their accusations (προσκαλεσάμενος αὐτοὺς, 3.23), and he speaks to them in parables. His teaching concludes with the saying concerning blasphemy against the Holy Spirit (3.28–29). Gnilka notes that the scribes openly attack Jesus and he addresses his teaching concerning the sin against the Holy Spirit to them.[34] It is noteworthy, moreover, that Jesus' family have not yet arrived at the house. The explanatory clause ὅτι ἔλεγον, Πνεῦμα ἀκάθαρτον ἔχει (for they said, 'He has an unclean spirit', 3.30) indicates that this saying is intended to be a warning to the scribes. The relatives of Jesus do not directly accuse him of being demon-possessed unlike the scribes.

Both the relatives' accusations of madness and the scribes' charge of demon possession illustrate the failure of human beings to understand the mission of Jesus. The presentation of Jesus' relatives, however, differs from that of the scribes, since the former act out of concern for him, misguidedly believing that they are helping him by attempting to remove him from his mission. The relatives of Jesus do not appear again, whereas the opposition of the scribes increases, and they are part of the group of religious leaders who condemn Jesus to death (8.31; 10.33; 14.1, 43, 53; 15.1, 31).

In the apocalyptic context of the Gospel, human beings are unable to understand the identity of Jesus until his death on the cross, when the Roman centurion recognizes him as the Son of God (15.39). Jesus' family fail to realize that Jesus' mission will cost him his life. In this way they behave like Peter in attempting to protect Jesus from suffering and death. In contrast, the scribes wish Jesus to die, but fail to understand that paradoxically their plans are working in accordance with God's will to redeem creation through Jesus. The intention of Jesus' relatives to take him from his mission does not succeed, whereas the plot of the scribes will succeed, at least in a superficial way as they form part of the group of religious authorities who will condemn Jesus to death. Jesus identifies the end of Satan's reign with the division of kingdoms and houses (3.24–25), and in this passage we see that Jesus' own house is divided, which is an indication of the presence of the end-time (cf. 13.12; Mic. 7.6; *Jub.* 23.16).

32. D.E. Nineham, *Saint Mark* (Pelican New Testament Commentaries; Middlesex: Penguin Books, 1963), 123.
33. Lambrecht, 'Relatives', 245–46.
34. Gnilka, *Evangelium*, 1.149.

4. *Discipleship*

In our account Jesus' mother, brothers and sisters misunderstand his mission, whereas the crowd who sit around him listening to his teaching are described as his true mother, brothers and sisters (3.35). This group become his new family, since they are the ones who do the will of God. Mark employs language associated with discipleship to highlight the contrasting responses of Jesus' family and his followers. Jesus' mission begins with the proclamation of the gospel (1.15). Throughout Mark there is an emphasis on the importance of hearing and understanding (4.3, 9, 10–12, 23; 8.18), and 'hearing' frequently represents the first action of those who end up following Jesus.

In chapter 4 those who hear Jesus' parables and approach him for further instruction are the ones who are given the mystery of the kingdom of God (4.10–12).[35] This pattern may also be seen in the narrative of the healing of the woman with the flow of blood, who hears of Jesus and follows him in the crowd (5.27), and in the account of the Syrophoenician woman, who hears of him and approaches him for healing (7.27). There is a contrast between those who 'hear' of Jesus and approach him seeking healing, and his relatives who hear what he is doing and wish to take hold of him (3.21). Those who are desperately ill respond to Jesus as the one who can bring them health, whereas his own people fail to understand him.

In our account the family of Jesus send to Jesus calling him (ἀπέστειλαν πρὸς αὐτὸν καλοῦντες αὐτόν, 3.31). As Marcus notes, the verb καλέω (to call) occurs in the call of James and John (1.20)[36] and in the selection of the Twelve (προσκαλεῖται οὓς ἤθελεν αὐτός, 3.13). Jesus calls his followers to come after him, whereas his relatives want Jesus to come to them. The verb ἀποστέλλω (to send) is a discipleship term, which occurs in the account of the selection of the Twelve who are chosen to be sent out to preach (ἵνα ἀποστέλλῃ αὐτοὺς κηρύσσειν, 3.14), and again in the description of the sending out of the Twelve (ἤρξατο αὐτοὺς ἀποστέλλειν δύο δύο, 6.7). In addition, Jesus refers to himself as the one sent by God (καὶ ὃς ἂν ἐμὲ δέχηται, οὐκ ἐμὲ δέχεται ἀλλὰ τὸν ἀποστείλαντά με, 9.37). God is the one who sends Jesus, and Jesus in turn will send his disciples to carry out his mission. In the apocalyptic context of the Gospel Jesus is engaged in a battle against Satan (1.12–13), and his disciples are called to continue this mission. Jesus' relatives, however, unwittingly attempt to summon Jesus from his mission instead of joining him inside the house. Jesus' family thus find themselves opposing God by attempting to call him from his mission.

In our passage Jesus' family stand outside the house where Jesus is teaching (ἔξω στήκοντες, 3.31), and they send word to him rather than enter the house. Their attitude contrasts with the faith of the four friends, who create a hole in the roof of a house to lower the paralysed man to Jesus (2.1–12), and with that of the Gentile Syrophoenician woman, who approaches Jesus in a house with a request for healing for her daughter (7.24–30). Jesus' family, therefore, who may be

35. Marcus, *Mark*, 301–7.
36. Marcus, *Mark*, 276.

expected to be insiders, act as outsiders to Jesus' mission. The spatial distance of Jesus' family from him expresses their misunderstanding of his mission. His family believe that he is mad (ἐξέστη, 3.21), which has the literal meaning 'he has stood outside'. As Marcus observes, they believe that Jesus is 'outside', yet they reveal themselves as outsiders by their response to him.[37] Their response, however, is not as culpable as that of the scribes who *do* enter the house, but with the purpose of threatening Jesus.

The house, as we have already seen, is the place associated with teaching and healing in 2.1–12. In other passages disciples approach Jesus in a house for further instruction (7.17; 9.28, 33; 10.10). Malbon argues that Jesus owns a house (cf. 2.15),[38] but apart from the initial reference to the house of Simon and Andrew (1.29), we are not given any indication of the owners of the houses (cf. 7.24; 9.28, 33; 10.10). The house thus becomes a symbolic term associated with the new community which forms around Jesus. In Mark's Gospel, however, the boundary of the house does not protect Jesus from his enemies (3.1–6). Jesus shows an openness to those who enter the house to the extent that even one of his chosen disciples betrays him.

In our passage Jesus is identified as the one who communicates the teaching of God to human beings. There is an emphasis on action, since the act of doing the will of God is defined as listening to Jesus' teaching. As Brown *et al.* note, the presence of the crowd indicates their 'openness to the will of God'.[39] In Matthew, Jesus identifies those who do the will of God as his disciples (12.49), whereas in Mark, Jesus refers to the larger, more fluid group of the crowd. Those who sit in a circle around Jesus (περὶ αὐτὸν κύκλῳ, 3.34) point forward to the group who later sit around Jesus with the Twelve (οἱ περὶ αὐτὸν σὺν τοῖς δώδεκα, 4.10).[40] They seek an explanation of Jesus' parables, and they are thus the ones who receive the secret of the kingdom of God (4.11). Jesus' family are described as standing outside (ἔξω, 3.31, 32), which foreshadows the 'outsiders' (ἔξω, 4.11) who receive everything in parables lest they turn to God and are forgiven (4.11–12).

The focus on the will of God (τὸ θέλημα τοῦ θεοῦ, 3.35) is an indication of the theocentric nature of Mark, and this emphasis is illustrated later in the Gospel by Jesus' citation of the great commandment (12.28–31). In Gethsemane, moreover, Jesus is portrayed as following the will of God even though this desire costs him his life (ἀλλ' οὐ τί ἐγὼ θέλω ἀλλὰ τί σύ, 14.36). Jesus addresses God as his father (ἀββα ὁ πατήρ, 14.36), and his identity as Son of God is shown by his desire to follow the will of God. Jesus acts as an example for his disciples, and as Best points out, all human beings are called to follow the way of the cross.[41] The verb θέλω (to wish), moreover, is used frequently in the teaching of Jesus about discipleship, as can be seen in the call to the disciples to follow the way of the

37. J. Marcus, *The Mystery of the Kingdom of God* (SBLDS, 90; Atlanta: Scholars Press, 1986), n. 62 93.
38. E.S. Malbon, 'TH OIKIA AYTOY: Mark 2.15 in Context', *NTS* 31 (1985), 282–92.
39. Brown *et al.*, *Mary*, 58.
40. Marcus, *Mark*, 302.
41. Best, 'Mark III', 319.

cross (εἴ τις θέλει ὀπίσω μου ἀκολουθεῖν, 8.34) and also in the definition of discipleship as service (εἴ τις θέλει πρῶτος εἶναι, ἔσται πάντων ἔσχατος καὶ πάντων διάκονος (9.35). These correspondences show that the new family around Jesus are those who follow the way of the cross.

5. *The Role of Women as Disciples*

In Mark, women are described as listening to Jesus' teaching, and they are included in Jesus' new family as his sisters and mothers (3.35). In our passage Mark uses the individual terms of brother and sister, whereas the masculine plural 'brothers' (οἱ ἀδελφοί) could have been used to refer to both men and women. Luke's Gospel, for example, does not list the singular feminine nouns of sister and mother, but uses the masculine inclusive plural term οἱ ἀδελφοί (8.19, 20, 21). In Mark, the inclusion of the feminine terms stresses the importance of women within the listening group. The positive description of women suggests that they had a prominent role within Mark's community.

Traditionally family terms are associated with the twelve tribes of Israel who correspond to the sons of Jacob.[42] As Wilkins observes, family terms are used in the Qumran literature, whose authors believed themselves to belong to the new Israel (1 QS 6.10, 22; CD 6.20; 7.1–2). Similar family terminology is used as a boundary marker in the Hellenistic Jewish novel *Joseph and Aseneth*. Joseph refuses to kiss Aseneth, the Gentile daughter of an Egyptian priest, because a man who worships God will kiss only 'his mother and the sister (who is born) of his mother and the sister (who is born) of his clan and family and the wife who shares his bed, (all of) who(m) bless with their mouths the living God' (8.6). As Barclay points out, primary social relations are here defined by religious boundaries.[43]

After her conversion Aseneth is rejected by her family because she refuses to worship their gods, and she describes herself as an orphan (11.3–5). God is described as 'the father of orphans' (11.13; 12.13), and she receives a new father in God (12.8, 14–15). Furthermore, her religious community is defined as her family. Similarly, in Mark those who sit around Jesus listening to his teaching find a new identity in their position as brothers, sisters and mother of Jesus who is the Son of God, and God is the father of the whole community. The fictive kinship terminology continues within the early church, as the terms ἀδελφός and ἀδελφή are employed as discipleship terms (Rom. 16.1, 17, 23; 1 Cor. 1.10, 11, 26).

Our account describes the dispute between Jesus and his family, which arises as a result of his mission. Jesus' experience foreshadows that of his followers who may also be rejected by their families. Crossan notes that the same order of family relationships ('brother', 'sister' and 'mother') in our passage may be seen in 10.29 ('brothers', 'sisters', 'mothers', and 'fathers').[44] He observes, moreover, that the

42. M.J. Wilkins, 'Brother, Brotherhood', *ABD*, I, 782–83.
43. J.M.G. Barclay, *Jews in the Mediterranean Diaspora from Alexander to Trajan (323 B.C.E.-117 C.E.)*, (Edinburgh: T. & T. Clark, 1996), 209.
44. Crossan, 'Mark', 98.

expected order of the family terms would be to place fathers before mothers, as Matthew does in the parallel passage (Mt. 19.29). As Crossan argues, Mark intentionally adopts the same order in his two passages because he wishes to draw out the correspondences between the rejection of Jesus by his family and the similar opposition that his followers will experience.

Disciples leave their own family to receive a large family which consists of all the followers of Jesus, but they will also experience persecution (10.30). The description of a hundredfold rewards (ἑκατονταπλασίονα) and the reference to persecution (μετὰ διωγμῶν, 10.30) recall the parable of the sower (4.1–20), in which the proclamation of the gospel will meet persecution (διωγμοῦ διὰ τὸν λόγον, 4.17), but those who accept the message will produce up to a hundredfold harvest (ἐν ἑκατόν, 4.20). In chapter 4 the parable of the sower concludes with a description of an abundant harvest (4.20). Similarly, Mark stresses that opposition will not prevail, since disciples not only receive abundant rewards in the present age but will receive the gift of eternal life in the age to come (10.30).

In our passage the opposition of Jesus' family is not a sign of the failure of his mission. As Gnilka observes, this account shows that the misunderstanding of Jesus' family and the accusations of the scribes do not halt Jesus' mission.[45] Instead, a huge crowd of followers are presented as his new family. Similarly, the disciples who leave relatives and home to follow Jesus may expect to receive a far larger family despite the experience of persecution, and in the age to come eternal life (10.29–30).

The portrayal of the disciples who leave everything behind to follow Jesus in chapter 10 raises the question of whether or not women are included in this group. Fander follows Theissen's differentiation of the Jesus movement into wandering charismatics and settled supporters, and she asserts that the reference to the brothers, sisters and mothers in 10.30 applies to settled supporters.[46] Fander, moreover, believes that women were primarily among the settled supporters.[47] In our passage, however, Jesus addresses his teaching to individual women and men who leave their birth families to become the sisters and brothers of Jesus in his new family (3.35). In chapter 10 there is also no indication that Mark refers only to men who leave their families and homes. The motive for leaving family and home is service of Jesus and of the gospel (ἕνεκεν ἐμοῦ καὶ ἕνεκεν τοῦ εὐαγγελίου, 10.29). This phrase is also used in the invitation to the crowd to follow Jesus on the way of the cross (8.35). The correspondence between these two passages suggests that Jesus' call to follow him is addressed to both women and men.

There is also little evidence in Mark for a sharp division between wandering charismatics and settled supporters. Schüssler Fiorenza points out that Theissen's theory is based on Luke's Gospel, which includes a reference to men who leave their wives on account of their mission (14.26; 18.29).[48] Mark and Matthew, however, do not include this reference, and Luke's interpretation appears to be an

45. Gnilka, *Evangelium*, 1.153.
46. Fander, *Stellung*, 330–31.
47. Fander, *Stellung*, 320–22.
48. Schüssler Fiorenza (*In Memory*, 145–46) refers to G. Theissen, *Sociology of Early Palestinian Christianity* (Philadelphia: Fortress Press, 1978), 12.

example of redaction. Luke is the only Gospel which implies that men are the only ones who leave their families and homes to carry out their mission.

In Mark a group of women have followed Jesus in Galilee and accompanied him to Jerusalem (15.40–41). These women have left their families and homes to follow Jesus. Fander accepts the possibility that Mary Magdalene is a missionary, and also the evidence that Peter's wife accompanied him (1 Cor. 9.5).[49] She does, however, downplay the references to women who travelled on mission, such as Phoebe who is a deacon of the church at Cenchreae (Rom. 16.1). There are other references to women and men who travelled as missionaries, for example, Prisca and Aquila (Acts 18.2–3; Rom. 16.3–5; 1 Cor. 16.19) and Junia and Andronicus (Rom. 16.7). In the *Acts of Paul and Thecla* Thecla is persecuted by her family because she leaves home to become a missionary. Her mother calls for her death because she refuses to marry Thamyris, her parents' choice of husband (*Acts of Paul and Thecla* 20).

6. *Excursus: Mark's use of the term* μαθηταί

Our passage portrays women who listen to Jesus' teaching, and who become members of his new family (3.35). They are described in terms of discipleship, but the feminine singular noun for disciple μαθήτρια does not occur in Mark or in any of the canonical Gospels. It does, however, appear once in Acts 9.36 to describe Tabitha, and it is used of Mary Magdalene in the *Gospel of Peter* (12.50). The term μαθητής (disciple) is associated with the followers of a teacher and etymologically refers to one who learns. The basic meaning of the cognate verb μανθάνω is 'to direct one's mind to something'.[50] Rengstrof argues that the female term is rare because of the lack of opportunities for women to develop their education.[51] He notes that Diogenes Laertius, *Pythagoras* 8.42 mentions that Pythagoras may have had a disciple (μαθήτρια) called Theano, and he refers to two women who are associated with the Platonic academy. Rabbinic literature also records few references to women studying the Law.[52] A notable exception, however, is Beruriah (*b. 'Erub.* 53b; *t. Kelim. BM* 1.6).[53] Archer, moreover, points out that the custom of

---

49. Fander, *Stellung*, 320–22.
50. K. H. Rengstorf 'μαθητής', *TDNT*, IV, 415–61.
51. Rengstorf, *TDNT*, IV, 460.
52. Ilan (*Jewish Women*, 190–204) observes that there was no official education system for girls, although some girls may have had the opportunity to learn to read and write at home.
53. D. Goodblatt ('The Beruriah Traditions', *JJS* 26 [1975], 68–85) has examined the references to Beruriah in rabbinic writings. He notes that Beruriah is identified as the wife of Rabbi Me'ir (*b. Ber.* 10a) and the daughter of Hananyah ben Teradyon and the wife of Rabbi Me'ir (*b. Pesah* 62b; *b. 'Erub.* 53b–54a). There are, however, also references to an unnamed daughter of Hananyah ben Teradyon (*t. Kelim BQ* 4.17; *Sifre Deut.* 307; *Sem* 12; *b. 'Abod. Zar.* 18a) and to an unnamed wife of Rabbi Me'ir (*Midr. Prov.* 31.1). Other sources refer to the father-in-law of Rabbi Me'ir as Ben Ziroz (*y. Demai* 2.1, 22c; *b. Hul.* 6b). Goodblatt notes that the citations which identify Beruriah as the daughter of Hananyah and the wife of Rabbi Me'ir are both from the Babylonian Amoraic tradition, and he proposes that the Babylonian tradition has elaborated and linked traditions concerning Beruriah identifying her as the daughter of Hananyah ben Teradyon and the wife of Rabbi Me'ir (cf. *b. Pesah* 62b and *b. 'Abod. Zar.* 18a–b). As Goodblatt points out,

early marriage curtailed the opportunities for a girl's education, and many women would give birth to their first or second child while still a teenager.[54]

In Mark the term μαθηταί is used of the disciples of Jesus and also of the disciples of John the Baptist (2.18; 6.29) and of the Pharisees (2.18). Mark only uses the masculine plural μαθηταί which may refer to men alone, or to women and men. This description raises the question of whether or not Mark applies μαθηταί (disciples) to women. We do not have in Mark a call of a woman to follow Jesus. Jesus calls Peter and Andrew, James and John to follow him (1.16–20), as well as the tax collector Levi (2.13–14). Later, he summons twelve male disciples to follow him in a more intensive way (3.13–19). Jesus chooses Twelve who have the particular purpose of 'being with Jesus', casting out demons and healing the sick. Jesus conveys authority to the Twelve, and they are sent out on a mission to continue the work of Jesus (6.6b–13).

In Mark the Twelve are Jesus' constant companions. Meye thus identifies the term μαθηταί with the twelve disciples.[55] Mark, however, uses the term disciple before the call of the Twelve (2.15, 16, 18, 23; 3.7, 9). Jesus also calls Levi to follow him, and Levi may be regarded as one of his disciples (2.18, 23; 3.7, 9), although he is not included in the later list of the Twelve (3.16–19). As Meier points out, Mark applies the term 'disciple' to a wider group of Jesus' followers, whereas Matthew frequently limits its use to the Twelve.[56] He notes that in Matthew, Levi's name is changed to Matthew, which means that all the disciples called by Jesus are members of the Twelve. Matthew's Gospel does not record the calling of the Twelve from a larger group of disciples, as Mark's does in 3.13–14.

In Mark a wider group of disciples is mentioned throughout the Gospel (4.10, 34; 8.34; 10.13, 32). The existence of a larger group prompts the question of whether or not women are to be included in the wider group. Throughout Mark women are depicted as being among the crowds who listen to Jesus' teaching. In our passage the women who listen to the teaching of Jesus become his new family (3.35). In Mark the women sit in a circle around Jesus listening to his teaching (περὶ αὐτὸν, 3.32, 34). This description foreshadows the account of those who hear Jesus' parables and approach him for further instruction (οἱ περὶ αὐτὸν σὺν τοῖς δώδεκα, 4.10). At the end of this passage Jesus refers to this group as his own disciples (τοῖς ἰδίοις μαθηταῖς, 4.34). This passage, therefore, implies that women are included among the wider group of Jesus' disciples.

moreover, in the Palestinian sources the teaching of Beruriah relates to household matters (*t. Kelim* BM 1.6), whereas the sources which indicate the formal rabbinic education of Beruriah all come from the Babylonian Amoraic tradition (*b. Ber.* 10a; *b. Pesah* 62b; *b. 'Erub.* 53b–54a). He, therefore, concludes that the Beruriah traditions do not provide evidence of the formal rabbinic training of Jewish women in Roman Palestinian traditions.

54. L.J. Archer, *Her Price Is Beyond Rubies: The Jewish Woman in Greco-Roman Palestine* (*JSOT*Sup, 60; Sheffield: Sheffield Academic Press, 1990), 95.

55. R.P. Meye, *Jesus and the Twelve* (Grand Rapids: Eerdmans, 1968), 110–15.

56. J.P. Meier, 'The Circle of the Twelve: Did it exist during Jesus' Public Ministry?', *JBL* 116 (1997), 638.

The main evidence for the existence of women disciples is the reference to the group of women who accompany Jesus to Jerusalem (15.40–41). These women are described as serving 'him' and following 'him', which implies a commitment to Jesus. Mark thus portrays this group of women in discipleship terms. The women have continuously followed Jesus in Galilee and they have journeyed with him to Jerusalem. They, therefore, may be considered as part of the discipleship group. The late reference to the women disciples (15.40–41) has led some commentators to argue that Mark does not regard women as disciples. Malbon proposes that on a narrative level Mark's audience would identify the term 'disciples' as the Twelve.[57] The prominence of women as witnesses of the crucifixion and resurrection, however, suggests that Mark's community would be aware that women were historically members of the group of disciples who travelled with Jesus.

Some feminist scholars, such as Kinukawa, propose that the group of twelve male disciples is not historical.[58] She believes that Jesus rejected boundaries between human beings (2.15–16, 18–22, 23–27; 3.35; 9.34–35; 10.13–16, 42–45). Mark's references to the Twelve, however, more likely reflect the historicity of this group of disciples.[59] The number twelve, moreover, has theological significance within the mission of Jesus. Jesus' choice of the twelve disciples recalls the expectations of the restoration of the twelve tribes in the end-time (*1 En.* 57.1; *4 Ezra* 13.32–50; *2 Bar.* 78.1–7; *T. Benj.* 9.2). On the other hand Best argues that in Mark the number twelve is not associated with the Old Testament concepts of 'twelve'.[60] His interpretation is unconvincing, since Jesus' choice of twelve disciples appears to be modelled on the twelve tribes of Israel (3.13–19). As Hooker suggests, the account of the call of the Twelve on a mountain recalls the formation of the people of Israel in Exod. 19–20.[61]

Jesus calls the Twelve to be with him and to be sent out on mission (3.13–19) and from this passage onwards the term μαθηταί appears to be primarily associated with the Twelve who accompany Jesus on his boat journeys (4.35–41; 6.45–52; 8.14–21). Jesus sends the Twelve out on mission (6.6b–13) and after their return he feeds the five thousand (6.30–44). The reference to the twelve baskets of leftovers recalls the twelve disciples and foreshadows the restoration of Israel. The number twelve is also significant in the miracle accounts which take place in a Jewish setting. For example Jesus heals the woman with the flow of blood who suffers from her illness for twelve years, and he raises Jairus' daughter who is twelve years old (5.21–43).

---

57. E.S. Malbon, 'Disciples/ Crowds/ Whoever: Markan Characters and Readers', *NovT* 28 (1986), n. 9 107.

58. H. Kinukawa, 'Women Disciples of Jesus (15.40–41; 15.47; 16.1)', in A.-J. Levine (ed.), *A Feminist Companion to Mark* (Sheffield: Sheffield Academic Press, 2001), 175.

59. Meier ('Circle', 663) argues that there was an identifiable group of twelve disciples during Jesus' mission. He refers to the multiple attestation of sources and forms in Mark (the list of the Twelve and the tradition of the betrayal of Judas), the separate tradition in John (6 and 20.24), the creedal formula in Paul (1 Cor. 15.3-5), probable L material (the variations in Luke's list of the Twelve), and a probable Q saying (Mt. 19.28//Lk. 22.30).

60. Best, 'Mark's Use', 35.

61. Hooker, *St. Mark*, 111.

In this way the number twelve represents the restoration of Israel, and it reflects the initial focus of Jesus' mission to Israel. Jesus, however, prophesies that the period between the resurrection and the parousia will be associated with the Gentile mission (13.10). In the Passion Narrative Judas betrays Jesus, and the circle of the Twelve is broken. In our passage the new group around Jesus does not give the Twelve any special status, which is particularly striking since it follows the call and selection of the Twelve (3.13–19). In the new community women and men have equal status in their relationships to Jesus. This account thus foreshadows the new eschatological community around Jesus in which the distinction between the Twelve and other disciples will no longer be apparent.

7. New Creation

In our passage there is a contrast between birth families and the new family which forms around Jesus. Jesus' identity as the Son of God is central, since others become his brothers, sisters and mothers by listening to his teaching (3.35). Barton, however, emphasizes that Jesus does not reject the concept of family, and his interpretation is supported by other passages in which Jesus condemns those who manipulate the Law in order to avoid caring for their families (7.9–13) and in which he prohibits divorce (10.1–12). In addition, Jesus tells the rich man to obey the ten commandments, which include the command to honour father and mother (10.17–22). Barton stresses that Jesus redefines the concept of family in accordance with the imminence of the kingdom of God, in which the decision to follow Jesus relativizes all other relationships.[62]

The discipleship group, however, differs from birth families. In 3.35 the new family around Jesus consists of brothers, sisters and mothers, but the category of father is omitted. Similarly, disciples who leave their natural families will receive brothers, sisters and mothers, but not fathers (10.30). Some scholars, such as Schüssler Fiorenza, regard this text as a rejection of the patriarchal family.[63] Dewey points out that this passage is particularly liberating for women because in the surrounding society they were expected to obey their fathers or husbands, and Jesus' teaching therefore sanctions a break with the norms of society.[64] Fander also argues that the new family around Jesus is not hierarchical, and the sexes are not ranked differently.[65]

God is understood in masculine terms, and the category of mother is not given equal prominence with that of father. Painter suggests that the inclusion of the term 'mothers' may reflect the presence of Jesus' mother in our passage.[66] The category of mother and not that of father, however, may also be seen in 10.30. The unique relationship of mother with child is thus undermined as disciples now may have several mothers, but only one father. In our passage Jesus also has a key role; those

62. Barton, *Discipleship*, 107.
63. Schüssler Fiorenza, *In Memory*, 146–48.
64. Dewey, 'Mark', 478.
65. Fander, *Stellung*, 332.
66. Painter, 'Mark 3.13-35', 512.

who do the will of God are the ones who sit around him listening to his teaching (τοὺς περὶ αὐτὸν κύκλῳ καθημένους, 3.34). The male category of son is central to the understanding of the relationship of disciples to God, since disciples are brothers, sisters and mothers of Jesus.

In the new community no human being can take the role of father, as God alone is regarded as father (cf. Mt. 23.9). The break with patriarchal families corresponds to other anti-hierarchical teaching in the Gospel. The one who wishes to be first must place herself or himself last of all and servant of all (9.35). This teaching is realized by Jesus, since he comes not to be served but to serve and to give his life as a ransom for many (10.45). Jesus identifies a child as the greatest in the community, and he teaches that whoever welcomes a child welcomes him and also God (9.35–37; 10.13–16). Schüssler Fiorenza, moreover, notes that the child has the lowest place within the patriarchal family, and she also points out that the same term may refer to a slave.[67] This identification may be seen in other Greco-Roman texts.[68] The role of God as father takes on a new meaning, since Jesus and God take the place of a slave. In this way power and domination structures are overcome in the new creation. The house was the basic social and economic structure within Greco-Roman society, and the male head of the family ruled the household. Mark's passage permits women to leave their birth households and join a community in which no man can take the role of father. Our passage thus acts against those who seek to take a patriarchal role for themselves within the community.

The conflict between Jesus and his family illustrates the cost of discipleship, since the desire to do the will of God may lead to division within families. Fander interprets Jesus' break with his family in the eschatological context of the end-time.[69] In Mk 3.20–35 we see the tension between Jesus and his family, which foreshadows his rejection by the people of his hometown (6.1–6). Jesus is compared to the scriptural prophets of the Old Testament who are rejected by their own people (e.g. Jer. 12.6). The rejection of the prophets thus foreshadows the necessity of Jesus' suffering. This portrayal locates the misunderstanding of Jesus by his family in the context of God's relationship to Israel. Their failure to follow him may be related to the mysterious purposes of God, which humanity is unable to comprehend.

Family divisions are also a reflection of the end-time struggles (Mic. 7.6; *Jub.* 23.16). In his prophecy of the end-time Jesus predicts family betrayal (13.12), and the severity of these conflicts is stressed since they lead to accusation, trial and death. The rule of Satan is in the process of being destroyed, and as part of this disintegration human allegiances are broken. Those who accept the proclamation of the kingdom of God come into conflict with those who are still aligned to the old age. In his parables Jesus teaches that a divided kingdom and a divided house are

---

67. Schüssler Fiorenza, *In Memory*, 148.

68. A. Oepke ('παῖς', *TDNT*, V, 636–54) notes that παῖς can refer to social position and may be translated as 'servant' or 'slave' as in Aeschylus, *Cho.* 653; Aristophanes, *Ach.* 395 and *Nub.* 132. The term παιδίον occurs in Plutarch, *Adut.* 24 (II, 65c) and 31 (II, 70e). He observes that the diminutive παιδίον may also refer to social status, as in Aristophanes, *Ran.* 37 and *Nub.* 132.

69. Fander, *Stellung*, 327.

signs of the end, and the phrase τέλος ἔχει (is coming to an end, 3.26) has eschato-logical associations, revealing that the breakup of the old world heralds the advent of the new. Similarly, the break with his natural family enables a larger new family to form.

Mark's account, however, refers not only to the breakup of families, but also to the active opposition of families who will even hand one another over to death (13.12). Best argues that Mark is writing to strengthen disciples who have encountered such opposition from their families, and in his view there is an underlying hope that the families may eventually respond in faith to Jesus.[70] Best's interpretation highlights the context of family opposition, but does not take into account that this opposition is a sign of the end (13.13). In chapter 13 Jesus prophesies the events of the end-time which include wars and rumours of wars (13.7). Graham rightly points out that Jesus' teaching alludes to the present experiences of the Markan community, and she notes that the experience of family breakup is located in the midst of social disruption.[71]

In our passage brothers and sisters are discipleship terms, and in chapter 13 the reference to brothers may be an indication that disciples are being betrayed by members of their own communities. As Graham observes, this experience is foreshadowed by the betrayal of Jesus by Judas, since Jesus would have considered Judas as a 'brother'.[72] Jesus is open to his enemies and vulnerable to betrayal, and even one of his twelve chosen disciples betrays him.

Nevertheless the purposes of God are being worked out even in the betrayal of Jesus by Judas. In the same way, Jesus prophesies that the community will be hated by all on account of his name (καὶ ἔσεσθε μισούμενοι ὑπο πάντων διὰ τὸ ὄνομα μου, 13.13). This period of suffering is particularly severe for women, as may be seen in the woes directed at pregnant women and women nursing babies (13.17). The betrayal that the community faces, however, may also be interpreted as a positive sign of the end-time, because their suffering is an indication of the breakup of the rule of Satan and the nearness of the parousia.

8. *Conclusion*

In chapter 3 Mark gives a negative portrayal of Jesus' mother, sisters and brothers. As we have seen, however, they act with the intention of protecting Jesus. Their failure to understand Jesus is linked to the human inability to recognize the necessity of Jesus' suffering and death. In contrast, the failure of the scribes is more culpable, since they identify the power of Jesus with that of Beelzebul. Their blindness leads them to plot to put Jesus to death. The passage contrasts the will of God which seeks to redeem creation through self-giving with the desires of human beings to

---

70. Best, 'Mark III', 317.

71. H.R. Graham, 'A Passion Prediction for Mark's Community: Mark 13.9-13', *BTB* (1986), 20–21.

72. Graham, 'Passion Prediction', 21.

stop Jesus' mission. The family of Jesus and the scribes respond negatively to Jesus' mission, but the women and men who listen to the teaching of Jesus do the will of God (3.35). Although their allegiance to Jesus leads to opposition, they will experience the eschatological gift of a new family, and in the age to come eternal life.

Chapter 4

THE HEALING OF THE WOMAN WITH THE FLOW OF BLOOD AND THE RAISING OF JAIRUS' DAUGHTER (5.21–43)

1. *Introduction*

Our second account of the healing of women describes the cure of a woman with a flow of blood and the raising of Jairus' daughter. After the exorcism of the Gerasene demoniac (5.1–20) Jesus returns to Jewish territory, and he is immediately approached by Jairus, the president of the synagogue, requesting help for his daughter, who is on the brink of death (5.23). As Jesus sets off to heal the sick girl, a woman with a flow of blood draws near him secretly and reaches out to touch his garment. Several commentators, such as Swartley, have noted the positive portrayal of women within this narrative, particularly the role of the woman with the flow of blood who is praised by Jesus for her faith (5.34).[1] In Tolbert's view the faith of the woman acts as a foil to the negative portrayal of the male disciples, who are criticized by Jesus for their fear and lack of faith (4.40; 6.50).[2] Marshall, however, highlights the woman's struggle between faith and fear, and argues that her faith is incomplete until she comes forward to tell Jesus 'the whole truth' (5.33).[3]

Other commentators, such as Selvidge, focus on the Jewish setting of the narrative, and argue that these stories illustrate the abandonment of the purity laws by Mark's community.[4] Selvidge proposes that the woman is isolated on account of the purity regulations of Lev. 15.19–30, but Jesus does not condemn her action of touching his garment. Similarly, Kinukawa highlights the action of the woman in touching Jesus' clothes, which in her view forms the impetus for the abandonment of the purity regulations.[5] These interpretations have been challenged by the work of Cohen, who argues that there is no clear evidence that women were quarantined in the Second Temple period; the first references to the quarantine of women occur in Jewish sources of the sixth and seventh centuries.[6] Josephus, however, states that

---

1. Swartley, 'Women', 19.
2. M.A. Tolbert, 'Mark', in C.A. Newsom and S.H. Ringe (eds.), *Women's Bible Commentary* (London: SPCK, 1992), 263.
3. C.D. Marshall, *Faith as a Theme in Mark's Narrative* (SNTSMS, 64; Cambridge: Cambridge University Press, 1989), 106–107.
4. M.J. Selvidge, 'Mark 5.25–34 and Leviticus 15.19–20: A Reaction to Restrictive Purity Regulations', *JBL* 103 (1984), 619–23.
5. Kinukawa, *Women*, 44–45.
6. S.J.D. Cohen, 'Menstruants and the Sacred in Judaism and Christianity', in S.B. Pomeroy

menstruating women are not permitted to enter the Temple (*War* 5.227) or to participate in the celebration of Passover (*War* 6.426–27). Marcus also notes earlier references to the quarantine of women (11QT 48.14–17; Josephus, *Ant.* 3.261; *m. Nid.* 7.4), and he points out that the third-century texts cited by Cohen, the *Epistle of Basilides* of Dionysius of Alexandria (ch. 2) and the *Didascalia Apostolorum* (ch. 26), cite our passage in relation to menstrual purity regulations.[7] It is also possible that there was a varied understanding of menstrual purity regulations within Jewish groups. Ilan, for example, proposes that Pharisaic women may have followed more stringent menstrual purity regulations than other Jewish women such as the Sadducees.[8]

Our account is set in Galilee, and D'Angelo[9] and Fonrobert[10] argue that the passage is not concerned with purity issues because purity regulations were associated solely with the Temple in Jerusalem. The description of the woman, however, implies that she is ritually unclean. As Selvidge notes, there are verbal similarities between the description of the woman's condition (οὖσα ἐν ῥύσει αἵματος, 5.25; ἡ πηγὴ τοῦ αἵματος αὐτῆς, 5.29) and the references to menstruating women in Leviticus (ῥέῃ ῥύσει αἵματος, 15.25 LXX; τῆς πηγῆς αἵματος αὐτῆς, 12.7 LXX).[11] The healing account, moreover, focuses on the power of Jesus' touch, which may be seen as particularly appropriate to concerns with ritual purity. According to the laws of Leviticus (15.19–30), anyone and anything the woman touches will be made unclean. Her blood is a source of impurity and threatens others, since blood was believed to contain life (Lev. 17.10–14). The woman may be expected to render Jesus unclean by her touch, but instead Jesus has the power to heal her and restore her to health. Jesus does not criticize her for touching his clothes, but praises her action. In this way our passage, which features a woman character, acts as a precedent for the abandonment of the purity regulations.

(ed.), *Women's History and Ancient History* (Chapel Hill: University of North Carolina Press, 1991), 278–81.

7.   Marcus, *Mark*, 357–58.

8.   Ilan (*Jewish Women*, 103–105) cites an account in the Tosefta in which the purity of a high priest is not affected by his meeting with a Sadducee even though he has come into contact with the man's spittle. The high priest has not been rendered impure because the wife of the Sadducee has observed the menstrual purity regulations and been examined by a sage (*t. Nidd.* 5.3). As Ilan observes, the high priests were usually Sadducees and this account may have been formulated at a later period because the rabbis wished to legitimate the Temple-service and thus claimed that the Sadducean women followed the same purity regulations as the Pharisaic women.

9.   M.R. D'Angelo, '(Re)Presentations of Women in the Gospels: John and Mark', in R.S. Kraemer and M.R. D'Angelo (eds.), *Women and Christian Origins* (Oxford: Oxford University Press, 1999), 140.

10. C. Fonrobert, 'The Woman with a Blood-Flow (Mark 5.24–34) Revisited: Menstrual Laws and Jewish Culture in Christian Feminist Hermeneutics', in C.A. Evans and J.A. Sanders (eds.), *Early Christian Interpretation of the Scriptures of Israel* (Sheffield: Sheffield Academic Press, 1997), 130.

11. Selvidge, 'Mark 5.25-34', 619.

2. *The Portrayal of the Women*

The woman with the flow of blood is anonymous, and we are not told the name of Jairus' daughter or of her mother, who is introduced at the healing of her daughter.[12] The anonymity of the women contrasts with the named male character, Jairus, and with the three named disciples, Peter, James and John (5.37). As we have seen, the predominance of male names is characteristic of first-century texts from Palestine.[13] The recording of Jairus' name may be an indication of his high social status as a leader of the synagogue (5.22). It is also possible that the name Jairus has symbolic associations, as Guelich notes that 'Jairus' may transliterate either יאיר which means 'he enlightens' (cf. Num. 32.41; Judg. 10.3–5; Est. 2.5) or יעיר which means 'he awakens' (cf. 1 Chron. 20.5).[14] Although Guelich is unconvinced by the symbolic significance of Jairus' name, the account does describe the awakening of Jairus' faith, particularly when he struggles between faith and fear on receiving the news that his daughter has died (Μὴ φοβοῦ, μόνον πίστευε, 5.36).

Jairus appears to be a prominent member of the community, since he is one of the presidents of the synagogue (5.22). His title may imply that he is also wealthy because synagogue presidents were often responsible for financial support of the synagogue.[15] In Mark's Gospel, the religious authorities are depicted as men, although Brooten has noted that this title is applied to women in synagogue inscriptions in Greece and Asia Minor from the second to the fifth century.[16] Mark does not mention whether or not Jairus has other children, whereas Luke describes the girl as an only daughter (θυγάτηρ μονγενὴς, 8.42). As Ilan points out, Luke's description may be an indication of his compositional technique of narrating corresponding stories concerning female and male characters; his reference to the girl as an only child parallels his account of the healing of the only son of the widow at Nain (7.12).[17] Ilan also notes that the birth of a daughter was not always viewed positively.[18] In our passage, however, the love of Jairus for his daughter leads him

---

12. Guelich (*Mark*, 295) notes that the woman with the flow of blood is named in later tradition as Veronica (*Gos. Nic.* 7) and Bernice (*Acts. Pil.* 7).

13. Ilan, 'Notes', 186–200.

14. Guelich, *Mark*, 295.

15. Guelich, *Mark*, 295.

16. B. Brooten (*Women Leaders in the Ancient Synagogue: Inscriptional Evidence and Background Issues* [BJS 36; Chico, CA: Scholars Press, 1982], 5–33) cites three surviving inscriptions that refer to women as presidents of the synagogue (Rufina in Smyrna, Ionia around the 2nd century; Sophia of Gortyn in Kastelli Kissamou, Crete around the 4th–5th century, and Theopempte, in Myndos, Crete, at least 4th–5th century). According to Brooten's analysis, these titles are not merely honorific, but are evidence of the role of women as administrators and teachers in their synagogues.

17. Ilan, *Jewish Women*, n. 22 52.

18. Ilan (*Jewish Women*, 44–52) notes that the birth of a daughter was often regarded as a disappointment. She cites Sir. 22.3: 'It is a disgrace to be the father of an undisciplined son, and the birth of a daughter is a loss', and the tannaitic tradition 'Anyone who does not have a son is as if dead' (*Gen. R.* 45.2). As Ilan observes, however, there are positive references to daughters in other texts, and she points out that the relationship between God and Israel is sometimes portrayed in

to seek help from Jesus, who is outwith his social sphere. The close relationship between parent and daughter is also depicted in the account of Herodias and her daughter (6.14–29) and the exorcism of the Syrophoenician woman's daughter (7.24–30).

The girl is twelve years old, which is regarded as the age of puberty, and some scholars, such as Pomeroy, note that girls often married at this age.[19] Ilan, however, disagrees with this view, and she cites examples of Jewish women who married at a later age.[20] Her argument is not convincing, since she cites only a few examples, which may be exceptions to the general pattern of early marriage. The girl is thus on the cusp of adulthood when her disease afflicts her. The girl's age of twelve, moreover, corresponds to the twelve years of the woman's illness. The woman has suffered from constant menstrual bleeding. Leviticus, however, differentiates between menstruants and women who suffer bleeding outwith their menstrual period. The woman's condition of a constant flow of blood implies that she is a zabah, and anything she touched could pass on ritual impurity, even household utensils. Ilan notes that any man who has a sexual relationship with a menstruating woman becomes unclean (Lev. 15.24; *Pss. Sol.* 8.12; CD 5.7).[21]

Our account is thus concerned with purity issues, and it recalls the account of the healing of the leper, which is also set in Galilee, since Jesus sends the healed man to a priest in order to make the offering for cleansing, which Moses commanded (1.44). As Marcus observes, Mark appears to have structured his narrative around three healings which are associated with purity regulations: the restoration of the leper (1.40–45), the healing of the woman with the flow of blood and the raising of Jairus' daughter (5.21–43).[22] He notes that these three healings correspond to the three categories of people who were to be excluded from the camp of Israel: those with a ritually unclean skin disease or a discharge, or anyone who has become unclean through touching a corpse (Num. 5.1–5). In Mark, Jesus restores the people of Israel by including those previously excluded on account of their diseases. The power of Jesus, therefore, is stronger than the forces of disease and death, which threaten to defile the camp of Israel.

The account of the woman's healing is intercalated into the account of the raising of Jairus' daughter, and commentators debate whether the intercalation is a Markan

terms of the love between father and daughter as in the account of the king who redeems his daughter from captivity (*Song R.* 1.9.5). She also notes the similarity between our passage and the account of the rescue of the daughter of Nehonia the welldigger by R. Hanina b. Dosa (*b. Yeb.* 121b; *b. B. Qam.* 50a).

19. Pomeroy, *Goddesses*, 164; Archer, *Her Price*, 151–52; Wegner, *Chattel or Person?*, 20–39.

20. Ilan (*Jewish Women*, 65–69) points out that the rabbis advocated that girls should marry shortly after puberty (*b. Sanh.* 76a), and they interpret the pubescent girl as one who is older than twelve and a half (*m. Nid.* 5.6–8). Ilan, however, argues that there are examples of girls who married at a later age, such as the Hasmonean Mariamme, who could have been eighteen or older when she married Herod, but not younger than sixteen. In support of Ilan's view, the Hellenistic Jewish text, *Joseph and Aseneth*, describes Aseneth as eighteen at the time of her marriage (1.4), and the seven virgins who attend on her are also eighteen (2.6).

21. Ilan, *Jewish Women*, 101.

22. Marcus, *Mark*, 367–68.

creation or whether the stories were linked in the pre-Markan tradition. Taylor, for example, believes that the connections between the two stories are historical.[23] Marshall, however, shows that the literary styles of the stories differ, since the account of the raising of Jairus' daughter is written in the historical present with a frequent use of καί (and) whereas the healing of the woman is written in the aorist and the imperfect tenses and has many participles.[24] Mark, then, has placed the passages together in order to draw correspondences between the woman who is an outcast and Jairus, the president of the synagogue. Both stories explore the response of faith, since the woman overcomes her fear to confess her faith (5.34), and Jairus is told by Jesus not to fear but to keep faith (5.36).

Mark's technique of intercalation draws attention to the similarities and contrasts between the woman with the flow of blood and Jairus' daughter. Both the woman and the young girl are so seriously ill that human means of healing are unable to help. The woman has suffered from a menstrual condition of continual bleeding for twelve years and has spent all her money on doctors, only to find that her illness has increased (5.26). Jairus' daughter is described as ἐσχάτως ἔχει (at her last, 5.23); her illness is so severe that it prompts her father, a synagogue leader, to seek help from an itinerant preacher. The two stories, moreover, are linked by the number twelve, since the woman has been ill for twelve years and we discover at the end of the account that the girl is twelve years old.

The account of the woman's illness is the only account in the Gospels of a disease that is particularly connected to gender. D'Angelo, however, suggests that the illness of Jairus' daughter may reflect the supposed condition of a closed womb, a disease diagnosed by doctors of the Greco-Roman world.[25] This condition was believed to afflict girls at the age of puberty, and as Rouselle notes, they were encouraged to marry early to avoid this illness.[26] Some girls were even married before menstruation. We are not, however, given any indication of the nature of Jairus' daughter's illness, but it is significant that the healing of both women is associated with the restoration of fertility. The woman's condition of constant menstrual bleeding would make her infertile, and the girl dies at the age of physical maturity.

The woman in our passage is alone, and her condition implies that she is unlikely to have a husband. The isolation of the woman is suggested by her hiddenness within the crowd, and her words are spoken secretly to herself (5.28). As Gnilka points out, our passage is striking in its description of the inner thoughts and reactions of the woman.[27] Jairus comes forward to make his request to Jesus before the crowds, whereas the woman has no one to act on her behalf.

23. Taylor, *St. Mark*, 289.
24. Marshall, *Faith*, 92.
25. D'Angelo, '(Re)Presentations', 143.
26. A. Rouselle, *Porneia: On Desire and the Body in Antiquity* (Oxford: Basil Blackwell, 1988), 63–77. See also M. R. Lefkowitz, *Heroines and Hysterics* (London: Duckworth, 1981), 12–25. Lefkowitz notes that the condition of hysteria among young women was attributed to the illness of the wandering womb.
27. Gnilka, *Evangelium*, 1.214.

These two women differ in that the older woman is defined in terms of her illness of menstrual bleeding, which would make her ritually unclean (Lev. 15.25–30), whereas the girl is the daughter of a synagogue leader. Although the young girl has a respected position as the daughter of a synagogue leader, the power of disease has shown no discrimination, and when she dies, she too becomes a source of ritual impurity (Num. 19.11). The two women both suffer from severe diseases, but they differ in their social status. The older woman may once have been rich, since only the wealthy could afford doctors. She has now spent all her money and appears to be destitute. As Cranfield points out, the phrase τὰ παρ αὐτῆς may be translated as her wealth (cf. Lk. 10.7; Phil. 4.18).[28] In addition, Marshall observes that Jairus and his family appear to be wealthy, since they live in a house with separate rooms (5.40), unlike the simple one-roomed houses of the poor.[29]

Marshall has noted several differences between the character of the woman and that of Jairus.[30] As he observes, the woman is anonymous, poor and ritually unclean, whereas Jairus is named, wealthy, and has the respected religious status of a synagogue leader. The woman approaches Jesus secretly, trying to avoid detection, whereas Jairus comes forward publicly and throws himself at Jesus' feet. The woman touches Jesus' garment, believing that this small action will make her healthy. Jairus, in contrast, requests Jesus to come to his house and heal his daughter by placing his hands on her. Jesus asks the woman to come forward and praises her for her faith (5.34), whereas he urges Jairus not to fear but to have faith (5.36), and he raises the girl in secret with only her parents and his inner circle of disciples present, whereas the woman is healed in a public place.

Jairus is portrayed as the active figure who seeks healing for his daughter, but Jesus also includes her mother at the raising of the girl (παραλαμβάνει τὸν πατέρα τοῦ παιδίου καὶ τὴν μητέρα, 5.40). Matthew characteristically abbreviates Mark's miracle accounts (cf. 3.7–12; 5.1–43; 6.14–39; 9.14–29),[31] and he makes no mention of the girl's mother (9.18–26), but Luke also refers to both father and mother (8.51). Mark's inclusion of the girl's mother, however, may reflect his concern for the equal status of women and men, which we have already seen in the teaching concerning the new community around Jesus, which includes women and men (3.35). Fittingly, the account concludes with the restoration of the girl to both her parents.

3. The Healing of the Woman with the Flow of Blood

Although the woman's disease makes her unclean, she is described as part of the large crowd that follows Jesus. The surging crowd, which pushes against Jesus, conveys an impression of the chaos of humanity in an age of evil. Marcus points out that the phrase ἐν ῥύσει αἵματος (in a flow of blood, 5.25) is reminiscent of the descriptions of the demoniacs ἐν πνεύματι ἀκαθάρτῳ (in an unclean spirit,

---

28. Cranfield, *St. Mark*, 184.
29. Marshall, *Faith*, 95.
30. Marshall, *Faith*, 104.
31. Davies and Allison, *Matthew*, 1.73.

1.23; 5.2).[32] The phrase is ambiguous as to whether the human being has an un-clean spirit within or whether he or she is subsumed within an unclean spirit. In the same way, the woman suffers from a condition of constant bleeding, but is also caught up in an age of evil associated with disease and suffering. The illness of the woman makes her unclean, and her condition contrasts with that of Jesus as the bearer of the Holy Spirit. At the baptism of Jesus, the Holy Spirit descends εἰς αὐτόν (on or into him 1.10), which suggests that it is both the power which rests upon him and the power which resides within him.

The woman's desire for healing is so great, however, that she is able to reach out to Jesus and risk arousing condemnation for breaking the purity laws. According to Lev. 15.25–30 an unclean woman pollutes anything she touches, including some-one's clothes. The laws of Leviticus also forbid a woman who has given birth to touch anything holy or to enter the sanctuary during the time of her blood-purifica-tion (Lev. 12.4). Furthermore the conclusion to the purity regulations warns the Israelites against bringing their uncleanness into the sanctuary in order that they may not die (Lev. 15.31). As we have seen, Jesus is anointed by the Holy Spirit (1.10), and the Spirit dwells in him (1.24). In this way the woman risks her life in ap-proaching Jesus; as she is unclean, she may be destroyed by coming into contact with the holy. The healing power of Jesus, however, leaves his body in response to the faith of the woman, bringing her freedom from her disease. The Spirit moves outwards from Jesus, casting out her disease, and she realizes through a physical change that she has been healed (ἔγνω τῷ σώματι, 5.29). In contrast, Jesus per-ceives spiritually that power has left him (ἐπιγνοὺς ἐν ἑαυτῷ, 5.30).

The woman takes the initiative in seeking healing from Jesus by struggling through the crowd to reach him. Kinukawa argues that she challenges Jesus to break the purity laws by touching Jesus' garments.[33] The woman, however, attempts to touch Jesus in secret, without drawing attention to herself. Jesus is aware only that power has left him, and he does not know who has been healed. Nevertheless, Kinukawa is correct to note that Jesus is not defiled by her action, since the power of Jesus acts to cast out disease. The term δύναμις (5.30) is associated with the power of God, and is used of the miracles of Jesus (6.2). When Herod hears of the acts of power carried out by Jesus, he mistakenly believes that Jesus is John the Baptist risen from the dead: διὰ τοῦτο ἐγεργοῦσιν αἱ δυνάμεις ἐν αὐτῷ (6.14). Barrett notes that the characteristic associations of δύναμις in Mark are eschato-logical, as in the prophecies about the kingdom of God in 9.1 and 13.26, which refer to the end-time.[34] Mark's presentation of the healing thus suggests that the power of Jesus to heal is God's power of the new age, and the nature of that power is to move outwards to humanity to restore it from disease. In this way the miracles of Jesus are acts of power that point forward to the future rule of God, when no disease or evil will remain.

32. Marcus, *Mark*, 357.
33. Kinukawa, *Women*, 42–44.
34. C.K. Barrett, *The Holy Spirit and the Gospel Tradition* (London: SPCK, 1947), 77.

The healing of the woman is unusual, since Jesus appears to have no control over his power. Malbon, moreover, observes that this healing narrative is unique in Mark's Gospel, since the woman's request is granted without the direct intention of Jesus.[35] He stops to ask who has touched his clothes (5.30), and thus he does not seem to be aware of whom he has healed. Matthew may wish to avoid this implication, since in his account Jesus turns round and speaks to the woman *before* she is made well (9.22). Scholars, such as Witherington, argue that the woman's desire to be healed by touching Jesus' clothes is an indication of her belief in magic, and Jesus' question is therefore designed to show that the grounds of her cure is her faith.[36]

This interpretation is unconvincing, since Mark includes references to other instances of human beings who are healed through touching Jesus' clothes in the summary account (6.56), which is generally associated with Mark's own influence. As Taylor notes, handkerchiefs and aprons were believed to hold the power of the healer (Acts 19.12) and even the shadow of Peter is a means of healing in Acts 5.15.[37] Taylor, therefore, regards the garment of Jesus as an extension of his person. At the baptism of Jesus, the Spirit descends upon him, and this description conveys the idea of the Spirit clothing Jesus (1.10). This concept is illustrated by baptismal accounts of early Christians, who leave behind their old clothes representing their old way of life, and put on new clothes, symbolizing their entry into the new age (cf. Gal. 3.27).

The woman, however, is described as terrified (φοβηθεῖσα καὶ τρέμουσα, 5.33). As Gnilka points out, fear and trembling is a characteristic human response to the revelation of God (Phil. 2.12; Exod. 15.16; Deut. 2.25; 11.25).[38] It is significant that the description of the woman's fear follows the description of her healing, as there are other examples in Mark of the fear of human beings arising in response to the miracles of Jesus. In the first boat journey, for example, the disciples are greatly afraid after Jesus has stilled the storm (ἐφοβήθησαν φόβον μέγαν, 4.41), and the women at the tomb are terrified by the news of the resurrection (ἐφοβοῦντο, 16.8). In these examples fear is an expression of awe at the occurrence of miracles, but these miracles also illustrate the gulf separating God from humanity; they suggest a contrast between the power of God and the powerlessness of human beings. Fear, therefore, is an incomplete response to God, since it reveals a lack of understanding and of trust in God's desire to redeem human beings.

The woman's fear points to her sense of awe at the miracle which has occurred, but other scholars, such as Kinukawa, also suggests that the woman fears condemnation for her action of contaminating Jesus.[39] Similarly, Marshall argues that the woman is afraid of being discovered by Jesus.[40] On the other hand Tolbert high-

---

35. Malbon, 'Fallible Followers', 36.

36. B. Witherington, *Women in the Ministry of Jesus: a Study of Jesus' Attitudes to Women and their Roles as Reflected in his Earthly Life* (Cambridge: Cambridge University Press, 1984), 72–73.

37. Taylor, *St. Mark*, 290.

38. Gnilka, *Evangelium*, 1.216.

39. Kinukawa, *Women*, 45.

40. Marshall, *Faith*, 107.

lights the change in the woman from an attitude of faith to one of fear.[41] She proposes that the woman acted boldly when she was regarded as an outcast, but now that she has been healed, she defers to the social conventions associated with the 'male world of honour and shame'. Marshall, however, is correct to point out that the woman is afraid of imminent discovery; her fear is a response to the questioning of Jesus.[42] He notes, moreover, that the knowledge of her healing (εἰδυῖα ὃ γέγονεν αὐτῇ, 5.33) gives the woman the power to come forward and tell Jesus what has happened.

In our passage the woman overcomes her fear to confess the truth (5.33), and Jesus calls the woman θυγάτηρ (daughter, 5.34). As Marshall observes, this address establishes a personal relationship between him and the woman.[43] Some commentators, such as Tolbert, interpret this address to the woman as an indication that she is now restored to society.[44] The address, however, signifies her entry not into society at large but into the new community related to Jesus. In an earlier healing account Jesus has called a paralysed man τέκνον (son, 2.5) when he has seen the faith of those who have brought the man to him. The terms θυγάτηρ and τέκνον recall the teaching of Jesus concerning the relationships in the new community that whoever does the will of God is his brother, sister and mother (ὃς ἂν ποιήσῃ τὸ θέλημα τοῦ θεοῦ, οὗτος ἀδελφός μου καὶ ἀδελφὴ καὶ μήτηρ ἐστίν, 3.35). The woman follows the will of God by responding to Jesus in faith and in approaching him for healing.

The woman is praised for her faith despite her action of ignoring the purity regulations. As Kinukawa points out, Jesus disregards the purity regulations by accepting the woman's action of touching his clothes and he thus identifies himself with someone who is ritually unclean.[45] Kinukawa's interpretation of our passage recalls the action of Jesus in touching the leper (1.40–45). In both narratives the act of touching another human being aligns Jesus with those who are ritually unclean. Fander suggests that the abandonment of the purity regulations indicates that Mark's community has rejected the social norms of society.[46] It is more likely that the discipleship group is to be regarded as an eschatological community that foreshadows the end-time in which no disease remains and the purity regulations are no longer required.

The address to the woman as θυγάτηρ (5.34) may be compared to the words of God, who designates Jesus as his beloved Son at his baptism (1.11) and his transfiguration (9.7), and to the words of the centurion at his death on the cross (15.39). All three instances depict the Sonship of Jesus in the context of his death and resurrection. In Gethsemane, moreover, Jesus reveals his Sonship since he chooses to obey the will of his father, and face trial and death (14.36). In our passage the

---

41. Tolbert, 'Mark', 355.

42. Marshall, *Faith*, 107.

43. Marshall, *Faith*, 107.

44. Tolbert, 'Mark', 268.

45. H. Kinukawa, 'The Story of the Hemorrhaging Woman (Mark 5.25–34) Read from a Japanese Feminist Context', *BibInt* 2 (1994), 292.

46. Fander, *Stellung*, 54–55.

woman is named 'daughter' because she has acted in accordance with the will of God; she too has risked her life and found healing through the power of God. The eschatological implications of the healing are further indicated by the use of the verb σώζω (5.34), which means both 'to heal' and 'to save'. The ambiguity of this verb conveys the cosmic dualism of Mark's depiction of the miracles: Jesus heals human beings and rescues them from the force of evil associated with the old age.

Jesus, moreover, tells the woman 'Go in peace', which means literally 'Go into peace' (ὕπαγε εἰς εἰρήνην, 5.34), a blessing which also may be seen in Judg. 18.6; 1 Sam. 1.17; 2 Sam. 15.9. Frequently those healed by Jesus are told to go (ὕπαγε, 1.44; 5.19; 10.52), and this instruction suggests that through their encounter with the healing power of Jesus, they move into the new age. The sending away of these people, however, also contributes to the sense of isolation around Jesus, since he remains behind to continue his mission by confronting the forces of evil through his proclamation of the kingdom of God.

4. *The Raising of Jairus' Daughter*

While Jesus speaks to the woman, news arrives from Jairus' house to report that his daughter has died (5.35). At this point, there is a movement away from the crowds, since Jesus takes only his three closest disciples with him to Jairus' house. There is a contrast between the secret request of the woman for healing and the public request of Jairus, and between the confession of the woman before the crowd and the secret healing of the young girl. The progression of the narrative heightens the impact of the miraculous raising of the girl from death and suggests that this miracle is to be concealed from those who are 'outsiders'. The inability of outsiders to understand Jesus is further illustrated by the group of mourners who mock Jesus when he tells them that the girl is only sleeping. In Matthew this group is described as professional mourners (τοὺς αὐλητάς, 9.23), and many scholars, such as Gnilka, interpret the Markan group in the same way.[47] As Taylor observes, however, it is more likely that Mark refers to members of the household, since there has been little time to arrange for professional mourners.[48]

The mourners reject Jesus because he claims that the girl is sleeping (καθεύδει, 5.39). This description, however, is ambiguous, since it may refer either to literal sleep or to the sleep of death (cf. 1 Thess. 5.10). Jesus has the power to raise human beings from death, and he can, therefore, turn death into sleep. In response to their mockery, Jesus casts these people out (5.40). The verb ἐκβάλλω is used, the same verb which is employed in Jesus' exorcisms (1.39; 3.22, 23; 7.26). In addition, Marshall points out that Jesus' action serves to separate unbelief from faith, thus emphasizing that miracles can take place only where faith is present (6.6).[49] Jesus

---

47. Gnilka (*Evangelium*, 1.217) notes that two flute players and a mourning woman are required by even the poorest household in *m. Ket.* 4.4. In addition Josephus records the practice of hiring flute players at the time of mourning (*War* 3.437).

48. Taylor, *St. Mark*, 295.

49. Marshall, *Faith*, 98.

removes those who actively oppose him and chooses only a small circle of people to witness the miracle.

The healing of Jairus' daughter follows the same pattern as that of the earlier healing of Simon's mother in-law (1.29–31) and the healing of the boy with a deaf and mute spirit (9.14–29). Jesus takes the girl by the hand and raises her to life (κρατήσας τῆς χειρός, 5.41; 1.31; 9.27). In the healing of Simon's mother-in-law Jesus seized the woman from the power of the fever, which enveloped her, but in this account he pulls the girl from the clutches of death. Behind Jesus' conflict with disease lies his battle against the power of evil, which seeks to destroy humanity. In our passage Jesus heals through his words as well as by his touch, as he speaks to the girl in Aramaic ταλιθα κουμ ('Little girl, get up', 5.41). This speech is recorded as the actual words of Jesus who spoke Aramaic, in contrast to Mark's audience who speak Greek.[50] Smith suggests that the preservation of this phrase indicates an interest of the early Christians in magical formulas.[51] The words of Jesus, however, bring an intimate sense of his presence to the account of the healing, and it is more likely that they are intended to stress his power to heal through both words and touch.

As we noted in our analysis of the account of the healing of Simon's mother-in-law, here too there are verbal associations with the account of Jesus' resurrection. Jesus commands the girl to rise (ἔγειρε, 5.41; cf. ἤγειρεν, 1.31; 9.27) and God will later raise Jesus (ἠγέρθη, 16.6). She arises (ἀνέστη, 5.42; cf. 9.27), and the same verb is used in the description of the resurrection of Jesus (ἀναστῆναι, 8.31; ἀναστήσεται, 9.31; 10.34). The verbal similarities may imply that Jesus raises Jairus' daughter with the same divine power that will rescue Jesus from death.[52] After she has been raised the girl walks (περιεπάτει, 5.42), which recalls the paralysed man who walks after his healing (ἔγειρε... περιπάτει, 2.9). The reference to walking also suggests the account of Jesus walking on water (ἔρχεται πρὸς αὐτοὺς περιπατῶν ἐπὶ τῆς θαλάσσης, 6.48). The walking of the girl, moreover, points forward to the action of Jesus, who goes ahead of his disciples to Galilee after his resurrection (14.28; 16.7). The instruction of the girl to be fed foreshadows the messianic feast (Isa. 25.6–8; *1 En.* 62.12–14; *2 Bar.* 29.5–8). The structure of the account thus consists of a pattern similar to that found in the healing of Simon's mother-in-law, in which a successful struggle against the force of evil is followed by a celebratory meal (1.29–31).

The reaction of those present is one of great amazement (ἐξέστησαν ἐκστάσει μεγάλῃ, 5.42), which is a characteristic response to the miracles of Jesus, pointing to the kingdom of God breaking into the world. Although Jesus commands the witnesses to let no one know what they have seen (5.43), it would be impossible to conceal the girl's return to life. As Wrede points out, Jesus' command is one of the key passages in the theory of the Messianic secret.[53] Matthew omits the command

50. Cranfield, *St. Mark*, 190.
51. M. Smith, *Jesus the Magician* (New York: Harper & Row, 1978), 95.
52. Marcus, *Mark*, 372–73.
53. W. Wrede, *The Messianic Secret* (trans. J.C. Greig; Cambridge: J. Clarke, 1971 [1901]), 50–51.

to secrecy; instead, the report spreads all through the district (9.26). In Mark, Jesus characteristically commands secrecy after his miracles, as in the commands to the unclean spirits not to reveal his identity (1.25; 3.12). He also commands human beings to secrecy, as in the instruction to the leper to tell no one of his cure except the priest, in order to carry out the sacrifice Moses requires (1.44).

A time limit is placed on the commands to secrecy at the account of Jesus' transfiguration, when he instructs his disciples to tell no one what they have seen until the Son of Man has risen from the dead (9.9). This time limit is relevant for understanding our story, because the raising of Jairus' daughter has similarities with the account of Jesus' transfiguration (9.2–8). Marshall notes the similar wording in the commands to secrecy (5.43; 9.9), and the same three disciples accompany Jesus in the two accounts.[54] These three disciples also accompany Jesus during his prayer in Gethsemane, when he struggles to follow the will of God in accepting the necessity of his death (14.32–42).

In our passage Jairus' daughter is transformed from death to life, and in the transfiguration account Jesus is also changed (μετεμορφώθη ἔμπροσθεν αὐτῶν, 9.2). The description of Jesus' shining white clothes (ἐστίλβοντα λευκὰ λίαν, 9.3) is reminiscent of those who have been raised to life in apocalyptic literature, as in Rev. 7.9, 13–14. The emphasis on a heavenly experience is stressed by the reference to Jesus' clothes, which are brighter than any fuller on earth could bleach (9.3). Thrall compares the appearance of Jesus to that of the young man at the tomb who is dressed in a white robe (περιβεβλημένον στολὴν λευκήν, 16.5).[55] The purpose of the young man is to tell the women that Jesus has been raised. She rightly notes that these allusions suggest that the transfiguration foreshadows the resurrection of Jesus.

Elijah and Moses, moreover, are present with Jesus in the transfiguration, and Nineham interprets Elijah and Moses as representatives of the prophets and the Law.[56] Jesus thus fulfils the Law and the prophets. Elijah is mentioned first in accordance with the eschatological expectation that Elijah would return before the end-time (9.11). Allison notes that Mal. 3.23–24 states that Elijah will return before the day of the Lord.[57] As Allison argues, Elijah is regarded as the forerunner to the Messiah because the Messiah is expected to come on the day of the Lord (cf. *b. 'Erub*. 43a–b). At the transfiguration Jesus is present with two figures (9.4), and this pattern foreshadows the request of James and John for the places on the right and the left of Jesus (10.37). At the crucifixion Jesus is executed between two rebels (15.27). The picture of a central figure accompanied by two others recalls the portrayal of a king with his retainers on either side of him. The inscription placed above Jesus' head reads 'King of the Jews' (15.26). Jesus is crowned king through his death on the cross (15.26), and thus the presence of the mother and father of the girl at her raising points to the two figures who will accompany Jesus at his death.

---

54. Marshall, *Faith*, 99.

55. M.E. Thrall, 'Elijah and Moses in Mark's Account of the Transfiguration', *NTS* 16 (1970), 311.

56. Nineham, *St. Mark*, 234–35.

57. D.C. Allison, 'Elijah Must Come First', *JBL* 103 (1984), 256–58.

The raising of Jairus' daughter foreshadows Jesus' own resurrection and reveals the power of Jesus to overcome death. Jesus commands those present to secrecy. Similarly, he instructs his disciples not to mention his transfiguration until after he is raised from the dead. As Marshall points out, the comparison between the two accounts suggests that the raising of Jairus' daughter may only be fully understood in the light of Jesus' own death and resurrection.[58] According to Hooker, the miracle is not to be told to those who are unable to understand the significance of the event.[59] Jesus, however, may command secrecy to the witnesses because they too are unable to understand the significance of her healing. Jesus has prophetic knowledge of the future, whereas human beings are unable to recognize his identity until his death on the cross (15.39).

5. *Priority in the Kingdom of God*

The account of the healing of the woman with the flow of blood and of the raising of Jairus' daughter raises the issue of priority in the kingdom of God. Jesus sets out to heal Jairus' daughter, who is on the point of death (ἐσχάτως ἔχει, 5.23), but stops on the way to talk to the woman he has healed. Jairus' daughter has high social status as the daughter of the synagogue president, whereas the woman is ritually unclean. The older woman who is an outcast and who has lost everything comes first, and the synagogue leader's daughter who is just reaching maturity comes last. Jesus' desire to stop to speak to the woman thus illustrates his teaching that many who are first will be last, and the last will be first (10.31).

In addition, the identification of the woman with the 'last' is suggested by her action in touching only the garment of Jesus. She believes that this small action can restore her health, whereas all the doctors she has consulted have failed. The emphasis on the smallness of her gesture is seen also in the minor agreement between Matthew and Luke, since they both mention that the woman touches the fringe of Jesus' garment (ἥψατο τοῦ κρασπέδου τοῦ ἱματίου αὐτοῦ, Mt. 9.20; Lk. 8.44). The woman's faith is depicted as greater than that of Jairus because she believes that she will be healed by the small gesture of touching Jesus' garment, whereas Jairus thinks that Jesus needs to come to his house to heal his daughter.

In Mark, the woman places herself among the least by not attempting to interrupt Jesus' journey to Jairus' daughter, and she does nothing which may detract from the healing of the girl. The woman places the girl's health first, but senses that she too can be healed along the way. Jesus, however, stops to talk to the woman. His action causes a delay, and while he is speaking to the woman, news arrives that the girl has died. The healing of the two women is thus deeply connected, since the woman is healed at the same moment that the girl dies. Blood stops flowing in both, bringing life to one and death to the other. Jesus gives priority to the woman who is an outcast, since her healing is incomplete without his acknowledgment of her. His action in speaking to her establishes a personal relationship illustrated by

58. Marshall, *Faith*, 99.
59. Hooker, *St. Mark*, 151.

his naming of her as 'daughter'. Marcus notes that the story may be trying to teach that time is not a factor in the kingdom of God, where stopping to help one person does not necessarily harm another.[60] These healings indicate the abundance of the kingdom of God and point to the feeding narratives in which abundant food is produced from a small number of loaves and fish, so that everyone may eat and be satisfied (6.42; 8.8).

6. *The Portrayal of the Woman as a Disciple*

In some ways the woman is portrayed as analogous to a disciple; she hears of Jesus (ἀκούσασα περὶ τοῦ Ἰησοῦ, 5.27) and approaches him from the crowd. Her action recalls the parable of the sower, in which insiders are those who hear Jesus' words and approach him for further teaching (4.10–11).[61] The woman comes up behind Jesus (ἐλθοῦσα ἐν τῷ ὄχλῳ ὄπισθεν, 5.27), which is reminiscent of Jesus' call to his disciples to come after him (δεῦτε ὀπίσω μου, 1.17). Jesus praises the faith of this woman (ἡ πίστις σου σέσωκέν σε, 5.34), and he summons human beings to believe in the gospel (πιστεύετε ἐν τῷ εὐαγγελίῳ, 1.15).

Disciples are called to follow Jesus on the way of the cross (8.34). There are, moreover, verbal parallels between the description of the woman's suffering and that of Jesus, as the adverb πολλά (greatly) and the verb πάσχω (to suffer) is used both of the woman (πολλὰ παθοῦσα, 5.26) and of Jesus (πολλὰ παθεῖν, 8.31; ἵνα πολλὰ πάθῃ, 9.12). Selvidge notes that the verb πάσχω is used only of the woman and Jesus, and similarly the woman's disease is described as a scourge (μάστιξ, 5.29) and Jesus is scourged (μαστιγώσουσιν, 10.34).[62] According to Selvidge these allusions suggest that the woman's suffering in society corresponds to the passion of Jesus.[63] Her isolation may be compared to that of Jesus in the Passion Narrative. Jesus is later abandoned by his disciples who are afraid to be arrested with him (14.50).

The stigma associated with the illness of the woman, moreover, points forward to the stigma of Jesus' death on the cross. As Hengel notes, crucifixion was regarded as a shameful death and as a punishment for slaves.[64] The woman's disease of constant bleeding corresponds to the pouring out of Jesus' blood as a sign of the new covenant (14.24). In the Passion Narrative Jesus suffers as a result of the plots of his human enemies. In the apocalyptic context of Mark's Gospel, the power of evil lies behind the force of disease and the evil actions of human beings. In the course of the narrative Jairus' daughter dies and is raised to life, just as Jesus also dies and is raised by God.

The woman is depicted as being like a disciple in that she follows the way of the cross through suffering and overcomes her fear to confess her faith. She is portrayed

60. Marcus, *Mark*, 370.
61. Marcus, *Mystery*, 225.
62. M.J. Selvidge, '"And Those Who Followed Feared" (Mark 10.32)', *CBQ* 45 (1983), 398.
63. Selvidge, 'Those who Followed', 99.
64. M. Hengel, *The Cross of the Son of God* (trans. J. Bowden; London: SCM Press, 1986), 143–55; 177–82.

as a Christ-like figure, for Jesus faces opposition, appears at trials before religious and political authorities, suffers death and is raised to life. The woman has struggled against disease, searching for a cure, and her struggle corresponds to the battle of Jesus against evil. She has spent everything she has on doctors in the attempt to find a cure for her illness, and she risks condemnation by ignoring the purity laws in order to be healed by Jesus. This woman, therefore, foreshadows those who will lose everything but paradoxically will save their lives (8.35).

Our passage thus portrays the woman as someone who suffers from the evil of disease, just as Jesus will later suffer at the hands of his human enemies in the Passion Narrative. The woman's suffering, however, is involuntary, whereas Jesus chooses to face death in Gethsemane (14.36). The verbal correspondences between the portrayal of the women and the description of Jesus in the Passion Narrative, therefore, emphasize that Jesus chooses to become aligned with the suffering of humanity. Jesus follows the will of God and takes the place of those who are persecuted by the rule of Satan. Jesus gives his life as a ransom for many, seeking to liberate humanity and inaugurate the new age (10.45).

The woman illustrates the reciprocity of discipleship, since she comes forward to tell Jesus the truth of what has happened after she has been healed (5.33). We have seen this feature of discipleship already in the account of the healing of Simon's mother-in-law (1.29–31), in which the woman serves Jesus and those present after she has been healed. The emphasis on reciprocity is seen in our passage, since Jesus tells the woman that her faith has saved her (5.34). Jesus heals others in the power of the Spirit, which leaves him as he heals. The self-giving of Jesus' mission is also indicated by his action in giving his life as a ransom for many (10.45). As Matera observes, Jesus brings healing to others and accepts their response, but he is unable to save himself, as the chief priests and scribes mockingly point out at the cross, 'He saved others; he cannot save himself' (15.31).[65]

As we have seen, Dahl[66] and Juel[67] believe that Mark aims to challenge the complacency of his community. In Mark, however, the exploration of the tension between faith and fear suggests that terror of persecution on account of Jesus and the gospel is a central issue for the community. Marcus points out that our passage has similarities with a trial, since the phrase πᾶσαν τὴν ἀλήθειαν (the whole truth, 5.33) frequently occurs in a judicial context (cf. Isocrates, *Antid.* 50; Plato, *Apol.* 16–17; Lycurgus, *Leocrates* 32).[68] He interprets the woman, on the level of the Markan community, as a hidden follower of Jesus who has experienced the power of God, but is afraid to confess her faith on account of possible persecution. The woman confesses the truth and is praised for her faith by Jesus (ἡ πίστις σου σέσωκέν σε, 5.34). In the next part of the story Jairus is asked to continue to have faith even though his daughter has died (μὴ φοβοῦ, μόνον πίστευε, 5.36). Jairus represents early Christians who have lost family and friends to death, and may

65. F.J. Matera, ' "He Saved Others; He Cannot Save Himself", A Literary-Critical Perspective on the Markan Miracles', *Int* 47 (1993), 23.
66. Dahl, 'Purpose', 32–33.
67. Juel, *Master*, 88.
68. Marcus, *Mark*, 360.

consequently be in danger of losing their faith. In this account Jesus shows that he has the power to raise the dead and that disease and human evil are unable to end the lives of those who have faith.

Jairus is portrayed as an active figure who intercedes for his daughter, whereas the girl is powerless in the face of the disease which afflicts her. Her condition recalls the account of the healing of Simon's mother-in-law, who is also portrayed as powerless (1.29–31). This woman, like Jairus' daughter, receives healing because of the people who tell Jesus about her. These accounts illustrate the importance of intercession and the role of the Christian community in supporting and caring for its members.

In our passage the woman with the flow of blood acts as a model of faith for Mark's audience. Although she lives on the margins of society, suffering from a terrible disease, she responds with greater faith to Jesus than those who have been called by him and who journey alongside him. Mark depicts outsiders with greater faith than the disciples (5.34; 10.52). Tolbert argues that the woman's faith acts as a foil to the negative portrayal of the male disciples, who are criticized for their fear (τί δειλοί ἐστε; οὔπω ἔχετε πίστιν; 4.40; μὴ φοβεῖσθε, 6.50).[69]

The portrayal of the woman, however, acts not so much as a foil to the disciples as an encouragement to the Markan community. In the boat journeys the disciples experience the same struggle between faith and fear that we have seen in the portrayal of the woman. The fear of the disciples arises in the context of the storms they encounter during their boat journeys, and these storms represent the persecution the disciples will meet as a result of their mission. Their fear is that their mission will lead to death, whereas faith points to the power of God which reaches beyond death.

The dangers that the disciples will face are illustrated by the prophecies of Jesus in chapter 13. Jesus warns his disciples of the events of the end-time in the period between his death and the parousia, and he describes a time of increased suffering, such as there has never been before, since the beginning of creation until the present (13.19). During this time the disciples will be brought to trial before sanhedrins, synagogues, governors and kings (13.9), but despite this opposition the purpose of the Markan community is to continue the proclamation of the gospel throughout the world (13.10). The disciples are not to worry beforehand about what they should say, as the Holy Spirit will be given to them (13.11). This experience recalls the boat journeys, in which the wind dies down at the sound of Jesus' voice (4.39) or at the presence of Jesus when he enters the boat (6.51). The struggle between faith and fear is an eschatological struggle between the old age and the new. The old age is characterized by fear and lack of understanding, whereas the Spirit brings knowledge of the hopeful shape of the new age.

The depiction of the struggle between faith and fear, which is shown in the account of the woman with the flow of blood and of Jairus' daughter, would act as an encouragement to the Markan community. These stories depict individuals overcoming disease and death through the healing brought by Jesus. The discipleship

69. Tolbert, 'Mark', 263.

community may be compared to the woman with the flow of blood, who has been afraid to tell the truth. In the case of the woman her knowledge of God's power, which has healed her, gives her courage to come forward (5.33). In the same way the Spirit will come to the disciples, bringing knowledge of what they should say during their trials. Her story acts to encourage Mark's community to continue their proclamation even in the face of death. The account of this woman and of Jairus' daughter does not ignore the severity of disease and death. The Markan community is not protected from suffering and persecution, but through hearing the stories of these women, they know that ultimately God will overcome evil.

7. The Restoration of Israel

The account of the healing of the woman with the flow of blood and of the raising of Jairus' daughter occurs in a section of the Gospel particularly concerned with the Jewish mission. Jesus returns to Jewish territory after the healing of the Gentile Gerasene demoniac (5.1–20), and he is immediately approached by a synagogue ruler. Despite Jairus' position in the synagogue he is powerless to heal his daughter. The woman with the flow of blood is unable to find healing from human doctors, and she also approaches Jesus. Both Jairus' daughter and the woman with the flow of blood are associated with the number twelve, since the woman has been ill for twelve years and the girl is twelve years old.

As we have noted, the number twelve is connected to the eschatological hopes for the restoration of the twelve tribes (*1 En.* 57.1; *4 Ezra* 13.32–50; *2 Bar.* 78.1–7; *T. Benj.* 9.2). This number also recalls Jesus' selection of twelve disciples who correspond to the twelve tribes (3.13–19). Twelve years signals the time for the end of the woman's suffering and also the time for the healing of the young girl. Mark, moreover, defers the reference to the girl's age until after she has been raised from death and thus links her age to the occasion of her healing. In contrast, Luke more logically moves the age of the girl to an earlier position in his account (8.42). The use of the number twelve is continued in the account of the feeding of the five thousand, in which there are twelve baskets of leftovers (6.43).

The woman has suffered from a menstrual disease which renders her ritually unclean (Lev. 15.25–30). Although she touches Jesus, however, he does not become ritually impure; instead, power leaves Jesus liberating her from her disease. As we have seen, the term 'power' is associated with the Holy Spirit. In Mark, the Spirit is the power of the new creation which moves out from the heavens to liberate the earth from evil (1.10). After his baptism the Spirit casts Jesus out into the desert to battle against Satan (1.12–13). In the same way, Jesus' mission leads him primarily to those possessed by unclean spirits, to those who suffer from diseases, and to those who would be considered unclean. Jesus eats with tax collectors and sinners (2.15–17). His priority is illustrated by his teaching that he comes to heal the sick not the healthy and that he comes to call sinners not the righteous (2.17). In the prologue John the Baptist prophesies that Jesus will baptise ἐν πνεύματι ἁγίῳ (in the Holy Spirit, 1.8). It is only through Jesus' death on the cross, however, when he gives up the Spirit (ἐξέπνευσεν, 15.37) that the boundary between pure and impure is broken and the new age is inaugurated. Through their baptism the Markan community are incorporated into Jesus' death and resurrection, and they are, therefore, no longer required to observe the purity laws.

In the Passion Narrative, however, Jesus himself is 'handed over' into the realm of evil (9.31; 10.33; 14.44; 15.1). In his mission Jesus has placed his hands on people to heal (1.41; 5.41; 8.23), but now he is struck by his enemies (14.65; 15.19). He has used spittle to heal (7.33; 8.23) and now he is spat upon (14.65; 15.19). He has healed the blind (8.25; 10.52), but now he is blindfolded (14.65). As Marcus points out, Jesus' cry of dereliction at the crucifixion signifies his entry into darkness.[70] In the passion Jesus takes the place of human beings, who are subject to the force of evil in its manifestation of disease. These correspondences recall the description of the suffering servant (Isa. 50.6; 53.5). The servant is struck down and wounded on account of the transgressions of the people, but his wounds become a source of healing. Similarly, Jesus takes on the afflictions of humanity and gives his life to redeem many (10.45). He is crucified at Golgotha, the place of the skull, which is associated with impurity and death. On the cross, darkness descends, expressing the judgement of the day of the Lord (Amos 8.9). Jesus dies on the cross as one who is cursed (Deut. 21.23; cf. Gal. 3.13). At his death he is possessed by evil, and his cry of dereliction on the cross (φωνή μεγάλη, 15.34, 37) corresponds to the earlier cries of the demoniacs (1.26; 5.7).[71]

At the crucifixion Jesus becomes aligned with impurity. Similarly, the blood of the woman is a source of impurity, and her menstrual blood corresponds to the blood of Jesus. Just as she loses her blood through her illness, Jesus loses his life-blood through his mission. The woman's suffering is caused by disease, while Jesus' suffering arises through human opposition to the gospel. But behind both the force of disease and human enemies lies the cosmic power of evil. Jesus does not respond to evil with oppressive force, but gives his life to redeem humanity. His blood, which would be considered unclean, becomes a source of life for his followers. Douglas takes an anthropological approach to the interpretation of this distinction when she discusses the power of blood, which is regarded as threatening within an everyday setting, but which becomes a creative source of power in a sacred setting.[72] At the Last Supper Jesus takes bread and wine and identifies them with his own body and blood (τοῦτό ἐστιν τὸ σῶμά μου, 14.22; τοῦτό ἐστιν τὸ αἷμά μου τῆς διαθήκης τὸ ἐκχυννόμενον ὑπὰρ πολλῶν, 14.24). His body becomes the bread, proleptic of the messianic feast in the kingdom of God (Isa. 25.6–8; *1 En.* 62.12–14; *2 Bar.* 29.5–8). His own blood is poured out for many and becomes a sign of the new covenant (14.24).

---

70. J. Marcus, 'Mark 4.10-12 and Marcan Epistemology', *JBL* 103 (1984), 571–72.

71. F.W. Danker, 'The Demonic Secret in Mark: A Reexamination of the Cry of Dereliction (15.34)', *ZNW* 51 (1970), 52.

72. M. Douglas, *Purity and Danger: An Analysis of the Concepts of Pollution and Taboo* (London: Routledge, 1966), 115, 120.

8. *New Creation*

Jesus heals the woman who has the flow of blood, liberating her from her disease, and he raises Jairus' daughter, overcoming the power of death. The two stories thus illustrate Jesus' battle against disease and death, and his miracles are signs of the new creation breaking into the world. In Genesis, God creates through acts of separating light from darkness, land from sea (1.3–10). Similarly, Jesus heals by casting out unclean spirits that possess human beings (1.21–28; 5.1–20), and he banishes disease (1.31; 5.42). The setting of our account also recalls the opening of Genesis. One of the first acts of creation is the separation of dry land from sea (Gen. 1.9–10). At the beginning of our passage Jesus is depicted at the boundary of land and sea (παρὰ τὴν θάλασσαν, 5.21). The land is the place associated with the sowing of the word (4.13–20), and the sea is linked with the forces of chaos and evil, where storms arise and threaten the mission of the disciples (4.35–41; 6.45–52). As Starobinski observes, the journey across the sea to the other side (τὸ πέραν) signifies the movement into unknown, uncharted territory.[73] It expresses the movement into death which the disciples are called to follow in the hope of finding life (8.34–35). In the boat journeys, moreover, Jesus has the power to still the sea, and to walk on the surface of the water, the margin between chaos and order.

The healing of the woman with the flow of blood is reminiscent of the creation of dry land from chaos. In our passage the disease of the woman is depicted in terms of a flow of blood (ἐν ῥύσει αἵματος, 5.25) and a fountain of blood (ἡ πηγὴ τοῦ αἵματος, 5.29). The healing of the woman is described as ἐξηράνθη (5.29), a verb which means 'to dry up'. The drying of the flow of blood is reminiscent of the creation of dry land in Gen. 1.9 (ἡ ξηρά, Gen. 1.9, 10 LXX). In Genesis God creates dry land as a place of fertility and growth (1.11–12), and similarly the healing of Jesus restores the woman's fertility. The verb ξηραίνω (to dry up), moreover, recalls the account of the exodus, in which the sea dries up to allow the Israelites to escape from slavery (ἡ ξηρά, Exod. 14.21, 22, 29 LXX). These correspondences suggest that the healing of the woman is a sign of the new creation.

The woman with the flow of blood has suffered from her disease for twelve years and she has spent everything she has in her attempts to regain her health. She is depicted as someone who has exhausted all human means of healing. The woman with the flow of blood has been unable to bear children on account of her menstrual disorder, but now her fertility is restored. In addition Jairus' daughter died at the age of puberty, and is now raised from death to life. The restored fertility of the two women foreshadows the overarching metaphor of the birth of the new age, as implied for example in Mark 13.8. The renewal of Israel, similarly, is depicted in terms of restored fertility in Isa. 54.1–3, and in apocalyptic writings the movement from the old age to the new is seen in terms of birth, as in *4 Ezra* 4.40–43; 5.46–55.

The healing of the woman's condition of menstrual bleeding, moreover, may relate to the account of Genesis. As Marcus notes, menstruation is associated with the sin of Eve and there are eschatological expectations which predict an end to

---

73. J. Starobinski, 'An Essay in Literary Analysis – Mark 5.1-20', *EcumRev* 23 (1971), 383.

menstruation in the new age (*b. 'Erub.* 100b; *'Abot R. Nat.* 42 [B]; *Tanḥuma on Lev* 15.25; cf. Ezek. 36.16–25; *Gen. R.* 20.5).[74] In addition, Be'er points out that menstruation is associated with sin (Lam. 1.8, 17; Ezra 9.11) and murder (Ezek. 36.17–18).[75] In our story, then, the woman's healing foreshadows the overcoming of evil in the new creation.

The woman with the flow of blood is described by a series of seven participles, which convey the increasing severity of her disease (5.25–27). In our passage the accumulation of participles expresses the burden the woman carries, and her deteriorating condition corresponds to the increasing evil of the rule of Satan at the end-time. Before the woman reaches death, however, Jesus intervenes to heal her. Similarly, Jairus' daughter is described as at her last (ἐσχάτως ἔχει, 5.23), and she dies in the course of the narrative. Nevertheless, Jesus is still able to raise the girl to life. As Marshall points out, the power of the kingdom of God is operative in the midst of human powerlessness.[76] The experience of these women, moreover, may be compared to that of the disciples. In chapter 13 Jesus prophesies a time of suffering such as has never been since the beginning of creation (13.19). God, however, will cut short the time of trial, and their suffering paradoxically is a sign of the imminence of the kingdom of God.

After her healing, Jairus' daughter walks (περιεπάτει, 5.42), and this verb also occurs in the healing of the paralysed man (2.9). In addition, Jesus asks that she may be given something to eat. On a form-critical level, the picture of the girl walking and eating confirms her restoration from death. These actions, however, also have an eschatological significance. As we have seen, both the healing of Simon's mother-in-law and that of Jairus' daughter are described in terms of a victory over the force of evil, as Jesus seizes both women by the hand in order to save them from disease and death (κρατήσας τῆς χειρὸς, 1.31; 5.41). In addition, the meals at the conclusions of the account foreshadow the messianic feast (Isa. 25.6–8; *1 En.* 62.12–14; *2 Bar.* 29.5–8).

9. *Conclusion*

The account of the healing of the woman with a flow of blood and of the raising of Jairus' daughter illustrates the power of faith to overcome disease and even the power of death. Jesus praises the faith of the woman who struggles through the crowd, seeking only to touch his garment as he hurries past to reach the sick girl. The account also shows the power of intercessory faith, since Jairus is urged to keep on believing that Jesus has the power to heal his daughter even after news arrives to say that the girl had died. The woman is ritually unclean through her condition of constant bleeding, and Jairus' daughter is unclean through death. Jesus, however,

---

74. Marcus, *Mark*, 358.

75. I. Be'er, 'Blood Discharge: On Female Im/Purity in the Priestly Code and in Biblical Literature', in A. Brenner (ed.), *A Feminist Companion to Exodus–Deuteronomy* (Sheffield: Sheffield Academic Press, 1994), 161.

76. Marshall, *Faith*, 94.

is identified with both women through his suffering and death. At his death he gives up the Spirit and inaugurates the new age, in which no disease or other evil will remain. The healing of the two women foreshadows the abundance of the kingdom of God, which breaks into the world in the midst of human suffering.

Chapter 5

HERODIAS AND HER DAUGHTER (6.14–29)

1. *Introduction*

The account of Herodias and her daughter is the second narrative that features a woman and a young girl. Earlier we heard the combined account of the healing of the woman with the flow of blood who is praised by Jesus for her faith (5.34) and of the raising of Jairus' daughter (5.21–43), and in chapter 7 Mark will relate another positive portrayal of women in his description of the persistence of the Syrophoenician woman in her search for healing for her daughter (7.24–30). The negative depiction of Herodias and her daughter widens the portrayal of women in the Gospel. Just as some men follow Jesus and others reject him, some women accept and others oppose the gospel.

Herodias and her daughter are members of the ruling class, and they live a privileged existence, surrounded by wealth. The description of the Herodian women gives insight into the world of Herod's court, a world far removed from Jesus' mission, which takes place primarily around the towns and countryside of Galilee before his final journey to Jerusalem. The prestige and riches of Herodias and her daughter, however, do not ultimately benefit them. Our passage is reminiscent of the parable of the sower in which the cares of the world, the deceit of wealth and desires for different things are depicted as barriers to the proclamation of the gospel (4.19).

In our account Herodias and her daughter act together to manipulate Herod into ordering the execution of John the Baptist. As Wainwright points out, Herodias and her daughter have a greater role in the death of John in Mark than in Matthew, since in the latter Herod also desires to kill John, and Herodias remains in the background (Mt. 14.1–12).[1] In our passage the women plot against John the Baptist because he has aroused the anger of Herodias by condemning her marriage to Herod (6.19). Our account thus illustrates Herodias' violent response to opposition, a reaction which foreshadows the rejection of Jesus by the religious authorities and Pilate.

Mark's description of the death of John the Baptist, however, differs from that of Josephus (*Ant.* 18.116–19). Mark's reference to the leading men of Galilee (6.21) suggests that our passage is located in Herod's residence at Tiberias in Galilee, whereas Josephus situates his account at the fortress of Machaerus near the Judean desert. The two accounts also differ in their description of the reasons behind John

---

1. E. Wainwright, *Towards a Feminist Critical Reading of the Gospel according to Matthew* (Berlin: Walter de Gruyter, 1991), 250–51.

the Baptist's execution. In Mark, Herodias desires the death of John because he criticizes her marriage (6.18). Josephus, on the other hand, attributes to Herod a fear of sedition posed by the followers of John. Mark focuses on the personal motives of Herod, Herodias and her daughter, whereas Josephus puts greater emphasis on political motives. Taylor attempts to reconcile the historicity of the two accounts by suggesting that the portrait of a vengeful woman is not incompatible with a motive of political expediency.[2] In fact Josephus does link Herod's abandonment of his first wife with a military defeat in 39 CE. Herod incurred the wrath of her father Aretas IV of Nabatea, and some Jews interpreted his attack on Herod as divine retribution for the execution of John (*Ant.* 18.119). Myers points out that the Herodians' personal relationships have political significance, since intermarriage within the Herodian family may have been intended to consolidate the power of their dynasty.[3]

The portrayal of Herodias in our passage recalls that of Jezebel who plots against Elijah in 1 Kgs 19. As Gnilka notes, both accounts depict a weak king who is manipulated by an evil queen.[4] John the Baptist acts like a prophet of old who fearlessly criticizes the actions of rulers, and he recalls the portrayal of Elijah, who denounces Ahab in 1 Kgs 16–19. Gnilka also points out the differences in the accounts, since Jezebel's evil plots come to nothing, whereas Herodias manages to gain her will. At the end of his life Elijah is taken up into the heavens (2 Kgs 2.11), whereas John the Baptist suffers a cruel death at the hands of his enemies.

Gnilka, however, argues against an explicit Elijah typology as he notes the influence of other Old Testament traditions and Greco-Roman literature on our story. He prefers to compare Herodias to the vengeful woman of Sir. 25.113–15 or the popular figures of revenge-seeking women such as are depicted in Plutarch's *Artaxerxes* 17. It is still significant that both Herodias and Jezebel are portrayed as determined and inflexible in seeking to enforce their will. Herodias is aligned with Roman rule, which is similar to the fact that Jezebel is a Gentile queen. Both women reject the rule of God to follow their own wishes. In the prologue, moreover, John the Baptist has been identified with Elijah by the description of his clothes of camel's hair and the leather belt around his waist (1.6), which is reminiscent of the portrayal of Elijah (2 Kgs 1.8).

Mark's account focuses on the theological significance of John's death, and as Gnilka notes, there are correspondences between the description of John's execution and other Jewish martyr accounts. These narratives characteristically portray the martyr as zealous for the law (e.g. 2 Macc. 6.18–31; 4 Macc. 5.1–6.30; *b. Ber.* 61b).[5] Similarly, John the Baptist criticizes the marriage of Herod and Herodias as unlawful (6.18). According to the Levirate law (Deut. 25.5), marriage to a brother's wife is only permitted if the brother has died, in order to produce heirs for the dead

---

2.   Taylor, *St. Mark*, 310–11.
3.   Myers, *Binding*, 214–15.
4.   Gnilka, *Evangelium*, 1.249.
5.   J. Gnilka, 'Das Martyrium Johannes' des Taufers (Mk 6.17-29)', in P. Hoffmann *Orientierung an Jesus: zur Theologie der Synoptiker. Für Josef Schmid* (ed. N. Brox and W. Pesch; Freiburg: Herder, 1973), 78–92.

man. As Ilan observes, moreover, some Jewish groups prohibit marriage between an uncle and niece as may be seen in the Qumran literature which regards these marriages as incestuous (CD 5.7–11; 11QT 66.16–17).[6] In Mark, John's criticism challenges the status of Herod as king because the true ruler was expected to uphold the law. As Gnilka indicates, John the Baptist acts like one of the martyrs by his willingness to suffer imprisonment and death on account of the law.[7]

Our passage is located between the sending out of the twelve disciples on a mission (6.6b–13) and their return (6.30). Some scholars, such as Schweizer, suggest that the story of Herodias and her daughter is intended to take up the time needed for the mission of the disciples and to form a narrative relief to the main plot.[8] The account of the persecution and execution of a prophet, however, also foreshadows the future arrest and crucifixion of Jesus. Herodias wishes to kill John the Baptist (6.19), just as the chief priests and scribes want to kill Jesus (14.1). The account also illustrates the nature of the opposition the Markan community may expect to encounter. Just as John and Jesus are arrested and killed, the disciples will be brought to trial before governors and kings (13.9–11).

2. *The Portrayal of the Women*

Herodias is the only woman named in Mark, apart from Jesus' mother, Mary (6.3) and the three women who are witnesses of the resurrection of Jesus (15.40). In her article on the distribution of women's names in Palestine, Ilan notes that in patriarchal society the names of women are recorded less frequently than those of men, and the recording of names is linked to social status.[9] In Mark the inclusion of Herodias' name may thus reflect her high social status. Herodias was a daughter of Aristobulus, the son of Herod the Great, and she was also a niece of Herod Antipas. Herodias' name is derived from the male name Herod, and it associates her with Herod the Great; indeed, many members of Herod's large family were named after him. Her name, therefore, reflects her status of subordination to the male head of the family within the patriarchal culture.

Herodias is introduced as 'Herodias, his brother Philip's wife' (6.17), which defines her identity in terms of her previous husband, in a similar way to the portrayal of Simon's mother-in-law, who is also described by her relationship to a man and in terms of her marriage (1.30). These descriptions are characteristic of the portrayal of women in a patriarchal society, and they highlight the significance of marriage in determining the social status of women. The words chosen, moreover, define Herodias in terms of her earlier marriage, a marriage she wishes to forget. Her past still affects her, just as Herod's execution of John continues to haunt him (6.14–16).

Mark names Herodias' first husband as Philip, but according to Josephus, he was also called Herod, and her second husband was Herod Antipas (*Ant.* 18.136). It is

---

6. Ilan, *Jewish Women*, 76.
7. Gnilka, 'Martyrium', 86.
8. Schweizer, *Mark*, 132.
9. Ilan, 'Notes', 187, 190–92.

possible that Mark may confuse her first husband with Philip the Tetrarch, but this mistake is more likely to have arisen through the frequent use of the name Herod within the dynasty. As Lane suggests, Herodias' first husband may have been called Herod Philip, which Mark has recorded as Philip.[10] According to Josephus, Herodias' daughter was named Salome, and she later married Philip, her father's brother (*Ant.* 18.137). There was frequent intermarriage within the Herodian family, and Ilan cites the example of Salome and Philip as evidence of the tendency to marry girls to their cousins or uncles in order to keep property within the ruling families.[11]

Herod is identified as king (6.14, 22, 25, 26), but there is no corresponding description of Herodias as queen. The title of king, however, is not historically accurate; Herod Antipas was a tetrarch subject to the authority of the Romans, and both Matthew (14.1) and Luke (3.19; 9.7) change his title to tetrarch. On the death of Herod the Great, the Romans divided his kingdom between his three sons, and Herod Antipas was tetrarch of Galilee and Perarea from 4 BCE until 49 CE. The use of the title king may derive from local custom or may reflect Herod's wish to be known as king, particularly as his request for this title ultimately led to his banishment by Caligula in 39 CE (Josephus, *Ant.* 18.240–56).

The Romans preferred to retain local rulers, but on condition that they were able to maintain peace, and the Herodians colluded with the Roman authorities in order to maintain power. Lane, moreover, points out that Herod's guest list includes οἱ χιλίαρχοι (6.21), who were military officers with a status equivalent to a Latin *tribunus militum*, 'a commander of a thousand'.[12] As Lane notes, Herod's guest list suggests that Herod is attempting to portray himself as an imperial ruler and to model his court after the Roman administration.

In Mark, John the Baptist threatens Herodias' marriage by arguing that it is unlawful (6.18). It is significant that John directs his criticism of the marriage to the king, whereas Herodias is excluded. In a patriarchal society ultimate authority belongs to Herod as the male ruler, and he has already divorced another wife to marry Herodias. Herodias' power comes only through her marriage; John's criticism, therefore, also threatens her position at the court. Herodias wishes to kill John, but she is unable to do so because of Herod's respect for the prophet. Herodias is overruled by Herod, but there is also an implication that Herodias does have some power, since Herod has to try to protect John from her. Tolbert even suggests that Herod may have imprisoned John in order to keep him safe from Herodias (διὰ Ἡρῳδιάδα, 6.17).[13] This imprisonment of John, moreover, becomes even more dangerous to Herodias, since Herod is then able to listen to John frequently in the privacy of prison without Herodias interfering (6.20).

John becomes a source of contention between Herod and Herodias. As Gnilka notes, Herodias is dominated by revenge and wants to kill John, whereas Herod seeks to protect him.[14] Delorme argues that Herod's perplexity (6.20) indicates the

10. Lane, *Mark*, 216.
11. Ilan, *Jewish Women*, 77.
12. Lane, *Mark*, 220.
13. Tolbert, 'Mark', 272.
14. Gnilka, 'Martyrium', 82.

division within him as Herod desires Herodias, but is also attracted by the teaching of John the Baptist.[15] The relationship between Herodias and Herod is full of distrust, since Herodias fears that John will be able to threaten her marriage, and Herod suspects that Herodias will ignore his wishes and attempt to put John to death.

In some early manuscripts (e.g. ℵ, B, D) Herodias' daughter is described as θυγάτηρ αὐτοῦ Ἡρῳδιάδος (his daughter, Herodias, 6.22), which implies that she is also the daughter of Herod Antipas and that she has the same name as her mother. Josephus, however, describes the girl as the daughter of Herodias' first marriage, and names her Salome. Mark may refer to her as 'daughter' because she is Herod's stepdaughter. As Marcus points out, there is an overtone of incest in the portrayal of the relationship between the girl and her stepfather, which may reflect the licentiousness of the Herodian court.[16]

The girl is described as a κοράσιον (young girl, 6.22, 28), which is reminiscent of the description of Jairus' daughter (5.41, 42). Jairus' daughter is twelve, which is associated with an age of physical maturity, since girls were frequently married at twelve.[17] The correspondences between the two accounts of a woman and a young girl may imply that Herodias' daughter is of a similar age. Herodias' daughter appears to be unmarried, since there is no mention of her husband's name. In the patriarchal context of the time, the girl is in a precarious position because she cannot inherit, and any son born to her mother and stepfather will take precedence over her.[18] A threat to the marriage of her mother and Herod is also a threat to her own security, and this situation forms the background to the girl's close relationship with her mother.

The account takes place at the birthday celebration of Herod, and his guests consist of the courtiers, military officers and leading men of Galilee (6.21). The men gather in the public setting of a banquet, whereas Herodias and her daughter are portrayed outside the main room. As Corley notes, Mark's description reflects the practice of Greco-Roman banquets in which men dined apart from women.[19] Schwank, moreover, compares our passage to the excavations at Machaerus in which two dining rooms have been discovered alongside one another, suggesting that upper-class Jewish women attended public banquets but dined separately from men.[20] Although our account takes place in Galilee, Schwank's comments help-

---

15. J. Delorme, 'John The Baptist's Head–The Word Perverted: A Reading of a Narrative (Mark 6.14-29)', *Semeia* 81 (1998), 120.

16. Marcus, *Mark*, 396.

17. Pomeroy, *Goddesses*, 164; Archer, *Her Price*, 151–52; Wegner, *Chattel or Person?*, 20–39.

18. For a discussion concerning the ability of women to inherit property, see p. 18 n. 8.

19. K. Corley, *Private Women, Public Meals. Social Conflict in the Synoptic Tradition* (Peabody, MA: Hendrickson, 1993), 94. Corley (183) notes that women and men dined separately in ancient Greece, but women were included at some formal banquets within the Roman period (see Cornelius Nepos, *Praef.* 6–7). She cites the presence of women at private meals (Plutarch, *Praec. ger. rei publ.* 140A; *Cupid. divit.* 528B; Achilles Tatius, *Leuc. Clit.* 1.5) and at public banquets (Dio Chrysostom, *Ven.* 7.65–68; Plutarch, *Gen. Socr.* 594 D–E; *Otho* 3.5–6; Dio Cass. 57.12; Petronius, *Satyr.*).

20. B. Schwank, 'Neue Funde in Nabatäerstädten und ihre Bedeutung für die neutestamentliche Exegese', *NTS* 29 (1983), 429–35.

fully illustrate the influence of Hellenistic banquets on the dining practices in Palestine.

In our account Herodias and her daughter are excluded from the banquet. Corley, however, argues that Herodias and her daughter are present at the dinner in Matthew (14.1–12).[21] She notes that Matthew omits the reference to the military officers and the leading men of Galilee (Mk 6.21), and there is no need for the girl to enter as she is already 'in the midst' (ἐν τῷ μέσῳ, Mt. 14.6). Corley thus argues that Matthew is the most gender-inclusive of the Synoptic Gospels, since it is the only Gospel to depict men and women dining together. This impression, however, may reflect Matthew's desire to shorten Mark's account rather than an aim to indicate the presence of the women at the meal (cf. Mk 3.7–12; 5.1–43; 6.14–29; 9.14–29).[22] Matthew may have regarded the references to the entrances and exits of the girl as unnecessary, and Mt. 14.6 thus refers to her dance in the midst of the guests. Corley, nevertheless, rightly points out the impropriety of the girl's dance before the male guests, since women who attended such meals were usually courtesans. She cites, for example, the account of Philodamus who is reluctant to permit his daughter to attend such a dinner arguing that it is not the Greek custom for women to attend men's banquets (Cicero, *Against Verres*, 11.1.26.66–67).

In Mark, there is a distinction between the public male setting of the banquet and the private conversation of the women which takes place in secret. Herodias' daughter disrupts the male gathering in order to dance before Herod and his assembled company, and her entrances and exits delineate the structure of the narrative (εἰσελθούσης, 6.22; ἐξελθοῦσα, 6.24; εἰσελθοῦσα, 6.25). The girl is on the cusp between adulthood and childhood, and her age enables her to transgress the boundary separating men and women, while her mother waits outside.

Some commentators portray Herodias' daughter as an innocent girl manipulated by her mother, whereas others stress the girl's own part in John's death. Schweizer, for example, regards Herodias as responsible for the girl's action, arguing that she is prepared to sacrifice the honour of her daughter to gain her will.[23] On the other hand, Lane describes the girl's dance as 'lascivious', and as intended to manipulate Herod into granting her wish.[24] Glancy, however, argues that male scholars' concepts of gender have led them to exaggerate the role of Herodias and her daughter in the execution of John the Baptist, and she places more emphasis on Herod's responsibility for John's death.[25]

Herodias' role is downplayed by Glancy, who interprets Herodias' wish to kill John as a 'human' desire because John threatens Herodias' status at the court.[26] Glancy argues that women are frequently condemned for acting in aggressive ways that would be regarded as acceptable in men, and she regards Herodias as neither a monster nor sexually depraved. Glancy's interpretation, however, ignores the

---

21. Corley, *Private Women*, 158–59.
22. Davies and Allison, *Matthew*, 1.73.
23. Schweizer, *Mark*, 134.
24. Lane, *Mark*, 221.
25. Glancy, 'Unveiling Masculinity', 34–50.
26. Glancy, 'Unveiling Masculinity', 50.

cruelty of the women: Herodias instigates the plot to put John the Baptist to death, and her daughter adds that his head should be brought in on a dish (6.24).

Although Glancy notes that Mark does not state at whose volition the girl dances before the guests, she suggests that Herod may have ordered her to dance.[27] Her interpretation, however, does not appear to be convincing, since there is no prior mention of the girl's presence before Herod, and her entrance appears to be unexpected. Initially the girl is with her mother outside the banquet (6.21–22), which may suggest that the dance is planned by Herodias. There is also no indication that either Herodias or her daughter are opposed to the dance before Herod and his guests. The girl quickly responds to Herod's offer of a gift and swiftly exits to consult her mother (6.24–25).

The execution of John is Herodias' idea, particularly as Herodias' desire to kill John has been mentioned earlier (6.19). The girl does conspire with her mother, since Mark stresses the haste of the girl to gain her victim (εὐθὺς μετὰ σπουδῆς, ἐξαυτῆς, 6.25), and the girl adds the request that John's head be brought upon a dish (6.25). The girl, therefore, is responsible for the associations of John's death with a cannibalistic meal. In the text, then, both mother and daughter act to bring about the death of John, and Mark stresses their desire to do so (6.19; 6.25). Herod, however, is also partly responsible for John's murder, since he gives the order for the execution to the guard. He could refuse the women's demand, but his guilt lies in his desire to fulfil his oaths and maintain his status before his guests.

The dance of the girl is not described, and our attention is focused instead upon the response of Herod and his guests (6.22). Marcus notes that the verb ἤρεσεν (pleased) has sexual connotations in the Septuagint as in Gen. 19.8 and Job 31.10.[28] As Aus observes, the description of a beautiful girl who attracts the attention of a king suggests parallels with the story of Esther.[29] He notes that the term τὸ κοράσιον (young girl, Mk 6.22, 28) occurs in Esther LXX (2.2, 3, 7, 8, 9, 12).[30] There are other verbal similarities between the two accounts, as in ἤρεσεν τῷ Ἡρώδῃ (6.22; cf. ἤρεσεν αὐτῷ τὸ κοράσιον, Est. 2.9 LXX). Herod offers the girl up to half his kingdom (6.23), which is reminiscent of Artaxerxes' offer of half his kingdom to Esther (Est. 5.3).[31] Anderson notes that in a patriarchal culture the power of a woman is frequently linked to her ability to please men.[32] Herod is willing to share half of his kingdom with his stepdaughter rather than with his wife. Herodias as an older woman lacks power to influence her husband, and she must act through her daughter.

27. Glancy, 'Unveiling Masculinity', 40.

28. Marcus, *Mark*, 396.

29. R. Aus, *Water into Wine and the Beheading of John the Baptist* (BJS, 150; Atlanta: Scholars Press, 1988).

30. Aus, *Water into Wine*, 50.

31. Aus, *Water into Wine*, 53–54.

32. J.C. Anderson, 'Feminist Criticism: The Dancing Daughter', in J.C. Anderson and S.D. Moore (eds.), *Mark and Method: New Approaches in Biblical Studies* (Minneapolis: Fortress Press, 1992), 121.

Herodias and Esther both use their beauty to manipulate kings into granting their wishes. Esther, however, uses her beauty to save her people from genocide, whereas Herodias' daughter uses hers to condemn a prophet to death. A further correspondence, moreover, may be seen in *Est. R.* (4.11), in which the head of Vashti is brought to the king on a platter, and in our account in which Herodias' daughter requests the head of John the Baptist to be brought in on a platter (6.25).[33]

The girl pleases Herod and the other men present at the banquet, and Herod stresses his authority as king: he is the only one with the power to offer the girl up to half his kingdom. The contrast in social status between Herod and the girl is emphasized in the phrase εἶπεν ὁ βασιλεὺς τῷ κορασίῳ (the king said to the girl, 6.22). The simple description of Herodias' daughter as a girl suggests innocence and powerlessness, particularly as this word has earlier been used to describe Jairus' daughter (5.41, 42). It is ironic, therefore, that the girl's apparent vulnerability allows her to gain power over the king. The change in her behaviour is indicated by her commanding reply to the king θέλω ἵνα ἐξαυτῆς δῷς μοι ('I want you to give me at once', 6.25).

Throughout the account Mark describes the wishes of human beings. Herodias desires to put John the Baptist to death (6.19) whereas Herod likes to listen to him (6.20). Herod asks the girl what she desires (6.22) and she wants the head of John the Baptist (6.25). Girard interprets the account of John's execution as a story of mimetic desire, and focuses on the desire of Herodias to kill John.[34] Initially Herod imitates the desire of his brother and marries his brother's wife Herodias. She, however, loses power over Herod once they are married because he is no longer competing against his brother for her. Herodias desires the death of John the Baptist because he criticizes her marriage. Girard describes Herodias' daughter as a child who has no desire of her own, since she asks her mother what she should request from Herod. At this point the girl's desire mirrors that of her mother, so that mother and daughter become interchangeable. Girard's analysis also emphasizes that the desire of Herodias' daughter is imitated by the guests at the feast, who all wish the death of John. John the Baptist is interpreted as a random victim who becomes a ritual sacrifice with the function of reconciling the desires of all the other characters.

This interpretation, however, appears to impose a theory of mimetic desire upon the passage rather than to interpret the motives of the characters within the text. Meltzer, for example, points out that Herodias' daughter is not described as lacking any desire, for her initial reaction to Herod's offer is to seek out her mother's advice.[35] The daughter's initial desire, therefore, is her wish to please her mother. This interpretation is confirmed by the end of the account, where the girl passes the platter with the head of John the Baptist to her mother. The death of John, moreover, does not bring a resolution of the characters' desires. When Herod hears the

33. Aus, *Water into Wine*, 62–64.

34. R. Girard, 'Scandal and the Dance. Salome in the Gospel of Mark', *New Literary History* 15 (1984), 311–24.

35. F. Meltzer, 'A Response to Rene Girard's Reading of Salome', *New Literary History* 15 (1984), 328–29.

girl's request, he is described as περίλυπος (deeply troubled, 6.26), and the residual conflict within Herod is illustrated by Herod's fear that Jesus is John risen from the dead (6.14–16).

The daughter acts as an intermediary who carries out the wish of her mother. She asks her mother for advice, and she adds the request that the head of John the Baptist be delivered on a platter (6.25). This request may reflect the girl's desire to hand the head of John the Baptist to her mother as a gift (6.28). The portrayal of Herodias and her daughter contrasts with other narratives in which parents intercede for the health of their children. We have previously heard the request of Jairus for Jesus to heal his daughter (5.21–43), and later the Syrophoenician woman will plead with Jesus to cast a demon from her daughter (7.24–30). In our passage the prominence of the mother is emphasized by the initial reference to Herodias' desire to kill John (6.19) and the final description of the girl handing the platter to her mother (6.28). The girl, however, is also in the middle of the relationship between her mother and her stepfather. Herodias is an older woman who watches her daughter arouse the sexual desire of her husband. She takes advantage of his offer to the girl to trick him into complying with her request. Herodias, therefore, takes revenge not only on John but also on Herod. As Herod betrays her in his offer to her daughter, she betrays him by making her own request, which she knows to be contrary to his will.

There are similarities in the portrayals of Herodias, the woman with the flow of blood (5.24–34), and the Syrophoenician woman (7.24–30). All three women are depicted as persistent, and they act independently. The woman with the flow of blood has spent all her money on doctors and has only grown worse, but she still seeks healing by touching Jesus' clothes (5.28), and the Syrophoenician woman ignores the initial rebuttal of Jesus (7.28). In the same way Herodias does not give up hope in her desire to put John the Baptist to death, despite Herod's opposition. All three take the initiative when an opportunity arises for their wishes to be realized.

Herodias' daughter, however, is more active than Jairus' daughter and the Syrophoenician woman's daughter, who are both ill. Just as children may be possessed by evil spirits, they may also act in the power of evil desires. The girl breaks social boundaries, and in this way her action is characteristic of the portrayal of women in Mark. The woman with the flow of blood breaks the purity laws to touch Jesus' clothes (5.27), and later the Gentile Syrophoenician woman approaches Jesus, a Jewish man, for the healing of her demon-possessed daughter. The disruption of a banquet with male guests points forward to the woman who disturbs a meal to anoint Jesus (14.3–9). The persistence and determination of Herodias and her daughter echo these qualities in other women in Mark, but their actions have a destructive effect as they are intended to bring about the cruel death of John the Baptist.

3. *Discipleship*

The account of Herodias and her daughter offers an evil counterpart to the faithful women we see elsewhere in the Gospel (5.21–43; 7.24–30; 14.3–9). The Herodian women are driven by evil desires to bring about the death of John the Baptist, a purpose which is in opposition to the life-giving aim of Jesus' mission. Throughout the account there are repeated references to the wishes of human beings, high-lighted by the use of the verb θέλω (to wish). Herodias wishes to kill John the Bap-tist (ἤθελεν αὐτὸν ἀποκτεῖναι, 6.19) but is unable to execute John as Herod fears John, recognizing him as a holy and righteous man (ἄνδρα δίκαιον καὶ ἅγιον, 6.20). Herod fears John, just as the demoniac in the synagogue fears Jesus as ὁ ἅγιος τοῦ θεοῦ (the holy one of God, 1.24). As Marcus notes, Herod is attracted and repelled by John, just as the demoniacs fall down before Jesus and even seem to worship him, but also fear that he will destroy them (1.24; 5.7).[36] Herod's reac-tion reveals the power of the gospel as both disturbing and life-giving.

Herod's fear of John the Baptist, however, is overcome by his desire for Herodias' daughter. He offers the girl up to half his kingdom, again using the verb θέλω (αἴτησόν με ὃ ἐὰν θέλῃς, καὶ δώσω σοι, 6.22), and the strength of his desire is seen in the repetition of his offer with oaths (6.23). Herod, however, does not have the power to give away half his kingdom, since he is subject to Roman authority. His offer of only half his kingdom contrasts with the teaching that disciples should give away everything in order to follow Jesus (10.29–30). The girl replies by demanding the head of John the Baptist (θέλω ἵνα ἐξαυτῆς δῷς μοι, 6.25). As Derrett points out, Herod makes an oath 'to give' something to the girl, but John the Baptist is not a possession to be given away.[37] Herod's execution of John thus turns him into an object to be handed over to the girl.

When Herod hears the girl's request, he is described as περίλυπος (6.26), a term expressing strong fear and distress, which is also used of Jesus in Gethsemane (14.34). In Gethsemane Jesus struggles to follow the will of God, although he is aware that his acceptance of it will lead to his death (ἀλλ᾽ οὐ τί ἐγὼ θέλω ἀλλὰ τί σύ, 14.36). The girl's wish provokes contrasting desires within Herod in the same way that the will of God creates conflict within Jesus, but Herod's desire to protect John is overcome by his greater wish to keep the oaths he has made before the honoured guests at his banquet. He chooses earthly power and status in prefer-ence to the will of God, and again the verb θέλω is used to express this choice (οὐκ ἠθέλησεν ἀθετῆσαι αὐτήν, 6.26).

There is some ambiguity over Herod's response, since he does not wish to deny the girl, and the preceding clause stresses that he is unwilling to break his word before his guests (διὰ τοὺς ὅρκους καὶ τοὺς ἀνακειμένους, 6.26). As Taylor notes, the plural 'oaths' implies repeated oaths.[38] Herod's fear of breaking his oaths is ironic, as his oaths are made before God, yet he fears breaking his oaths more than he fears the one before whom oaths are made. In the Greco-Roman world oaths made at banquets were expected to be honoured. These banquets could pro-vide opportunities for women to gain their will despite the opposition of male rulers. As Gnilka observes, for example, Herodotus relates the account of King Xerxes who was constrained by law to grant a request to his wife, Amestris, at a

---

36. Marcus, *Mark*, 401.
37. J.D.M. Derrett, 'Herod's Oath and the Baptist's Head', *BZ* 9 (1965), 52.
38. Taylor, *St. Mark*, 316.

banquet celebrating his birthday (*Hist.* 9.108–13).[39] In a similar way to Herodias, Amestris takes advantage of the banquet to demand the death of her enemy.

In our passage Herod wishes to protect John, but he is ruled by his desire to maintain his status before his guests. There is an implication that Herod's company of guests are more likely to think badly of Herod for breaking his oath than for his murder of John. Davies and Allison point out that Mark's portrait of Herod is more ambiguous than that of Matthew, since Matthew identifies Herod as the one who wishes to kill John the Baptist.[40] As Marcus notes, Herod's dependence on the opinions of his guests is an indication of his lack of power and authority. Herod is presented as a man who is torn apart by conflicting desires, and is depicted as the antithesis of a true ruler because others manipulate his emotions.[41] Tolbert interprets Herod as an example of the thorny ground, as initially he listens to John eagerly, but the cares of the world and his desires choke his response (4.19).[42]

Herod foreshadows Pilate, who condemns Jesus to death despite his belief in Jesus' innocence. Pilate knows that the chief priests have handed Jesus over on account of envy (15.10). There is a verbal parallel, moreover, between the offer of Herod to the girl (6.22) and Pilate's offer to the crowd τί οὖν θέλετε ποιήσω ('Then what do you wish me to do', 15.12). Herodias instructs her daughter to request the head of John the Baptist (6.24), and the chief priests incite the crowd to cry out for the release of Barabbas rather than Jesus (15.11). Herod wishes to uphold his dignity before his guests (6.26), and Pilate desires to please the crowd (15.15). Both Herod and Pilate are depicted as weak rulers, who knowingly hand over innocent men to death in order to preserve their own status.

The portrayal of the desires of the Herodians may be compared to the wishes of the disciples. There are verbal similarities between Herod's conversation with the girl (αἴτησόν με ὃ ἐὰν θέλῃς, καὶ δώσω σοι, 6.22; θέλω ἵνα ἐξαυτῆς δῷς μοι, 6.25) and the request of James and John to Jesus (θέλομεν ἵνα ὃ ἐὰν αἰτήσωμέν σε ποιήσῃς ἡμῖν, 10.35; δὸς ἡμῖν, 10.37). James and John want the seats next to Jesus when he rules in glory, but unlike Herod, Jesus replies that their request is the province of God alone. Jesus asks the brothers if they are willing to endure the same baptism he faces, and they reply that they are. James and John act as disciples in their desire to follow Jesus. Although they flee at Jesus' arrest, they are still given the opportunity to renew their discipleship (14.28; 16.7).

Herodias, her daughter and Herod contrast with the disciples in that they do not seek God's will but only their own. The use of the verb θέλω recalls the teaching of Jesus that those who do τὸ θέλημα τοῦ θεοῦ (the will of God, 3.35) are members of Jesus' family. The verb is also prominent in Jesus' teaching about discipleship that those who want to come after him must deny themselves, take up their crosses and follow him (εἴ τις θέλει, 8.34). Similarly, those who wish to save their lives

39. Gnilka, 'Martyrium', 88.

40. Davies and Allison, *Matthew*, 2.471.

41. Marcus (*Mark*, 399) points out that the antityrannical theme in Mark may also be seen in the Old Testament (the portrayal of Pharaoh in Exodus and the king in Daniel), and in Greco-Roman writings (Plato, *Resp.* 9.573b–80a; 587b–e and Arrian, *Epict. diss.* 1.19.2–3; cf. 1.24.15–18).

42. Tolbert, 'Mark', 272.

will lose life, but those who lose life on account of Jesus and the gospel will save their lives (ὃς γὰρ ἐὰν θέλῃ, 8.35). Jesus invites rather than compels disciples to follow him, but the desire to follow him draws the disciples into a close identification with Jesus. They will not only share the same opposition and persecution (13.9), but those who endure to the end will find abundant life (13.13).

The desires for status and self-preservation act as forces in opposition to the call of Jesus to follow the way of the cross. Unlike the Herodians, those who suffer diseases and live as social outcasts express desires which are compatible with the will of God. The leper asks if Jesus is willing to make him clean (ἐὰν θέλῃς δύνασαί με καθαρίσαι, 1.40), and Jesus replies that he does want to heal him (θέλω, καθα-ρίσθητι, 1.41). Later, Jesus asks the blind beggar τί σοι θέλεις ποιήσω ('What do you want me to do for you?') and he replies ἵνα ἀναβλέψω ('let me see again', 10.51). The desires of Herodias, her daughter and Herod bring torment and death to others. In contrast, the leper and Bartimaeus recognize their need for healing, illustrating the will of God to bring life.

Those who are outcasts and powerless desire health, whereas those who have wealth and high social status seek to preserve their power. Herodias seeks to preserve herself when threatened by John, the girl desires to please her mother, and Herod desires the approval of his guests. As Jesus teaches, they kill John according to their will (ἐποίησαν αὐτῷ ὅσα ἤθελον, 9.13). Wealth and the cares of the world are depicted as barriers to discipleship (4.19). The rich man desires eternal life but is unable to leave his possessions in order to follow Jesus (10.22), whereas the blind beggar, Bartimaeus, immediately throws down his garment to be healed by Jesus (10.50). Those who suffer diseases recognize their need for health, but often those who have high social status, such as Herodias and her daughter, do not recognize their spiritual blindness. The desires for status and wealth are aligned with the destructive power of Satan who rules the world, whereas ultimate authority belongs to God alone.

4. *The Messianic Feast*

The setting of the account is a banquet given in honour of Herod's birthday. In the Greco-Roman world the birthday of a ruler was regarded as an opportunity to celebrate the gift of life, and frequently birthday banquets were the occasion for requests to be granted or prisoners to be released. Marcus, however, notes that a birthday feast, particularly of a king, was regarded as idolatrous by the rabbis (*m. 'Avod. Zar.* 1.3) and in the writings of the church fathers (Origen, *Comm. Matt.* 10.22), and they were not celebrated in ancient Judaism (see *EncJud*, 4.1054).[43] Despite these associations banquets celebrating birthdays may have been characteristic of the Herodians, since Josephus mentions a similar feast in honour of Agrippa (*Ant.* 19.321).[44]

43. Marcus, *Mark*, 395.
44. Lane, *Mark*, n. 71 220.

Herod's birthday feast is the occasion of the death of John the Baptist. It is ironic that the term τὰ γενέσια signifies a day set aside in memory of the dead in classical Greek, but occurs in Plato, *Leg.* 784D and in later Greek with a meaning similar to τὰ γενέθλια 'a birthday feast'.[45] The original meaning thus foreshadows the situation in which Herod's birthday becomes an opportunity for the remembrance of his execution of John the Baptist. Our passage, moreover, begins with Herod's memory of his responsibility for the execution of John, and the account of John's death is narrated in the form of a flashback. The story concludes with a description of the burial of John in a tomb, and as Delorme suggests, the term μνημεῖον (tomb) may also be translated as a 'place of memory'.[46] According to Delorme, the tomb may hide the body, but it also becomes a place of remembrance. Herod fears the consequences of his execution of John the Baptist, and the theme of memory thus pervades the whole passage.

Herod invites the most prominent people in his society to his birthday celebration (τοῖς μεγιστᾶσιν αὐτοῦ καὶ τοῖς χιλιάρχοις καὶ τοῖς πρώτοις τῆς Γαλιλαίας, 6.21). This list of prominent guests aligns Herod with the scribes who are criticized by Jesus because of their desire to have the highest positions (πρωτοκαθεδρίας ἐν ταῖς συναγωγαῖς καὶ πρωτοκλισίας ἐν τοῖς δείπνοις, 12.39). In contrast, Jesus' meals are open to tax collectors and sinners, and he is described as eating at the house of a leper (14.3–9). The use of πρῶτοι (first, 6.21) also looks forward to the teaching of Jesus that many who are first will be last, and the last first (πολλοὶ δὲ ἔσονται πρῶτοι ἔσχατοι καὶ οἱ ἔσχατοι πρῶτοι, 10.31). Herod surrounds himself with prominent people, unaware of the imminent eschatological reversal in which the poor and vulnerable will come first.

Herod's birthday banquet is given to his male hierarchy of courtiers, and Herodias along with her daughter is excluded. The dance of the girl, however, creates an opportunity for the women to participate in the meal, as occurs when Herodias' daughter requests that the head of John the Baptist should be brought to her on a platter (6.25). As Anderson indicates, the presentation of John's head on a platter depicts John as food being brought before the guests at the banquet.[47] Now, through her daughter's request, Herodias is served 'food' from the banquet, and the women's desires are satiated at Herod's birthday celebration.

The women's actions recall the celebration of some of the other meals in Mark. Marcus notes that there are verbal similarities between the account of the execution of John and the feeding narratives (6.30–44; 8.1–10).[48] The executioner gives the platter to the girl, who then hands it to her mother (ἔδωκεν, 6.28). In the feeding narratives Jesus gives the bread to the disciples to distribute (ἐδίδου, 6.41; 8.6). These meals foreshadow the Last Supper in which Jesus breaks bread and gives it to his disciples (ἔδωκεν, 14.22). At the Last Supper Jesus is aware that he is facing death, and he identifies his body as bread given to bring life (14.22). John the Baptist, however, is suddenly executed without warning and we are not told anything

45. Taylor, *St. Mark*, 314.
46. Delorme, 'John the Baptist's Head', 126.
47. Anderson, 'Dancing Daughter', 132.
48. Marcus, *Mark*, 403.

about his death. Marcus suggests that Herod's banquet is portrayed as a demonic caricature of the eucharist.[49] Anderson notes that similar connections are frequently depicted in medieval paintings of the death of John the Baptist.[50]

The feeding narratives and the Last Supper foreshadow the abundance of the messianic feast (Isa. 25.6–8; *1 En.* 62.12–14; *2 Bar.* 29.5–8). Everyone eats and is fully satisfied in the feeding narratives (6.42; 8.8), and at the Last Supper Jesus' blood is poured out for many (14.24) in order that his death may bring redemption to humanity. Jesus gives his own life as food for many others, whereas the Herodians take John's life and the platter is given to only one person, Herodias.

In other accounts women are particularly linked with serving food, such as Simon's mother-in-law who serves a meal after her healing (1.31) and the women who follow and serve Jesus in Galilee (15.40–41). The positive association of women with the service of food in Mark recalls the angels who serve Jesus while he is tested by Satan in the prologue (1.13). During this time he is also described as being among the wild animals. The description of the Herodian women is reminiscent of the reference to the wild animals, since the women are described in cannibalistic terms because Herodias' daughter gives her mother the head of John the Baptist on a platter.

The Herodian women do not have the authority to gain their desires and they manipulate Herod into ordering the execution of John the Baptist. Herod is depicted as an imperial king whose commands are obeyed immediately. He sends orders for John to be imprisoned (ἀποστείλας ἐκράτησεν, 6.17), and later he sends an executioner to behead him (ἀποστείλας ὁ βασιλεὺς σπεκουλάτορα ἐπέταξεν, 6.27). As Marcus notes, the use of the verb ἀποστέλλω (to send) recalls Jesus' choice of twelve disciples in order to send them out on a mission (3.14) and the sending out of the twelve (6.7).[51] On their return they are described as οἱ ἀπόστολοι (6.30). In the prologue a messenger is sent to prepare the way (1.3), and the use of the verb ἀποστέλλω is also associated with the action of God in the definition of Jesus as the one sent by God (9.37).

Marcus regards the use of this same verb in the present passage as a continuation of the theme of demonic caricature that pervades the pericope. In addition, he points out that the same verb is used of Herod's command to the executioner as is employed for Jesus' instructions to the people in the feeding narrative (ἐπέταξεν, 6.27, 39). Herod takes the role of king, but his commands cause suffering and death, whereas Jesus' instructions are intended to bring life to others. The Herodian women are not depicted as guests at the banquet, and Herodias does not appear at the meal. Nevertheless, she takes a leading role from behind the scenes, and her daughter carries out her plans. The two Herodian women may thus be compared to Simon's mother-in-law (1.29–31) and the group of Galilean women (15.40–41) who serve Jesus. In contrast the Herodian women seek only to serve themselves, and bring death to others.

49. Marcus, *Mark*, 403.
50. Anderson, 'Dancing Daughter', 127.
51. Marcus, *Mark*, 394.

5. *New Creation*

The account of the death of John the Baptist describes the fulfilment of the evil wishes of human beings. Herodias' determination to kill John, her daughter's desire for the head of John the Baptist, and Herod's wish to please his guests are all fulfilled. Mark gives the impression, however, that the realization of these desires brings no peace to the Herodians. Herodias feared the influence of John the Baptist because he criticizes her marriage, but ironically she is likely to threaten her own marriage by ignoring her husband's wishes. In addition, she has witnessed her husband succumbing to the attractions of her daughter, which may cause repercussions in her relationships both with her husband and with her daughter.

Similarly, Herod is tormented by his role in bringing about the death of John (6.16). When Herod hears the girl's request, he is described as περίλυπος (deeply troubled, 6.26), but he still gives the order for John's execution. His wish to keep his oaths and his status before his guests indicates his weakness in response to the cares of the world, the deceit of wealth and the desire for things other than those of God (4.19). Herod acts like a Roman king by inviting the hierarchy of Galilee to celebrate his birthday. He is overcome by his emotions and kills a man he believes is a prophet. He is condemned by his own action, as he later realizes (6.16). As Gnilka observes, his belief that Jesus is John the Baptist, risen from the dead, is an indication of his disturbed conscience.[52]

The use of the flashback technique at the beginning of the passage places the account of John's death in the context of Herod's guilt and fear of God. The introduction emphasizes that the discontent of Herod extends from the execution of John into the later time of Jesus' mission. The references to the spread of Jesus' name and the debates over his identity suggest that the power of God is at work in the world despite the execution of John. Herod's anguish is evident in his assertion that Jesus is John the Baptist risen from the dead (6.16). The use of the divine passive, moreover, stresses that he fears that his evil action has been overturned by God (ἠγέρθη, 6.16). This term also foreshadows the message of the young man at the tomb that Jesus has been raised (ἠγέρθη, 16.6).

Herod is aware of various interpretations of Jesus' identity: John the Baptist, Elijah or a prophet like one of the prophets of the past (6.14–16), but he is convinced that Jesus is John the Baptist whom he beheaded. He associates Jesus' power to perform miracles with the raising of John the Baptist from the dead (διὰ τοῦτο ἐνεργοῦσιν αἱ δυνάμεις ἐν αὐτῷ, 6.14). John the Baptist, however, is not known to have carried out any miracles (cf. Jn 10.41). Herod believes that John's power has become greater after his death than it was during his lifetime. Although Herod has exerted his utmost power by executing John, his fears point to his belief in a power greater than his own.

Herodias and her daughter appear to have prevailed in their execution of John the Baptist, but the meaning behind events is concealed from human beings. The use of apocalyptic terminology, moreover, stresses that events are following the

52. Gnilka, *Evangelium*, 1.249.

purposes of God. At the beginning of the passage Herod hears reports about Jesus (φανερὸν γὰρ ἐγένετο τὸ ὄνομα αὐτοῦ, 6.14). The reference to Jesus' name recalls the messianic secret, in which Jesus commands the unclean spirits not to reveal his identity (καὶ πολλὰ ἐπετίμα αὐτοῖς ἵνα μὴ αὐτὸν φανερὸν ποιήσωσιν, 3.12) and human beings are told not to speak of his miracles (5.43; 7.36). The use of the term φανερὸν (evident, visible) is also reminiscent of the teaching of Jesus that nothing is hidden except with the purpose of being revealed (φανερωθῇ; φανερόν, 4.22). In our account the spread of Jesus' name is thus an indication that events are following the purposes of God, despite the manipulations of the Herodian women and Herod's subjection to them.

The death of John the Baptist, moreover, foreshadows Jesus' teaching about his own suffering and death. As Gnilka notes, Herod's three interpretations of Jesus' identity (6.14–16) are repeated by the disciples prior to Jesus' first passion prediction (8.31).[53] Each of his passion predictions (8.31; 9.31; 10.32–34) stresses that his death is in accordance with scripture. These references put the passion of John and that of Jesus in the wider context of God's purposes of bringing about the new creation. On a human level, the evil wishes of human beings, including the Herodian women, are carried out, but on the divine level God's will prevails.

Throughout the Gospel John the Baptist takes the role of Elijah (1.6; cf. 2 Kgs 1.8). At the transfiguration Jesus associates John the Baptist with Elijah as the one who comes to restore all things (9.11–13). It was believed that Elijah would return before the end-time (Mal. 3.1; 4.5). As Lane points out, the phrase ἀποκαθιστάνει πάντα (to restore all things, 9.12) recalls the prophecy of the return of Elijah (ἀποκαταστήσει, Mal. 4.6 LXX).[54] John calls the people to prepare the way of the Lord, and he proclaims a baptism of repentance for the forgiveness of sins (1.4). John's purpose of restoration appears to have failed, however, since the Herodians have treated him as they wished. Jesus still stresses that his death will happen in accordance with the scriptures (καθὼς γέγραπται ἐπ᾽ αὐτόν, 9.13).

Herodias, moreover, seeks an opportune time to gain her desire to kill John (εὐκαίρου, 6.21), and this term occurs again in the description of the desire of Judas to find an opportunity to betray Jesus (εὐκαίρως, 14.11). Marcus points out that the term εὐκαίρου also recalls the use of εὐαγγέλιον (gospel) and καιρός (time) in 1.15. The use of καιρός in this verse includes the arrest of John the Baptist, which signals the time of the start of Jesus' mission (1.14). As Marcus argues, the opportune time in 6.21 is a counterpart to the time of fulfilment proclaimed by Jesus.[55] These opportune times are moments of decision which change the course of events, but they are also foreseen moments in the unfolding of God's plan.

In our passage Herodias and her daughter are depicted as the enemies of John the Baptist, and as such they oppose a prophet sent by God. John the Baptist acts as the forerunner to Jesus (1.7–8), and this role is stressed by the use of similar terms to describe the two figures. The verb παραδίδωμι (to hand over) is used of the

53. Gnilka, 'Martyrium', 79–80.
54. Lane, *Mark*, n. 27 322.
55. Marcus, *Mark*, 401.

arrest of John (1.14) and foreshadows the arrest of Jesus (9.31; 10.33; 14.41, 42, 44, 46) and his disciples (13.9, 11, 12). Herod seizes and binds John (ἐκράτησεν; ἔδησεν, 6.17), and Jesus is seized and bound in the Passion Narrative (ἐκράτησαν, 14.46; δήσαντες, 15.1). The plot of Herodias and her daughter is inserted into an account of the sending out of the Twelve and their return. Initially the Twelve have a successful mission, but the account of John's death depicts the sort of opposition disciples may encounter. Just as John is arrested and handed over, so will Jesus and the disciples be (13.9–13).

The women show no compassion for John, and he is executed at their whim. After his death John's disciples gather to bury his body (τὸ πτῶμα, 6.29), and the same term is used of Jesus' corpse (15.45). John's death is bleak, and Schweizer notes that the love of John's disciples is the only positive feature at the end of the account.[56] There is a sense of poignancy as John dies without any expectation that his mission will continue. John fades from the narrative to be replaced by the mission of Jesus and his disciples.

Herodias and her daughter appear to have gained their will since John's mission is now over. As Gnilka points out, John's death is not vindicated in the course of the narrative.[57] His vindication awaits the death and the resurrection of Jesus, when the new creation will be inaugurated. John the Baptist speaks out in criticism of Herod, and he is put to death. John prepares the way for Jesus, who will also be executed. The strongest human power is the ability to kill, and the human action of murder is aligned with the destructive power of Satan. Death is a negation of creation itself, but God has the power of resurrection, which is a form of new creation. Life is not only a contrast with death, because God brings life out of death. At the beginning of creation, God creates from chaos, bringing light out of darkness and separating the two (Gen. 1.3–4). At the resurrection of Jesus he brings life out of death and separates the new creation of life from the old age which is characterized by death.

6. *Conclusion*

In our passage Herodias and her daughter are instrumental in bringing about the death of John the Baptist. The women are not invited to Herod's banquet, but the young girl is able to please Herod and, guided by her mother, she manipulates him into agreeing to the execution of John. The women take advantage of the banquet and Herod's wish to please his powerful guests. These evil desires are destructive and bring suffering to others. The strongest power of the Herodians is the human ability to kill, but God's power is stronger as it can bring life out of death. John the Baptist is the forerunner of Jesus, and the murder of John brings about the greater power of Jesus. In this way the plot of Herodias and her daughter ultimately proves futile, as Herod himself senses when he hears the rumours about the miraculous powers of Jesus.

---

56. Schweizer, *Mark*, 134.
57. Gnilka, *Evangelium*, 1.251.

Chapter 6

THE SYROPHOENICIAN WOMAN AND HER DAUGHTER (7.24–30)

1. *Introduction*

The account of the exorcism of the Syrophoenician woman's daughter is the third narrative depicting a woman and young girl. We have seen the positive portrayal of the healing of the woman with the flow of blood and of the raising of Jairus' daughter (5.21–43), followed by a negative description of women in the account of the plot of Herodias and her daughter to execute John the Baptist (6.14–29). The third story, which is of a woman who seeks healing for her daughter, is a positive account portraying the faith of a Gentile woman. The earlier two accounts present women in a Jewish context, but now Jesus moves into the Gentile area surrounding Tyre, and the woman who requests help for her daughter is a Syrophoenician. Her child is possessed by an unclean spirit, indicating that the power of disease and evil extends over Gentile land as well as over Israel.

Initially, Jesus appears reluctant to heal the woman's daughter, but the Syrophoenician woman refuses to give up her request. The account of the Syrophoenician woman is striking in its portrayal of the courage and determination of the woman. Her refusal to give up hope recalls portraits of other persistent women who successfully debate with powerful men as in 2 Sam. 14.1–20, Lk. 18.1–8 and *b. 'Erub.* 53. Feminist interpreters, such as Fander, argue that the Syrophoenician woman changes Jesus' mind.[1] Ringe, moreover, suggests that the faith of the woman allows Jesus to come to a new understanding of the relationship between Jews and Gentiles.[2] Kinukawa proposes that the woman is the one who challenges Jesus to ignore the barriers between Jews and Gentiles.[3] As Rhoads points out, the persistence of the Syrophoenician woman reveals the power of faith to overcome obstacles.[4] Her courage and determination thus portray this woman as a prototype of the faith of the Gentiles.

The portrayal of the Syrophoenician woman is similar to that of the woman with the flow of blood (5.24–34), since each account depicts the courage of women and their ability to act independently. Both women appear alone and risk condemnation

---

1. Fander, *Stellung*, 74.
2. S.H. Ringe, 'A Gentile Woman's Story', in A. Loades (eds.), *Feminist Theology: A Reader* (London: SCM Press, 1985), 56.
3. Kinukawa, *Women*, 60.
4. D. Rhoads, 'Jesus and the Syrophoencian Woman in Mark: A Narrative-Critical Study', *JAAR* 62 (1994), 348–52.

in their approach to Jesus. The woman with the flow of blood seeks healing by reaching out to touch Jesus' clothes, and her action points to the abandonment of the purity regulations. In our passage the Syrophoenician woman appears as a prophetic figure, who ignores the religious and social barriers between Jews and Gentiles in order to seek help from an itinerant Jewish teacher, and her story indicates that the mission of Jesus is for both Jews and Gentiles.

2. *The Portrayal of the Syrophoenician Woman*

The Syrophoenician woman and her daughter are both anonymous, and the mother is introduced simply as a woman (γυνή, 7.25) in a manner similar to that of other women in Mark (5.25; 14.3). She is defined by her daughter's illness (ἧς εἶχεν τὸ θυγάτριον αὐτῆς πνεῦμα ἀκάθαρτον, 7.25), which suggests that her life is dominated by her child's suffering. Matthew portrays the woman as a Canaanite (15.22), but Mark describes her in greater detail as ῾Ελληνίς, Συροφοινίκισσα τῷ γένει (Greek, a Syrophoenician by race, 7.26). As Rhoads observes, this phrase is a typically Markan two-step progression in which a general description is followed by a more specific term (1.32; 6.53; 14.3).[5] In our passage Mark emphasizes that the woman is not only Greek-speaking, but also a Gentile by race. Taylor argues that the description Syrophoenician is intended to distinguish the woman from Libyphoenicians who are from the area around Carthage.[6] As Marcus points out, however, Mark may use this term to indicate that the woman is from the Phoenician area of Syria instead of the Coele-Syrian area, or the description may suggest that the woman is a descendant of the intermarriage of Phoenicians with Syrians.[7]

The narrative takes place in the region around the city of Tyre, and some manuscripts include a reference to Sidon, but the latter may have been inserted, since these cities are frequently linked together, and Jesus later visits Sidon (7.31). Tyre and Sidon are portrayed negatively in the Old Testament (Isa. 23.1–12; Jer. 47.4; Ezek. 26–28; Joel 3.4–8; Amos 1.9–10; Zech. 9.2–4). The description of the woman's background, therefore, not only defines her as a Gentile, but also links her with the people of Tyre who were traditionally regarded as the enemies of the Jewish people (cf. Josephus, *Apion* 1.70). This conflict, moreover, continues in the first century as Josephus refers to hostilities between the Jewish people and the inhabitants of Tyre at the time of the Jewish War (*War* 2.478).

The Old Testament references to Tyre and Sidon often condemn the wealth and materialism of these cities (Isa. 23.8–9; Ezek. 27–28; Joel 3.4–6; Zech. 9.2–4). Theissen highlights the socio-economic features in the account in his examination of the social and historical context which lies behind the relationship between the Galileans and the inhabitants of Tyre and Sidon.[8] Tyre was a wealthy trading city which lacked land suitable for agriculture, and Tyre therefore bought food supplies

---

5. Rhoads, 'Syrophoenician', 353.
6. Taylor, *St. Mark*, 349.
7. Marcus, *Mark*, 462–63.
8. G. Theissen, *The Gospels in Context: Social History and Political History in the Synoptic Tradition* (Minneapolis: Fortress Press, 1991), 72–75.

from Galilee. Theissen argues that there were considerable tensions between the two areas, since the Galileans went hungry in times of food shortage in order to supply the people of Tyre.

In our passage the social status of the woman may be indicated by the description of her as a Greek (7.26). Theissen notes that the term ʹΕλληνίς suggests that the woman is immersed in Hellenistic culture, which may imply that she is a member of the upper classes.[9] As he observes, the woman may be wealthy, since her child lies on a bed (κλίνη, 7.30), rather than on the mats that were used by poor people (κράβαττος, 2.4, 9, 12; 6.55).[10] The apparent wealth of the woman is reminiscent of the portrayal of the woman with the flow of blood (5.24–34) who initially had sufficient means to enable her to pay doctors in her search for a cure for her illness. The social status of the Syrophoenician woman, however, is not as high as that of Herodias and her daughter, who are members of the aristocracy of Galilee, but her position contrasts with that of the majority of the poorer people of Galilee. The inhabitants of Tyre are traditionally associated with sufficient wealth to buy whatever grain they need from their poorer Jewish neighbours. In our passage these roles are reversed as a representative from the wealthy area of Tyre is portrayed as seeking 'bread' from Jesus, a Galilean.

Not all associations of Tyre and Sidon in the Old Testament, however, are negative. Gnilka points out that there is a promise of salvation for Tyre and the neighbouring peoples in Ps. 87.4.[11] In addition Derrett notes the similarities between our passage and the story of the widow of Zarephath who encounters the prophet, Elijah, in the vicinity of Sidon (1 Kgs 17).[12] In 1 Kings Elijah requests that the woman serves him first before sharing her last meal with her son, which is similar to the way Jesus in our account wants his people to be fed before the Gentiles. Both passages feature the healing of Gentile children, since Elijah raises the widow's son from death and Jesus casts out a demon from the Syrophoenician woman's daughter. The widow of Zarephath, moreover, acts as a prototype of faithful Gentiles elsewhere in the New Testament (cf. Lk. 4.16–30). The positive response of the Syrophoenician woman to Jesus may thus foreshadow the future success of the Gentile mission.

The Syrophoenician woman and Jesus each represent separate worlds, since they differ in race, social status and gender. She is portrayed as a member of the Hellenistic world, cultured and wealthy, whereas Jesus is a Jewish man who lives as an itinerant teacher. The woman's need for help for her daughter prompts her to seek out someone outside her world to find healing for her child. Just as Jairus, the president of the synagogue, had to move out from the synagogue to find healing for his daughter (5.21–43), so the Syrophoenician woman seeks help from someone outwith the Gentile world. In both passages there is an implication that the present

9.   Theissen, *Gospels*, 70.
10.   Theissen, *Gospels*, 71.
11.   Gnilka, *Evangelium*, 1.291.
12.   J.D.M. Derrett, 'Law in the New Testament: The Syro-Phoenician Woman and the Centurion of Capernaum', *NovT* 15 (1973), 16.

world of the suppliant is unable to heal, and this lack of power prompts individuals to approach someone beyond their familiar experience.

The Syrophoenician woman acts independently, without anyone to help on her behalf, and there is no reference to her husband or to any male relatives. Rhoads argues that the gender of the Syrophoenician woman is not essential to the story, since the account of the relationship between Jews and Gentiles could have featured a Gentile man.[13] The gender of the woman, however, is highlighted by her willingness to ignore social conventions in order to speak to Jesus.[14] Respectable women were not expected to go out unaccompanied or to approach strangers, particularly men. A woman on her own was also vulnerable to attack, and therefore the Syrophoenician woman risks her security for the sake of her child, since she enters the house alone to speak to Jesus. The Syrophoenician woman's trust in Jesus, however, enables her to disregard the social boundaries between Jews and Gentiles to seek help from a Jewish man. In this way she is similar to the woman with the flow of blood (5.24–34) and the woman who anoints Jesus (14.3–9), as they also appear to be alone.

The issue of gender plays a role in both our passage and in the account of the woman with the flow of blood (5.24–34). Although the woman with the flow of blood is ritually impure, she still touches Jesus' clothes (5.27). In our account the Syrophoenician woman disregards the religious and social barriers between Jews and Gentiles in her search for healing for her daughter, and Jesus casts the unclean spirit from the Gentile child. The abandonment of the purity regulations, therefore, is prompted in both accounts by the actions of women, and is justified by the healing of women.

On one level the encounter between Jesus and the Syrophoenician woman is an account of a mother's request for healing for her sick daughter, but on another, this meeting has deeper implications for the relations between Jews and Gentiles. Sugirtharajah[15] notes that Jesus does not ask the Syrophoenician woman to give up her status as a Gentile or to follow him, and Perkinson[16] raises the question of

---

13. Rhoads, 'Syrophoenician', 367.

14. Pomeroy (*Goddesses*, 149–89) notes that upper-class Roman women had more freedom to travel outside their homes in order to attend public dinners, games and political gatherings than their counterparts in classical Athens. She also observes (*Goddesses*, 190–204) that the lives of poorer women were not as secluded as those of the upper classes, since women worked at trades and in taverns. Clark (*Women in the Ancient World* [Oxford: Oxford University Press, 1989], 17–21) takes a similar view in her analysis of the lives of women. She points out that Roman women attended dinner parties with men (Cornelius Nepos, *Praef.* 6). See also E. Cantarella, *Pandora's Daughters: the Role and Status of Women in Greek and Roman Antiquity* (trans. M.B. Fant; Baltimore: John Hopkins University Press, 1987). Cantarella (134) accepts the increasing freedom of Roman women, but argues that it was intended to educate upper-class women in male values and to prepare women for the role of wife and mother. The Syrophoenician woman, however, not only travels on her own to visit Jesus, but meets him in a private place. Her unexpected appearance and Jesus' reluctance to heal her daughter imply that she has not been invited to the house, and there is also no indication of the presence of any other people.

15. R.S. Sugirtharajah, 'The Syrophoenician Woman', *ExpTim* 98 (1986), 13–15.

16. J. Perkinson, 'A Canaanite Word in the Logos of Christ; or The Difference the Syrophoenician Woman Makes to Jesus', *Semeia* 75 (1996), 61–85.

whether or not the Syrophoenician woman retains her religious differences after her encounter with Jesus. Our passage, however, is not a call narrative. In the context of the gospel the Gentiles are not subsumed within the Jewish mission, since Jesus abandons the food laws (7.19). The exorcism of the Syrophoenician woman's daughter is a sign of the kingdom of God breaking into the world. Mark characteristically portrays the healing of an individual as representative of the action of God in redeeming the world. As we have seen, the account of the healing of the woman with the flow of blood and of the raising of Jairus' daughter (5.21–43) foreshadows the restoration of Israel. Our passage describes the exorcism of a Gentile woman's daughter in a way that points forward to the extension of the salvation of Israel to the Gentiles.

3. *The Portrayal of the Syrophoenician Woman's Daughter*

The daughter of the Syrophoenician woman is anonymous like her mother, and we are given little information about her apart from her illness. The girl is first described as being possessed by an unclean spirit (πνεῦμα ἀκάθαρτον, 7.25), and later there are two references to the demon which possesses her (7.26, 29). She is subject to an outside evil force which renders her unclean. As we have seen, the descriptions of human beings possessed by evil spirits (ἐν πνεύματι ἀκαθάρτῳ, 1.23; 5.2) are ambiguous. Individuals may have the unclean spirit within them, or they may be regarded as submerged within the evil age of Satan.[17] In one sense an outside evil force has taken control over the girl. On the other hand this description suggests that illness comes about as a result of the inability of an individual to adapt to an evil environment. The child is possessed by an unclean spirit because she is vulnerable to the power of the evil age in which she lives. Jesus, therefore, seeks both to heal the individual and to redeem creation.

Although the girl's condition is not portrayed in detail, the Markan audience is aware of the severity of demon possession, since we have already heard the description of the torments of the Gerasene demoniac who lived among tombs, tearing himself with stones (5.1–20). The Gerasene demoniac has been abandoned by his community, who seek only to restrain him. The Syrophoenocian woman, however, refuses to abandon her child. In the Greco-Roman world girls were less highly valued than boys, and they were more likely to be exposed as infants (*P.Oxy.* 744; Apuleius, *Metam.* 10.23).[18] Ringe, moreover, notes that they were costly to their

17. Marcus, *Mark*, 192.

18. For a discussion on the exposure of female infants, see Pomeroy, *Goddesses*, 164–65 and Cantarella, *Pandora's Daughters*, 115–16. D. Engels ('The Problem of Female Infanticide in the Greco-Roman World', *CP* 75 [1980], 112–20) argues that the stable population figures indicated that there was not a high rate of the exposure of female infants in the Greco-Roman world. M. Golden ('Demography and the Exposure of Girls at Athens', *Phoenix* 35 [1981], 316–31), however, counters Engel's argument and shows that female infanticide was a factor in the low rate of population growth. G. Clark (*Women in the Ancient World* [Oxford: Oxford University Press, 1989], 25) notes that there is evidence for a shortage of upper-class women since Augustus allowed well-born men not of the senatorial class to marry the daughters of freedmen (Dio 54.16.2).

families and required a dowry in order to marry.[19] The desire of the Syrophoenician woman to seek healing for her daughter, however, indicates the value she places on her child. This portrayal is similar to that of Jairus' daughter. The concern of both parents to find healing for their daughters at personal cost to themselves challenges negative views of the status of women and particularly of daughters in the first century.[20]

Children are the most vulnerable members of the community and suffer the onslaught of disease associated with the increasing evil of the end-time (cf. 13.19). They are members of the last generation in whose lifetime the kingdom of God will come (9.1; 13.30). The healing of Jairus' daughter and the Syrophoenician woman's daughter thus point forward to the new age when no disease or evil will remain. Mark, however, gives different presentations of the healing of these children. As Taylor points out, the girl in our passage is healed at a distance and there is no reference to healing either by the touch (1.31; 5.41) or by the word of Jesus (1.25; 5.8; 9.25).[21] This account contrasts with the healing of Jairus' daughter, as in that passage Jesus seizes the girl by the hand and addresses her directly (ταλιθα κουμ, 5.41). The present exorcism is depicted as a battle between Jesus and the power of evil. Jesus is asked to cast the demon from the girl (ἵνα τὸ δαιμόνιον ἐκβάλῃ, 7.26). The verb ἐκβάλλω (to cast out) is a violent verb expressing the force necessary to free the girl from evil. After her healing the girl is thrown onto her bed (βεβλημένον ἐπὶ τὴν κλίνην, 7.30), and Rhoads notes that this description implies that a violent struggle has taken place.[22] The narrative depicts the after-effects of the exorcism, and the final picture of the girl is one of the peace attained after a battle.

As in the earlier accounts of exorcisms (1.21–28; 5.1–20), however, there is still a lack of resolution to the conflict since we are not told where the demon has gone. The healing of the girl is poignant because she appears to be alone in the climactic moments of her struggle against evil. This situation contrasts with the healing of Jairus' daughter in which Jesus, his four disciples, and the girl's mother and father are present (5.40). Jairus' daughter rises from death to the presence of her family, and she is given food by them (5.43). As Hooker observes, the healing of the daughter of the Syrophoenician woman is reminiscent of the healing of another Gentile, the centurion's servant who is also healed at a distance (Mt. 8.5–13; Lk. 7.1–10).[23] These healings, therefore, are indications of the power of Jesus to move beyond

---

J. Boswell (*The Kindness of Strangers. The Abandonment of Children in Western Europe from Late Antiquity to the Renaissance* [London: Allen Lane, The Penguin Press, 1989], 74) argues that the practice of the exposure of children in the Greco-Roman world should not be confused with infanticide because children were often left in places where they could be collected and brought up by strangers. Some were adopted as foster children (*Dig.* 34.1.15; 34.1.14.1; 36.3.26). Boswell (111–13), however, also notes that a large number became slaves or prostitutes (Terence, *Haut.* 640; Justin, *1 Apol.* 27).

19. Ringe, 'Gentile Woman's Story', 55.
20. Ilan, *Jewish Women*, 44–48.
21. Taylor, *St. Mark*, 348.
22. Rhoads, 'Syrophoenician', 352.
23. Hooker, *St. Mark*, 184.

Israel to the Gentiles. As the Gentile mission is particularly associated with the period between the resurrection and the parousia (13.10), these healings without the physical presence of Jesus are proleptic of a power to heal that will continue after his death.

4. *The Meeting of Jesus with the Syrophoenician Woman*

At the beginning of our passage Jesus travels north into the Gentile area of Tyre and enters a house with the desire of remaining hidden. Immediately the Syrophoenician woman hears of him and she approaches him within the house with a request that he release her daughter from the power of an unclean spirit. Mark, however, begins with Jesus' reply rather than the request of the woman. Jesus' words are shocking in their severity since he appears unwilling to heal the sick child ('Let the children be fed first for it is not right to take the children's bread and throw it to the dogs', 7.27). In the opening chapters of the Gospel, by contrast, we have seen Jesus responding immediately to the needs of those who seek healing (1.29–31; 1.40–45; 2.1–12). When Jairus, the president of the synagogue, requests help for his daughter, Jesus sets off immediately to his house (5.24). In our account, then, expectations are overturned, since Jesus seems reluctant to help the Syrophoenician woman's daughter.

Various interpretations have been suggested to explain the harshness of Jesus' reply. Some give a psychological explanation; Taylor, for example, cites the beginning of our passage in which Jesus enters a house and wishes to remain concealed (7.24). He suggests that Jesus seeks privacy in order to reflect on the scope of his mission, and he is speaking to himself as well as to the woman.[24] Lane, moreover, proposes that Jesus tests the woman to ensure that she does not regard his miracles as magic or superstitions.[25] These interpretations are unconvincing, however, since Mark does not describe Jesus' motives and there is no indication that the woman has a false understanding of Jesus.

Other commentators, such as Myers, focus on the action of the woman, proposing that Jesus' rejection of the woman is to be expected, because the behaviour of the Syrophoenician woman in approaching an unknown man in a private house was unconventional and insulting to Jesus.[26] Similarly, Kinukawa argues that the

---

24. Taylor, *St. Mark*, 349–50.

25. Lane, *Mark*, 262.

26. Myers, *Binding*, 203. Tolbert ('Mark', 269) suggests that Mark's audience may have compared the woman's unconventional behaviour to that of the Cynics who were called 'dogs' because of their disregard of social conventions. F.G. Downing ('The Woman from Syrophoenicia, and her Doggedness: Mark 7.24–31 (Matthew 15.21-28)', in G.J. Brooke (ed.), *Women in the Biblical Tradition* [Studies in Women and Religion, 31; Lewiston: Edwin Mellen Press, 1992], 134) also argues that the use of the term 'dog' implies that the woman is portrayed as a Cynic. Downing, moreover, compares the skill of the Syrophoenician woman in argument to that of the Cynic Hipparchia (Diogenes Laertius, 6.97–98). The Syrophoenician woman, however, does not articulate any of the teaching of the Cynics, and she is portrayed as a mother who is anxious to return home to her daughter rather than as an itinerant philosopher who has rejected social norms.

woman's approach to Jesus brings disgrace to him, because the act of bowing was only accepted among men.[27] Her argument is influenced by her experience of the social conventions of Japanese society, which are not reflected in our passage. Both Myers' and Kinukawa's interpretations fail to consider the praise and acceptance Jesus gives to the woman with the flow of blood, who also kneels before him (5.33).

In our passage, rather, the reason behind Jesus' refusal is indicated by the clause δέ (but) in 7.26: the woman is Ἑλληνίς, Συροφοινίκισσα τῷ γένει, implying that Jesus is reluctant to heal the child because of her race. The woman and her daughter are Gentiles and are thus outside the Jewish nation. Jesus contrasts the Syrophoenician's daughter with the term for children, τέκνα (7.27), which may also be translated as descendants, and thereby portrays the Jewish people as the children of God (cf. Deut. 14.1; Isa. 1.2; Hos. 11.1; *m. 'Abot* 3.15). Jesus, moreover, insults the Gentile child and portrays her as an outsider, since he compares her to a dog. The reference to dogs (κυναρίοις, 7.27) occurs in other biblical texts as a term of abuse for Gentiles (1 Sam. 17.43; 2 Kgs 8.13).

There are only a few positive references to dogs in the Old Testament (Tob. 6.2; 11.4). Dogs were regarded as scavenger animals who roamed on the outskirts of towns. In the Old Testament Elijah prophesies that Jezebel will be eaten by dogs (1 Kgs 21.23), and in Greco-Roman literature Herodotus writes of Masistes' wife whose mutilated body is thrown to the dogs (*Hist.* 9.112). Jesus' reference to dogs, therefore, depicts the Gentile world as a threatening environment. As Theissen notes, in other New Testament texts Jesus teaches that his disciples should not throw that which is holy to dogs (Mt. 7.6) and opponents and heretics are described as 'dogs' in 2 Pet. 2.22; Phil. 3.2 and Rev. 22.15.[28] The term 'dogs' is used in association with meals by the author of the *Didache* when he prohibits anyone who is not baptized from sharing the community meal; in so doing he cites the teaching of Jesus 'Do not give what is holy to dogs' (9.5).

The comparison between the children and dogs portrays the woman and her daughter as outsiders. Rhoads, however, attempts to soften the severity of Jesus' response by suggesting that the portrayal of the woman as a scavenger dog is playful.[29] He argues that the term κυνάριον (dog, 7.27) is a diminutive, which may be regarded as a term of 'endearment' referring to a puppy rather than a dog. As Guelich observes, κυνάριον is only one of a series of diminutives in this passage (θυγάτριον, 7.25; ψιχίων, 7.28; παιδίον, 7.30).[30] It is therefore more likely that the use of the diminutive is intended to strengthen the correspondence between the dogs and the Syrophoenician woman's daughter, since she is described with another diminutive, θυγάτριον in 7.25.

Jesus' harsh answer implies that the woman requests that 'food' be taken from the Jewish children in order to 'feed' her own Gentile daughter. The use of πρῶτον (first, 7.27), however, indicates that Jesus does not deny food to the Gentile girl,

27. Kinukawa, *Women*, 54.
28. Theissen, *Gospels*, 62.
29. Rhoads, 'Syrophoenician', 356–57.
30. Guelich, *Mark*, 386.

but argues that she must wait until the Jewish children are fully fed. The concept of priority in eating recalls texts such as Exod. 23.11, in which the surplus produce of the land is intended for the poor of the people and anything left over is for the wild animals. The prospect of throwing food to dogs, therefore, has connotations of wastefulness.

The Syrophoenician woman asks Jesus to heal her daughter, but Jesus replies with a saying about food. Rhoads thus notes that Jesus' words in our passage may be interpreted as a 'carefully crafted allegory'.[31] Throughout Mark Jesus' parables may be interpreted allegorically (4.1–20; 7.14–15; 12.1–11). Similarly, Jesus' reply may be read as an allegory which relates to the timing of the Gentile mission. His words may also be compared to a parable. Parables act as a means of revelation in apocalyptic literature (cf. *1 En.* 37–71; *4 Ezra*). Marcus observes that Jesus' parables characteristically act as a means of revelation which divide those who hear them into insiders and outsiders (4.10–12).[32] In chapter 4 Jesus teaches the parable of the sower to the crowd, and insiders are those who approach him for further instruction. They are the ones who receive the secret of the kingdom of God.

The Syrophoenician woman is a Gentile who may be considered an outsider, but she shows herself to be an insider, since she responds to Jesus' parable with one of her own. Jesus proposes that the children must be fully satisfied before the dogs are fed. The woman contradicts Jesus' saying with an observation from everyday life, arguing that the dogs under the table eat at the same time as the children from the abundance of the children's crumbs. Her response emphasizes that she does not want to deprive anyone else of food; she merely wants to benefit from others' surplus.

Whereas Jesus speaks of throwing the children's bread to dogs, the woman introduces a reference to a table (τράπεζα, 7.28). As Dufton notes, Jesus refers to scavenger dogs which are outside the house, while the woman is speaking of household dogs under the table.[33] In addition, the Syrophoenician woman replaces the Jewish term for children, τὰ τέκνα (7.27), with τὰ παιδία (7.28). As Pokorny points out, the Syrophoenician woman's daughter is described as τὸ παιδίον (7.30) at the end of the passage.[34] The term τὸ παιδίον is a general word for child and is used for the synagogue president's daughter (5.40) and of the Syrophoenician woman's child (7.30) as well as in the teaching of Jesus (9.36–37; 10.13–15). In our passage Jesus speaks of giving bread to the children first, and the Syrophoenician woman reminds him that her daughter is also a child.

Behind the account of the request of the Syrophoenician woman is the issue of salvation history. Jesus argues that his mission is directed first to the Jews and then to the Gentiles. This chronological order occurs in Rom 1.16 (Ἰουδαίῳ τε πρῶτον καὶ ῞Ελληνι) in which the term ῞Ελληνι recalls the initial description of the woman as ῞Ελληνίς (7.26). A similar priority of mission may be seen in other New Testament texts such as Rom. 2.10; Acts 13.46 and Acts 18.6. In our passage the

---

31. Rhoads, 'Syrophoenician', 355.

32. Marcus, *Mark*, 305.

33. F. Dufton, 'The Syro-Phoenician Woman and her Dogs', *ExpTim* 100 (1989), 417.

34. P. Pokorny, 'From a Puppy to a Child: Some Problems of Contemporary Biblical Exegesis Demonstrated from Mark 7.24-30/Matt 15.21-28', *NTS* 41 (1995), 337.

order of Jews and Gentiles has an eschatological focus. There are several Old Testament texts which refer to the positive response of the Gentiles after the restoration of Israel (cf. Isa. 2.2–4; 19.19–25; 60.3; 66.18–24; Mic. 4.1–2; Zech. 9.10).[35] In Matthew, Jesus describes his mission to the lost sheep of Israel (10.6; 15.24), and the mission to the whole world is commanded only by the risen Jesus (Mt. 28.19). In John, the positive response of Gentiles occurs at the close of Jesus' mission, and is interpreted by Jesus as a sign of the end-time (Jn 12.20–23). In our passage the advent of the Syrophoenician woman is also a foreshadowing of the faithful response of the Gentiles in the end-time, since Jesus particularly associates the mission to the Gentiles with the period between the resurrection and the parousia (13.10). The Syrophoenician woman's response indicates that the time has drawn near for the Gentile mission.

Jesus' reply suggests that the initial focus of his mission is Israel. Burkhill proposes that our passage has developed over a period of time from a saying of Jesus (Mk 7.27b) expressing the priority of his mission to Israel to a narrative supporting the future mission to the Gentiles.[36] Although the Gentile mission appears to have been supported by the early Christians, Sanders points out, that there was considerable debate over the terms of the Gentile mission among Christian groups.[37] The sharing of meals between Jews and Gentiles was a contentious issue in the early church (Gal. 2.1–14; Acts 10). It is significant, therefore, that our passage focuses on the sharing of food between Jews and Gentiles.

Jesus' speech, moreover, contains verbal similarities to the accounts of the feeding of the five thousand (6.30–44) and of the four thousand (8.1–10). The phrase λαβεῖν τὸν ἄρτον (to take bread, 7.27) is similar to the description of Jesus' action of taking bread to feed the crowds in the feeding narratives (λαβὼν... ἄρτους, 6.41; 8.6). In our passage Jesus wants the children to be fully fed (χορτασθῆναι, 7.27), and this verb recalls the account of the feeding of the five thousand in which the crowd eats and is fully satisfied (ἐχορτάσθησαν, 6.42). The feeding of the five thousand (6.30–44) has several features which suggest a Jewish setting. The number twelve is prominent in the account; the twelve disciples help to distribute the food, and there are twelve baskets of leftovers (6.43). The number twelve is associated with the gathering of the twelve tribes and the restoration of Israel (Isa. 27.12–13; Hos. 11.11; 2 Macc. 1.27; *4 Ezra* 13.32–50; *2 Bar.* 78.1–7). The feeding of the five thousand, therefore, shows that the Jewish people have already been fully fed (6.42) and points to the restoration of Israel.

Jesus' encounter with the Syrophoenician woman acts as a turning point in the Gospel. After the healing of the Syrophoenician woman's daughter Jesus moves to the area of the Decaoplis, where many Gentiles lived (7.31), and he feeds a crowd of four thousand (8.1–10). The crowd with Jesus have travelled a great distance (ἀπὸ μακρόθεν ἥκασιν, 8.3), and Danker observes that this phrase is associated with Gentiles (Josh. 9.6, 9) and is used of the inclusion of Gentiles in the salvation

---

35. See J. Jeremias, *Jesus' Promise to the Nations* (London: SCM Press, 1958), 55–73.

36. T.A. Burkhill, 'The Historical Development of the Story of the Syrophoenician Woman (Mark vii: 24-31)', *NovT* 9 (1967), 161–78.

37. Sanders, *Jesus and Judaism* (London: SCM Press, 1985), 220.

of Israel (Isa. 60.4).[38] The reference to four thousand people may allude to Gentiles, since there were eschatological expectations that people would travel from the four corners of the earth to Israel at the end-time (Ps. 107.3; Isa. 43.5–6). On this occasion there are seven baskets of leftovers (6.43). The number seven is associated with completion, since the world was created in seven days, and the Sabbath is regarded as the fulfilment of creation (Gen. 2.2–3).

The significance of the feeding narratives and hence of our feeding parable, moreover, can only be understood in the context of the Last Supper. As Taylor points out, there are verbal similarities between the blessing and distribution of bread in the feeding narratives and the action of Jesus at the Last Supper (λαβὼν ἄρτον... εὐλογήσας ἔκλασεν...ἔδωκεν, 14.22).[39] Jesus blesses bread (εὐλόγησεν, 6.41) as he blesses bread at the Last Supper (14.22). In the feeding of the four thousand he breaks the bread after having given thanks (εὐχαριστήσας, 8.6), a sequence that is also repeated at the Last Supper (14.23). At the Last Supper Jesus identifies his body with the bread which is broken and shared among his followers (14.22). Jesus also identifies the wine as his blood of the covenant which is poured out for many (14.24). His action alludes to his death on the cross, which brings salvation to humanity. The broken bread foreshadows the death of Jesus which redeems all human beings, both Jews and Gentiles.

The feeding narratives (6.30–44; 8.1–10) and the Last Supper (14.22–25), look forward to the messianic feast. As Schweitzer notes, the Last Supper has an eschatological focus, since Jesus tells his disciples that he will not drink the fruit of the vine until he drinks it in the kingdom of God (14.25).[40] In the feeding narratives everyone eats and is fully satisfied (6.42; 8.8), and the messianic feast is characterized by abundance (Isa. 25.6; *1 En.* 62.14; *2 Bar.* 29.5–6; *4 Ezra* 6.51; *Pirque Aboth* 3.20; Mt. 8.11; Rev. 19.9). In the parallel passage in Matthew, the woman refers to the table of the Lord (κύριος, 15.27). The woman's reference to the table in our passage may also allude to the Lord's table (cf. 1 Cor. 10.21; Isa. 65.11; Mal. 1.7–12). Furthermore, in the reference to our passage in Ps.–Clem. *Hom.* 2.19 there is a direct allusion to the 'table of the kingdom'.

Allusions to the presence of Gentiles at the messianic feast are also to be found in Jewish writings. Marcus points out that righteous Gentiles are depicted as domestic dogs at the eschatological banquet (*Midr. Ps.* 4.11), and he suggests that the description of the presence of dogs at a banquet may be a known term for the inclusion of Gentiles at the end-time.[41] In our passage the woman places herself in the last

38. F.W. Danker, 'Mark 8.3', *JBL* 82 (1963), 215–16.

39. Taylor, *St. Mark*, 324; G.H. Boobyer ('The Eucharistic Interpretation of the Miracle of the Loaves in St. Mark's Gospel', *JTS* 3 [1952], 161–71) argues that the language used in the feeding narratives is not intended to foreshadow the eucharist. He notes that the references to the blessing and the distribution of the bread may be seen in meals which are not eucharistic (cf. Acts 27.35). In the literary context of Mark's Gospel, however, there are verbal correspondences between the feeding narratives and the account of the Last Supper which suggest that these accounts all allude to the eucharist.

40. A. Schweitzer, *The Mystery of the Kingdom of God* (London: A. & C. Black, 1925), 172–73.

41. Marcus, *Mark*, 464.

position content with the crumbs which fall from the table. The Syrophoenician woman's desperation to find a cure for her daughter enables her to recognize the power of Jesus to heal. In Jesus' exorcisms and healings the kingdom of God breaks into the world and his miracles are proleptic of the new age. The Syrophoenician woman appears as a prophetic figure whose word indicates that the time has drawn near for the Gentile mission.

Jesus is the Messiah who overcomes the power of disease and evil through his death on the cross, and his victory is celebrated by the messianic feast. Jesus, therefore, 'feeds' both Jews and Gentiles through the giving of his life. In our passage the Syrophoenician woman asks Jesus to heal her sick child and he replies with a saying about food. In earlier passages too healing is associated with eating. In response to her healing Simon's mother-in-law serves a meal to those present (1.31), and after Jairus' daughter is raised from death, Jesus asks that she be given something to eat (5.43). Simon's mother-in-law and Jairus' daughter, therefore, both eat after their struggle against disease. In these accounts food is both a confirmation of their healing and a foreshadowing of the messianic feast which celebrates the victory over evil. In our passage the Syrophoenician woman's determination to find healing for her daughter is a prophetic sign of the faith of the Gentiles which will be realized in the future mission of the Markan community (13.10).

5. *The Gentile Mission*

At the beginning of Mark's Gospel Jesus begins his mission in Galilee, and he calls twelve disciples who may be regarded as representatives of the twelve tribes of Israel (3.13–19). He later heals the woman with the flow of blood who has been ill for twelve years and raises a twelve-year-old girl to life (5.21–43). In the feeding of the five thousand there are twelve baskets of leftovers (6.43). The use of the number twelve in these accounts points forward to the restoration of Israel. At the same time, however, the news of the gospel moves on ahead of Jesus, attracting crowds from the Gentile area around Tyre and Sidon (3.8). As Burkill notes, the places named in this summary statement are later visited by Jesus during his mission.[42] The power of the word breaks the boundary between Jews and Gentiles, and Gentiles respond positively to Jesus' teaching.

Jesus, moreover, has already healed the Gentile Gerasene demoniac (5.1–20). Farrer suggests that this man is a representative of the Jews from the Diaspora.[43] This interpretation is unlikely, since the Decapolis is a Gentile area, and the reference to the herd of pigs implies a Gentile setting. In this account the Gerasenes are afraid of Jesus and ask him to leave their district. Rhoads, therefore, argues that the negative response of the Gerasenes leads Jesus to believe that it is not the right time for the Gentile mission.[44] Jesus, however, does not abandon Gentiles; he sends

42. T.A. Burkill, 'The Syrophoenician Woman: The Congruence of Mark 7,24-31', *ZNW* 57 (1966), 32–33.
43. A. Farrer, 'Loaves and Thousands', *JTS* 4 (1953), 2.
44. Rhoads, 'Syrophoenician', 361–62.

the healed man to his own house and his own people to bear witness to what the Lord has done for him (5.19). The sending out of this man is unusual, since Jesus characteristically commands silence when he has healed someone (1.44; 5.43). Jesus' action, however, foreshadows his sending out of the Twelve (6.6b–13). Jesus does not reject the Gentile mission, for this Gentile man has the role of continuing Jesus' mission.

In this section there is a positive portrayal of the Jewish mission, but at the same time there are instances of opposition to Jesus. Jesus' family (3.20–35) and his hometown (6.1–6a) fail to understand him. The religious authorities oppose him (2.1–3.6; 3.22–30; 7.1–23), and the Pharisees and the Herodians desire to put him to death (3.6). In our passage Jesus moves into the same area and wishes to remain concealed (οὐδένα ἤθελεν γνῶναι, 7.24), following the account of the execution of John the Baptist at the instigation of the Herodian women (6.14–29). The introduction to our passage is reminiscent of the account of the flight of Elijah, who goes into hiding after he is threatened by Jezebel (1 Kgs 19.1–3). In 1 Kings Elijah is driven north into Gentile territory, and similarly, there is an implication that opposition to Jesus leads him to move to Gentile areas.

Opposition to Jesus' mission is suggested by the storm which arises during the second boat journey. After the feeding of the five thousand Jesus sends his disciples on ahead to Bethsaida (6.45). A strong wind appears to blow the boat off course and they land at Gennesaret (6.53). At the beginning of our passage Jesus enters Gentile territory and enters a house with the desire of remaining hidden (7.24). As Marcus notes, the appearance of the Syrophoenician woman indicates that Jesus is unable to remain hidden and suggests that the power of the gospel cannot be concealed (7.24).[45] He and the disciples do not reach Bethsaida until 8.22, and the intervening section relates Jesus' teaching, healing (7.31–37) and miraculous feeding of Gentiles (8.1–10). After Jesus and the disciples reach Bethsaida they begin to make their way to Jerusalem. This structure is reminiscent of Paul's argument that the opposition of Israel leads to the Gentile mission but that ultimately Israel will come to faith through the Gentiles (Rom. 9–11).

The course of Jesus' mission thus shows an initial priority of Israel. At the same time the word of God transcends the boundaries of Israel and attracts Gentiles. Jesus encounters opposition from the Jewish authorities, which drives him into Gentile territory (7.24). The progression of events implies that the arrival of the Syrophoenician woman is intended to indicate that the time has drawn near for the Gentile mission. In Mark, Jesus teaches that the disciples are to carry out the Gentile mission in the period between the resurrection and the parousia (13.10). The Jewish mission is not rejected, since the first disciples are Jewish. In chapter 13, moreover, Jesus addresses his teaching about the events of the end-time to four of the Twelve, who act as representatives of the community who are to carry out the Gentile mission.

Several features of the Gentile cycle in Mark allude to the period between the resurrection and parousia. On the second boat journey Jesus sends his disciples on

---

45. Marcus, *Mark*, 467.

ahead of him while he prays on a mountain (6.45–46). The absence of Jesus in this narrative may point forward to the period following the death of Jesus. When the disciples experience difficulties, Jesus approaches them and intends to go past them (6.48), and this description is similar to the references to the resurrection in which Jesus goes ahead of his disciples to Galilee (14.28; 16.7). The numinous quality of Jesus' appearance is indicated by the fear of the disciples that he is a ghost (φάντασμά, 6.49). The time of Jesus' appearance at the fourth watch of the night (περὶ τετάρτην φυλακὴν τῆς νυκτὸς, 6.48) is associated with the resurrection, since Jesus is raised from death before the women arrive in the early morning (16.2).

The account of the exorcism of the Syrophoenician woman's daughter continues these allusions to the period between the resurrection and the parousia. At the beginning of the narrative Jesus rises (ἀναστὰς, 7.24) and moves on to Gentile territory. The verb ἀνίστημι is used of Jesus' resurrection in the passion predictions (ἀναστῆναι, 8.31; ἀναστήσεται, 9.31; 10.34). Jesus, moreover, desires to remain hidden in the house, a description that might remind readers of the period after his death when he is physically absent from his followers. Jesus heals the Gentile child at a distance, and this description emphasizes that the power of Jesus is effective even when he is not physically present. Our passage, then, may allude to the way in which Jesus is able to become present to his followers during the time between the resurrection and the parousia.

The feeding of the four thousand which follows shortly (8.1–10) also has associations with the period between the resurrection and the parousia. The phrase ἐν ἐκείναις ταῖς ἡμέραις (in those days, 8.1) has eschatological connotations (cf. Joel 3.1 and Zech. 8.23), and it is used later in Mark to signify the end-time (13.17, 19, 24). On the present occasion the people have been with Jesus for three days in the desert (8.2), and this reference also has eschatological associations, since it corresponds to the period between the death and the resurrection of Jesus (8.31; 9.31; 10.34). Jesus does not want to send the people away hungry (νήστεις, 8.3), a description that recalls the passage in which Jesus is asked why his disciples do not fast (οὐ νηστεύουσιν, 2.18). Jesus replies that they do not fast because the bridegroom is with them, which suggests that the presence of Jesus is associated with a feast. Jesus, however, prophesies that he will be taken from them, and this time is linked with mourning (2.20). Mark locates both the feeding of the five thousand and that of the four thousand within the earthly life-time of Jesus, but as we have seen, the Gentile cycle contains literary allusions to the period after the death and resurrection. This literary technique corresponds to the section we have identified between the two references to Bethsaida (6.45; 8.22). The Gentile mission does not replace the Jewish mission, but is placed within the context of the Jewish mission.

6. *The Markan Community*

The account of the exorcism of the Syrophoenician woman's daughter is preceded by a series of debates on purity issues (7.1–23). The Pharisees and some scribes criticize some of Jesus' disciples, who eat without first washing their hands. The Pharisees were noted for their aim to develop personal holiness by extending law observance to the everyday life of the people.[46] In response Jesus propounds a parable that says that nothing from outside can enter a person and make that person unclean. Instead impurity originates from within a human being (7.14–15). The narrator concludes this passage with the statement that Jesus has declared all foods to be clean (7.19). These debates are followed by the account of the exorcism of the Syrophoenician woman's daughter.

The girl is initially described as possessed by an unclean spirit (πνεῦμα ἀκάθαρτον, 7.25), whereas Mark refers to her condition as demon possession later in the passage (7.29–30). As Focant observes, the phrase πνεῦμα ἀκάθαρτον may be intended to allude to the earlier debates about impurity (7.1–23).[47] The Syrophoenician woman enters the house where Jesus is present, but she does not make Jesus unclean. Similarly, the unclean spirit has entered the child, but Jesus has the power to cast the demon out of her. Jesus, moreover, interprets the woman's request for healing in terms of sharing a meal between Jews and Gentiles.

The conflict over the sharing of meals between Jews and Gentiles has led scholars, such as Sanders, moreover, to argue that Jesus did not carry out a Gentile mission during his lifetime, and that this mission was the initiative of the early church.[48] Loader proposes that Jesus may have had a conservative attitude towards the Law, and there are traces of his view in our passage in Jesus' initial rejection of the woman.[49] Räisänen believes that the parable about the nature of defilement (7.15) is not authentic, since it would have been used to support those who wished to abandon the food laws.[50] Riches, however, shows that Jesus' redefinition of purity in this parable is compatible with his other teaching such as the love of enemies and his meals with tax collectors and sinners.[51]

It is significant, nevertheless, that the declaration that Jesus has made all food clean is an editorial comment from Mark (7.19). As Marcus observes, the passage begins with a debate about hand washing and develops into teaching concerning the abandonment of the food laws.[52] He points out that the account may start with a debate in the lifetime of the historical Jesus and end with an issue in the current disputes between the Pharisees and the Markan community.

On the level of the Markan community, some members may wish to retain the food laws. The compassion of Mark's audience, however, is engaged by the

46. D. R. de Lacey, 'In Search of a Pharisee', *TynBul* 43 (1992), 353–72.

47. C. Focant, 'Mc 7,24-31 par. Mt 15, 21-29. Critique des Sources et/ou Étude Narrative', in C. Focant (ed.), *The Synoptic Gospels: Source Criticism and the New Literary Criticism* (BETL, 110; Leuven: Leuven University Press, 1993), 48.

48. Sanders, *Jesus and Judaism*, 212–21.

49. W. Loader, 'Challenged at the Boundaries: A Conservative Jesus in Mark's Tradition', *JSNT* 63 (1996), 45–61.

50. H. Räisänen, 'Jesus and the Food Laws: Reflections on Mark 7.15', *JSNT* 16 (1982), 79–100.

51. J.K. Riches, *Jesus and the Transformation of Judaism* (London: Darton, Longman & Todd, 1980), 136–44.

52. J. Marcus, 'Scripture and Tradition in Mark 7', in C.M. Tuckett (ed.), *The Scriptures in the Gospels* (BETL 131; Leuven: Leuven University Press, 1997), 145–63.

account of the suffering of the woman and her child; the barriers between Jews and Gentiles are swept away in order to heal a sick child. Mark portrays the abandonment of the food laws in the lifetime of Jesus, but this is proleptic of the post-Easter situation, and the healing of the Gentile child functions as a prototype for the Gentile mission. In Jesus the power of God breaks into the world and foreshadows the new creation, which comes about through his death and resurrection, since the period between the resurrection and the parousia will be the real time of the Gentile mission (13.10).

7. *Discipleship*

The Syrophoenician woman acts like a disciple: she has heard about Jesus, and this news prompts her to approach Jesus (ἀκούσασα... περὶ αὐτοῦ, 7.25). She may be compared to the woman with the flow of blood who also seeks Jesus after hearing about him (ἀκούσασα περὶ τοῦ Ἰησοῦ, 5.27). The Syrophoenician woman enters a house to speak to Jesus, and this location is frequently depicted as a discipleship setting (3.31–35; 9.28, 33; 10.10). She falls at Jesus' feet in an attitude of worship (προσέπεσεν πρὸς τοὺς πόδας αὐτοῦ, 7.25), and this description recalls the portrayal of the woman with the flow of blood, who also kneels before Jesus (προσέπεσεν αὐτῷ, 5.33). The woman in the present story may be regarded as a model of discipleship, since she places herself and her child last, content with the crumbs which fall from the table. As Rhoads points out, she makes herself 'least' in order to help her daughter.[53]

Ringe wishes to avoid interpretations of the passage which concentrate on the relations between Jews and Gentiles, and she focuses on the social and economic background of the account.[54] She proposes that Jesus is reluctant to heal the child because the Syrophoenician woman is a representative of the wealthy inhabitants of Tyre who exploit the poor people of the region. Ringe, however, does not take into account the tensions between Jews and Gentiles which are reflected in the economic situation. Theissen, moreover, observes, that the Syrophoenician woman may be portrayed as a representative of the wealthy inhabitants of Tyre who have taken food from the Galileans.[55]

In this case an apparently rich Hellenistic woman is willing to give up her privileges and place herself last. Her response foreshadows Jesus' teaching that those who wish to be first should make themselves last of all and servants of all (9.35). Her willingness to come last illustrates Jesus' teaching about the eschatological reversal in the kingdom of God, in which many who come first will be last and the last first (10.31).

The speech of the Syrophoenician woman also has deeper implications than she may realize. She addresses Jesus as κύριε (7.28), which may be understood as a

---

53. Rhoads, 'Syrophoenician', 366.
54. S.H. Ringe, 'A Gentile Woman's Story Revisited: Rereading Mark 7.24-31', in A.-J. Levine (ed.), *A Feminist Companion to Mark* (Sheffield: Sheffield Academic Press, 2001), 79–100.
55. Theissen, *Gospels*, 75.

term of respect, but which is also a Christological title in the phrase κύριος Ἰησοῦς (Rom. 10.9 and 1 Cor. 12.3). Fander, moreover, argues that the woman's address of κύριε foreshadows the confession of the Roman centurion that Jesus is the Son of God (15.39). As Fander points out, elsewhere in Mark this title occurs only in scripture citations (1.3; 11.9; 12.11, 29, 30, 36) and in the words of Jesus (5.19; 12.37; 13.20, 35).[56] While the other three Gospels include examples of human beings addressing Jesus as Lord, this passage is the only occasion in Mark in which this happens.[57] Gnilka, moreover, argues that it is significant that this title is used by a woman who becomes a prototype for the faithful Gentiles.[58] The title κύριος also occurs in the account of the exorcism of the Gerasene demoniac, who is a Gentile, Jesus instructs the man to proclaim what the Lord has done for him (ὁ κύριος, 5.19), although the man speaks of Jesus' action in healing him (5.19–20).

In Fander's view, the confession of the woman indicates that she has been given the secret of the rule of God.[59] Rhoads, however, argues that while the woman shows faith in Jesus' ability to heal her daughter, her faith does not imply that she is aware of Jesus' identity as the Messiah.[60] Rhoads' argument is convincing, since the woman responds to Jesus in everyday language. Her desperation for healing for her daughter gives her insight into Jesus' parable. She acts as a prophetic figure, and her word foreshadows the future sharing of food between Jews and Gentiles.

Jesus heals the girl on account of the word the woman speaks (διὰ τοῦτον τὸν λόγον, 7.29) which may be translated 'because of this word'. Fander argues that the woman's reply leads Jesus to change his mind.[61] She even compares the conversation between the woman and Jesus to the controversy debates with the religious authorities (2.1–3.6). In these debates Jesus characteristically concludes with an authoritative saying (2.17; 2.27–28; 3.3–4). Fander stresses that this account is the only passage in which someone other than Jesus has the last word. This narrative, however, differs from the controversies, since the woman is not hostile towards Jesus. Her faith in the power of Jesus to heal her daughter leads her to challenge him.

The Syrophoenician woman is persistent in her request for healing for her daughter despite Jesus' initial refusal. She acts as a model of discipleship on account of her courage and her refusal to give up hope. The woman has faith in Jesus' power to heal, just as disciples have to place their trust in Jesus. She continues to hope for a cure for her daughter, and her action brings a message of perseverance. In the prophecies of the end-time Jesus teaches his disciples that the one who endures to the end will be saved (13.13). The account of the Syrophoenician woman conveys a sense of hope in the midst of despair, which points forward to the power of God to bring life out of death. Her story may encourage members of Mark's community who face persecution and fear that Jesus will not respond to them (cf. 4.38). This

56. Fander, *Stellung*, 80.
57. Fander, *Stellung*, 80.
58. Gnilka, *Evangelium*, 1.293.
59. Fander, *Stellung*, 81.
60. Rhoads, 'Syrophoenician', 346.
61. Fander, *Stellung*, 74.

message continues to appeal to the members of Mark's audience, who also wait for the return of Jesus and the dawn of the new age.

8. *The Relation between the Syrophoenician Woman and the Twelve*

The Syrophoenician woman responds in faith to Jesus, and her speech reveals that the time has drawn near for the Gentile mission. The positive portrayal of this woman leads Fander to compare her favourably with the twelve male disciples.[62] Fander suggests that the Syrophoenician makes a Christological confession whereas the Twelve lack understanding of the nature of Jesus' identity. As we have seen, the Syrophoenician woman acts as a prophet, since her word looks forward to the messianic feast which has abundant food for both Jews and Gentiles. In contrast, the Twelve have difficulty in understanding the Gentile mission. After the feeding of the five thousand the failure of the disciples to recognize Jesus is linked to their inability to understand the significance of the feeding of the five thousand (οὐ γὰρ συνῆκαν ἐπὶ τοῖς ἄρτοις ἀλλ᾽ ἦν αὐτῶν ἡ καρδία πεπωρωμένη, 6.52). On the third boat journey Jesus expects the disciples to be able to understand the significance of the two feeding narratives (8.14–21).

The disciples have been present throughout Jesus' mission and they have witnessed the two feeding miracles, but they do not understand the significance of the events they have witnessed. Farrer interprets Jesus' references to the number of loaves in the feeding narratives by examining the account of the description of the disciples who pluck grain on the Sabbath (2.23–28).[63] In his debates with the Pharisees Jesus defends the disciples by referring to the action of David who took five loaves from the bread of the presence in order to feed his soldiers (1 Sam. 21). Farrer argues that the five loaves in the feeding of the five thousand correspond to five of the twelve loaves of the bread of the presence (Lev. 24.5–8). There are thus seven presentation-loaves left to feed the Gentiles in the feeding of the four thousand (8.1–10). In the feeding of the five thousand the twelve baskets allude to the restoration of Israel, and in the feeding of the four thousand the Gentiles are added to indicate the redemption of the whole of humanity.

The disciples have forgotten to bring bread and they have only one loaf. Gibson suggests that the disciples have deliberately 'forgotten' to bring additional loaves because they wish to deny bread to the Gentiles.[64] The disciples, however, fail to understand the significance of the bread which they do have in the boat. As Manek points out, the symbolic significance of the numbers in the feeding narratives suggests that the reference to one loaf is also to be taken symbolically.[65] In the feeding of the five thousand and that of the four thousand the crowds are fed through the breaking of bread, which foreshadows the Last Supper, where Jesus will identify the bread with his body (14.22). In the period between the resurrection

---

62. Fander, *Stellung*, 83.
63. A. Farrer, *A Study in St. Mark* (Oxford: Oxford University Press, 1952), 303.
64. J.B. Gibson, 'The Rebuke of the Disciples in Mark 8:14-21', *JSNT* 27 (1986): 35–36.
65. J. Manek, 'Mark viii 14-21', *NovT* 7 (1964), 12–13.

and the parousia Jesus takes the place of the bread of the presence. The disciples will continue Jesus' mission, and the breaking of the bread points to the presence of Jesus in their midst.

The disciples are accused of having hardened hearts (6.52; 8.17), which recalls the description of the Pharisees and Herodians (3.5). In the Old Testament God is frequently described as the one who hardens the human heart. In Exodus, God hardens the heart of Pharoah (Exod. 7.3; 8.15; 9.35; 11.10), and there are references to the hardening of Israel in other texts (Deut. 29.18; Isa. 63.17). Matera explores the New Testament background of the description of the hardened hearts.[66] He compares the hardening of the hearts of the disciples to the hardening of Israel, so that Israel does not recognize the Messiah (Jn 12.40; Rom. 11.7, 25; 2 Cor. 3.14). As Matera points out, God is the agent of hardening the heart, and human beings are able to understand only through the revelation of God. Matera rightly emphasizes that the hardening of the heart is not a moral failure, but it may be an indication of moral failure. In Mark the hardening of the disciples' hearts reflects their inability to understand the mystery of Jesus' identity, and they fail to recognize Jesus as the Messianic shepherd. He notes that the disciples are not as culpable as the religious and political authorities, since they wish to understand and follow Jesus, whereas the authorities plot to put him to death (3.6).

The disciples, moreover, differ from Jesus' enemies, since Jesus asks if they do not *yet* understand (οὔπω, 8.17, 21). As Marcus observes, the use of οὔπω suggests that they *will* understand in the future.[67] At the end of this section the disciples arrive in Bethsaida, and after the healing of the blind man Peter recognizes Jesus as the Messiah (8.29). Peter thus gains understanding of Jesus' identity, but at this stage he is unable to comprehend that the Messiah is to suffer and die. The significance of the feeding narratives can only be understood in relation to the Last Supper, when Jesus identifies the bread with his body (14.22). Jesus' identity is revealed as he gives his life for others. In the same way, no human being is able to understand Jesus' identity until the Roman centurion recognizes him as Son of God at his death on the cross (15.39).

Mark characteristically portrays individuals in the healing narratives who show faith and courage beyond that of the Twelve. The woman with the flow of blood risks criticism for breaking the purity regulations, and she overcomes her fear to tell Jesus the truth (5.33). Similarly, Bartimaeus does not allow the crowd to forbid him from calling out to Jesus (10.48). Those who suffer from debilitating diseases recognize their need for healing, whereas the religious and political authorities who have power and status are unable to put their trust in Jesus. Individuals in the healing narratives are often at the extremities of life, at the boundary between life and death. They respond to Jesus because the power of God is revealed at the point of human hopelessness. Jesus overcomes evil though his death on the cross, and his identity as Son of God is revealed as he gives his life to redeem humanity.

---

66. F.J. Matera, 'The Incomprehension of the Disciples and Peter's Confession (Mark 6,14-8,30)', *Bib* 70 (1989), 157–58.

67. Marcus, *Mark*, 508.

In our passage the Gentile woman acts as a model of discipleship, but she does not become a disciple herself. The Twelve do continually follow Jesus, and they are portrayed positively in that they leave everything to follow him (1.18; 1.20; 10.28). Nevertheless, they learn the implications of Jesus' teaching only as they follow him. Disciples are called to follow Jesus on the way of the cross, and discipleship involves struggles between faith and fear, lack of understanding and understanding.

The Gentile woman contrasts with the twelve male disciples who act as representatives of the twelve tribes of Israel. Her faith points forward to the Gentile centurion who recognizes Jesus as the Son of God (15.39) and also to the future faith of the Gentiles (13.10). The disciples, however, are the ones who question Jesus inside the house about the meaning of the parable about purity (7.15). They are insiders who receive the private teaching of Jesus which dispenses with the food laws (7.19). In the feeding of the five thousand they have the role of distributing the food (6.41), which foreshadows their service of the eucharist. The disciples, moreover, are instructed to undertake the Gentile mission in the period between the resurrection and the parousia (13.10).

The Syrophoenician woman contrasts with the Twelve according to gender and race. She is an outsider who responds in faith to Jesus and who does not render him unclean. She illustrates the teaching that there is nothing from outside a person that can enter and defile the person. Instead impurity originates in the human heart (7.14–15). The power to pollute the community, moreover, comes from within the community itself, as is shown in the example of Judas, one of the Twelve, who betrays Jesus (14.45). In chapter 13 Jesus warns his disciples of betrayal within families, which may allude to betrayal within the discipleship community, since family terminology is associated with discipleship (3.31–35; 10.29–30).

Mark's audience has greater understanding than the characters within the narrative, and they are shown the struggles of the disciples to understand. The difficulties with the Gentile mission are current debates for Mark's community, and the faithful response of the Gentile woman highlights these issues. As we have seen, the woman with the flow of blood overcomes her fear to confess her faith (5.33), and her story acts as an encouragement to those who risk persecution on account of the gospel. In our passage the Syrophoenician woman reveals the courage and persistence of the Gentiles, and thus acts as a model of discipleship for Mark's community.

9. *New Creation*

In Mark, creation is under the rule of Satan, and Jesus, the Son of God, has come to liberate human beings and inaugurate the new creation. As we have seen, Jesus heals the woman with the flow of blood and raises Jairus' daughter to life in a Jewish setting that points forward to the time in which there will be no disease or evil. In our passage the Syrophoenician woman's request for the healing of her daughter indicates that Gentiles are also plagued by unclean spirits, and that Gentile land as well as Israel is under the rule of Satan. Jesus first heals two Jewish women, and now he casts out an unclean spirit from a Gentile child. Just as the account of the healing of the woman with the flow of blood and the raising of Jairus' daughter foreshadows the restoration of Israel (5.21–43), our passage reveals that the Gentiles are to be incorporated into the salvation of Israel.

Jesus' initial response to the Syrophoenician woman refers to the priority of his mission to Israel (7.27). We have already seen the issue of priority in association with the account of the healing of the woman with the flow of blood and of the raising of Jairus' daughter (5.21–43). Jesus stops to speak to the woman with the flow of blood who has been an outcast, and while he is speaking to her the daughter of the president of the synagogue reaches the point of death. Jesus assigns priority to the woman, who would be regarded as among the least in her community, and the young girl dies. The earthly realm is characterized by limited time and resources. Jesus, however, has the power of the Spirit and is able to overcome the force of death and raise the girl to life. His healing of the two women foreshadows the abundance of the new creation. In our passage the priority of the Jewish mission is aligned to the old age. In the new creation the boundaries between Jews and Gentiles are overcome.

The new creation is inaugurated through the death and resurrection of Jesus. In his death on the cross Jesus dies as one who is cursed (Deut. 21.23; cf. Gal. 3.13); he becomes aligned with impurity in order that humanity may be redeemed. In the new creation the boundaries between Jews and Gentiles no longer exist (cf. Gal. 3.28). In the account of the woman with the flow of blood and of the raising of Jairus' daughter, the purity regulations are disregarded. In his debates with the Pharisees Jesus has declared all food clean (7.19), overcoming one of the main boundaries between Jew and Gentile. The two accounts are thus signs of the new creation breaking into the world, in which purity regulations and the food laws are no longer required.

The Syrophoenician woman's desire for the healing of her daughter leads her to ignore the division between Jews and Gentiles and to ask Jesus for help. She replies to Jesus' parable with a saying which indicates that the time for the Gentile mission has drawn near. The Syrophoenician woman speaks a prophetic message (λόγος, 7.29). The term λόγος (word) is associated with the proclamation of the gospel (1.45; 4.1–20; 8.32), and the word Jesus speaks has the power to teach, heal and cast out demons. In the parable of the sower the proclamation of the gospel (λόγος, 4.14–18) leads to the abundance of the kingdom of God (4.20). The focus on the creative power of speech, moreover, recalls the account of creation in Genesis. At the beginning of Genesis, God speaks and his word separates creation from chaos. The word of God separates land from sea, and the purpose of creation is that the land may bear abundant fruit (Gen. 1.11–12).[68] In Mark the proclamation of the gospel itself is a sign of the power of God breaking into the world. In our passage the word of the woman is aligned to the proclamation of the gospel.

In his analysis of the creation accounts in the Old Testament Levenson points out that God combats evil in order to bring creation into being, and creation is

---

68. Levenson, *Creation*, 47.

celebrated with a victory banquet.[69] On the first day of Jesus' mission in Caper-naum, similarly, he casts out demons and heals, and Simon's mother-in-law serves a meal (1.21–31). Jesus then carries out his mission by teaching, healing and mira-culously feeding a crowd in a Jewish setting (5.21–43; 6.30–44). After the meeting with the Syrophoenician woman Jesus follows a similar pattern as he teaches, heals and feeds a crowd of Gentiles (7.24–30; 7.31–37; 8.1–10). Both sections culminate with a miraculous feeding of the crowds, and these feedings are associated with the Last Supper. At the Last Supper Jesus identifies the bread as his body given to redeem humanity. His action points forward to the messianic feast in which his victory over evil will be celebrated.

Just as evil is overcome only through the death of Jesus on the cross, so Jesus' own identity is realized through his death on the cross (15.39). Jesus is revealed as Messiah and Son of God at the point when he wins the battle against evil through his death on the cross. In Mark, Jesus does not struggle against evil alone. In the prologue he is served by angels who sustain him during his testing by Satan (1.13). In our passage the Syrophoenician woman serves Jesus in the midst of his testing by human enemies by bringing him the word of God (7.29). It is only in the Passion Narrative, when Jesus is handed over into the power of evil, that he will be abandoned by his disciples (14.50) and will have to face his enemies alone.

10. *Conclusion*

The Syrophoenician woman is portrayed as a woman who is alone and in great need of help for her sick child. Her desperation leads her to ignore religious and social conventions and to approach an itinerant Jewish teacher. She refuses to be dissuaded by Jesus' initial parabolic rejection of her request, and she acts as an in-sider by responding to his parable with one of her own. The woman skilfully trans-forms the imagery of Jesus' parable into a saying that leaves room for the healing of her daughter. Her response reveals her faith in the power of Jesus to heal her daughter. The woman acts like a prophet, since she looks beyond a situation of dis-ease and division to catch a glimpse of the messianic feast, where there will be abundant food for everyone. In the apocalyptic context of the Gospel, her word points to the new creation, in which the division between Jews and Gentiles will be overcome and no disease or evil will remain.

69. Levenson, *Creation*, 29–32.

Chapter 7

THE POOR WIDOW (12.41–44)

1. *Introduction*

The account of the poor widow, who throws her last two coins into the Temple treasury, continues Mark's presentation of women on the periphery of life whose actions are hidden from the powerful. Jesus compares her small gift favourably to the large offerings of the rich because it represents her whole living (12.43–44). Traditionally the widow has been regarded as a paradigm of Christian giving and discipleship. Taylor, for example, suggests that the account of this woman is used to introduce a 'significant saying of Jesus about almsgiving'.[1] Witherington[2] interprets the offering of the widow as a 'clear model of devotion' and Swartley[3] describes the widow as an example of 'true piety'.

These interpretations, however, have tended to spiritualize the passage and have failed to take into account the severity of the widow's poverty. Wright challenges these views by interpreting the account of the poor widow in the context of the surrounding verses, which condemn the actions of the scribes (12.38–40), and which prophesy the destruction of the Temple (13.2).[4] This context encourages Wright to describe Jesus' attitude to the widow's gift as 'downright disapproval and not as approbation'. Sugirtharajah, similarly, argues that Jesus condemns the religious authorities who are in control of the Temple, and asserts that the widow's gift to the Temple treasury is, therefore, a 'misguided gesture'.[5]

The woman is in a desperate situation and she gives away her whole living. Wright and Sugirtharajah correctly raise the issue of whether or not the Temple treasury is an appropriate destination for her gift. These scholars, however, are harsh in their interpretation of the widow's action. She is destitute, and she gives her last two coins as an offering to God. Throughout chapters 11–12 Jesus counters hostile questions from the religious leaders who refuse to accept his authority, and the widow is the only person who acts with self-giving. Malbon, moreover, disputes Wright's emphasis on the immediate context of the passage, preferring to interpret

---

1. Taylor, *St. Mark*, 496.
2. Witherington, *Women*, 18.
3. Swartley, 'Role', 20.
4. A.G. Wright, 'The Widow's Mite: Praise or Lament?–A Matter of Context', *CBQ* 44 (1982), 261–63.
5. R.S. Sugirtharajah, 'The Widow's Mites Revalued', *ExpTim* 103 (1991), 43.

our account in relation to several 'overlapping contexts'.[6] For example, she associates the widow's gift of her 'whole life' with the giving of Jesus' life (10.45).[7] Although the widow's gift may be considered unreasonable, she points out that Peter makes the same charge about the giving of Jesus' life (8.31–33). Malbon is right to note that the woman acts with self-giving, but there is a difference between the sacrificial action of the woman and that of Jesus, since Jesus gives his life to redeem humanity (10.45).

The widow acts generously placing her trust in God, but she devotes her last two coins to the Temple treasury. There is a tension in our narrative between the positive portrayal of the woman's self-giving and the negative portrayal of the Temple treasury, which is described by Jesus as a 'den of thieves' (11.17). The instruction of Jesus about the widow's offering is his last teaching in the Temple. It acts as a transition to his prophecies of the end-time, which begin with his prediction of the destruction of the Temple (13.1–2). The account of the widow thus serves to illustrate the corruption of the religious authorities and of the Temple itself. In the new age, however, there will be an eschatological reversal in which many who are first will become last and the last first (10.31). Jesus prophesies the coming judgement of the scribes (12.40), whereas this widow who is presently one of the most vulnerable in society, will be one of the first in the kingdom of God.

2. *The Portrayal of the Woman*

The woman is alone and unnamed (μία χήρα πτωχή, 12.42), which recalls the portrayal of the woman with the flow of blood (5.24–34) and the Syrophoenician woman (7.24–30). This woman differs from these earlier women, however, in that she is introduced as a widow. Widows were regarded as among the most vulnerable members of society, and the prophets repeatedly defend widows and orphans (Isa. 1.23; 10.2; Jer. 22.3; Zech. 7.10). In the Old Testament there are positive accounts of the resourcefulness of widows such as the widow of Zarephath (1 Kgs 17) and the destitute widow who seeks help from Elisha (2 Kgs 4.1–7). Other widows are praised because they use their widowhood to devote themselves to God, for example, Judith in the Apocrypha and Anna, the daughter of Phanuel, in Luke, who remained a widow to the age of eighty-four (Lk. 2.36–8).

In the patriarchal society of the first century a young girl was under the supervision of her father until she married, and after marriage her husband became the head of the household.[8] As Ilan points out, divorce and widowhood could bring freedom to a woman giving her legal autonomy.[9] In her analysis of the status of women in the Mishnah, Wegner points out that the legal autonomy of a widow reflects the fact that no man has a claim to her biological function.[10] In contrast the biological

6.   E.S. Malbon, 'The Poor Widow in Mark and Her Poor Rich Readers', *CBQ* 53 (1991), 595.

7.   Malbon, 'Poor Widow', 596.

8.   Archer, *Her Price*, 45–49; Wegner, *Chattel or Person?*, 40–45.

9.   Ilan (*Jewish Women*, 147) cites *m. Qidd.* 1.1: 'And she acquires her freedom by a bill of divorce or by the death of her husband.'

10.   Wegner, *Chattel or Person?*, 14–17, 144.

function of dependent women such as young girls, wives and Levirate widows was controlled by men.

Widows were able to carry out their own financial affairs, and could live independently. The state of widowhood, however, could also lead to poverty, since women were then no longer entitled to receive maintenance (*b. Git.* 12b). Women were unable to inherit from their husbands, and were only entitled to their *ketubbah* (*m. B. Bat.* 8.1). These regulations made financial circumstances difficult for many widows. Ilan notes that the rabbis urged women to remarry and sought ways of making remarriage easier for women. Only one witness was necessary to prove the death of a husband instead of the usual two witnesses, and this witness could also be a woman (*m. Yeb.* 16.5–7; *b. Yeb.* 115a). Ilan also observes that there are a few examples of women who remained widows after the death of their husbands.[11] These women, however, were wealthy women of high social status who did not need to remarry on account of financial reasons.

When a woman became a widow she was entitled to be paid her *ketubbah* from her husband's estate. Ilan observes that the Mishnah records that widows could choose to stay with their husband's children and be supported by them for as long as they wished in Galilee and Jeruslem, or they could stay until their *ketubbah* had been paid in Judea (*m. Ketub.* 4.12; cf. 12.3; *m. B. Bat.* 9.1).[12] Although it is difficult to ascertain the extent to which the laws in the Mishnah were observed at the time of the New Testament, the marriage contract of a second-century woman, Babatha, does support these points.[13]

In our passage the widow is alone, and there is no indication that she has any family or friends. The woman's identity as a poor widow is stressed by the repetition of this description (χήρα πτωχή, 12.42, 43). In addition, she appears to be destitute, since she has only two coins left (12.42). The portrayal of this single poor woman contrasts with the reference to the many rich people (πολλοὶ πλούσιοι, 12.41). In our passage the number of rich people is greater than the number of the poor, which is unusual, since the majority of people were poor in the first century. The reference to the many rich people may reflect the timing of Passover, when many pilgrims attended the temple with special gifts. The timing of Passover is particularly associated with almsgiving (*m. Pes.* 10.1), but the crowds of rich people in our account are blind to the presence of this poor widow in their midst.

---

11. Ilan (*Jewish Women*, 149–50) cites the widow of R. Eliezer b. R. Shimon as the only example of a woman in rabbinic writings who desired to remain a widow after the death of her husband (*y. Šabb.* 10.5, 12c; *Eccl. R.* 11.2.1). Josephus, to be sure, mentions Hasmonean women who remained widows, such as Alexandra, the daughter of Hyrcanus II (*War* 1.185; *Ant.* 14.125) and Cypros, the mother of Herod (*War* 1.226; *Ant.* 14.280–1). As Ilan points out, remarriage may have been difficult for these women on account of their relationship to a political ruler.

12. Ilan, *Jewish Women*, 170.

13. The marriage contract of the Judean woman, Babatha (dated around 125 CE) includes a clause stating that she may reside in her late husband's house until her *ketubbah* has been paid. For a translation and an analysis of Babatha's *ketubbah*, see Yadin, Greenfield and Yardeni, 'Babatha's Ketubba', 75–101.

The widow is defined by her poverty, and she gives two small coins to the Temple treasury. As Taylor notes, the λεπτόν was the smallest coin in circulation.[14] The small financial value of her gift is given greater precision by the twofold description of her offering, λεπτὰ δύο, ὅ ἐστιν κοδράντης (two copper coins, which make a penny, 12.42). In contrast to the offering of the poor widow, there is a lack of definition in the references to the rich people and their many gifts (πολλοὶ πλούσιοι ἔβαλλον πολλά, 12.41).

The female gender of the woman, moreover, contrasts with the use of masculine plural terms to describe the rich (πολλοὶ πλούσιοι, 12.41). It is possible that the one poor widow is intended to contrast with the many rich men. The series of contrasts highlights the solitary nature of the widow. As Dewey points out, she is 'triply oppressed': as a woman, as a widow and as poor.[15] Her poverty and her status as a widow push the woman to the margins of society. She is hidden in the crowd, and as Tolbert suggests, the widow may be presented as invisible on account of her lack of legal, religious and social status.[16]

The account of the poor widow contrasts with the earlier narratives which feature women, in that there is no description of a meeting between the woman and Jesus. There is also no indication that the widow has heard of Jesus, unlike the woman with the flow of blood (5.27) or the Syrophoenician woman (7.25). There is a sense of poignancy to this woman's story, since she is unaware of Jesus' presence. This portrayal contrasts with the account of the woman with the flow of blood, who is healed by Jesus and called 'daughter' (Θυγάτηρ, 5.34). In our passage there is no relationship established between the widow and Jesus, and the account finishes with a lack of resolution of the woman's need. The story leaves her as she enters into a situation of total vulnerability, and we do not know the consequences of her action in giving away all she has to live on.

3. *Discipleship*

Initially the story is told through Jesus' eyes (ἐθεώρει, 12.41) as he watches the crowd making their gifts to the treasury. Jesus sees the crowd of rich people first, then the woman, and she is singled out from the crowd only because Jesus notices her. Individuals characteristically emerge from the crowd to seek help from Jesus, as in the account of the healing of the woman with the flow of blood (5.24–27) and that of Bartimaeus (10.46–52). This woman, however, does not approach Jesus, but goes to the Temple treasury to make her offering. As Tannehill notes, Jesus is the evaluator of human action and the audience is intended to interpret the behaviour of the other characters through his eyes.[17] The widow's gift thus becomes a source for Jesus' teaching.

The account of the widow is addressed to the disciples rather than to the crowd, and Jesus sits down, taking up the position of a teacher (cf. 4.1; 13.3). Jesus' action

---

14. Taylor, *St. Mark*, 497.
15. Dewey, 'Mark', 499.
16. Tolbert, 'Mark', 270.
17. Tannehill, 'Disciples', 138.

of calling together the disciples (προσκαλεσάμενος, 12.43) appears to be Markan redaction, since this verb is one of his most frequently used expressions (3.13, 23; 6.7; 8.1, 34; 10.42). In the previous section Jesus was pictured addressing a large crowd (ὁ πολὺς ὄχλος ἤκουεν αὐτοῦ ἡδέως, 12.37). There is a characteristic Markan move from the public teaching of the crowd to the private teaching of the disciples (12.43). A similar division between Jesus' teaching of the crowd and his teaching of his disciples may also be seen in 4.10; 7.1–17; 9.30–31; 10.10 and 10.23. The significance of the woman's action is explained to the disciples, not to the crowd, which indicates that the account of the widow conveys teaching suitable only for insiders.

The specific reference to the teaching of the disciples leads commentators such as Gnilka to place emphasis on the role of the passage as instruction for Mark's present community. Gnilka argues that Mark's community consists of a far greater number of poor people than of rich people.[18] The poor widow is held up as an example to the community because the poor among them are in danger of being despised. Mark encourages his community to follow the generous example of the widow and to support those who are in the same situation as her. Similarly, Fander regards the widow in the account as an example of teaching concerning the economic practice within the Christian community, and she argues that the widow is presented as a positive role model for the disciples.[19]

The story of the widow's offering, however, gives an account of Jesus' attitude to wealth and poverty. It is reminiscent of stories in which the gifts of the poor are praised. Lohmeyer cites a close parallel in rabbinic literature, in which a poor woman makes an offering of a handful of flour, which is rejected by a priest. Later, he is warned in a dream: 'Despise her not; it is as if she offered her life' (*Lev. R.* 3.105).[20] Our passage is similar to the rabbinic story, since both are concerned with the evaluation of the gifts of the poor. In *Leviticus Rabbah*, moreover, the poor woman's gift of flour is compared to her life, and in our passage the widow gives away her whole living (12.44).

The passages, however, also differ, since Mark mentions that Jesus sits opposite the Temple treasury (κατένατι τοῦ γαζοφυλακίου, 12.41), a position that conveys an attitude of judgement. Jesus' teaching is associated with true perception of the significance of the events. In our passage there is a direct contrast between the large gifts of the many rich people and the small offering of the single poor widow. The woman's gift of two small coins is small in the eyes of the world, but it is of greater value than the offerings of the rich because her gift represents her entire livelihood (12.44). There is, moreover, a contrast between the circumstances of the woman and those of the rich. The rich give from their abundance (ἐκ τοῦ περισσεύοντος αὐτοῖς), whereas she gives from her 'lack' or 'need' (ἐκ τῆς ὑστερήσεως αὐτῆς). There is an impression of injustice in this description, since the rich have more than enough while the widow does not have enough to live on.

18. Gnilka, *Evangelium*, 2.178.
19. Fander, *Stellung*, 116.
20. E. Lohmeyer, *Das Evangelium des Markus* (Göttingen: Vandenhoeck & Ruprecht, 1967), 266.

The widow's gift also contrasts with the action of Herod, the wealthy ruler, who offers Herodias' daughter only half his kingdom (6.23). Herod keeps back half for himself, and the rich people in our passage reserve some of their wealth. This woman, however, gives away her whole living, her entire means of survival. She is dependent on God's help because she has no human support. She gives everything she has (πάντα ὅσα εἶχεν, 12.44). In the same way the woman who anoints Jesus breaks open the jar pouring out everything. Jesus praises her profligate action, saying 'what she had she has done' (ὃ ἔσχεν ἐποίησεν, 14.8). Each woman carries out a sacrificial action by not keeping anything for herself.

The widow's action is depicted as sacrificial, but her desire to give away her last two coins is poignant. The portrayal of the widow, moreover, contrasts with the earlier account of a rich man whose wealth acts as a hindrance to his discipleship (10.17–22). There is a verbal correspondence between the two narratives, since the widow gives out of her lack (ἐκ τῆς ὑστερήσεως αὐτῆς, 12.44), while the rich man lacks only one thing (ἕν σε ὑστερεῖ, 10.21). The widow gives away everything she has, whereas the rich man is unwilling to sell his possessions and give the proceeds to the poor. The widow gives up her livelihood, while the rich man wishes to know what he must do in order to inherit eternal life (10.17). The woman's action illustrates self-giving, whereas the rich man's request suggests that he is seeking a way in which he can place God under an obligation to grant him eternal life.

In our passage the presence of the many rich people highlights the poverty of the widow. The rich worship God, but fail to obey the command of God to care for the poor. Similarly, in the account of the rich man there is an allusion to the oppression of the poor by the rich. In response to the request of the rich man, Jesus quotes the commandments from the second table of the Decalogue, which is concerned with relations among human beings. His list of commandments, however, includes the command 'Do not defraud' (μὴ ἀποστερήσῃς, 10.19), which is not in the Decalogue. Nineham suggests that this commandment may correspond to the tenth commandment, 'Do not covet'.[21] In addition, Bühner points out that the verb ἀποστερέω may be translated as 'to steal' or 'to rob'.[22] The use of this verb may thus imply that this man has gained his wealth through the oppression of others. The relationship between wealth and poverty is stressed, since the man is not only told to give his money away, but that he has to give it specifically to the poor (10.21).

The rich man, however, rejects the offer of Jesus and he leaves sorrowful (λυπούμενος, 10.22), a description which recalls the portrayal of Herod at the request of Herodias' daughter (περίλυπος, 6.26). The rich man and Herod are both confronted with a decision for or against the kingdom of God, and both make a wrong decision. In Gethsemane Jesus feels similar emotions (περίλυπός ἐστιν ἡ ψυχή μου ἕως θανάτου, 14.34), since he is torn between the desire to follow his own will and the desire to obey the will of God (14.36). He, however, makes the

21. Nineham, *St. Mark*, 274.
22. J.-A. Bühner ('ἀποστερέω', *EDNT* 1.142) cites 1 Cor. 6.8, in which Paul accuses the Corinthians of defrauding one another, and 1 Cor. 7.5, in which Paul instructs married couples not to refuse each other. In Jas. 5.4 the verb is used in association with those who keep wages back by fraud.

right decision, unlike Herod or the rich man. Mark, then, contrasts those who do the will of God by giving away everything they have, with those who seek to keep hold of their possessions.

The rich man has obeyed the commandments from his youth, but lacks one thing (ἕν σε ὑστερεῖ, 10.21). He is commanded to act immediately and to follow Jesus, but he cannot because he is unwilling to give up his wealth. Paradoxically, the wealth of the man becomes a lack or hindrance. In contrast, the poverty of the woman enables her to give away her possessions freely and reveals her wealth in the kingdom of God. The rich give out of their abundance (ἐκ τοῦ περισσεύοντος αὐτοῖς, 12.44), whereas she gives out of her lack or need (ἐκ τῆς ὑστερήσεως αὐτῆς, 12.44). Wealth, moreover, is portrayed negatively in the interpretation of the parable of the sower, where it is regarded as one of the barriers to the kingdom of God (4.1–20). In this passage wealth is described as deceptive (ἡ ἀπάτη τοῦ πλούτου, 4.19).

Jesus emphasizes how difficult it is for the rich to enter the kingdom of God (10.24–25), but the abundance of the kingdom of God is such that all things are possible for God (10.27). The willingness to give everything cuts across the values of the world, which are concerned with status and power. The world is concerned with survival, whereas the gospel is concerned with the paradox that saving life involves giving life away (8.34–38).

The self-giving of the widow is indicated by the description ὅλον τὸν βίον αὐτῆς (12.44). This phrase is ambiguous, since the term βίος means both life and livelihood.[23] In this way the woman is not making a small gesture, but is offering her whole life. The use of ὅλος (all), moreover, recalls Jesus' citation of the commandment, 'You shall love the Lord your God with all your heart, and with all your soul, and with all your mind, and with all your strength' (ἀγαπήσεις κύριον τὸν θεόν σου ἐξ ὅλης τῆς καρδίας σου καὶ ἐξ ὅλης τῆς ψυχῆς σου καὶ ἐξ ὅλης τῆς διανοίας σου καὶ ἐξ ὅλης τῆς ἰσχύος σου, 12.30). As Fander notes, there is a relationship between this commandment and the woman's sacrificial action. She argues that human beings should love God with all the means at their disposal, including their material possessions, since a human being cannot separate the use of money from service of God.[24]

The action of the woman in the present story may be compared to Jesus' teaching, 'the measure you give, will be the measure you get, and still more will be given you' (4.24). This teaching expresses the paradoxical giving and receiving which is at the heart of the kingdom of God. The giver not only receives back that which she or he has given, but something more besides. A similar pattern is seen in the account of the feeding narratives, in which the crowd have only a few loaves and fish. They give what little they have (6.38; 8.5) and are granted an abundance in return. In the feeding of the four thousand, moreover, there is a verbal correspondence between the reference to the seven baskets of leftovers (ἦραν περισσεύματα κλασμάτων

---

23. H.J. Ritz ('βίος', *EDNT* 1.219) notes that this term may be translated as 'life' in Lk. 8.14 or as 'livelihood' in Lk. 8.43. The meaning 'possessions' or 'wealth' may also be seen in Lk. 15.12, 30 and 1 Jn 3.17.

24. Fander, *Stellung*, 116.

ἑπτὰ σπυρίδας, 8.8) and the term for abundance in our passage (ἐκ τοῦ περισσεύοντος αὐτοῖς, 12.44). In the feeding narratives, Jesus miraculously multiplies
the bread to feed the hungry crowds, and his action foreshadows the abundance of
the kingdom of God. Wealth and poverty are depicted in an eschatological context
in which the one who gives up everything will have treasure in heaven (10.21).

The rich man wishes to inherit eternal life (cf. *Pss. Sol.* 16.6). In Mark, eternal
life is the eschatological gift of the new age, received by those who are prepared to
give up everything in order to follow Jesus. This definition of eternal life may be
seen in the teaching of the disciples which follows the account of the rich man
(10.29–30). The disciples have left everything to follow Jesus, and their rewards
are described in two stages: the rewards of the present age and of the age to come.
In the present age they will receive a hundredfold houses, brothers, sisters, mothers,
children, lands and persecution, but in the age to come they will receive eternal life
(10.30). The disciples receive additional family relationships and homes by becom-
ing members of the new community formed by Jesus. In this way the widow's self-
giving acts as a model for disciples who are called by Jesus to leave their homes
and families behind in order to follow him. Although the disciples are promised
rewards, they also face persecution (10.29). They must be prepared to put their
trust in God just as the poor widow does in our passage.

4. *The Context of the Widow's Offering*

Jesus calls disciples to give up everything in order to follow him, whereas the
widow gives her livelihood to the Temple treasury. Wright suggests that the widow
should take care of her own needs rather than give away her last two coins.[25] He
believes an attitude of praise is inconsistent with Jesus' teaching about korban in
7.10–13. In this passage Jesus is critical of those who claim to dedicate their money
to God in order to avoid their responsibilities to their parents. According to Wright,
Jesus' korban saying sets limits on almsgiving. The two passages, however, are
dissimilar, since Jesus directs his criticism at those who use the korban regulations
in order to keep their money for themselves, not at those who give it away.

Wright is more convincing in his emphasis on the significance of the immediate
context of our passage. The preceding verses relate the denunciation of the scribes
by Jesus (12.38–40), and the following verses record Jesus' prophecy of the destruction of the Temple (13.1–2). There are clear connections between the preceding
verses and our passage. The omission of Jesus' name in the opening verse (ἐθεώρει,
12.41) links our passage to the preceding section. As Wright notes, there are verbal
correspondences between the description of the scribes who devour widows' houses
(κατεσθίοντες τὰς οἰκίας τῶν χηρῶν, 12.40) and our passage, which is concerned with a poor widow (χήρα πτωχὴ, 12.42, 43). There is an additional verbal
link between the reference to the greater judgement (περισσότερον κρίμα, 12.40)
and the abundance of the rich (ἐκ τοῦ περισσεύοντος αὐτοῖς, 12.44). The juxta-

25. Wright, 'Widow's Mite', 261–62.

position of the two passages leads Wright to suggest that the poverty of our widow has come about as a result of the actions of the scribes.

The scribes are one of the main groups of opponents who reject Jesus in Galilee (3.22; 7.1–5) and in Jerusalem (8.31; 11.18; 10.33). The scribes are concerned with status and wealth (θελόντων ἐν στολαῖς περιπατεῖν καὶ ἀσπασμοὺς ἐν ταῖς ἀγοραῖς, 12.38), and they seek public approval, as is indicated by the references to three public places: marketplaces, synagogues and banquets (12.38–39). The repetition of the πρωτο- root (first) in the references to the best seats in the synagogues and the places of honour at banquets (πρωτοκαθεδρίας, πρωτοκλισίας ἐν τοῖς δείπνοις, 12.39) illustrates the wish of the scribes to be first among the people. It recalls the choice of prominent guests at Herod's birthday party (τοῖς μεγιστᾶσιν αὐτοῦ καὶ τοῖς χιλιάρχοις καὶ τοῖς πρώτοις τῆς Γαλιλαίας, 6.21). The emphasis on hierarchy in the case both of the scribes and of Herod reveals their desire to reinforce their power and authority in public. Painter, moreover, rightly observes that the desire of the scribes for social status contrasts with the teaching of Jesus that if his disciples wish to be first (πρῶτος, 9.35; 10.44), they should act as servants and place themselves last of all (8.34–38; 9.33–37; 10.35–45).[26]

The high social status of the scribes contrasts with that of the widow, who lives on the margins of society unnoticed by everyone but Jesus. The scribes are associated with the social elite, whereas the poor widow is one of the least in social terms. They seek privileged places in public, while the widow in our passage is hidden among the crowd. The widow, moreover, contrasts with the scribes because women were excluded from the role of religious authorities.[27] The scribes have the authority to interpret the scriptures, but they ignore the prophets' teaching to take care of widows and orphans.

The scribes are not only contrasted with widows; they also oppress widows, since they are described as devouring the houses of widows (12.40). According to Taylor, Jesus accuses the scribes of defrauding the widows.[28] Other commentators link the description of the scribes in 12.40a to the reference to their long prayers in 12.40b (καὶ προφάσει μακρὰ προσευχόμενοι, 12.40). Cranfield argues that the term προφάσει may be translated as 'alleged motive or cause' or as 'pretext or pretence'; since it has connotations of falsehood which are illustrated by its use in Phil. 1.18, where it is employed as a contrast to ἀληθεία (truth).[29] Cranfield, therefore, compares the scribes in our passage to Josephus' account of some Pharisees

26. J. Painter, *Mark's Gospel: Worlds in Conflict* (London: Routledge, 1996), 169.

27. Brooten (*Women Leaders*, 5–33) has identified several inscriptions which refer to women as presidents of the synagogue. For an analysis of Brooten's work, see note 222 on page 71–72. Ilan (*Jewish Women*, 33) points out that there are only two laws in rabbinic literature which are attributed to the authority of a woman. One is related to Beruriah (*t. Kelim*. BM. 1.6), and the other to the daughter of Ḥananiah b. Tardian (*t. Kelim. BQ* 4.17). For a discussion of the study of Torah by women, see Ilan (*Jewish Women*, 190–204). She observes that there was no official education system for girls, although some girls may have had the opportunity to learn to read and write at home. Women, however, did pass on to one another knowledge of laws concerning household matters.

28. Taylor, *St. Mark*, 495.

29. Cranfield, *St. Mark*, 385.

who deceive widows (*Ant.* 17. 41–42), and he suggests that the scribes take advantage of the generosity shown to them by the widows.

The specific reference to widows (12.40), however, suggests that the state of widowhood in itself makes these women vulnerable to the destructive influence of the scribes. Derrett, for example, regards the portrayal of the scribes as a reference to the abuse of Jewish inheritance laws.[30] In the case of widows and orphans an estate may be administered by a trustee, who could be a scribe, and some scribes abused their position by managing the estates for their own benefit. Derrett, moreover, argues that the term προφάσει does not mean 'false pretext' in this account, but may be more accurately translated as 'true reason' or 'occasion'.[31] The scribes, therefore, were able to use their public reputation for piety in order to misappropriate the property of the widows. Derrett cites evidence from *b. Giṭ.* 52b and Maimonides Mishneh Torah 13.5.10.6–7. These texts, however, are from a later date than our passage. Derrett also points out that there are similar examples of religious authorities who take advantage of vulnerable people in the *As. Mos.* 7.6–7 and the *Pss. Sol.* 4.10–13.[32] These examples, however, do not specifically refer to inheritance laws. The poverty of the woman in our passage is such that she appears unlikely to have an estate.

The juxtaposition of the two passages, moreover, suggests a link between the scribes who devour the houses of widows and the poor widow in our passage. Sanders notes that the Temple required scribes as copyists and as legal experts, and he suggests that many scribes were priests and Levites.[33] Josephus refers to Temple scribes (*Ant.* 11.128; 12.142). This proposal is supported by Mark's association of the scribes with Jerusalem (3.22; 7.1). In addition, the scribes are frequently linked with the chief priests (8.31; 10.33; 11.18, 27; 14.1, 43, 53; 15.1, 31) and are thus portrayed as belonging to the Temple authorities. A further association of the scribes with the Temple is indicated by Jesus' condemnation of the false prayers of the scribes (12.40) and his teaching that the Temple should be a 'house of prayer' (11.17). The scribes' prayers are used to conceal their evil intentions and to deceive others. Their prayers are a pretence, since their actions are far from God. Fleddermann compares the account of the scribes who devour the houses of widows (12.40) to the description of the Temple as a 'den of thieves' (11.17).[34] According to Fleddermann the house of the widow in our passage has been devoured by her gift to the Temple treasury.

Behind the greed of the scribes lies the force of evil. The description of the scribes who devour widows' houses associates the behaviour of the scribes with that of the wild animals in the prologue (1.13). The use of the verb κατεσθίω (eat up, devour, 12.40) suggests greed and destruction and also recalls the description

---

30. J.D.M. Derrett, ' "Eating Up the Houses of Widows": Jesus' Comment on Lawyers?', *NovT* 14 (1972), 1–9.

31. Derrett, 'Eating Up', 7–8.

32. Derrett, 'Eating Up', 6–9.

33. E.P. Sanders, *Judaism: Practice and Belief 63 B.C.E.–66 C.E.* (London: SCM Press, 1992), 180–82.

34. H. Fleddermann, 'A Warning about the Scribes (Mark 12.37b-40)', *CBQ* 44 (1982), 61–67.

of the birds, who eat the seed in the parable of the sower (κατέφαγεν, 4.4). In the interpretation of the parable the birds represent Satan, who takes away the word sown in human beings (4.15).

The scribes' prayers are used to conceal their evil intentions and to deceive others. Their prayers are pretence, since their actions are far from God. Their portrayal is similar to that of the political authorities who rule over the Gentiles and lord it over them (οἱ δοκοῦντες ἄρχειν τῶν ἐθνῶν κατακυριεύουσιν αὐτῶν, 10.42). As Marcus points out, the earthly rulers only appear to rule.[35] Their authority is aligned to the old age, which is passing away. In the same way the scribes only appear to have authority from God. Jesus' conclusion is ominous, since he prophesies eschatological judgement upon them (λήμψονται περισσότερον κρίμα, 12.40). At present the scribes oppress widows, but in the future they will be judged. Hooker notes that this phrase may be translated 'the greater judgment', and as she points out, the scribes are judged more severely because they use their false piety to oppress the poor.[36] The scribes place themselves first and they seek the service of others. The term πρῶτος (first) has eschatological connotations, since Jesus teaches that many who are first (πρῶτοι) will be last, and the last first (10.31). As we have seen the scribes will be judged, but the widow can expect a reversal in her condition. She is one of the last in the present age who will be first in the kingdom of God.

The account of the widow is placed within a section of the Gospel concerned with the setting of the Temple (11–13), and our passage forms a conclusion to a series of debates between Jesus and the religious authorities (11.27–12.40). Some scholars, such as Gnilka, offer a positive interpretation of the widow's gift, and he observes that it is remarkable that the Temple offerings are approved without qualification in our passage.[37] Wright, however, as we have already seen, has interpreted the account of the widow's gift in the context of Jesus' prophecy of the destruction of the Temple which follows immediately in 13.1–2.[38] In this context the woman's contribution is 'misguided', and the final irony is that her gift is a 'waste'.

Mark's attitude to the Temple treasury is indicated by the setting of our passage. Jesus is described as sitting opposite the Temple treasury, which suggests an attitude of judgement (κατέναντι τοῦ γαζοφυλακίου, 12.41). Similarly, Jesus leaves the Temple and then takes up a position on the Mount of Olives opposite the Temple (κατέναντι τοῦ ἱεροῦ, 13.3).[39] One of the disciples exclaims at the magnificence of the Temple building (13.1), and this statement leads to Jesus' prophecy of the destruction of the Temple (13.2). The magnificence of the Temple, moreover, further highlights the poverty of the widow in our account.

Wright correctly notes that Jesus is critical of the Temple. In an earlier account Jesus' attitude to the Temple has been illustrated by his action of overturning the tables of those who buy and sell, and driving them out of the Temple precincts

---

35. Marcus, 'Epistemology', 558.
36. Hooker, *St. Mark*, 295.
37. Gnilka, *Evangelium*, 2.178.
38. Wright, 'Widow's Mite', 263.
39. Myers, *Binding*, 321.

(11.15). Jesus proclaims that the Temple should be a house of prayer for all nations, citing Isa. 56.7, and he condemns those who have made the Temple a den of thieves (σπήλαιον ληστῶν, 11.17), which recalls Jer. 7.11. Fleddermann, therefore, believes that Mark opposes the Temple cult with prayer.[40]

In Mark, however, Jesus does not condemn the Temple worship, but focuses on the exploitation of the authorities who have turned the Temple into a den of thieves. In the phrase 'den of thieves' the term ληστής (11.17) is used which may also be translated as 'brigand' (cf. 14.48; Josephus, *Ant.* 14.421). The use of ληστής instead of κλέπης 'thief' suggests that the Temple authorities have usurped the Temple for their own purposes rather than for God's. Hooker notes the context of Jer 7.11, which describes God's condemnation of those whose worship is insincere on account of the injustices they commit.[41] In Jeremiah the people rob God of genuine worship, and Hooker argues that the people in Mark act in a similar way. There is also, however, a concern for the poor in Jer. 7.6 and the description 'den of thieves', in our passage suggests that Jesus condemns those who exploit the poor.

Jesus' action, moreover, has been interpreted as a prophetic sign foreshadowing the destruction of the Temple. As Telford points out, Mark intercalates the action of Jesus in the Temple into the account of the cursing of the fig tree (11.12–14; 20–25). The tree has leaves and thus appears to be fruitful, but it does not bear fruit because the time is not right (11.13). Telford examines the Old Testament background to the cursing of the fig tree, and he proposes that five passages point to the eschatological context of Jesus' action (Jer. 8.13; Isa. 28.3–4; Hos. 9.10, 16; Mic. 7.1; Joel 1.7, 12).[42] As Telford observes, the fig tree was expected to bear fruit in the messianic age, and in the same way the Temple was expected to show signs of fruitfulness.

Jesus, however, accuses the Temple authorities of turning the Temple into a 'den of thieves' (11.17). Behind the corrupt Temple authorities lies the power of evil. In Mark, Jesus drives out from the Temple those who buy and sell. The verb ἐκβάλλω (to cast out) is the same term used in connection with Jesus' exorcisms (1.34; 6.13; 7.26; 9.18). This correspondence suggests that his action in the Temple may be interpreted as an exorcism in which he casts evil out from the Temple. There is, moreover, a verbal similarity between the reference to Jesus action of preventing anyone from carrying vessels through the Temple (τὰ σκεύη, 11.16), and the reference to plundering 'goods' in the parable of the strong man (τὰ σκεύη αὐτοῦ, 3.27). Mark depicts the world under the rule of Satan; but Jesus, the Son of God, has come to liberate humanity from this slavery.

The corruption of the Temple is further indicated by Jesus' prophecy of the end-time, which culminates with the description of the abomination of desolation which takes possession of the Temple (τὸ βδέλυγμα τῆς ἐρημώσεως, 13.14). The use of the masculine participle ἑστηκότα (13.14) suggests a personal agent behind the

40. Fleddermann, 'Warning', 64.
41. Hooker, *St. Mark*, 264.
42. W.R. Telford, *The Barren Temple and the Withered Tree* (*JSNT*Sup, 1; Sheffield: JSOT Press, 1980), 142–56.

desolation.[43] The description ἐρημώσεως (desolation) has a similar root to the word for desert (ἔρημος). The desert is portrayed as the home of demons in the Old Testament (Deut. 32.17; Isa. 34.14), and in Mark it is the location of the testing of Jesus by Satan (1.12–13). In the end-time the home of Satan is thus located within the Temple itself (13.14).

The juxtaposition of the two scenes, therefore, contrasts the portrayal of the scribes with the description of the poor widow. The scribes act with a false piety seeking public recognition, whereas the widow gives away everything she has, hidden from the eyes of the world. The scribes, however, are not only contrasted with the widow; they also exploit the vulnerability of widows. Their actions thus contradict the teaching in the Old Testament which demands special care for widows (Isa. 1.23; 10.2; Jer. 22.3; Zech. 7.10). The scribes devour the houses of widows while they make a pretence of praying. The Temple has been turned into a 'den of thieves' when it should be a house of prayer for all nations (11.17). Behind these sayings we gain a picture of scribes possessed by evil and a Temple possessed by evil practices. In the apocalyptic context of the Gospel the evil in the Temple reflects the increasing evil of the end-time, and Jesus prophesies its destruction. In this context Jesus does not praise the destination of the widow's offering. The woman's gift to the Temple treasury is poignant, since she gives her last two coins to a Temple which has been turned into a den of thieves.

Some feminist critics, such as Dewey[44] and Kinukawa,[45] argue that the woman is used as an exemplar for the male disciples, rather than to empower women as disciples in their own right. Women are not regarded as disciples, and there is no need, therefore, for Jesus to establish a relationship with the woman. Our analysis of 3.20–35, however, suggests that women have prominent roles within Mark's community, and the teaching on discipleship in our passage thus applies to both women and men. Kinukawa draws attention to the fact that Jesus does not intervene to help the woman.[46] She suggests that Mark may not wish to explore this issue or perhaps he aims to challenge his audience to seek answers. It is more likely that Mark intends to leave us with a picture of the poverty of the widow.

The location of the account of the widow's gift acts as a transition to the Passion Narrative. Schweizer, moreover, points out that the story of the woman who places all her trust in God serves as a fitting end to Jesus' mission.[47] The woman gives her whole life, and her action foreshadows the gift of Jesus' life in the Passion Narrative. In the Passion Narrative Jesus faces his religious and political opponents alone and they condemn him to death. The widow is alone and destitute and her gift to the Temple treasury indicates her desire to devote her last two coins to God. As van Iersel observes, our passage is not only concerned with the generosity of the widow, but may also be intended to illustrate her trust in God.[48] In Mark, the disciples must

43. Taylor, *St. Mark*, 511–12.
44. Dewey, 'Mark', 508.
45. Kinukawa, *Women*, 107–22.
46. Kinukawa, *Women*, 77.
47. Schweizer, *Mark*, 259–60.
48. Van Iersel, *Mark*, 386.

be prepared to lose their lives on account of Jesus and the gospel (8.35). In a similar way to the widow, they too must place their trust in God at the point of their human powerlessness.

The lack of resolution to the widow's poverty is reminiscent of the omission of any vindication of John the Baptist in the account of his execution (6.14–29). It also points forward to the increasing evil of the Passion Narrative when Jesus is handed over into the power of his enemies. On the cross Jesus gives his life to redeem human beings and to inaugurate the new age. In the present age evil prevails but the new creation is characterized by abundance for everyone.

5. *New Creation*

The Gospel moves from a situation of hiddenness to one of revelation (4.21–22). The old age of human misunderstanding and blindness is being overcome by the truth. The account of the widow focuses on the nature of perception. The widow acts with self-giving, whereas the rich give only from their abundance (12.44). The rich, moreover, are blind to the presence of the poor widow in the Temple. Jesus' teaching brings sight to his disciples, and he attempts to teach them how to distinguish between truth and falsehood, the kingdom of God and the realm of Satan. The end-time is a time of revelation, and Jesus uncovers the things not seen by the 'world'. Jesus brings to light the true motives of the scribes who use their piety to deceive others and to oppress the poor. He prophesies that they will be judged for their actions. The Temple has been corrupted and Jesus prophesies its destruction (13.1–2). The suffering of the widow may be ignored by the world, but it is not unseen by God.

In our passage the poor widow faces destitution and gives away her last two coins to the Temple treasury. Jesus' observation of the widow's gift prompts him to leave the Temple. The widow's suffering thus leads to the first direct prediction of the destruction of the Temple to Jesus' disciples (13.1–2). In the course of the Gospel the synagogue is replaced by the 'house' which is the place associated with the private teaching of the disciples (9.28; 33; 10.10).[49]

This situation applies also to the Temple, as is indicated by the events of the Passion Narrative when the Temple veil tears at Jesus' death, foreshadowing the destruction of the Temple (15.38). At his trial the opponents of Jesus state that he claimed to destroy the Temple made with hands and build another not made with hands in three days (14.58; 15.29). The reference to three days alludes to the resurrection of Jesus (8.31; 9.31; 10.33–34). As Juel points out, the Temple not made with hands relates to the Christian community.[50] This concept may also be seen in other texts such as 1 Cor. 3.16; 2 Cor. 6.16 and Eph. 2.20–22.

---

49. See E.S. Malbon, *Narrative Space and Mythic Meaning in Mark* (Sheffield: JSOT Press, 1991), 150.

50. D.H. Juel, *Messiah and Temple: The Trial of Jesus in the Gospel of Mark* (SBLDS, 31; Missoula, MT: Scholars Press, 1973), 168.

In our passage there is no resolution to the widow's poverty. The present age has poverty and oppression in which some use their status and power to oppress others. In the eschatological reversals of the new creation the scribes will receive the greater judgement, but the widow as one of the last will be first in the kingdom of God (10.31). Jesus' death, however, has a redemptive effect for the whole of humanity (10.45). In Jesus' death the destructive power of evil is overcome, not through retaliation or force, but through the generous giving of his life on the cross. The conflict between the kingdom of God and the old age will be resolved only through the death and resurrection of Jesus.

In this account the woman throws away everything she has (ἔβαλεν, 12.42). In a similar way the woman who anoints Jesus breaks the whole jar, giving away everything (14.3). Both actions correspond to the abundance of God who gives the Holy Spirit to Jesus at his baptism (1.10). There are pictures of abundant giving within nature in the parable of the sower, in which the sower scatters seed indiscriminately across land and path. Only a small amount of the seed will grow and produce an abundant harvest (4.1–20). The tiny mustard seed also produces a plant in which the birds will nest (4.30–32). The production of abundance from a small amount is also seen in the feeding of the five thousand (6.30–44) and the feeding of the four thousand (8.1–10). The feeding narratives are proleptic of the abundance of the new creation (*T. Jud.* 25.4; *4 Ezra* 14.13; *Sib. Or.* 3.378; 8.208; *b. Šabb.* 151b; *b. Pes.* 50a).[51]

The desire to risk everything is a characteristic of the women in Mark. The woman with the flow of blood spends all she has on doctors trying to recover her health (5.26) and the Syrophoenician woman seeks help from a man of a different race and religion (7.24–30). The widow's sacrificial action contrasts with the self-seeking standards of the world. Her self-giving corresponds to the willingness of Jesus to give his life to inaugurate the new age. The woman faces destitution and she does not spend her last coins on herself. Her action defies both the human desire for self-preservation and the power of death. Her offering illustrates her trust in God and the underlying hope that he will overcome evil.

6. *Conclusion*

The account of the poor widow depicts a woman who is destitute. The prophets call for care of widows and orphans, but this woman is ignored. The juxtaposition of the description of the scribes with the account of the widow highlights the contrast between the destructive greed of the scribes and the self-giving of the woman. Mark, moreover, portrays the scribes as responsible for the poverty of widows. Jesus points out the widow to his disciples. He compares her small offering favourably to the many large gifts of the rich, but he does not praise the destination of her gift. The widow's offering is poignant, since the religious authorities have turned the Temple into a 'den of thieves' (11.17). At the same time the woman acts as an

---

51. E. Bammel, 'πτωχός, πτωχεία, πτωχεύω', *TDNT*, VI, 885–915.

example for the disciples who find themselves caught up in the increasing evil of the end-time. Their struggle against evil may demand their whole lives, and they too must place their trust in God.

Chapter 8

THE WOMAN WHO ANOINTS JESUS (14.3–9)

1. *Introduction*

The account of the woman who anoints Jesus (14.3–9) is unique within Mark's Gospel in its portrayal of a woman who makes an extravagant gift to Jesus. In the period of increasing evil of the Passion Narrative, Jesus prepares to give his life to redeem humanity, and this woman's action represents the one response of love towards Jesus in the midst of human opposition. In earlier sections of the Gospel there were positive portrayals of women such as the woman with the flow of blood who was praised by Jesus for her faith (5.34) and the Syrophoenician woman whose word brought healing to her daughter (7.29). This woman, however, receives greater praise from Jesus than any other human being, for her action is to be remembered wherever the gospel is proclaimed (14.9). The woman acts like a prophet as she anoints Jesus' head with oil, an act which is associated with the anointing of kings in the Old Testament (1 Sam. 9.15–10.1; 16.12–13; 1 Kgs 1.38–40). Her action is a prophetic sign, since Jesus' identity as Messiah and king is not revealed until the time of his death on the cross (15.39). Jesus interprets the woman's act of anointing as preparation for his burial, and her gift encapsulates the message of the gospel because it foreshadows the new creation which comes about through Jesus' death.

The account of the anointing of Jesus by a woman occurs in all four Gospels, yet with differing portrayals of the woman and various descriptions of the act of anointing. Mt. 26.6–13 most closely resembles Mark with the presentation of an unknown woman who anoints Jesus' head with oil in the house of Simon the leper, and both Gospels locate the account in a key position at the beginning of the Passion Narrative. Luke, however, describes the woman as a repentant sinner who anoints Jesus' feet in the house of Simon the Pharisee, and he places the account earlier in his Gospel (7.36–50). The account in John (12.1–8) also depicts an anointing of Jesus' feet, and the setting is the house of Martha, Mary and Lazarus in Bethany. Mary is the woman who anoints Jesus, and Judas is the one who objects to the expense of the perfume.

The relationships between these accounts are complicated by the identical location in Mark and John (Bethany), their verbal similarities in the reference to the sum of three hundred denarii (Mk 14.5; Jn 12.5), and their similar description of the perfume itself (ἀλάβαστρον μύρου νάρδου πιστικῆς πολυτελοῦς, Mk 14.3; λίτραν μύρου νάρδου πιστικῆς πολυτίμου, Jn 12.3). As Munro points out, the reference to the perfume is particularly significant, since these examples are the only occurrences of the words νάρδου and πιστικῆς in the New Testament.[1] Luke and John also have shared material in the description of the anointing of Jesus' feet and in the reference to the woman's action of drying Jesus' feet with her hair.

Scholars have taken different approaches in the interpretation of the relationships between the accounts. Elliott regards the anointing of Jesus' head as the original account, but argues that Mark has downplayed the Messianic associations of the anointing, preferring to interpret the woman's gift as an act of devotion in preparation for Jesus' burial.[2] On the other hand Holst suggests that the anointing of Jesus' feet represents the earliest tradition, which Mark and Matthew have changed into a Messianic anointing of Jesus' head.[3] Schüssler Fiorenza, however, argues that it is more probable that the anointing of Jesus' head is historical than the anointing of his feet.[4] She points out that the anointing of the feet was an everyday occurrence and would not be likely to be recorded. Legault proposes that the accounts refer to two separate incidents: the first depicts a penitent woman who weeps over Jesus' feet at the house of a Pharisee in Galilee, and the second describes an anointing of Jesus' head by Mary in Bethany.[5] Brown rightly follows Legault, and he suggests that the strange reference to the woman who dries away the perfume in John may stem from the shared motif in the Lukan account in which the woman dries her tears from Jesus' feet.[6]

These relationships between the accounts suggest that our passage is a freestanding story within the tradition, which Mark has placed at the beginning of the Passion Narrative. Barton identifies Mark's characteristic use of intercalation in the location of the account between the plot of the scribes and chief priests to put Jesus to death (14.1–2) and the betrayal of Jesus to the chief priests by Judas (14.10–11).[7] He shows that the first passage could run smoothly into the last one, without the inclusion of the intervening account of the anointing of Jesus. As in the other Markan intercalations, the two accounts reflect and develop the significance of one another. In the midst of an atmosphere of betrayal and hostility, a woman anoints Jesus with perfume, an action described by Jesus as a beautiful deed (14.6). Her act contrasts with the malice of the enemies who surround Jesus, both the religious authorities and one of the Twelve, Judas. She gives a costly gift to Jesus, whereas Judas wishes to exchange him for money. The chief priests and scribes seek to execute Jesus (ἐζήτουν, 14.1), and Judas seeks to betray him (ἐζήτει, 14.11), whereas

1. W. Munro, 'The Anointing in Mark 14.3-9 and John 12.1-8' (SBLSP, 1; Missoula, MT: Scholars Press, 1979), 128.
2. J.K. Elliott, 'The Anointing of Jesus', *ExpTim* 85 (1974), 105–107.
3. R. Holst, 'The One Anointing of Jesus: Another Application of the Form-Critical Method', *JBL* 95 (1976), 435–46.
4. Schüssler Fiorenza, *In Memory*, xliii–xliv.
5. A. Legault, 'An Application of the Form-Critique Method to the Anointings in Galilee and Bethany', *CBQ* 16 (1954), 131–45.
6. R.E. Brown, *The Gospel according to John* (New York: Doubleday, 1966), 1.450–52.
7. S.C. Barton, 'Mark as Narrative: The Story of the Anointing Woman (Mark 14.3-9)', *ExpTim* 102 (1991), 231.

the woman takes the opportunity of the presence of Jesus at a public dinner to offer her gift.

The use of the technique of intercalation also emphasizes the timing of the betrayal of Jesus. Initially, the chief priests and scribes wish to arrest Jesus, but they decide to avoid the time of Passover (μὴ ἐν τῇ ἑορτῇ, μήποτε ἔσται θόρυβος τοῦ λαοῦ, 14.2). The intercalation, however, gives the impression that events are moving more quickly than the wishes of the chief priests and scribes. As Schweizer points out, Jesus is crucified during the festival, which suggests that events are progressing according to the will of God rather than the intentions of human beings.[8] In the following verses Jesus expects his imminent death, since he interprets the action of the woman who anoints him as preparation for his burial (14.8), and the plot progresses in the final passage as Judas approaches the religious authorities with his offer to betray Jesus (14.10–11).

The literary technique of intercalation also mirrors larger theological concerns of Mark. The action of the woman breaks into a hostile environment in the same way that the kingdom of God suddenly becomes manifest in the world ruled by evil. The good action of the woman contrasts with the evil intentions of the religious authorities and of Judas, one of the Twelve. The contrast between the actions of the woman and those of the men is highlighted by the exclusion of women from the status of religious authorities and from the group of twelve disciples. The costly gift comes from an anonymous woman outwith both those who have a high status as religious authorities and those whose status comes from their role as members of the Twelve. The religious authorities are depicted as an anonymous group, and even the identities of the chief priests are not given. Judas, however, is one of Jesus' closest followers, and his actions signal the breakup of the discipleship group. The Twelve will shortly flee at the arrest of Jesus (14.50), and Peter will deny him three times (14.66–72).

The woman's action is poignant, since it takes place in an atmosphere of betrayal and hostility. In one sense, her gift is futile, as Jesus is facing death. It is also hopeful, however, since she affirms the preciousness of life in the midst of death. The woman takes advantage of the presence of Jesus in order to anoint him before his death. Later, there will be an impression of loss related to a group of women who try to perform a similar action, going to Jesus' tomb but arriving too late to anoint his body (16.1–8). The description of the present woman's act of love lingers in the midst of the increasing evil of the Passion Narrative in which Jesus dies alone and is buried by strangers. In the context of Jesus' impending death, the gift of love from this woman anticipates the future response of love from humanity to Jesus.

2. *The Portrayal of the Woman*

The woman who anoints Jesus is anonymous and appears only in this passage. Her solitariness is characteristic of other women in Mark, as in the woman with the

---

8. Schweizer, *Mark*, 287.

flow of blood, who emerges from the crowd to touch Jesus' garment before she sets out again on her way (5.24–34), and the Syrophoenician woman who approaches Jesus in the house, then returns home alone to find her daughter healed (7.24–30). The woman who anoints Jesus, however, differs from these earlier women as she does not approach Jesus in order to seek healing for herself or another. This woman asks nothing of Jesus, which points to the mysterious and unexpected nature of her act of anointing. Her gift is depicted primarily as a response to the presence of Jesus rather than to his actions. The women who have been featured so far make a fleeting appearance and then depart. This woman is unusual, since her memory is to be connected to the gospel (14.9), and her story thus continues in a way that the stories of the other women do not. Instead of making a request she brings him a gift, and the extravagance of her gift suggests that her action is an offering of love to Jesus.

We are told nothing, however, of this woman's previous relationship to Jesus. Munro suggests that she may be a member of the group of women who have followed him from Galilee to Jerusalem (15.41).[9] The anonymity of the present woman, however, implies that she is not one of the discipleship group, since no one appears to recognize her at the meal. The woman also stands out from the disciples around Jesus on account of her wealth, as the disciples have given up everything to follow Jesus (10.28). Her gift is unusual in the extent of its extravagance, since the sum of three hundred denarii is almost equal to the year's wages of a labourer.[10] Her wealth also contrasts with the poverty of the destitute people Jesus usually encounters, such as the blind beggar Bartimaeus (10.46–52) and the poor widow (12.41–44). In comparison, the wealth of the woman in our passage is shocking and highlights the disparity of the living conditions among the people of the time.

The gender of the woman is highlighted, since she is the only woman who is directly mentioned at the meal. Schweizer suggests that the woman's action is unorthodox because she disturbs a company of men and anoints Jesus in the middle of a meal.[11] As we have seen, Herod invites only male guests to the banquet in honour of his birthday (6.14–29). On a literary level the dinner in our passage also appears to be given for men. The people named, Jesus and Simon, are both men, and although the masculine term τινες (14.4) may include women, the only woman directly mentioned is the anonymous woman who anoints Jesus. Our passage, however, describes a dinner in a private house rather than a formal public banquet.[12] It is possible that meal practices were less rigid in villages and among poorer people. Jesus, moreover, is criticized for his meals with tax collectors and sinners (2.15–17), which implies that he was not concerned with following prevailing dining

---

9. Munro ('Women Disciples', 240) raises the possibility that this woman is either part of the discipleship group or a member of the household of Simon.

10. Lane (*Mark*, n. 15 491) calculates the three hundred denarii as nearly the equivalent of a labourer's yearly wage, citing Mt. 20.2 where the daily wage is one denarius. Gnilka (*Evangelium*, 2.224), moreover, notes that the extravagant cost of the perfume is not incredible, as Pliny the Elder refers to anointing oil costing over four hundred denarii per pound (*Nat. Hist.* 13.3).

11. Schweizer, *Mark*, 290–91.

12. Munro, 'Women Disciples', 227; Corley, *Private Women*, 104.

customs. Earlier in Mark, Jesus has shown an openness to both the men and women who are depicted in a house sitting around him, listening to his teaching (3.34).

This woman's action, nevertheless, is unusual in that she anoints Jesus as he is reclining at the table in the middle of the meal (κατακειμένου, 14.3). Her entrance commands the attention of those present, and her disruptive action corresponds to earlier portrayals of women in Mark. This woman takes the initiative in seeking out Jesus just as the woman with the flow of blood interrupts Jesus' journey to heal Jairus' daughter (5.24–34) and the Syrophoenician woman disturbs Jesus' desire to remain hidden (7.24–30). The woman's entrance in the middle of a meal, more-over, recalls the entrance of Herodias' daughter at the birthday feast of Herod and his powerful male guests (6.14–29). On each occasion the entrance of a woman provokes a significant change in the course of events. The account of the woman with the flow of blood illustrates the breaking of the purity regulations, and the account of the Syrophoenician woman foreshadows the Gentile mission. The epi-sode concerning Herodias' daughter brings about the execution of John the Baptist, and in our passage the woman's act of anointing leads to Jesus' prophecy of his own death.

The present woman's action also disturbs the meal in that her gift is intimate and contrasts with the propriety of behaviour associated with public meals. She acts sensuously with her gift of perfume, which pours down over Jesus' body. Graham associates the women in Mark with an epistemology connected with touch rather than with speech.[13] Although the speech of the woman with the flow of blood (5.24–34) and that of the Syrophoenician woman (7.24–30) challenges Graham's argument, her interpretation is cogent in the case of our passage, which focuses on the woman's act of anointing Jesus. Throughout the account, moreover, the woman is silent, and she does not attempt to defend herself against her critics, leaving her action to speak for itself. The outpouring of the perfume is free and uncontrollable, and the portrayal of Jesus receiving her gift points to his increasing vulnerability in the Passion Narrative, which will culminate in his being handed over to the power of his enemies.

3. *The Significance of the Anointing of Jesus*

The practice of anointing was carried out frequently in antiquity and in ancient texts often signifies well-being and peace; see for example Ps. 133.2 and Prov. 27.9.[14] Jesus instructs his followers to conceal their fasts by anointing their heads with oil (Mt. 6.17–18). In addition Josephus records a description of Claudius whose anointed head suggests that he has just returned from a banquet (*Ant.* 19.238). The anointing of Jesus, however, has deeper connotations because of his identity as the Messiah, which literally means 'the anointed one'. In the Old Testa-ment the anointing of the head with oil was primarily associated with the consecra-

13. Graham, 'Silent Voices', 145–58.
14. Wainwright, *Matthew*, 126–27.

tion of kings (1 Sam. 9.15–10.1; 16.12–13; 1 Kgs 1.38–40) and of priests and prophets (Exod. 28.41; 1 Kgs 19.16). The individuals who carried out the anointing of kings were traditionally priests and prophets, such as Zadok (1 Kgs 1.45) and Samuel (1 Sam. 10.1; 16.1). These allusions suggest that this woman is taking on a role usually associated with men.

In our passage the woman's act of anointing points forward to the revelation of the kingship of Jesus in the Passion Narrative. As Matera points out, Jesus is first described as a king during the Passion Narrative, when he is called king six times (15.2, 9, 12, 18, 26, 32).[15] Jesus enters Jerusalem acclaimed as a king (11.1–10), and our passage continues this portrayal with Jesus' consecration. The question of Jesus' identity is the focus of the accusations made against him at his trials (14.61), and the title of king is the key accusation in the trial before Pilate (15.2). Human beings, however, fail to recognize his identity and he is condemned to death (15.15).

The misunderstanding of Jesus' true identity is stressed by the mockery of Jesus by the Roman soldiers who dress him in purple, place a crown of thorns on him and worship him as King of the Jews (15.16–20). The soldiers strike Jesus on the head with a reed, an action which directly contrasts with the woman's gift of anointing his head with oil.[16] Jesus' crucifixion, moreover, is depicted as a coronation. The inscription above Jesus' cross reads 'King of the Jews' (15.26), and the chief priests mock Jesus with a combination of the titles Messiah and King of Israel ὁ χριστὸς ὁ βασιλεὺς Ἰσραὴλ (15.32). The chief priests mock Jesus as one who saves others but cannot save himself (15.31); they fail to understand that Jesus is demonstrating his royal nature by giving up his life to save others (10.45). In the Passion Narrative Jesus is revealed as a king, but not as a worldly king, since his kingship is revealed in his death.

The anointing of Jesus' head is thus a prophetic sign which points to his kingship. The woman enters the room and chooses Jesus as the one to be anointed. She acts as a prophet, and the focus of the narrative is upon her action. The woman, however, is silent throughout the account, and Jesus is the one who interprets her action. The woman anoints Jesus' head, whereas Jesus speaks of his body which she has prepared for burial (14.8). Jesus refers to his body, since it was customary to anoint bodies before burial.[17] Jesus, moreover, uses the verb μυρίζω (to pour perfume upon) rather than ἀλείφω (to anoint). The verb μυρίζω is reminiscent of the μύρον (myrrh), which is used in association with the burial of the dead (2 Chron. 16.14; Josephus, *Ant.* 17.199). As Nineham notes, the woman's act of breaking the

---

15. F.J. Matera, *The Kingship of Jesus: Composition and Theology in Mark 15* (SBLDS, 66; Chico, CA: Scholars Press, 1982), 74.

16. The Markan references to the purple cloak, crown of thorns and reed correspond to Josephus' account of the burial of Herod the Great, since Herod is dressed in purple robes with a gold crown and he has a sceptre beside his right hand (*Ant.* 17.197).

17. Taylor (*St. Mark*, 533) notes that the practice of anointing the dead is referred to in *m. Šabb.* 23.5: 'They may make ready (on the Sabbath) all that is needful for the dead, and anoint it, and wash it, provided that they do not move any member of it.'

jar has further associations with death, since there was a practice of leaving the broken anointing jars in the tombs.[18]

The woman's prophetic act of anointing Jesus also has eschatological associations. Our passage is reminiscent of Psalm 23 since both the psalmist and Jesus are anointed on the head with oil at a meal. In Psalm 23 the speaker is anointed in the presence of his enemies, whereas in our passage Jesus is anointed as he prepares to face his opponents in the events of the Passion Narrative. Despite his enemies the psalmist hopes to dwell in the house of the Lord forever, and similarly in the passion predictions Jesus expresses his belief that he will be raised from the dead (8.31; 9.31; 10.32–34). As Allison notes, Psalm 23 was interpreted eschatologically in ancient Judaism and Christianity.[19] Our passage has an eschatological focus, since the woman's action is a prophetic sign which will be included in the proclamation of the gospel throughout the world (14.9). This comparison suggests that Jesus will also be vindicated by God. In Psalm 132 (LXX), moreover, the description of the oil which pours onto the head of Aaron (μύρον, 132.2 LXX) is associated with the blessing of eternal life (ζωὴν ἕως τοῦ αἰῶνος, 132.3 LXX). The act of anointing with myrrh (Χρίσονται μύρον, 25.7 LXX) is also included in a description of the messianic feast in Isaiah 25. As Michaelis notes, the reference to eating and drinking in the Masoretic text of Isa. 25.6 is replaced with the phrase Χρίσονται μύρον in the Septuagint.[20] These allusions suggest that the action of the woman not only looks forward to Jesus' death but also foreshadows his resurrection.

4. *The Role of the Woman as a Prophetic Figure*

The woman appears to be a prophetic figure, since her action expresses Jesus' identity as Messiah and king. In the Old Testament God reveals to Samuel the identity of the kings he is to anoint (1 Sam. 9.15–16; 16.12) and Elijah is instructed by God to anoint Jehu and Elisha (1 Kgs 19.16). These prophets carry out the actions ordained by God. In the Markan Passion Narrative there is also an implication that God is mysteriously arranging the events which are taking place. Before the entry into Jerusalem Jesus predicts that his two disciples will find a colt for him (11.1–7). Later, he prophesies that the two disciples who are sent to prepare the Passover will meet a man carrying a jar of water who will lead them to the room already prepared for Passover (14.12–16). In our passage the woman also appears to be sent by God to anoint Jesus in preparation for the events of the Passion Narrative.

The anointing of Jesus by the woman may be interpreted as a prophetic sign which has the effect of a parable, dividing those present into two groups. Marcus points out that the parable theory (4.10–12) defines insiders as those who hear the parables and approach Jesus for further instruction, whereas those on the outside do not seek understanding.[21] Paradoxically, this division is a sign that the gospel is

---

18. Nineham, *St. Mark*, 374.
19. D.C. Allison, 'Psalm 23 (22) in Early Christianity: A Suggestion', *IBS* 5 (1983), 132–37.
20. W. Michaelis, 'μύρον, μυρίζω', *TDNT*, IV, 800–801.
21. Marcus, *Mystery*, 224–25.

taking effect. In our passage, similarly, the woman's action arouses condemnation from some of those present (ἦσαν δέ τινες ἀγανακτοῦντες πρὸς ἑαυτούς, 14.4), and the description of her critics (ἐνεβριμῶντο, 14.5) signifies strong criticism.[22] The reference to τινες, however, suggests that others do not oppose her action. This effect is similar to the division provoked by Jesus in the series of controversies with the religious authorities in which *some* of the scribes (τινες τῶν γραμματέων, 2.6) question him.

The identity of the woman's critics is not stated in Mark, in contrast to Matthew, who refers to the disciples (Mt. 26.8) and John who refers to Judas (Jn 12.4). In Mark, the critics are a less defined group and the division between those who accept and oppose Jesus has a wider focus. Those who witness the woman's action represent those who hear the proclamation of the gospel: some will respond, while others will reject the mission. As Fander notes, the more provoking a prophetic sign is, the greater the opposition, and she stresses that opposition to Jesus increases at the points at which his identity as the suffering Messiah is revealed.[23] In the present account it is significant that those who condemn the woman speak out, whereas those who approve are silent. These contrasting responses foreshadow the reactions to Jesus in the course of the Passion Narrative. His enemies are vocal and take action against him, whereas his friends fail to speak out on his behalf.

The woman appears as a prophetic figure with a message that proclaims Jesus' identity as the Messiah. Kinukawa argues that the woman's action of anointing Jesus' head indicates that she is the only human being to recognize Jesus as a suffering Messiah.[24] Tolbert, similarly, suggests that the woman has heard Jesus' passion predictions (8.31; 9.31; 10.32–34).[25] We are not told, however, whether or not the woman is aware of the significance of her action. She takes advantage of the opportunity to anoint Jesus, and she makes her gift while she can. The woman is silent throughout the account, and Jesus is the one who interprets her act of anointing as a preparation for his burial (14.8). In a similar way, the Syrophoenician woman uses a metaphor from everyday life in order to convince Jesus to heal her daughter, but Jesus is the one who draws out the deeper meaning of her words in association with the λόγος of the gospel (7.29). Both women show insights into the kingdom of God. The action of the woman in our passage conveys a prophetic recognition of the identity of Jesus, and her extravagant gift may be interpreted as an expression of her love for him.

5. *The Attitude of Jesus towards the Poor*

In the story the critics argue that the perfume could have been sold and the money given to the poor (14.5). Jesus, however, praises the action of the woman (14.6–9), and his response raises the issue of his attitude towards the poor. Gnilka argues that

22. Taylor, *St. Mark*, 532.
23. Fander, *Stellung*, 131.
24. Kinukawa, *Jesus*, 83–84.
25. Tolbert, *Sowing*, 274.

the criticism of the opponents is primarily directed against the woman, but indirectly against Jesus for permitting the action.[26] But as Lane points out, concern for the poor is part of the Law, and almsgiving is particularly associated with the eve of Passover (*m. Pes.* 10.1).[27] Those who criticize the woman may thus expect Jesus to support their view.

Jesus, however, criticizes the woman's opponents for their harshness towards her, and deflects their arguments back to their own responsibility to the poor. Jesus does not neglect the poor, but cites the Law which requires the care of the poor (Deut 15.11). As Gnilka points out, the addition of the phrase ὅταν θέλητε δύνασθε αὐτοῖς εὖ ποιῆσαι (14.7) ironically calls into question the honesty of those who criticize the woman.[28] There is an implication that the critics condemn the woman's generosity while they fail to give alms.

Throughout the Gospel we have seen Jesus respond to the outcasts and the poor, from his initial healing of the man with the unclean spirit in the synagogue (1.21–28) and his healing of the leper (1.40–45) up to his healing of Bartimaeus (10.46–52). The rich man, moreover, is told to sell everything he has, give his money to the poor, and to follow Jesus (10.17–22). Jesus condemns the scribes who devour the houses of widows (12.40), and he shows compassion for the poor widow (12.41–44). These accounts suggest that Jesus is indeed concerned for the poor. It appears unlikely that Jesus would place himself above the poor, particularly since he teaches that he has come not to be served, but to serve (10.45).

Jesus describes the woman's action as a good deed (καλὸν ἔργον, 14.6). As Daube points out, in rabbinic writings there is a distinction between almsgiving and good deeds such as the burial of the dead.[29] Good deeds are regarded as more praiseworthy since they respond to a demand for immediate action, whereas almsgiving may be carried out at any time (*t. Pe'ah* 4.19; *b. Sukkah* 49b). In addition, Lane argues that the contrast is not between Jesus and the poor, but between always having the poor and not always having Jesus.[30] Lane's argument is supported by the parallel structure of the verses (πάντοτε γὰρ τοὺς πτωχοὺς ἔχετε...ἐμὲ δὲ οὐ πάντοτε ἔχετε, 14.7). Jesus is facing death, and the woman is to be praised because she takes advantage of Jesus' presence to offer a gift to him. Earlier, Jesus has described his presence with his followers as a time of feasting, but has warned them soon he will be taken from them (2.19–20). The woman in our passage takes the opportunity of a feast to anoint Jesus shortly before he is to be arrested and executed. In Jesus' teaching and miracles the kingdom of God breaks into the world and takes precedence over all other concerns.

Sugirtharajah points out that charitable gifts are insufficient to alleviate the needs of the poor, and he argues that Jesus' citation of Deut. 15.11 is intended to allude to the Sabbatical year in which all debts are cancelled and wealth is

---

26. Gnilka, *Evangelium*, 2.224.
27. Lane, *Mark*, 493.
28. Gnilka, *Evangelium*, 2.225.
29. D. Daube, *The New Testament and Rabbinic Judaism* (London: Athlone Press, 1956), 315.
30. Lane, *Mark*, 494.

redistributed.[31] In his analysis Sugirtharajah rightly emphasizes the need for a radical restructuring of wealth, but he does not take into account the apocalyptic context of the Gospel. The present age is characterized by limited resources, whereas the new age is one of abundance, foreshadowed by the feeding narratives, where everyone eats and is fully satisfied (6.42; 8.8). Jesus is about to give his life in order to redeem humanity and inaugurate the new age. Jesus' mission overturns the values of the world and he aligns himself with the poor by following the way of the cross. In this sense the poor will experience the abundance of the kingdom of God through Jesus' own death.

The critics of the present woman, however, describe her gift as a waste of the perfume (ἀπώλεια, 14.4). The term ἀπώλεια may be translated as 'waste' or 'loss'. The 'waste' of the perfume thus corresponds to the 'loss' of Jesus' life, and recalls the teaching of Jesus on discipleship, in which the cognate verb ἀπόλλυμι is used to show that only those willing to lose life will save life (8.35). The critics fail to see that paradoxically the loss of the perfume corresponds to the abundance of God's giving. The paradoxical nature of the gospel reveals that losing life means gaining the abundant life of the new age. The critics refer to the selling of the perfume, which suggests an exchange of buying and selling, whereas the gospel is concerned with giving and receiving. Judas hands Jesus over for money as if he were something to be sold (14.11), whereas Jesus interprets his mission in terms of giving his life as a ransom for many (10.45). The loss of Jesus' life leads to the redemption of humanity and the inauguration of the new creation.

In the light of his impending death Jesus is portrayed as one of the poor. Danker relates the portrayal of Jesus in the Passion Narrative to that of the righteous sufferer in the psalms of lament, and he points out that the righteous sufferer is identified as poor (πτωχός, Ps. 34.10; 68.29; 108.22 LXX).[32] In the Passion Narrative Jesus loses the support of his friends, he is rejected by the religious authorities and is executed as a criminal. On the cross he feels abandoned by God (15.34). Jesus participates in the suffering of human beings, and he thus becomes aligned with the poor. He gives his life as a ransom for many (λύτρον ἀντὶ πολλῶν, 10.45). The term λύτρον may be translated as the price required to redeem a slave, and Jesus' life is thus regarded as the equivalent of the life of a slave.[33] Jesus takes the role of a slave in dedicating himself to serve others by giving his life to bring life to others. In the apocalyptic context of the Gospel Jesus gives his life to redeem humanity which is enslaved to evil. The new age comes through the death of Jesus, and his loss of life brings abundance to everyone. As Bammel notes, there are expectations of the absence of poverty in the new age in the pseudepigrapha (*T. Jud.* 25.4; *4 Ezra* 14.13; *Sib. Or.* 3.378; 8.208) and in the rabbinic writings (*b. Šabb.* 151b; *b. Pes.* 50a).[34] In our passage, moreover, the abundance of the new age is foreshadowed by the woman's costly gift of perfume.

31. R.S. Sugirtharajah, '"For You Always Have the Poor With You": An Example of Hermeneutics of Suspicion', *AJT* 4 (1990): 102–107.

32. F.W. Danker, 'The Literary Unity of Mark 14.1-25', *JBL* 85 (1966), 468.

33. E. Bammel, 'λύτρον', *TDNT*, IV, 340.

34. Bammel, *TDNT*, IV, 895.

6. *Discipleship*

The woman breaks the jar in her desire to anoint Jesus, and the use of the strong verb συντρίψασα (14.3) implies that the jar is shattered so that it is unable to be used again, and all the perfume is poured out.[35] The objection of the critics to the 'waste' of perfume also suggests that all the perfume has been used; otherwise there would still be an opportunity to sell what was left over. The woman is thus portrayed in terms similar to that of a disciple, since she is willing to give away everything she has.

Jesus, moreover, vindicates the woman before her critics, and he praises her by saying ὃ ἔσχεν ἐποίησεν (14.8), which literally means 'what she had she has done'. The use of the verb ποιέω rather than one such as δίδωμι is unusual. The verb ποιέω, however, places emphasis on the woman's action and recalls the teaching of Jesus that his family consists of who ever does the will of God (ὃς ἂν ποιήσῃ τὸ θέλημα τοῦ θεοῦ, 3.35). In our passage the Greek grammatical structure establishes a contrast between the previous state of the woman in which she had the perfume and her present state which is one of loss. Her action leads to loss but paradoxically she will be remembered by her gift, since what she has done (ὃ ἐποίησεν) will be told in memory of her (14.9).

Discipleship means following Jesus, and the woman breaks the jar and gives everything she has, just as Jesus loses his life, giving away everything (10.45). Barton interprets the woman as a Christ-like figure, comparing her actions to those of Jesus.[36] As Barton notes, the woman's action arouses opposition, just as Jesus is condemned by his enemies. The woman is silent in the face of her critics, as Jesus is silent at his trials (14.61; 15.5) and the vindication of the woman by Jesus foreshadows the vindication of Jesus by God.

The account of the anointing of Jesus also illustrates the reciprocity of discipleship. The woman responds to the presence of Jesus with her gift, and he responds to her gift by defending her before her critics. The woman receives higher praise than anyone else from Jesus, and her action is to be remembered forever in connection with the proclamation of the gospel (14.9). She is praised in a way that the twelve male disciples chosen by Jesus are not. Kinukawa contrasts the woman's action of anointing Jesus as Messiah with Peter's confession that Jesus is the Messiah (8.29).[37] Peter fails to understand that it is necessary for the Messiah to suffer and die, and he attempts to dissuade Jesus from his mission (8.32). Myers, similarly, contrasts the attempt of the male disciples to avoid Jesus' death with the woman's action of preparing Jesus' body for burial.[38] Unlike the male disciples,

---

35. Lane (*Mark*, 492) notes that alabaster jars were filled with enough oil for one application and then sealed in order to preserve the fragrance. The jar had to be broken to use the perfume. Lane cites Pliny the Elder who claims that unguents are best preserved in alabaster boxes (*Nat. Hist.* 13.3.19).

36. Barton, 'Mark', 232–33.

37. Kinukawa, *Women*, 84.

38. Myers, *Binding*, 359.

she shows solidarity with Jesus, and her action supports him as he faces his passion. As Myers notes, she also foreshadows the women who remain with Jesus at his crucifixion (15.40–41) while the male disciples flee at his arrest (14.50).

Jesus' praise of the woman is also distinctive, since the Gospel is associated with the action of the woman rather than with that of Jesus. Gnilka relates Jesus' words to God's remembrance of human beings, which is mentioned in apocalyptic texts such as *1 En.* 104.1; 103.4 and *T. Job* 40.4.[39] The woman is to be remembered not only by God, but also by human beings, since Jesus' prophecy points forward to the period after the resurrection when the purpose of the Markan community will be to proclaim the gospel to all nations (13.10).

In one sense, Jesus' prophecy is ironic, since the woman is remembered, but we are not told her name. Schüssler Fiorenza interprets the omission of her name as a reflection of the patriarchal bias of the tradition.[40] We are told the name of Simon, the host of the meal (14.3), and in the following pericope the name of Judas, the betrayer of Jesus (14.10), but the name of the woman who performs this most memorable action is not recorded. The omission of the woman's name, however, focuses our attention on her gift. The woman is to be remembered for what she has done (ἐποίησεν, 14.8), not for who she is. This theme recalls the emphasis on the action in the teaching of Jesus that those who do the will of God are members of his new family (ὃς ἂν ποιήσῃ, 3.35). The desire of human beings for status within the community is criticized, since disciples are to be last of all and slaves of all (10.44). Their identity comes through giving everything away and following Jesus. Thus the name of the woman is unimportant, for the identity of a disciple is found only in relation to Christ.

The lack of information about the woman also enables her to be portrayed as a representative of humanity and as a role model within the community. Her unexpected appearance conveys a sense of the mystery of response of human beings to the gospel. Jesus teaches the crowds about the kingdom of God, and some people respond positively while others reject him. In the parable of the seed growing secretly the positive human response to the kingdom occurs in secrecy, suddenly revealing itself as if from nowhere (4.26–29). In the Passion Narrative, conversely, the religious authorities oppose Jesus and his closest followers abandon him (14.50). The woman in the present story, however, is the first of a series of previously unmentioned individuals, such as Simon of Cyrene (15.21) and Joseph of Arimathea (15.43), who appear unexpectedly and support Jesus.

7. *The Messianic Feast*

The anointing of Jesus takes place during a meal at Bethany in the house of Simon the leper. The setting of the meal corresponds to the many other meals in the Gospel, such as the meals with tax collectors and sinners (2.15–17), the feeding narratives (6.30–44; 8.1–10) and the Last Supper (14.22–26). These meals have an eschato-

---

39. Gnilka, *Evangelium*, 2.225.
40. Schüssler Fiorenza, *In Memory*, xliii–xliv.

logical focus, pointing forward to the messianic feast in which there will be food for everyone, as in Isa. 25.6; *1 En.* 62.12–14 and *2 Bar.* 29.5–8. These meals often have a marginal setting; the feeding narratives, for example, take place in desert places (6.35; 8.4), and the woman in our passage anoints Jesus in Bethany, a suburb of Jerusalem, rather than in Jerusalem itself.

As the opposition of the religious authorities increases, Jesus takes refuge in a place outside the city. Myers suggests that Jesus and his disciples are increasingly regarded as a 'fugitive' group.[41] Jesus' preference for the margins of society, moreover, is seen throughout his mission, which began in the villages and towns of Galilee. Jerusalem is the focus of opposition to Jesus, even at the start of his mission (3.22), and he avoids this city until his final journey there. The preference for outlying places recalls the beginning of the Gospel, which is located in the desert (1.4, 12–13). This setting corresponds to the eschatological hopes of salvation associated with the desert (see for example Isa. 40.3).

Furthermore, the description of the host of the meal, Simon the leper, also portrays the scene as a marginal setting because association with lepers rendered others unclean (Lev. 13.45–46; Num. 5.1–3; 11QT 45.17–18). The presence of Jesus in the house of a leper is reminiscent of the healing of the leper at the beginning of his mission (1.40–45) and continues his association with the ritually unclean that was illustrated in 5.24–34. Schweizer argues that the presence of Jesus at a public meal with a leper implies that the man has now been healed.[42] In this account, however, there is no mention of the healing of Simon. As Barton points out, it is significant that Jesus is anointed in the house of a leper rather than in the Temple.[43] Similarly, he is anointed by an unknown woman rather than by a male prophet or a priest. In these ways the anointing of Jesus subverts worldly standards. His preference for outcasts rather than the powerful reflects the bias of his mission, since he comes to heal the sick, not the healthy, and to call sinners, not the righteous (2.17).

In our passage the woman anoints Jesus during a meal, and her action of breaking the jar and pouring the oil recalls the accounts of the feeding narratives in which Jesus breaks bread to feed the hungry crowds (6.30–44; 8.1–10). In the feeding narratives abundance comes from brokenness, and everyone eats and is fully satisfied (6.42; 8.8). At the Last Supper, moreover, Jesus gives his disciples bread, identifying the bread with his own body (τοῦτό ἐστιν τὸ σῶμά μου, 14.22), and then takes the cup and gives thanks (εὐχαριστήσας, 14.23) and describes his blood as the blood of the covenant (τὸ αἷμά μου τῆς διαθήκης τὸ ἐκχυννόμενον ὑπὲρ πολλῶν, 14.24). As bread is broken and wine is poured out, his life is given to redeem humanity. Jesus prophesies that he will not drink wine until he drinks it new in the kingdom of God (14.25). In our passage, similarly, the extravagance of the gift of perfume foreshadows both the loss of Jesus' life and the abundant life all will receive in the new creation.

41. Myers, *Binding*, 354.
42. Schweizer, *Mark*, 289.
43. Barton, 'Mark as Narrative', 232.

Furthermore, the description of the central action of breaking and giving, which occurs in the Last Supper account, also takes place in the narrative of the woman who anoints Jesus. She breaks open the jar and pours the perfume upon Jesus. Jesus interprets her action as preparation for his death, and in this sense the giving of the perfume corresponds to Jesus' actions of thanksgiving and blessing before he shares the bread. The woman blesses him in preparation for the giving of his body to bring life to others. The extravagance of the gift of perfume corresponds both to the loss of Jesus' life and to the abundant life all will receive in the kingdom of God.

Jesus interprets the anointing as preparation of his body for burial (σῶμα, 14.8), and the word σῶμα (body) is prominent in the account of the Last Supper, in which Jesus interprets the bread as his body (14.22). The woman anoints Jesus' body, which is the source of life to redeem humanity. In the Passion Narrative, however, his body becomes the focus of abuse by his enemies. In his miracles, Jesus heals by placing his hands on people (1.41; 8.23) and by his spittle (7.33; 8.23). In the Passion Narrative there is a reversal as his enemies strike him (14.46, 65) and spit at him (14.65; 15.19). Jesus is executed as a criminal, but paradoxically his death brings life to others. At the Last Supper Jesus and his disciples celebrate the feast of Passover, commemorating the liberation of the Israelites from slavery in Egypt. At his final meal, he gives his body as bread to be broken for the liberation of all humanity from the power of Satan that grips the world.

8. New Creation

The woman's prophetic action points forward to the revelation of Jesus' identity as Messiah and king at the crucifixion. She anoints Jesus in preparation for his death, through which he redeems human beings and inaugurates the new age. The action of the woman in anointing Jesus may be compared with what happens at the baptism of Jesus (1.9–11), in which Jesus' identity as Son of God is also proclaimed. At his baptism he appears amongst many others who are being baptized, but he is the one who is singled out. Apocalyptic events are described as the heavens are torn apart (σχιζομένους τοὺς οὐρανούς, 1.10) and the Spirit descends. As Juel points out, the verb σχίζω (tear) implies that the heavens are torn in such a way that they can never again be closed, thus signalling that a cosmic change has taken place.[44] The association of the tearing of the heavens with the descent of the Spirit suggests that the power of the Spirit is the force that tears the heavens apart.

In the prologue God addresses Jesus directly, and events are described from the perspective of Jesus (εἶδεν, 1.10). No one else appears aware of the significance of the events that are taking place, and the identity of Jesus remains hidden from human beings. The action of the woman in anointing Jesus, however, dramatizes on a human level the cosmic events that are inaugurated in the prologue. The woman enters the room where the guests are dining, identifies Jesus as the one who is to receive her gift, and pours perfume over his head.

44. Juel, *Master of Surprise*, 34.

The pouring out of the perfume echoes the descent of the Spirit upon Jesus at his baptism (1.10). In our passage Mark gives an extended description of the perfume (μύρου νάρδου πιστικῆς πολυτελοῦς, 14.3). As Taylor notes, the adjective πιστικῆς is of uncertain origin, but may derive from the root πιστός and have the meaning 'pure' or 'genuine'.[45] Brown points out that the literal meaning of πιστι-κῆς is 'faithful',[46] and his interpretation points to the gift of the Spirit as a sign of the faithfulness of God. Moreover, the adjective πολυτελοῦς, which means 'costly', is reminiscent of the cost of discipleship, as in the teaching of Jesus that only those willing to lose life will save it (8.35). The portrayal of the extravagance and costliness of the perfume may thus point to the abundance of God in his gift of the Spirit.

The gift of the Holy Spirit is associated with the act of anointing in Isa. 42.1 and Isa. 61.1.[47] With this Old Testament background in mind, it can be said that the woman pours out the perfume upon Jesus as God has poured out the Spirit upon him. The Spirit descends εἰς αὐτόν (1.10), which is an ambiguous phrase that can mean both 'upon him' and 'into him'. This description also corresponds to the perfume, which is both poured out upon Jesus and at the same time absorbed into his body. The act of anointing is linked with the gift of power.[48] God anoints Jesus with the power of the Holy Spirit at his baptism and the woman in our passage is portrayed as bestowing power upon Jesus. At Jesus' baptism God proclaims Jesus as his beloved son (1.11), and at the start of the Passion Narrative the woman's action also expresses his identity as Messiah and king.

The Spirit, which is symbolized by the anointing oil, is the eschatological gift of the new age (Joel 2.28–29, Isa. 44.3, Ezek. 36.26–27). God's action in giving the Spirit sets a new series of events in motion. In the prologue the Spirit is the force which casts Jesus out from the presence of God into the desert to be tested by Satan (1.12–13). At the beginning of the Passion Narrative, Jesus is again anointed before he is handed over into the power of his enemies (14.41). The woman breaks open the jar and pours out the perfume (κατέχεεν, 14.3). At the Last Supper, moreover, Jesus identifies the cup of wine as the blood of the covenant which is poured out for many (τὸ ἐκχυννόμενον ὑπὲρ πολλῶν, 14.24). There is a verbal correspondence with the description of the pouring out of the Spirit at the end-time (ἐκχεῶ ἀπὸ τοῦ πνεύματός μου, Joel 3.1, 2 LXX). At the death of Jesus the old age is torn apart, and he gives up the Spirit to bring about the new creation (ἐξέπνευσεν, 15.37).

The eschaton, moreover, is often described in terms of a new creation in the Old Testament (Isa. 65.17; 66.22) and in apocalyptic writings (*1 En.* 45.4; *4 Ezra* 7.30;

---

45.   Taylor, *St. Mark*, 530–31.

46.   Brown, *John*, 1.448.

47.   The texts are ἔδωκα τὸ πνεῦμά μου ἐπ᾽ αὐτὸν (Isa. 42.1 LXX) and πνεῦμα κυρίου ἐπ᾽ ἐμέ, οὗ εἵνεκεν ἔχρισέ με (Isa. 61.1 LXX).

48.   T.M. Finn, 'Anointing', *EEC* 1.56–58. Finn also notes that the practice of anointing at baptism in the early church is associated with the gift of the Holy Spirit in order to combat Satan (Hippolytus, *Trad. ap.* 21; Cyril of Jerusalem, *Catech. mys.* 2.3; 3.1–6; John Chrysostom, *Catech.* 2.21–27).

2 Bar. 32.6).[49] In Genesis the Spirit is present, hovering over the waters before God speaks, and thus brings creation into being. The Spirit is the creative power of God, which separates land from sea, light from darkness. In the apocalyptic world-view of Mark, however, the world no longer flourishes, since Satan has invaded the earth, and his destructive power causes demon-possession and disease. But at the baptism of Jesus the Spirit descends upon him, and he carries out his mission of teaching, healing and exorcism in the power of the Spirit. His miracles are signs of the kingdom of God breaking into the world, and they point to the new age, when evil will be banished from the earth.

In our passage, then, the woman pours the perfume upon Jesus as God has poured out the Spirit upon him. The perfume, therefore, is associated with the Holy Spirit, the power which raises Jesus from death. The woman's act of anointing Jesus is connected to the proclamation of the gospel. The term εὐαγγέλιον may be translated as 'good news', and it is first used in the opening verse of Mark. As Marcus notes, the cognate verb is associated with a battle victory in Deutero-Isaiah (Isa. 40.9; 41.25–27; 52.7) as well as in secular Greek (Philostratus, *Vit. Apoll.* 5.8).[50] In our passage, similarly, εὐαγγέλιον refers to the victory of Jesus over the forces of evil. The allusions to the creation account in Genesis, therefore, suggest the new creation of the world, which comes about through the death and resurrection of Jesus.

The description of the woman's gift also recalls the terminology associated with God's acts of creation in Genesis. The woman gives what she has (ὃ ἔσχεν ἐποίησεν, 14.8) and the use of the verb ποιέω is reminiscent of the creative acts of God (Gen. 1.1, 7, 16, 21, 25, 26, 27, 31; 2.2 LXX). The woman's action, moreover, is described by Jesus as a καλὸν ἔργον (14.6), and the use of the adjective καλόν has connotations of beauty and goodness, which are reminiscent of God's acts of creation. In Genesis the work of God is described at the end of each day as καλόν (Gen. 1.4, 8, 10, 12, 18, 21, 25, 31 LXX). The term καλόν expresses the completeness and the satisfaction of God with creation, which culminates in the Sabbath rest. The allusions to creation are continued by the use of ἔργον, which is used of God's works of creation in Gen. 2.2, 3. In our passage the woman's action of breaking the jar thus releases a mysterious creative power into the world and also points to the abundance which come through Jesus' death.

The woman reminds us of earlier episodes in which women are portrayed as messengers. The woman with the flow of blood prompts Jesus to ignore the purity laws (5.21–43), and the Syrophoenician woman convinces Jesus of the necessity of the Gentile mission (7.24–30). The present woman's act of preparing Jesus' body for burial recalls the prophecy at the beginning of the Gospel to prepare the way of the Lord (ἑτοιμάσατε τὴν ὁδὸν κυρίου, 1.3). In the prologue God sends a messenger before Jesus to prepare his way (1.2), and in our account the woman has the role of a prophet who anoints Jesus in preparation for his death and resurrection. In

---

49. For analysis of the apocalyptic concept of new creation in Mark, see p. 13 of the Introduction.

50. Marcus, *Mark*, 146.

the Passion Narrative references to preparation are continued as Jesus dies on the day of preparation, the day before the Sabbath (15.42), which suggests perhaps that his death is preparation for the new creation. The woman in our passage is also reminiscent of the angels or messengers who serve Jesus in the prologue (1.13). Although Jesus is subject to testing by Satan, he is also given the sustaining support of the angels. The woman who anoints Jesus thus continues the mysterious service of women to Jesus which we have seen throughout the Gospel (1.31; 5.34; 7.29).

9. *Conclusion*

In our passage the woman who anoints Jesus is portrayed as a prophetic figure whose action expresses Jesus' identity as Messiah and king. Jesus interprets her gift as the preparation of his body for burial, since his kingship is revealed at his death when he gives his life for others. Her action is also eschatological since her act of anointing points forward to Jesus' death and resurrection. In the prologue Jesus is anointed by the Spirit before his mission, and in our account the woman anoints Jesus at the beginning of the events of the Passion Narrative. Throughout his mission Jesus provokes extreme emotional responses of love and hatred. The Passion Narrative depicts the opposition of the religious authorities, the failures of his disciples and the rejection of Jesus by the crowds; even those crucified with Jesus mock him. Jesus dies crying out to God from the depths of abandonment (15.34). The gift of this woman represents a different response to Jesus, a response of love which points to the heavenly reality concealed by the evil of the Passion Narrative. Her action foreshadows the action of God who will intervene in the midst of human hopelessness to raise Jesus from death.

Chapter 9

THE WOMAN WHO CHALLENGES PETER (14.53–54; 66–72)

1. *Introduction*

The account of the woman who anoints Jesus (14.3–9) paints a positive picture of a woman at the beginning of the Passion Narrative. We now move to an account in that same section of the Gospel of a woman who recognizes Peter and accuses him of being a follower of Jesus. This account frames the trial of Jesus (14.55–65). Just as the high priest questions Jesus, the woman in our passage puts Peter on trial. The high priest, however, is the leader of the Sanhedrin, the highest religious council of Jerusalem, whereas the woman who confronts Peter is a maidservant. While Jesus confesses his identity as the Messiah and Son of God (14.61–62), Peter seeks to preserve his life by denying all association with Jesus. Anderson proposes that Mark aims to highlight the contrast between the weakness of Peter under gentle persuasion and the fortitude of Jesus under a severe test.[1] The woman's charge, however, could lead to Peter's arrest and execution. If discovered Peter could face the same fate as Jesus.

2. *The Portrayal of the Woman*

The woman is introduced as one of the maids of the high priest (μία τῶν παιδισκῶν τοῦ ἀρχιερέως, 14.66). She is anonymous, as are most of the female characters in Mark, and she is defined as one of a group of servants rather than as an individual. Women are usually portrayed in relation to their family background (1.30; 5.23; 15.40), but this woman is defined in terms of her work. The description παιδίσκη is the feminine diminutive of the term παῖς, and this description suggests that the woman is a servant working in the courtyard. Bühner notes that the term παιδίσκη may refer to a young woman who is either a servant or a slave.[2] He observes that the description is used of a servant called Rhoda (παιδίσκη ... ὀνόματι Ῥόδη) in the house of Mary, the mother of John Mark (Acts 12.13). He points out, however, that the term may refer to a slave as in the account of the woman who has a spirit of divination in Acts 16.16, since this woman's powers bring her owners much gain (οἱ κύριοι αὐτῆς, Acts 16.19). The use of παιδίσκη

---

1.   H. Anderson, *The Gospel of Mark* (NCB; London: Oliphants, 1976), 325.
2.   J.-A. Bühner, 'παιδίσκη, ης, ἡ', *EDNT* 3.5.

to refer to a slave may also be seen in the description of Hagar in Galatians (4.22, 23, 30, 31).

In our account the term παιδίσκη is an indication of the woman's low social status. Unlike wealthy women of high social standing, this woman's work as a servant requires her to be present in a public courtyard among a company of men late at night. As Schottroff points out, we have few descriptions of the work of women in the Greco-Roman period, but she suggests that this woman has the job of keeping the fire going or of opening the gate (Jn 18.16).[3] In John's Gospel, the woman is described as the portress, which explains her ability to observe the movements of Peter in and out of the courtyard. Mark, however, does not give a clear account of her work, since we are told only that she recognizes Peter when she catches sight of him sitting at the fire (14.67).

The woman is presented as a marginal figure who may easily blend in with the crowd of servants in the courtyard. Her anonymity is similar to that of other Markan women (cf. 5.24–34; 7.24–30; 14.3–9). The low status of the servant woman, moreover, contrasts with Peter's role as the leading disciple of the Twelve. Peter is one of the first disciples called by Jesus (1.16–18), and he is chosen along with James and John to witness the raising of Jairus' daughter (5.37–43), the transfiguration of Jesus (9.2–8), and the prayer of Jesus in Gethsemane (14.32–42). He is also the first disciple to recognize Jesus as the Messiah (8.29), but he fails to understand the necessity of Jesus' suffering and death (8.32). He is, besides, the first disciple to protest when Jesus predicts that his disciples will abandon him (14.29). Peter and the other members of the Twelve reply that they are willing to die with Jesus (14.31). In our passage Peter's actions illustrate that he still lacks understanding of Jesus' mission and of the nature of discipleship, since he is not able to lose his life on account of Jesus and the gospel (8.34–35).

The woman lives in Jerusalem, whereas Peter is from Galilee, and she thus differs from Peter in terms of region as well as in terms of gender. In the account of the exorcism of the Syrophoenician woman's daughter we saw a contrast between Jesus and the woman in terms of gender, race, and social status (7.24–30). The Syrophoenician woman, however, ignored these divisions to seek help for her daughter, and Jesus healed the young girl and thus inaugurated his mission to the Gentiles. In our passage the woman rejects Peter, and the divisions which separate human beings are left intact.

The motivations behind the woman's challenge to Peter are not given, and we are not told if she fears Peter as an enemy or seeks a reward. The woman notices Peter while he is sitting at the fire, and she may question him because she recognizes him as a stranger, or because she remembers seeing him with Jesus (14.67). Theissen, however, argues that Peter's identity as a Galilean in itself made him suspicious (14.70).[4] He points out that there was an influx of Galileans into Jerusalem during Passover. Josephus, moreover, records that additional guards were stationed at the Temple during festivals (*Ant.* 20.106). A fear of sedition is apparent

---

3.   Schottroff, *Lydia's Impatient Sisters*, 83.
4.   Theissen, *Social Reality*, 102.

in Mark, since the authorities fear that the arrest of Jesus may lead to a riot (14.2). In Mark, Jesus has been arrested with a crowd carrying swords and clubs as if he were a rebel (ληστής, 14.48). Mark, however, does not indicate that the woman fears Peter as a rebel, and neither the woman nor the bystanders directly accuse him of being a brigand.

Initially the woman challenges Peter with the accusation that he was with Jesus (14.67). In this instance Peter could have agreed with her without further repercussions. The fact that Peter has been with Jesus does not necessarily imply that he is one of Jesus' disciples. Anderson, for example, notes that Peter could have spoken the truth in answer to the first question without much danger to himself.[5] Peter's repeated denials (14.68, 70), however, prompt the woman to question him further, and she becomes determined to prove that she has correctly recognized Peter. She calls to the bystanders to support her even though her accusations could lead to Peter's arrest. As someone who threatens Peter, the woman's actions are comparable with those of Herodias and her daughter (6.14–29), wealthy women of high social status who nevertheless are subject to the wishes of King Herod. Herodias desires the execution of John the Baptist because he has criticized her marriage to Herod, but she has no authority to order John's death. Instead, Herodias and her daughter take advantage of the opportunity of Herod's oath before his guests to trick him into carrying out their wishes. In our account the servant woman is powerless, but she takes an opportunity to exercise power over Peter through her recognition of his identity.

It is surprising that this woman is portrayed negatively, since Jesus teaches his disciples that they should act like servants and slaves (9.35; 10.43–44). Jesus, moreover, shows a concern for those who are poor and outcasts in his healing miracles (1.40–44; 5.1–20; 24–34). The vulnerability of slaves is suggested by the earlier account of the arrest of Jesus in which the ear of a slave of the high priest is cut off (14.47). But such exceptions to the rule occur elsewhere in Mark. Although religious leaders are usually portrayed negatively, for example, Jairus is depicted as a positive example of someone who is a religious leader (5.21–43). Similarly this woman appears to be a negative example of a servant, whereas servants are usually featured positively in the teaching of Jesus.

The portrayal of the woman as a servant raises the question of the focus of the service of human beings. The woman is described as one of the servants of the chief priest (14.66), and her service is thus directed to an enemy of Jesus. Jesus, however, does not ask others to serve him, since he teaches that he has come not to be served but to serve (10.45), and he instructs his disciples to be servants and slaves not of him but of all the members of the community (πάντων διάκονος, 9.35; πάντων δοῦλος, 10.44). In Mark, God initiates Jesus' mission to redeem humanity and to inaugurate the new creation. The focus of Jesus' service is thus the good of human beings and creation, whereas the woman's allegiance is given to the high priest who opposes Jesus.

---

5.   Anderson, *Mark*, 332.

3. *Discipleship*

The woman is one of a larger group of anonymous servants, and she emerges from the crowd of people within the courtyard to confront Peter. She comes forward on her own initiative as other women have done in the past (ἔρχεται, 14.66; cf. 5.26; 7.25; 12.42; 14.3). She catches sight of Peter (ἰδοῦσα, 14.67) while he warms himself at the fire, and her initial glance at Peter leads her to look more closely at him. As Cranfield points out, the verb ἐμβλέψασα (14.67) implies looking straight at someone.[6] Jesus has taught his followers to listen and to watch carefully (4.24), and his disciples have been those who have listened and approached Jesus for further instruction, whereas his enemies have seen without understanding (4.10–12). Although she recognizes Peter as a follower of Jesus, her perception is faulty since she does not understand that Jesus is the Messiah and Son of God.

The charges of the woman relate to the identity of Peter as a disciple. The woman first challenges Peter by claiming that he has been with the Nazarene, Jesus (14.67). Her accusation reminds us that one of the first definitions of the role of disciples is that they should be with Jesus (ἵνα ὦσιν μετ᾽ αὐτοῦ, 3.14). She points out to the bystanders that Peter is one of them (οὗτος ἐξ αὐτῶν ἐστιν, 14.69), and the bystanders, moreover, agree with her (ἀληθῶς ἐξ αὐτῶν εἶ, 14.70). This description is ambiguous, since it may also mean that Peter is 'out of them'. Their comment is true because the denials of Peter mean that he is no longer one of Jesus' followers. The term ἀληθῶς, moreover, has connotations of judgement, and it contrasts with the confession of the Roman centurion who states that Jesus is truly the Son of God (ἀληθῶς οὗτος ὁ ἄνθρωπος υἱὸς θεοῦ ἦν, 15.39). The charge that Peter is a Galilean is reminiscent of the call of Peter which takes place in Galilee (1.16–18). As Barton points out, the account of Peter's denial is a 'tragic reversal' of his action at the beginning of the gospel, when he immediately gave up everything to become a disciple of Jesus (1.16–18).[7] On that occasion Peter left everything behind to follow Jesus, but now he denies all knowledge of his experience as a disciple.

Peter's replies, moreover, reveal his failure as a disciple. He attempts to evade the woman's questions, and he claims not to know or understand what she is saying (οὔτε οἶδα οὔτε ἐπίσταμαι σὺ τί λέγεις, 14.68; οὐκ οἶδα, 14.71). The use of verbs associated with knowledge is ironic, since Peter reveals that he does not understand who Jesus is. The inability of Peter to understand is reminiscent of the account of the transfiguration, where Peter does not know what to say (οὐ γὰρ ᾔδει τί ἀποκριθῇ, 9.6), and also of Gethsemane where the disciples do not know how to answer Jesus (οὐκ ᾔδεισαν, 14.40). The woman is the one who refers to Jesus by name, whereas Peter refers to the man she is talking about (14.71).

The woman's questions threaten Peter, since they may lead to his arrest and trial, but they also give Peter the opportunity to confess his identity as a disciple of Jesus. Jesus teaches that those who wish to save their lives should be prepared to lose their lives (8.35). Disciples are called to follow Jesus on the way of the cross.

---

6. Cranfield, *St. Mark*, 446.
7. S. C. Barton, *People of the Passion* (London: SPCK, 1994), 28.

In our passage the charges of the women lead to Peter's movements away from Jesus. At the beginning of the account Peter follows Jesus inside the courtyard, and the inner location is emphasized by the phrase ἕως ἔσω εἰς τὴν αὐλὴν (14.54). At the second charge of the woman, however, Peter moves further away into the fore-court (εἰς τὸ προαύλιον, 14.68). Her word creates a conflict between Peter's desire to be loyal to Jesus and his desire to escape. The struggle within Peter is illustrated by his gradual movement further away, and the spatial setting thus expresses the failure of Peter's discipleship. Our account is reminiscent of 3.20–35, in which the family of Jesus stand outside the house while those who sit inside the house listening to Jesus' teaching are described as his family (3.35). Similarly, in 4.10–12 there is a division between those who listen to Jesus and approach him for further instruction, and those who remain on the outside.

As we have seen, the account of the denial of Peter (14.53–54; 66–72) frames the trial of Jesus in which Jesus is condemned to death (14.55–65). This literary technique provides an opportunity to compare and contrast the two narratives. As Brown points out, the introductory phrase, 'while Peter was below' (14.66) emphasizes that Peter's denial takes place at the same time as the trial of Jesus before the Sanhedrin.[8] The first and the last sections both contain a reference to the action of Peter warming himself at the fire (14.54; 14.67). Peter is thus described warming himself at the fire while Jesus is interrogated by the religious authorities. In Mark, moreover, the same woman continues to question Peter, whereas a different person is used in the other Gospels (Mt. 26.71; Lk. 22.56, 58, 59). Mark's account focuses on the development of the charges, since they are all linked to the woman who first recognizes Peter. This progression suggests that the woman has a similar role to that of a prosecutor in a trial who cites evidence and calls in witnesses to support her charges.

The role of the woman, then, may be compared to that of the high priest, who instigates the charges against Jesus. There are several similarities between the trials, since the accusations of the woman and the high priest follow a threefold structure. In addition, the servant woman and the high priest both focus on the question of the identity of the accused. The persistence of the woman in challenging Peter is comparable to the action of the high priest, since both are relentless in their pursuit of their opponent. They follow a similar strategy, moreover, by summoning others to join their condemnation. The woman looks for support from the bystanders (14.69) in the same way that the high priest seeks agreement from the Sanhedrin (14.64).

Jesus remains silent at the first two false charges, and he speaks only to confess his identity as the Messiah and Son of the Blessed (14.61–62). In contrast, Peter's denials of Jesus become increasingly forceful, and he concludes by cursing himself and Jesus (ὁ δὲ ἤρξατο ἀναθεματίζειν καὶ ὀμνύναι, 14.71). Taylor[9] argues that Peter curses himself if he is lying, and Cranfield[10] suggests that Peter may also

---

8.   R.E. Brown, *The Death of the Messiah: From Gethsemane to the Grave: A Commentary on the Passion Narratives in the Four Gospels* (ABRL; New York: Doubleday, 1994), I, 592.

9.   Taylor, *St. Mark*, 575.

10.   Cranfield, *St. Mark*, 447.

imply a curse on those who claim he is a disciple. As Brown notes, however, there is no direct object given for the verb ἀναθεματίζω (to curse), which may suggest that Peter is cursing Jesus.[11] Peter curses Jesus in order to save his own life, whereas Jesus gives his life in order to redeem others (10.45). At the end of the trial before the Sanhedrin Jesus is mocked as a prophet (14.65), but, as Juel notes, at this very time Jesus' prophecy that Peter will deny him is coming true.[12]

The woman's challenge to Peter illustrates the opposition which the disciples of Jesus will face. Jesus warns his disciples that they will be brought to trial before sanhedrins and synagogues, governors and kings (13.9), and they will be betrayed by members of their families (13.12–13). The questioning of the woman indicates that accusations are not always associated with the powerful leaders of society but could also come from unexpected sources. Our passage is similar to accounts of individuals who are accused of being Christians. As Johnson notes, the verb ἀπαρνέομαι (deny, disown, 14.72; cf. 14.30) is almost a technical term in the Gospels (cf. the Q saying Mt. 10.32–33/Lk. 12.8–9).[13] The act of accepting or denying Christ is depicted as the boundary marker of Christian identity (cf. 1 Cor. 12.3). Lane, moreover, observes that the form of Peter's denials 'I do not know what you are saying' is similar to that of a legal denial in rabbinic law (*m. Šebu.* 8.3, 6), and also in *T. Jos.* (13.2).[14] Pliny gives an account of female slaves who were accused of being Christians, and these women were told to curse Christ to prove their innocence (Pliny, *Ep.* 10.96–97). Brown also records that some Christians denounced each other under the persecution of Nero (Tacitus, *Ann.* 15.44). The language of our account thus points forward to the future persecution of Jesus' followers and may even reflect the present experiences of Mark's community.

Peter is accused first by the woman and then by a larger group, which may correspond to the experience of disciples. The failure of Peter not only acts as a warning to the community but also as an encouragement, because Peter is offered hope of restoration in Galilee (14.27–28; 16.7). There is evidence, moreover, that Peter died a martyr's death in Rome (*1 Clem.* 5; Eusebius, *Hist. eccl.* 2.25). Mark's audience, therefore, may be encouraged by the change in Peter to overcome their own fears of persecution. The charges of the servant woman foreshadow the accusations which are made against women as well as against men. In Mark, Jesus teaches the crowd and his disciples that they must deny themselves, take up their crosses and follow him (8.34). As we have seen, the crowd and the discipleship group consist of both men and women. Elsewhere in the New Testament we hear that Paul persecutes men and women (ἄνδρας καὶ γυναῖκας, Acts 8.3; 9.2). It is significant, moreover, that women are accused in the case reported by Pliny (*Ep.* 10.96–97), and we have other examples of the trials and persecution of women who are Christians (cf. *Acts of Paul and Thecla*, 20). Lefkowitz and Fant cite the later records of women who died on account of their faith such as Perpetua who

11. Brown, *Death of the Messiah*, 1.604–605.
12. Juel, *Messiah and Temple*, 68–69.
13. E.S. Johnson, *A Commentary on the Gospel According to St. Mark* (Black's New Testament Commentaries; London: A. & C. Black, 1991), 233.
14. Lane, *Mark*, 544.

was martyred in Carthage after Septimus Severus banned conversion to Judaism and Christianity (203 CE).[15] They also note the martyrdom of Chione, Irene and Agape, three women from Thessalonica, who died under the persecution of Diocletian in the early fourth century.

4. *New Creation*

Peter follows Jesus at a distance under the cover of darkness, and the woman discovers Peter as he sits at the fire (πρὸς τὸ φῶς, 14.54). The usual term for fire is πῦρ, although φῶς (light) is occasionally used (cf. Xenophon, *Cyr.* 7.5.27), and in our passage this word carries connotations of illumination (cf. 1 Macc. 12.29).[16] Peter desires to remain hidden, but the light from the fire reveals his identity to the woman and also illuminates his character. Our account takes place at night, and darkness is associated with the time of increasing evil. As Dewey notes, in rabbinic literature demons were believed to have power during the night until cockcrow (*Gen. R.* 36.1; *Lev. R.* 5.1).[17] It is only when the cock crows that Peter remembers the words of Jesus, and is overcome with remorse. The use of the term φῶς is also reminiscent of the creation account in Genesis, in which God separates light from darkness (φῶς, Gen. 1.3–5, LXX). The movement from hiddenness to revelation has earlier been seen in the parable of the light which cannot be concealed (4.21–22). Although Peter attempts to deceive the woman, his true identity is revealed.

The woman acts as the accuser of Peter in a way similar to the action of the high priest who accuses Jesus. In the Old Testament Satan is associated with the role of an adversary or of an accuser in a legal context (see for example Job 1–2 and Zech. 3.1–2), and in Rev. 20.7 he is a deceiver.[18] When Peter attempts to dissuade Jesus from his mission Jesus calls him Satan (8.33). Jesus draws a distinction between thinking the things of God and thinking the things of human beings. As Osborne notes, Jesus' response recalls the teaching about the two spirits at Qumran (1 QS 3.13.13–4.26) in which the evil thoughts of human beings are prompted by the angel of darkness and the spirit of falsehood.[19] In Gethsemane Jesus prays that his disciples may withstand the time of trial (πειρασμός, 14.38), and in our passage the woman tests Peter as a disciple. Her role thus corresponds to that of Satan and the human enemies who test Jesus (1.13; 8.11–13; 10.2; 12.13–17).

Our passage, moreover, has several correspondences with an exorcism account. Robinson notes the similarities between the debates of Jesus and his exorcisms.[20] As representatives from the supernatural realm, the unclean spirits recognize Jesus' identity as the Son of God (1.24; 3.11; 5.7). In the debates Jesus silences his oppo-

15. M.R. Lefkowitz and M.B. Fant, *Women's Life in Greece and Rome* (London: Duckworth, 1982), 265–70.

16. Taylor, *St. Mark*, 565.

17. K. Dewey, 'Peter's Curse and Cursed Peter (Mark 14.53-54, 66-72)' in W.H. Kelber (ed.), *The Passion in Mark: Studies on Mark 14-16* (Philadelphia: Fortress Press, 1976), n. 21 102.

18. C. Breytenbach and P.L. Day, 'Satan', *DDD*, 1369–70.

19. B.A.E. Osborne, 'Peter: Stumbling-Block and Satan', *NovT* 15 (1973), 187–90.

20. Robinson, *Problem*, 44–45.

nents (2.17; 2.27–28; 11.33; 12.17; 12.34), and likewise he silences the demons in the exorcisms (1.25–26; 3.12). In our passage the woman challenges Peter with knowledge of his identity (14.67, 69), just as the unclean spirits recognized Jesus. The woman approaches Peter after she catches sight of him (ἰδοῦσα, 14.67, 69), as the unclean spirits cry out when they catch sight of Jesus (ἐθεώρουν, 3.11), and the Gerasene demoniac approaches Jesus after seeing him from a distance (ἰδὼν, 5.6).

In exorcisms there is frequently a struggle before the demon leaves its victim. At the end of our passage Peter appears to throw himself to the ground (ἐπιβαλὼν ἔκλαιεν, 14.72). This phrase is difficult to interpret because it lacks an object, and suggested translations include 'he covered his face', 'he pulled on his cloak' and 'he threw himself down'.[21] The verb ἐπιβάλλω has the same root as the verb ἐκβάλλω (to throw out), which is used of Jesus' acts of casting demons. In the account of the Syrophoenician woman's daughter, the demon leaves the girl, after having thrown her onto her bed (βεβλημένον ἐπὶ τὴν κλίνην, 7.30). In other exorcisms there are struggles between the unclean spirits and the human beings they possess (σπαράξαν αὐτόν, 1.26; κράξας καὶ πολλὰ σπαράξας ἐξῆλθεν, 9.26). In our account, similarly, Peter throws himself to the ground after his struggle with evil. The power of Satan may have led Peter to betray Jesus, but Peter's memory of the words of Jesus fills him with remorse.

From the tearing of the heavens (1.10) to the tearing of the Temple veil (15.38) metaphors of destruction are used in association with the new creation. The kingdom of God breaks into the world, tearing the old order apart. The breaking of the rule of evil allows a new situation of growth to begin. The metaphors of cosmic breaking are paralleled by the description of Peter who breaks down in tears (ἐπιβαλὼν ἔκλαιεν, 14.72). Peter fails to understand or accept the prophecy of Jesus (14.27–31), but the power of Jesus' words will lead to revelation. In our account Peter's blindness is destroyed, and his encounter with the woman ends in a new self-understanding.

5. *Conclusion*

Our narrative depicts an anonymous servant woman who succeeds in challenging Peter, the leading disciple. She is persistent in her questioning and she refuses to be silenced by his denials of any knowledge of Jesus. Her charges mirror the accusations of the high priest. She takes the role of the accuser, which is traditionally associated with Satan. Her questions give Peter the opportunity to profess his loyalty to Jesus, but Peter denies Jesus in order to save his life. The woman's accusations also foreshadow the charges the Markan community may face from their persecutors. This passage illustrates that those who accuse the community may not be powerful leaders; unexpected people may bring charges against them. In our passage a male disciple is challenged, but as Pliny's letter shows, Peter's experience also relates to the persecution and trials of women, since women could face imprisonment or death if they were accused of being followers of Jesus.

21. Hooker, *St. Mark*, 365.

Chapter 10

THE WOMEN AT THE CRUCIFIXION AND THE BURIAL OF JESUS (15.40–41, 47)

1. *Introduction*

In 15.40–41 a group of women are mentioned for the first time as being present at the crucifixion of Jesus. These women have followed and served Jesus in Galilee before accompanying him on the way to Jerusalem. They are the last remaining followers of Jesus, and they are present at the crucifixion, despite the apparent failure of his mission. At the end of the Gospel three of the women, Mary Magdalene, Mary and Salome, go to the tomb to anoint Jesus, and they are the first human beings to receive the news of his resurrection (16.1–8). The reference to this group of women at such a late stage in the text has given rise to contrasting interpretations of their role. Schüssler Fiorenza identifies the women as the 'true disciples' of Jesus who have continued to follow him up to the time of his death.[1] Tolbert compares the women favourably to the male disciples, and she describes the presence of the women at the crucifixion as a 'hopeful sign'.[2] Munro also regards the women as disciples, but she argues that Mark has attempted to conceal their presence on account of his embarrassment at the prominence of women in Jesus' public ministry and in the early church.[3]

Women, however, have not been absent in the previous narrative, they have been included among the crowd who listen to Jesus' teaching and who are described as doing the will of God (3.35). Malbon, moreover, points out that there are positive portrayals of women in the earlier chapters, for example in the narratives of the healing of the woman with the flow of blood, the raising of Jairus' daughter (5.21–43) and the exorcism of the Syrophoenician woman's daughter (7.24–30).[4] Although these individual women have been positively portrayed (5.24–34; 7.24–30; 14.3–9), they appear only once in the narrative, whereas the present group of women have continually followed Jesus. The late reference to the presence of the women at the crucifixion of Jesus has therefore raised several questions. Why has Mark not mentioned the presence of these women before the crucifixion? Does Mark intend to highlight or to downplay the role of women? What is the relationship between this group of women and the Twelve?

---

1. Schüssler Fiorenza, *In Memory*, 320.
2. Tolbert, 'Mark', 273.
3. Munro, 'Women Disciples', 234–36.
4. Malbon, 'Fallible Followers', 36–37.

2. *The Names of the Women*

Mark names three women, Mary Magdalene, Mary the mother of James the younger and Joses, and Salome (Μαρία ἡ Μαγδαληνὴ καὶ Μαρία ἡ Ἰακώβου τοῦ μικροῦ καὶ Ἰωσῆτος μήτηρ καὶ Σαλώμη, 15.40). The first woman listed is Mary Magdalene, who has a key role as a witness to the resurrection in all of the Gospels (Mt. 28.1–10; Lk. 24.1–12; Jn 20.1–18). She is not identified by her male relatives as women normally were, but by her hometown, just as Simon of Cyrene and Joseph of Arimathea are (15.21, 43). Magdala is a town on the northwest coast of the Sea of Galilee, and therefore Mary is a Galilean like Jesus and the Twelve.[5] The reference to Magdala links Mary to the area associated with the beginning of Jesus' mission (1.14–15). As Schottroff points out, this designation would only have arisen after Mary had moved away from Magdala, since the town's inhabitants would not refer to her as Mary Magdalene.[6] Her name is thus an indication of her role as a disciple who has left her home and family to follow Jesus during his mission.

Mark does not record information concerning the background of Mary Magdalene. In Luke's Gospel Jesus casts seven demons from Mary Magdalene (8.2), but there is no indication in Mark that she has been healed by Jesus.[7] Mary Magdalene is regarded as a prominent figure in the early church, and there are several traditions that describe her as a teacher and as a missionary. She appears as a rival to Peter in the *Gospel of Thomas* (114) and as a companion to Jesus in the apocryphal gospels (*Gos. Phil.*). These traditions suggest that the Markan community may have heard of Mary Magdalene, and Mark, therefore, does not need to include additional information about her.

The second woman is described as 'Mary, of James the younger and of Joses, the mother' (Μαρία ἡ Ἰακώβου τοῦ μικροῦ καὶ Ἰωσῆτος μήτηρ, 15.40). Some scholars, such as Gundry, have argued that this woman may be identified with Mary, the mother of Jesus.[8] Gundry cites the reference to Mary's sons in 6.3, and he points out that James and Joses are the first two names recorded. The exegetes' desire to identify this Mary with the mother of Jesus may partly be an attempt to reconcile Mark's account with the reference to Jesus' mother at the crucifixion in John's Gospel (19.25), and partly an effort to overcome the negative portrait of Mary in Mark 3.31–35. Gundry's interpretation is unconvincing, since Mark makes

5.   Judas may not be a Galilean, since as Davies and Allison note (*Matthew*, 2.157), the description Judas Iscariot (Mk 3.19) may imply that he is a 'man of Kerioth', a town which is located in Judah.

6.   L. Schottroff, 'Women as Followers of Jesus in New Testament Times: An Exercise in Social-Historical Exegesis of the Bible', in N.K. Gottwald (ed.), *The Bible and Liberation* (Maryknoll, NY: Orbis Books, 1983), 419.

7.   A later ending to Mark mentions that Mary Magdalene has been healed of seven demons (16.9), but it is likely that this statement derives from Luke (8.2). Similarly, the account of the two disciples who meet Jesus (Mk 16.12-13) appears to be a condensed version of Lk. 24.13-35.

8.   R.H. Gundry, *Mark: A Commentary on His Apology for the Cross* (Grand Rapids: Eerdmans, 1993), 977.

no direct reference to this woman as the mother of Jesus, and only two male names are mentioned instead of the four that appear in 6.3. In the earlier references to Mary, moreover, she is always linked to Jesus as his mother (3.31, 32; 6.3), and Matthew and Luke both show no awareness of this interpretation in their presentation of the women at the crucifixion.

There is, however, an inconsistency between the description of the woman who is present at the burial of Jesus, Mary of Joses (Μαρία ἡ Ἰωσῆτος, 15.47) and of the woman who goes to the tomb, Mary of James (Μαρία ἡ τοῦ Ἰακώβου, 16.1). Some critics, such as Pesch, suggest that our passage refers to four women, since there is a textual variant in the manuscripts B, Ψ and 131, which place the definite article ἡ before Ἰωσῆτος μήτηρ.[9] Pesch argues that Mark could have placed μήτηρ (mother) before the two male names if he wished to indicate that they were both sons of Mary. It is unlikely, however, that Mark refers to four women since the name Mary appears only twice, whereas according to his interpretation three of the women are named Mary. The three named women at the crucifixion are more likely intended to correspond to the three women who go to the tomb, thus giving continuity to the witnesses of the events of the Passion Narrative.

It is difficult to interpret the relationship between the three descriptions of the second woman. Brown suggests that there were two older traditions, one of which referred to the presence of three women at the crucifixion (Mary Magdalene, another Mary and a third woman) and a second tradition which mentioned Mary Magdalene and some other women at the tomb.[10] The names of the women at the tomb were then harmonized and abbreviated to agree with the names of the women at the crucifixion. In this way Mary is described as the mother of James and Joses in 15.40 and the mother of James in 16.1. Brown also proposes that at a later stage the reference to Mary of Joses at the burial of Jesus (15.47) was added to correspond to the description of Mary as the mother of James and Joses in 15.40.

It is strange, however, that Mark has not harmonized the two different designations of Mary in 15.47 and 16.1, particularly since they are consecutive verses in his narrative. The differing descriptions of this woman may derive from the sources Mark received. It is possible that she was described as Mary of Joses in the pre-Markan passion narrative and as Mary of James in his source for the resurrection. The description Μαρία ἡ Ἰακώβου τοῦ μικροῦ καὶ Ἰωσῆτος μήτηρ (15.40) may thus be an attempt of Mark to reconcile the two versions of 15.47 and 16.1. In any case the interpretation of the description of the second woman is tentative, and Matthew avoids the confusion in the description of this woman by referring to her in the later passages as the other Mary.

The third woman is identified only by the name of Salome, and there is no additional information given regarding her relatives or hometown. In Matthew this woman is designated as the mother of James and John (27.56), but there is no reference to the mother of these disciples in our Gospel. Luke mentions the presence at

9. R. Pesch, *Das Markusevangelium* (HTKNT, 2; 2 vols.; Freiburg: Herder, 1976), II, 505–508.

10. Brown, *Death of the Messiah*, 2.1277.

the crucifixion of some women mourners from Jerusalem (23.27–31) and a group of women from Galilee (23.48–49), but he does not record their names. In a later passage he names the women who pass on the message of the resurrection to the disciples as Mary Magdalene, Joanna and Mary the mother of Joses, and he also refers to additional unnamed women (αἱ λοιπαὶ σὺν αὐταῖς, 24.10). As Fander observes, Luke's passage may reflect his attempt to reconcile the Markan list of names with the different names he received in his own tradition (Lk. 8.2–3).[11]

There is no mention of the husbands or fathers of Mary Magdalene and Salome. Stegemann and Stegemann note that these women are not defined in terms of their relationship to a man of high social status, and they argue that this omission is an indication that the followers of Jesus come from the lower stratum of society.[12] Kraemer, moreover, observes that the women in the Jesus movement are rarely presented as the 'virginal daughter, respectable wife, and mother of legitimate children'.[13] The lack of references to the women's husbands also raises the question of whether or not they were married. Heine proposes that the women were unmarried, and she regards their celibacy as a reflection of the itinerant nature of the group around Jesus and their expectations of the imminent end-time.[14] Heine's comments are supported by the lack of any references to the wife of Jesus in the Gospels particularly passages which mention his family (see for example Mk 3.20–35; 6.1–6a).

Women, however, married at an early age and marriages were arranged by parents. It is unlikely that many women would have the opportunity to choose to remain unmarried. Philo records that members of the community of the Therapeutae were unmarried (*Contemp.* 68–69), but the celibacy of these women appears to be an exception to the lives of most women in the first century. Ilan, moreover, argues that it was unusual for Jewish women to be unmarried, and she has discovered only one reference to an unmarried woman.[15] She observes, moreover, that there are other women in the Gospels who are not defined in terms of their husbands, for example, Susanna (Lk. 8.3) and Martha and Mary (Lk. 10.38–39; Jn 11.1). We are also not told whether the male disciples are married, although we know that Peter was because Jesus healed his mother-in-law (1.29–31).

Some of the women disciples may have followed Jesus with their husbands, some may be widowed and some divorced. The omission of any reference to the husbands of Mary Magdalene and Salome may reflect the lack of information available to the Gospel writers, but may also indicate that women acted independently of their families within the Jesus movement. Jesus calls men and women to leave their families and homes to follow him, and it is possible that the lack of

    11. Fander, *Stellung*, 138.
    12. Stegemann and Stegemann, *Jesus Movement*, 385.
    13. R.S. Kraemer, *Her Share of the Blessings: Women's Religions among Pagans, Jews and Christians in the Greco-Roman World* (Oxford: Oxford University Press, 1992), 133.
    14. S. Heine, *Women and Early Christianity* (London: SCM Press, 1987), 69.
    15. Ilan (*Jewish Women*, 64–65) cites a restored Greek funerary inscription from Tiberias (*CII* no. 984) of a seventy-five-year-old woman which states that she was never married, ἄγα(μον). Ilan notes, however, that this inscription is of uncertain date.

references to family relationships reflects the tensions between disciples and their birth families (cf. 3.20–35).

In our passage the reference to several named women is striking, since we have been given the names of only two women in the earlier chapters. The first is Mary (6.3), which reflects her place in the tradition as the mother of Jesus. The other is Herodias, and this is an indication of her high social status as the wife of Herod (6.14–29). The woman with the flow of blood (5.24–34), the Syrophoenician woman (7.24–30), the poor widow (12.41–44), and the woman who anoints Jesus are all anonymous (14.3–9). Tolbert argues that the record of the names of the women in our account may be an indication of a negative portrayal, since she associates names with worldly status and power.[16] The naming of characters is not always negative, since the names of Jesus and John the Baptist are given. These women, moreover, risk persecution by their presence at the crucifixion, which suggests that Mark views them positively.

The recording of the names of these three women stresses their importance as witnesses to the death, burial and resurrection of Jesus, and may also reflect their prominent status within the early Christian communities. Mark depicts a progression from a large group of women (15.40a) to three individual women (15.40b). This literary technique corresponds to other examples we have seen of individuals emerging from the crowds in response to Jesus (4.10–12; 5.24b–34). A large number of women have accompanied Jesus on the way of the cross to Jerusalem, but only two are mentioned at the burial of Jesus (15.47) and three at the empty tomb (16.1).

The naming of the women, moreover, depends on the names available to Mark in the early tradition. Munro suggests that Mark has deliberately omitted names of women that were present in his sources.[17] John, however, does not record a greater number of women's names than the Synoptic Gospels do, even though he seems to have access to traditions that are independent of the synoptics. Many of the Gospel's names occur in the Passion Narrative, which may reflect the early existence of a pre-Markan passion narrative which recorded the names at an early stage in the transmission of the traditions. Some names only occur here: Simon of Cyrene, Alexander and Rufus (15.21), and Joseph of Arimathea (15.43). The list of the women's names in our passage may reflect the presence of women's names in the pre-Markan passion narrative.

3. *The Portrayal of the Women*

In Luke there is a reference to a group of female residents of Jerusalem who mourn Jesus (23.27–31). The women in Mark, however, are specifically linked with Galilee, the starting place of Jesus' mission, a location which indicates their association with him throughout his mission. Munro argues that Mark has deliberately omitted any earlier reference to these women, and he mentions them now only because they

16. Tolbert, *Sowing*, 293.
17. Munro, 'Women Disciples', 240.

are witnesses to the death, burial and resurrection of Jesus.[18] Munro's analysis is unconvincing, since she does not explain Mark's reference to the many other women present at the crucifixion (ἄλλαι πολλαὶ, 15.41). If Mark intended to restrict the role of women, he would have no need to mention the presence of so many other women, who do not have any function within the remaining narrative.

According to Munro the earlier chapters suggest that Jesus travels on his mission with a small group of male disciples, and he meets women only in private.[19] She suggests that women are associated with the private domestic sphere of the house, whereas men are linked with the public ministry of Jesus. The separation between the private and the public spheres, however, is artificial. Crowds form around Jesus listening to his teaching in houses in passages such as 2.1–12 and 3.20–35, and in these passages the crowd consists of both men and women. In later passages the house becomes the setting for private teaching of the disciples (7.17; 10.10). Jesus, moreover, does not meet women only within the private sphere of the house. The woman with the flow of blood approaches Jesus in the midst of a crowd, and he calls her forward to praise her in front of the onlookers (5.24–34). Although the Syrophoenician woman encounters Jesus in a house (7.24–30), this account does not depict a conservative domestic setting. The Syrophoenician woman enters a house of a man she does not know, and one who belongs to a different culture.

In Mark the women are described as coming up to Jerusalem with Jesus (συναναβᾶσαι αὐτῷ εἰς Ἱεροσόλυμα, 15.41). Selvidge compares these women to the description of those who follow Jesus to Jerusalem (ἀναβαίνοντες εἰς Ἱεροσόλυμα, 10.32).[20] If those in 10.32, then, are 'followers' (οἱ ἀκολουθοῦντες) so probably are those in 15.41. In our passage, moreover, the use of the prefix συν- (with-) stresses the same close association of the group of women with Jesus as is suggested by the call of the Twelve to 'be with Jesus' (μετ᾽ αὐτοῦ, 3.14).

Although Sanders accepts that the women accompanied Jesus to Jerusalem for Passover, he proposes that the reference to women in our passage does not imply that they were constant members of the discipleship group.[21] Mark, however, first mentions that the women followed Jesus and then that they served him (15.41). The close association of the two verbs ἀκολουθέω (to follow) and διακονέω (to serve) implies that the women were members of the group who accompanied Jesus on his mission. Mark's emphasis that the women have been part of the group of Jesus' followers during his mission in Galilee is highlighted by a comparison with Luke's Gospel. Luke states that the women have followed Jesus from Galilee (23.49), which may imply that they have only joined the disciples in order to accompany them to Jerusalem.

The women at the crucifixion thus appear to have been constant members of the discipleship group. Corley proposes that the three named women are the only members of the discipleship group, whereas the other women have only accompanied

---

18. Munro, 'Women Disciples', 236.

19. Munro, 'Women Disciples', 229.

20. Selvidge, 'Those who Followed', 400.

21. E.P. Sanders, *The Historical Figure of Jesus* (London: Penguin Books, 1993), 109–11.

Jesus to Jerusalem on the pilgrimage to Jerusalem.[22] Mark, however, refers to two groups of women. The first group includes Mary Magdalene, the other Mary and Salome among them (ἐν αἷς, 15.40) and these women followed and served Jesus in Galilee and the second group (ἄλλαι πολλαί, 15.41b) consists of additional women who have accompanied Jesus and his followers to Jerusalem. The names of the three women also appear to be recorded only because they serve as witnesses to the crucifixion, burial and resurrection of Jesus. As Ricci observes, there is independent attestation to the historicity of the group of women who followed Jesus in Lk. 8.1–3.[23]

Stegemann and Stegemann argue that the action of the women in travelling in public with a group of men suggests that they would be regarded as disreputable women.[24] They note that Jesus eats with tax collectors and sinners (2.15) and he permits a woman to anoint him at a dinner (14.3–9). These actions reflect unconventional public behaviour, which would damage the reputations of the women who were his followers. Women, particularly those from the upper stratum of society, were associated with the private sphere of the home (cf. Philo, *Spec. Leg.* 3.169; *Flacc.* 89; 2 Macc. 3.19; Sir. 42.11–12). Stegemann and Stegemann thus suggest that the public behaviour of these women implies that they are from the lower stratum of society. Corley, moreover, proposes that the women, possibly Salome, may be servants or runaway slaves.[25] She notes the references to slavery in Jesus' parables (Mt. 18.23; Lk. 14.17; Mt. 21.34/Lk. 20.10; cf. *Gos. Thom.* 65; Lk. 19.13/Mt. 25.14) and that runaway slaves were members of the movement associated with Simon b. Giora (Josephus, *War* 4.508). Although there is little evidence to support Corley's proposal, Jesus does refer frequently to servants and slaves in his teaching on discipleship (διάκονος, 9.35; 10.43 and δοῦλος, 10.44). It may be possible that there were servants and slaves among the members of Mark's community.

In Mark, the women are portrayed more favourably than the male disciples, because they remain after the male disciples have fled (14.50). It is puzzling that Mark has not mentioned the women earlier. In one sense the presence of the women has been concealed by the focus on the Twelve. The Twelve are the disciples chosen to be with Jesus (3.14), and they are his constant companions until his arrest (14.50). Mark and Matthew are the only two Gospels which make no reference to the male followers of Jesus at the cross. Luke attempts to rehabilitate the male disciples, since he does not record the flight of the disciples at Jesus' arrest. He implies that men who are associated with Jesus are present at the crucifixion as well as the group of women (Εἱστήκεισαν δὲ πάντες οἱ γνωστοὶ αὐτῷ, 23.49). In John's Gospel, moreover, the beloved disciple stands with Jesus' mother, Mary the wife of Clopas and Mary Magdalene (19.25–27).

22. K.E. Corley, 'Slaves, Servants and Prostitutes: Gender and Social Class in Mark', in A.-J. Levine (ed.), *A Feminist Companion to Mark* (Sheffield: Sheffield Academic Press, 2001), 198.

23. C. Ricci, *Mary Magdalene and Many Others* (Kent: Burns & Oates, 1994), 28.

24. Stegemann and Stegemann, *Jesus Movement*, 385.

25. Corley, 'Slaves', 191–221.

The women, nevertheless, are not portrayed entirely positively, since they are described as watching from a distance (ἀπὸ μακρόθεν, 15.41). Selvidge notes that the phrase ἀπὸ μακρόθεν is placed after γυναῖκες, and she argues that the order of the sentence implies that Mark refers to the place of origin of the women.[26] The women have come from a distance to the crucifixion rather than that they stand at a distance. Selvidge's interpretation, however, is unconvincing, since Mark does not link this phrase with his reference to Galilee (15.41). On the other hand Tolbert suggests that this statement may be a negative description: the women stand at a distance because they are unwilling to be too closely associated with Jesus.[27]

The women, however, may be unable to move closer on account of the presence of the soldiers. Schottroff notes that the families and friends of those who were executed as revolutionaries could also face persecution (Tacitus, *Ann.* 6.10, 19; Suetonius, *Tib.* 61; Philo, *Flacc.* 72; Josephus, *War* 2.253).[28] It is possible, therefore, that the women stand at a distance on account of the soldiers who crucify Jesus and the presence of the chief priests and scribes (15.31). Kinukawa argues that women did not face the same dangers as men, but that women were not expected to be prominent in a public place.[29] As Schottroff points out, however, women also faced persecution, and she cites Josephus, who records the crucifixions of women and children ordered by Florus (*War* 2.307).[30] Brown believes that Jesus was not a revolutionary and he notes that the followers of Jesus were not rounded up and arrested by either the Jewish police or the Roman soldiers.[31] Brown, however, downplays the political features of Jesus' mission. Jesus is arrested as a revolutionary (ληστής, 14.48) and he is crucified along with two revolutionaries (15.27). At his trial before the Roman governor he is accused of the political charge of claiming to be the King of the Jews (15.2), and this title is inscribed above his cross (15.26). Jesus' followers flee at his arrest, which suggests that they fear that they too may be persecuted (14.50).

The women are afraid to stand near Jesus, and instead they observe the crucifixion from a distance. The phrase ἀπὸ μακρόθεν, moreover, recalls the Psalms of the Righteous Sufferer (Ps. 37.11; 87.18 LXX).[32] These psalms play a significant

---

26. Selvidge, 'Those who Followed', 399.

27. Tolbert, *Sowing*, 292–93.

28. L. Schottroff, *Let the Oppressed Go Free. Feminist Perspectives on the New Testament* (Louisville: Westminster John Knox Press, 1993), 171–72. Tacitus records the execution of Vitia, the mother of Fufius Geminus, because she had mourned the killing of her son (*Ann.* 6.10) and he refers to Tiberius' executions of both women and men who supported Sejanus (*Ann.* 6.19). Suetonius notes that Tiberius prohibited relatives to mourn those he had executed (*Tib.* 61) and Philo records that the friends and relatives of victims of executions were persecuted in Alexandria (*Flacc.* 72). Josephus also observes that Felix persecuted anyone who was a follower of the brigand leader, Eleazar (*War* 2.253).

29. Kinukawa, *Women*, 96.

30. Schottroff, *Let the Oppressed*, 172.

31. Brown, *Death of the Messiah*, 2.1157.

32. There are verbal similarities between 15.40 (ἀπὸ μακρόθεν) and Ps. 37.11 LXX (μακρόθεν οἱ ἔγγιστά μου μακρόθεν ἔστησαν) and Ps. 87.18 LXX (Ἐμάκρυνας ἀπ' ἐμοῦ φίλον, καὶ τοὺς γνωστούς μου ἀπὸ ταλαιπωρίας).

role throughout the Passion Narrative; several features of the account of Jesus' death may be compared to the afflictions of the righteous sufferer in the Psalms, such as the division of Jesus' clothes (15.24; Ps. 22.18), his cry of dereliction (15.34; Ps. 22.1), and the offer of vinegar to him (15.36; Ps. 69.21). The psalmist's friends, however, stand aloof during his suffering, whereas in our passage the women show concern for Jesus by remaining at the scene of the crucifixion.[33]

The description of the women may be interpreted in the apocalyptic context of the Gospel, since no human being is able to stay close to Jesus. At the Last Supper Jesus prophesies that when the shepherd is struck the sheep will be scattered (14.27). When Jesus is handed over into the power of evil, the male disciples flee (14.50). The presence of the women at a distance is a sign of the increasing evil of the Passion Narrative which separates human beings from Jesus. The distance of the woman from Jesus suggests that Jesus is unaware of their presence. The allusion to the Psalms of the Righteous Sufferer thus stresses the isolation and bleakness of Jesus' death. In Mark passers-by (15.29–30) and the chief priests (15.31–32) mock Jesus. Even those crucified with him revile him (15.32). Mark emphasizes that Jesus dies alone, feeling that he is abandoned by God (15.34).

Mark, then, portrays Jesus as surrounded by enemies, while his friends stand at a distance. Brown compares the women negatively to the Roman centurion who stands opposite Jesus.[34] He points out that the women are silent, whereas the Roman centurion recognizes Jesus as the Son of God (15.39). The centurion, however, only reappears once in order to confirm that Jesus is dead (15.45). Brown's interpretation ignores the care of the women who continue to serve him after his death. Two of the women observe the burial of Jesus (15.47), and three of them go to the tomb to anoint Jesus (16.1–8). In our passage the women stand powerless, afraid to intervene in the events that are taking place. Nevertheless, they show courage and faithfulness by their very presence at the crucifixion. They follow the command of Jesus that his disciples should be with him (3.14; 8.34–35), and they are with him at his death.

4. *Discipleship*

The women in our passage are described as having followed and served Jesus in Galilee before accompanying him to Jerusalem (15.41). Brown argues that this information is recorded here in order to clarify their identity because they have not been previously mentioned.[35] Mark, however, describes these women in terms associated with discipleship. Jesus calls disciples to follow him. Peter and Andrew follow him (ἠκολούθησαν αὐτῷ, 1.18) and Levi follows (ἠκολούθησεν αὐτῷ, 2.14). The disciples are also described as following Jesus in 6.1 and 10.28. As

---

33. J. Marcus, *The Way of the Lord. Christological Exegesis of the Old Testament in the Gospel of Mark* (Edinburgh: T. & T. Clark, 1992), 172–74.
34. Brown, *Death of the Messiah*, 2.1157–58.
35. Brown, *Death of the Messiah*, 2.1153.

Munro points out, the verb ἀκολουθέω (to follow) does not only refer to a physical following but implies a commitment to Jesus when it is applied to him.[36]

There are, however, several references to the crowds who follow Jesus (2.15; 3.7; 5.24) and some of these people are described in terms suggestive of discipleship, such as the woman with the flow of blood who emerges from a crowd which is following Jesus (5.27). Similar terminology is used in the account of the healing of the blind beggar, Bartimaeus, who follows Jesus on the way (ἠκολούθει αὐτῷ, 10.52). The woman and Bartimaeus, moreover, are both portrayed as models of discipleship, since they are praised by Jesus for their faith (5.34; 10.52).

There is also an example of a general call to follow Jesus which is addressed to the crowds and to the disciples. Jesus calls the crowd as well as his disciples together (προσκαλεσάμενος τὸν ὄχλον σὺν τοῖς μαθηταῖς, 8.34), and invites them to follow him (Εἴ τις θέλει ὀπίσω μου ἀκολουθεῖν, ἀπαρνησάσθω ἑαυτὸν καὶ ἀράτω τὸν σταυρὸν αὐτοῦ καὶ ἀκολουθείτω μοι). In this passage the verb ἀκολουθέω is repeated, stressing that discipleship may be defined as following Jesus on the way of the cross (8.31).

The crowd follow Jesus, but they are not constantly with him. These women, on the other hand, have continually followed Jesus in Galilee, as well as accompanying him to Jerusalem. Malbon argues that the disciples and the crowds complement one another, and she rightly notes that discipleship is open to all, but is not easy.[37] Mark suggests that discipleship involves following Jesus, but not everyone who follows is a disciple. The women are portrayed as disciples because they are the last remaining followers of Jesus.

The second verb used to describe the women in our passage is διακονέω (to serve). As we have noted, the verb διακονέω has the concrete meaning 'to wait at table'.[38] Beyer notes that διακονέω has connotations of 'to provide, care for', and that this meaning is particularly associated with the work of women. In Lk. 10.40, for example, διακονία (service) is used in the description of Martha being distracted by many tasks (περιεσπᾶτο περὶ πολλὴν διακονίαν), and in Jn 12.2 she serves at the dinner at Bethany (διηκόνει). Some critics, therefore, interpret διακονέω in our passage in terms of domestic care of Jesus. Carrington, for example, relates the reference to the service of the women to the account of Simon's mother-in-law, who serves Jesus and his companions after she has been healed (διηκόνει, 1.31).[39]

Other scholars, such as Gnilka, interpret the verb διακονέω in terms of the financial support which the women give Jesus.[40] Gnilka's interpretation recalls the group of women in Luke who accompany Jesus (8.2–3). In Luke, these women are also described as serving Jesus through their material resources (διηκόνουν αὐτοῖς ἐκ τῶν ὑπαρχόντων αὐταῖς, 8.3). The women in Mark, however, differ from the women in Luke. Apart from Mary Magdalene, Luke lists different names: Joanna,

36. Munro, 'Women Disciples', 231.
37. Malbon, 'Disciples', 124.
38. Beyer, *TDNT*, II, 82.
39. P. Carrington, *According to Mark* (Cambridge: Cambridge University Press, 1960), 331.
40. Gnilka, *Evangelium*, 2.326.

the wife of Herod's steward, Chuza, and Susanna (Lk. 8.3). Joanna may be a woman of high social status, since she is described as the wife of Herod's steward. In Mark, however, there is no indication that the women have high social status or are wealthy. As Corley suggests, Luke may intend to portray these women as respectable Greco-Roman patronesses in order to avoid criticism of the group as disreputable.[41] In Mark, on the other hand, Jesus does not appear to encourage his followers to bring their wealth with them to support the group. In contrast, he tells the rich man to give his money to the poor, then to follow him (10.21), and he calls his disciples to a precarious existence devoid of the usual means of support (6.8–11).

In Mark's Gospel the use of the verb διακονέω does suggest that the women supported Jesus by preparing and serving meals during the mission. Schottroff argues that the term must have a wider range of meaning than traditional household work, since Jesus and his disciples were an itinerant group who were poor and homeless.[42] Although the women may have prepared and served food during the mission, Schottroff is right to stress that the women are not portrayed in conventional roles, since they have left their homes to travel with a group of women and men who are not their relatives.

The verb διακονέω (to serve), moreover, is a key discipleship term in Jesus' teaching, particularly in the section in which he is on the way to Jerusalem. During this journey Jesus teaches his disciples that they should take on the role of a servant (διάκονος, 9.35; 10.43). As Collins points out, the term διάκονος may be translated as a household servant or slave who has a position which lacks power and honour.[43] The one who serves meals is usually the person who has the lowest social status in the group. This comparison suggests that the women have taken the positions of lower status within the discipleship group and have not held positions of power. The section concludes with Jesus' definition of his mission that he has come not to be served but to serve, and to give his life a ransom for many (ὁ υἱὸς τοῦ ἀνθρώπου οὐκ ἦλθεν διακονηθῆναι ἀλλὰ διακονῆσαι καὶ δοῦναι τὴν ψυχὴν αὐτοῦ λύτρον ἀντὶ πολλῶν, 10.45).

Jesus takes on the role of a servant or a slave in order to redeem human beings. This description is reminiscent of the portrayal of the suffering servant of Isa. 53.11. Barrett, however, disputes this interpretation by arguing that there are no linguistic correspondences between 10.45 and Isaiah 53.[44] As he observes, διακονέω does not occur in Isaiah 53 or any of the servant passages, and a different verb is used in Isa. 53.11 (εὖ δουλεύοντα πολλοῖς). Watts, however, points out that διακονέω is absent not only in Isaiah 53 but in the entirety of the LXX, and he suggests that by the time of the New Testament the verb stems δουλ- and διακον- had undergone a semantic shift in which the verb διακονέω took over some of the connotations of

41. Corley, *Private Women*, xix.
42. Schottroff, 'Women as Followers', 421.
43. Collins (*Diakonia*, n.1 248) cites Herodotus, *Hist.* 4.72; 9.82; Est. 1.10; 6.1, 3, 5 LXX.
44. C.K. Barrett, 'The Background of Mark 10.45', in A.J.B. Higgins (ed.), *New Testament Essays: Studies in Memory of Thomas Walter Manson* (Manchester: Manchester University Press, 1959), 4.

δουλεύω (to serve as a slave).[45] Watts observes that Paul frequently uses the δουλ-stem in relation to service towards Christ and God (Rom. 14.18; 16.18; 1 Thess. 1.9) and the διακον- stem in connection with service which is still 'in Christ', but which is directed towards others (cf. Rom. 13.4; 15.8; 2 Cor. 3.6; 5.18). In this way the use of διακονέω in 10.45 is intended to reflect Jesus' service in giving his life on behalf of many.

The associations of Jesus with the suffering servant, moreover, are continued in the account of the Last Supper, in which Jesus speaks of his blood as the blood of the covenant which is poured out for many (14.24; cf. Isa. 53.12). The celebration of Passover recalls the liberation of the Israelites from slavery in Egypt. God tells Moses that he will redeem Israel from captivity (λυτρώσομαι ὑμᾶς, Exod. 6.6 LXX). In 10.45 Jesus teaches that he gives his life as a ransom (λύτρον) for many. The term λύτρον may be translated as the price required to free a prisoner taken in war or to redeem a slave.[46] Jeremias, moreover, draws attention to the inclusive sense of the term πολλοὶ (many, 14.24) which may be translated as 'all'.[47] He compares the use of this term in 14.24 to Jesus' teaching that he gives his life as a ransom for many (ἀντὶ πολλῶν, 10.45). In Mark human beings are enslaved to the power of evil. Jesus, therefore, serves by giving his life as the manumission fee in order to redeem humanity. Mark aligns the women's service with the purpose of Jesus in giving his life for others. Their hidden service illustrates Jesus' teaching that disciples should place themselves last and become servants of all (9.35; 10.43).

The role of women in serving food is also associated with discipleship. As Munro points out, the male disciples distribute bread in the feeding narratives (6.41; 8.6).[48] She, therefore, proposes that the women's act of serving food does not imply that they cannot be regarded as disciples. In addition to Munro's analysis, the serving of food has theological significance within the Gospel. These meals foreshadow the Last Supper, in which Jesus and his disciples celebrate Passover, commemorating the liberation of the Israelites from slavery in Egypt. At the Last Supper Jesus identifies the bread as his body (14.22) and the wine as the blood of the covenant which is poured out for many (14.24). Jesus gives his life to inaugurate the new creation, and his action looks forward to the messianic feast of the kingdom of God (Isa. 25.6–8; *1 En.* 62.12–14; *2 Bar.* 29.5–8).

Throughout Mark's Gospel the celebration of meals signifies the kingdom of God breaking into the world. Jesus eats with tax collectors and sinners (2.15–17), and Jesus' mission is described as a time of feasting (2.18–20). The serving of food is also associated with healing; Simon's mother-in-law serves food after she has been healed (1.31), and Jesus asks that Jairus' daughter be given food to eat (5.43). In the account of the exorcism of the Syrophoenician woman's daughter, moreover, healing is equated with eating (7.27–28), and Jesus feeds the hungry crowds miracu-

45. R.E. Watts, 'Jesus' Death, Isaiah 53, and Mark 10.45: A Crux Revisited', in W.H. Bellinger, Jr and W.R. Farmer (eds.), *Jesus and the Suffering Servant, Isaiah 53 and Christian Origins* (Harrisburg: Trinity, 1998), 137–38.

46. F. Büchsel, 'λύτρον', *TDNT*, IV, 340–49.

47. J. Jeremias, *The Eucharistic Words of Jesus* (Philadelphia: Fortress Press, 1966), 179–82.

48. Munro, 'Women Disciples', 234.

lously (6.30–44; 8.1–10). Jesus' service in giving his life as a ransom for many is thus linked with serving food. In this way the service of the women looks forward to the service of Jesus.

There is, however, a difference between the service of Jesus and that of the women. Jesus gives his life as the Son of God to redeem human beings. His death is a unique event which inaugurates the new creation. The women's service is directed to Jesus as the one who serves all humanity. Jesus gives his life as food and he teaches his disciples to be servants. The association of διακονέω with discipleship is further indicated by the use of the term διάκονος for a leader of the early church. Paul refers to himself and other missionaries as διάκονοι (1 Cor. 3.5; 2 Cor. 3.6; 6.4; 11.23). In Phil. 1.1 Paul addresses ἐπίσκοποι and διάκονοι, who appear to hold leadership positions within the community. In Colossians the term is used of Tychicus (Col. 4.7). This role can be applied to women, as Phoebe is described as a διάκονος in Rom. 16.1. In the period between the resurrection and the parousia, moreover, part of their service is distributing the eucharist. In later texts, as Collins notes, the term διάκονος appears as a church office which is associated with serving the eucharist (*Did.* 14.1–3, 15.1; *1 Clem.* 42.4) and there is also a reference to διάκονοι who distribute the eucharist in Justin (*1 Apol.* 1.65.5).[49]

The association of the verb διακονέω with serving food may also be seen in the account of the angels who serve Jesus in the prologue (διηκόνουν, 1.13). As representatives of the heavenly realm, the angels appear to have been sent by God to help Jesus during his testing by Satan (1.12–13). The service of the angels is undefined, but the Old Testament correspondences imply that they sustain Jesus by bringing him food. As we have noted, the service of the angels is reminiscent of the account of Adam and Eve who ate the food of angels in Eden (*L.A.E.* 4.1–2; *b.Sanh.* 59b) and also of the angel who serves Elijah with food (1 Kgs 19.5–8). Munro, however, interprets Mark's temptation account in relation to Ps. 91.9–13, in which angels act as protectors, and she argues that the angels support Jesus in his conflict with evil.[50] Although Munro downplays the associations of service with food, her analysis does add insights into our understanding of the role of women. In the prologue the angels protect Jesus during his conflict with Satan. The women disciples have prepared meals but have also had a role in supporting Jesus in his struggle with his human enemies.

Our analysis of the verbs ἀκολουθέω and διακονέω thus suggests that they are discipleship terms. This raises a question about Munro's contention that Mark wishes to downplay the role of women, and that he has introduced these terms in order to explain the presence of the women.[51] Her interpretation is unconvincing, since Mark has described the women in terms associated with discipleship. If he intended to mention them only because they were witnesses to the events of the Passion Narrative, he could have employed different vocabulary. In chapter 15, moreover, the women have specifically followed 'him' and served 'him'. The

49. Collins, *Diakonia*, 238–43.
50. Munro, 'Women Disciples', 233–34.
51. Munro, 'Women Disciples', 234–36.

repetition of the single pronoun αὐτῷ (him, 15.41) implies a specific commitment to Jesus through following and serving him alone. This refutation of Munro also applies to Stegemann and Stegemann, who argue that the service of the women depicts them in the traditional female role of preparing meals and reflects the evangelists' desire to relativize the role of women as disciples.[52] His analysis does not take into account the portrayal of the women in the literary context of Mark's narrative, and he ignores the significance of service and meals within the teaching of Jesus that he serves by giving his life as a ransom for many (10.45).

5. *The Role of the Women in Relation to the Twelve*

In our passage women are portrayed in terms of discipleship. Mark, moreover, implies that they are members of the wider group of disciples because they have continually followed Jesus. Women have left their families and homes to follow Jesus and they have accompanied him to Jerusalem for Passover. It is probable that the women were present at the Last Supper, since the men and women have travelled together to Jerusalem. The instructions to celebrate Passover are given to the whole congregation of Israel (Exod. 12.43–49) and it was customary for men and women to celebrate Passover together. Although the Mishnah is dated later than Mark's Gospel, it also records that men and women eat Passover together (*m. Pes.* 7.13) and women, moreover, are not permitted to celebrate Passover with no men present (*m. Pes.* 8.7). Ilan also notes the participation of women in the pilgrimages to Jerusalem for Passover (*b. Ned.* 36a).[53] These Galilean women are part of Jesus' wider discipleship group, and it would be strange for the men to celebrate Passover separately from the women.

In Mark there seems to be a wider group of disciples than the Twelve at the Last Supper. Jesus sends two disciples on ahead to prepare the Passover (14.13–16). These two disciples do not appear to be members of the Twelve, since Jesus is later described as arriving with the Twelve (14.17). At the meal Jesus states that he will be betrayed by one who is eating with him (14.18) and then narrows this group to one of the Twelve (14.20). If Jesus and the Twelve were the only people present at the meal, there would be no need for Jesus to make a specific reference to the Twelve. It is also possible that Mark includes women amongst all those who flee at the arrest of Jesus (14.50). As we have seen, Jesus prophesies that he will be abandoned by all his followers (14.27). Mark, moreover, emphasizes that everyone deserts Jesus (ἔφυγον πάντες, 14.50).

It is noteworthy, however, that no male disciples are present at the crucifixion, whereas the women are his last remaining followers. Women and men have followed Jesus, but only women are linked to the verb διακονέω (1.31; 15.41). Jesus, moreover, has taught the Twelve that they should act as servants (9.35; 10.43) and recorded their failures to serve. The teaching of Jesus on the subject of service is linked to the predictions of his death (8.31; 9.31; 10.32–34). After each passion

52. Stegemann and Stegemann, *Jesus Movement*, 384.
53. Ilan, *Jewish Women*, 180.

prediction the Twelve show their inability to understand the nature of Jesus' identity as the suffering Messiah. Peter is the first human being to recognize Jesus as the Messiah (8.29), but he lacks an understanding that Jesus' mission involves suffering and death (8.32). After the first passion prediction (8.31), Peter attempts to dissuade Jesus from his mission, and Jesus calls him 'Satan' (8.32–33). The disciples do not understand the second passion prediction and they are afraid to ask Jesus about its significance (9.31). This prediction is followed by a discussion among Jesus' followers as to which one is the greatest (9.33–37), and Jesus specifically calls the Twelve together and teaches them that the one who wishes to be great must be the servant of all (9.35).

The third passion prediction is the most detailed, describing the rejection and suffering Jesus will encounter in Jerusalem, and it is given to the Twelve alone (10.32–34). After this prediction James and John request the seats of honour on either side of Jesus (10.35–40). In response, the other ten members of the Twelve become indignant with James and John, and Jesus then teaches all Twelve that the true nature of discipleship is service. This teaching has a cumulative function, since it concludes with the definition of the purpose of Jesus' mission as service. Jesus interprets his mission in terms of giving his life as a ransom for many (10.45). Mark thus links the inability of the Twelve to understand the passion predictions and their failures in discipleship. He highlights the contrast between the willingness of Jesus to give his life for others on the one hand, and the self-seeking desires of the Twelve on the other. Their desire for a powerful Messiah is linked to their own desire for power.

These women thus act as foils to the Twelve. We see the male disciples acting in ways that are contrary to Jesus' teaching on service, and then we discover that the women have been illustrating service (15.41). The service of the women has been unobtrusive and hidden. Their actions have been concealed by the focus on the desire of the male disciples for status and power on the way to Jerusalem. As women are excluded from membership in the Twelve, they have not been involved in the struggle for status and power within this group.

The failures of all human beings, however, are depicted as being within the wider purposes of God. At the Mount of Olives Jesus prophesies that the disciples will abandon him (14.27), but he promises that after the resurrection he will go ahead of them to Galilee (14.28; 16.7). He quotes Zech. 13.7, but he changes the verse 'strike the shepherd' to 'I will strike the shepherd'. Beneath the animosity and evil of the Passion Narrative, then, God's purposes are being worked out. In the Passion Narrative Judas, one of the Twelve, betrays Jesus. Judas is repeatedly identified as one of the Twelve (3.14–19; 14.10; 20, 43), and his betrayal signals the breakup of the discipleship group. The disciples desire to remain faithful to Jesus (14.31), but they are unable to resist the power of evil unleashed during the passion of Jesus. In Gethsemane Peter, James and John are overcome by sleep, which is portrayed as a struggle between the spirit and the flesh (14.38). At the arrest of Jesus everyone flees (14.50). When Jesus is handed over into the hands of his enemies, no human being is able to withstand the power of evil. In the same way the women in our passage stand at a distance from the crucifixion (15.40).

There are further correspondences between the portrayal of the Twelve and that of the women. Munro argues that the description of the women forms a counterpart to the presentation of the male disciples.[54] In both groups there is a larger group who follow Jesus and a smaller group of three named disciples. Peter, James and John witness significant events such as the raising of Jairus' daughter (5.37), the transfiguration (9.2–8), and Jesus' prayer in Gethsemane (14.32–42). Mary Magdalene, the other Mary and Salome, similarly, are witnesses of the crucifixion (15.40). Mary Magdalene and the other Mary emerge from a larger group of women to witness the burial of Jesus (15.47), and Mary Magdalene, the other Mary and Salome are the ones who go to the empty tomb and thus become the first witnesses to the resurrection (16.1–8).

Peter, moreover, is described as following Jesus at a distance (ἀπὸ μακρόθεν, 14.54), in the same way that the women who are present at the crucifixion are described as standing at a distance (ἀπὸ μακρόθεν, 15.40). Malbon argues that both men and women are fallible followers because the men flee at the arrest of Jesus (14.50) and the women stand at a distance at the crucifixion.[55] Peter, however, denies Jesus three times (14.66–72). The women are more faithful than the male disciples, since they are present at the crucifixion. Two of the women act as witnesses to his burial (15.47), and three of them show their loyalty by going to the tomb to anoint his body (16.1–8). It is not until the end of the Gospel that the women flee from the tomb (ἔφυγον, 16.8), recalling the earlier description of the flight of the male disciples at the arrest of Jesus (ἔφυγον, 14.50).

The comparison between the women and the Twelve reveals that the service of the women is a model of discipleship for the whole community of both women and men. The positive association between women and service corresponds to other favourable portraits of women such as the woman with the flow of blood who is praised for her faith (5.34) and the Syrophoenician women who breaks down the barriers between Jews and Gentiles (7.24–30). It is a characteristic of Mark's Gospel that those on the margins are portrayed in terms associated with discipleship and are presented as models for the community to follow. The favourable portrayal of these characters emphasizes that the Markan community should not be a closed group. The line between insiders and outsiders is not defined in terms of membership of the discipleship group but in terms of doing the will of God (cf. 3.35). Jesus acts to heal the diseased and include those who are outcasts. His purpose is to proclaim the kingdom of God which involves all human beings and the whole of creation.

6. *The Women at the Burial of Jesus (15.47)*

The role of women as witnesses continues in the account of the burial of Jesus (15.47). Mary Magdalene and the other Mary observe the preparations carried out by Joseph of Arimathea, and the same verb of sight is used in both passages (θεωροῦσαι, 15.40; ἐθεώρουν, 15.47). The account of the burial is thus sandwiched

---

54. Munro, 'Women Disciples', 230–31.
55. Malbon, 'Fallible Followers', 43.

between two references to the women who keep watch, and their presence indicates their support of Jesus. The women, however, do not appear to be actively involved in the burial arrangements. Joseph is the one who requests Jesus' body, buys the cloth, buries the body and seals the tomb. There is no communication, moreover, between the women and Joseph, and they do not act together to arrange Jesus' burial.

Joseph of Arimathea is a respected member of the council, and he may be more likely to receive the body of Jesus because of his high social status (15.43). In contrast, the women have low social status, and they would be unlikely to be granted such a request. Brown, however, challenges the positive portrayal of Joseph of Arimathea by arguing that Joseph may be a member of the Sanhedrin who have condemned Jesus to death.[56] Brown proposes that Joseph is more concerned with preserving the holiness of Passover than with Jesus. Frequently the bodies of those crucified were left on crosses to act as a deterrent to others and burials were refused (cf. Suetonius, *Aug.* 13.1–2). The corpse of a crucified person could bring pollution to the land (Deut. 21.23). This interpretation is unconvincing because Joseph does not attempt to arrange burials for the two revolutionaries who are crucified with Jesus. He also appears to be a more positive figure than Brown's interpretation permits. His action of plucking up his courage (τολμήσας, 15.43) to request the body of Jesus implies that he is not as aligned with the Sanhedrin as Brown proposes.

The women observe Joseph's actions and do not take part in the burial of Jesus. Brown suggests that the women are portrayed negatively because they do not directly intervene in the situation.[57] The women, however, risk arrest by their presence at the tomb, and they will later return to anoint Jesus (16.1–8). The distance of the women from Joseph strengthens the role of women as witnesses of the events of the Passion Narrative. The women stand apart watching Jesus' burial. Joseph buries Jesus with no anointing, which suggests a hasty burial. The view that Jesus has not been given a proper burial may prompt them to return to the tomb with spices. It is noteworthy that the women make no contact with Joseph to arrange their visit, since they discuss among themselves the difficulty of removing the stone from the entrance of the tomb (16.3).

7. New Creation

The women are witnesses of Jesus' death and burial, and later they will go to the tomb and discover the resurrection (16.1–8). They are the only followers of Jesus who are present at the crucifixion, but they are not mentioned until after the death of Jesus. Malbon interprets the reference to the group of women at this late stage in the narrative in terms of the literary theory of Gerard Genette.[58] She defines our passage as a 'repeating analepsis', an 'analepsis on paralipses'. This literary technique is a retrospective section that fills in information previously missing from the narrative. The women are mentioned at this late stage not in order to obscure their

---

56. R. E. Brown, 'The Burial of Jesus (Mark 15:42-47)', *CBQ* 50 (1988), 233–45.
57. Brown, *Death of the Messiah*, 2.1158.
58. Malbon, 'Fallible Followers', 41.

presence but to clarify their role. She argues that the service of the women can only be understood in relation to the service of Jesus, which is illustrated by the giving of his life.

The delayed reference to the women, moreover, may be interpreted within the apocalyptic context of Jesus' death. Jesus' identity is concealed from human beings until his death on the cross when the Roman centurion recognizes him as the Son of God (15.39). Jesus' service has an eschatological focus, since he serves by giving his life to redeem human beings and to inaugurate the new creation. The service of the women has also been hidden and is mentioned now only at the time of Jesus' crucifixion. The death of Jesus is a time of revelation which uncovers the difference between the values of God and those of human beings. The human rulers of the world have only appeared to rule. Satan has usurped the world, but ultimately God is in control of events.[59] The old age is characterized by the human desire for power, status and self-preservation, whereas the new age is associated with self-giving.

The presence of the women at the crucifixion aligns them with Jesus' suffering and death. As Rhoads points out, the proclamation of the gospel attracts opposition and persecution, and the suffering of Jesus comes about on account of his desire to be faithful to his mission.[60] Lee-Pollard, moreover, rightly defines God's power as 'the power to renounce power'.[61] The self-giving power of Jesus' life for others, however, paradoxically turns out to be more powerful than worldly concepts of power. The strongest worldly power is the power to kill, but God's power is able to raise Jesus from death.

Furthermore, the service of the women illustrates the anti-hierarchical teaching of Jesus in which a child comes first in the kingdom of God (9.33–37; 10.13–16). Women are not included among the religious and political authorities and they are not members of the Twelve. This situation enables women to develop relationships based on mutuality and reciprocity. Jesus dies as a slave, and his death is interpreted as service. Women have acted as servants, and Jesus becomes aligned with them in his death because he takes the role of a slave in order to redeem human beings.

At the crucifixion, however, the women stand at a distance and Jesus is aware of no human help, as he faces the power of Satan alone. The opposition to Jesus culminates in his trial and crucifixion, and Mark depicts the crucifixion as the testing of Jesus. Mark's account of the crucifixion recalls features in the description of the temptation of Jesus in the desert where he is described as being with wild animals and served by angels (1.12–13). At the crucifixion the religious authorities taunt Jesus to save himself (15.31–32) and those crucified with him revile him (15.32). As Danker points out, the opponents of Jesus behave in a similar way to the enemies

59. Marcus, 'Epistemology', 558.

60. D.M. Rhoads, 'Losing Life for Others in the Face of Death. Mark's Standards of Judgement', *Int* 47 (1993), 362–63.

61. D.A. Lee-Pollard, 'Powerlessness as Power: A Key Emphasis in the Gospel of Mark', *Scot. Journ. of Theol.* 40 (1987), 173–74.

who are depicted in the Psalms of the Righteous Sufferer as wild animals (Ps. 21.12–13, 16–17, 21 LXX).[62] The women's service is, therefore, part of the cosmic battle against evil. In the course of the Gospel Jesus is tested by his human enemies and he is served by women (1.31; 15.41). Only at the cross is the role of the women discovered but their service is described in the past tense (διηκόνουν, 15.41).

Throughout the Gospel Mark's focus has been on the conflict between Jesus and his human opponents, but behind his human opponents has lain the cosmic power of evil. The women have served Jesus food, but their service has also supported him in his struggle against his human enemies. Jesus calls his disciples to be with him (3.14) and the continual presence of the women has sustained Jesus during his mission. The kingdom of God is portrayed as a family, since those who do the will of God are described as the brother, sister and mother of Jesus (3.35). At the crucifixion Jesus is mocked by his enemies (15.31–32) and those crucified with him (15.32). He is unaware of the presence of the women who stand at a distance (15.40) and he feels abandoned by God (15.34). The isolation of Jesus is associated with the evil of the old age and contrasts with the kingdom of God in which Jesus is identified as the Son of God (1.11; 9.7).

In the prologue there is no outcome to the testing of Jesus, but at the crucifixion he overcomes the power of Satan. The crucifixion signifies the turning point between the old and the new age. The death of Jesus is described in apocalyptic terms. Darkness descends upon the earth from the sixth hour until the ninth hour (15.33). The darkness is a cosmic sign of judgement alluding to the account of the darkness of the Day of the Lord which is associated with the mourning for an only son in Amos 8.9–10. As Allison points out, darkness is also depicted as a sign of the end-time in Jewish eschatological texts (cf. *Ass. Mos.* 10.5; *T. Levi* 4.1; *2 Bar.* 10.12; 46.2; 77.14).[63] The pervasive darkness is reminiscent of the darkness which covered the deep before God's acts of creation (σκότος ἐπάνω τῆς ἀβύσσου, Gen. 1.2 LXX). In Genesis God creates by bringing order from chaos, and in Mark, Jesus struggles against evil in order to inaugurate the new creation. On the cross Satan appears to have taken control of Jesus, and Jesus' death is depicted in terms of a violent battle. Jesus dies with a loud cry (φωνῇ μεγάλη, 15.34, 37), which echoes the tormented cries of the demoniacs as the unclean spirits depart (1.26; 5.7).[64] Jesus dies giving up the Spirit (ἐξέπνευσεν, 15.37) in order that the new creation may begin.

But the crucifixion of Jesus is also a time of revelation which signifies the in-breaking of the kingdom of God. A further apocalyptic sign is the tearing of the Temple veil (ἐσχίσθη, 15.38), which recalls the tearing of the heavens at the baptism of Jesus (σχιζομένους, 1.10). Brown notes that it is difficult to determine whether Mark refers to the inner veil separating the Holy of Holies or to the outer

---

62. F.W. Danker, 'The Demonic Secret in Mark: A Reexamination of the Cry of Dereliction (15.34)', *ZNW* 51 (1970), 60.

63. D.C. Allison, *The End of the Ages has Come: An Early Interpretation of the Passion and Resurrection of Jesus* (Philadelphia: Fortress Press, 1985), 29.

64. Danker, 'Demonic Secret', 52.

Temple veil.[65] Although Mark's audience may not be aware of the distinctions between the veils, Matera rightly points out that the term καταπέτασμα is used more frequently to refer to the inner veil.[66] The tearing of the Temple veil thus signifies the destruction of the boundary between the holy and the profane. Brown, however, primarily interprets the tearing of the Temple veil as a sign of the wrath of God (*T. Levi* 10.3; *Gos. Pet.* 5.20; 7.25; 8.20).[67] On the other hand, as Daube suggests, the tearing of the Temple veil also points to the grief of God, and he cites the example of Elisha who tears his robes at the departure of Elijah (2 Kgs 2.12).[68] His interpretation points to the suffering experienced by God at the death of Jesus.

In the apocalyptic context of the Gospel the tearing of the Temple veil indicates the destruction of the old age and the beginning of the new creation. According to Josephus the Temple veil depicted four colours representing the four elements which portray the universe (*War* 5.212–15). Levenson notes that the Temple may be viewed as a microcosm of the world (Ps. 78.69) and that the world may be portrayed as a Temple (Isa. 66.1–2).[69] The Temple is described at the centre of the world in *Jub.* 8.19 in which the Holy of Holies is believed to be situated in the garden of Eden. In this way the tearing of the Temple veil may symbolize the tearing apart of the old creation.

The tearing of the Temple veil (ἐσχίσθη, 15.38), moreover, is also reminiscent of the tearing of the heavens at the baptism of Jesus (σχιζομένους, 1.10). As Motyer observes, the tearing of the Temple veil from top to bottom (ἀπ᾽ ἄνωθεν ἕως κάτω, 15.38) recalls the descent of the Spirit upon Jesus (1.9–11).[70] He suggests that the end of the Gospel may be regarded as a 'Markan Pentecost'. Although there is no direct reference to the gift of the Spirit, Motyer rightly notes that John the Baptist prophesies that Jesus will baptize in the Holy Spirit (1.8). The violent action of tearing signifies the inbreaking of the power of God, and the radical disjuncture of the new age from the old age. God's presence moves out from the Holy of Holies, bringing new power into the world.

The blindness and misunderstanding caused by the power of evil begins to disperse and the Roman centurion is the first human being to recognize Jesus as the Son of God (15.39).[71] Now the courage and the faithfulness of the women is depicted for the first time. They have kept watch despite the apparent failure of Jesus' mission and despite the dangers of arrest. Even though they stand at a distance, their refusal to break their relationship with him is an indication of their resistance to the forces of evil and death. Women are associated with perseverance

65. Brown, *Death of the Messiah*, 2.1112–13.

66. Matera (*Kingship*, 138) argues that Mark refers to the inner veil as he points out that in the Septuagint καταπέτασμα is used in connection with both veils, whereas κάλυμμα is used only in reference to the outer veil. Although Josephus employs the term καταπέτασμα for both veils, Matera notes that καταπέτασμα refers to the inner veil in Heb. 6.19 and 9.3. As Matera proposes, the linguistic evidence suggests that it is more probable that Mark refers to the inner veil.

67. Brown, *Death of the Messiah*, 2.1101.

68. Daube, *Rabbinic Judaism*, 23–26.

69. Levenson, *Sinai and Zion*, 78–99; 137–45.

70. S. Motyer, 'The Rending of the Veil: A Markan Pentecost?', *NTS* 33 (1987), 155–57.

71. Marcus, 'Epistemology', 571.

and courage in the face of persecution and death. The act of watching, moreover, is evidence of an eschatological hope for a reality that is different from the present suffering.

The women are powerless to intervene in the events which are taking place, but they do have the strength to stand with Jesus at the time of his death. As Grey points out, remaining with Jesus is the only action possible for the women.[72] She defines their strength as a relational power which corresponds to the hidden power of God, which is also present with Jesus. At the crucifixion, God's presence is concealed from Jesus, but he is present in the midst of human powerlessness through the unseen women. Although the presence of the women is hidden from Jesus, their desire to remain with him will lead them to the empty tomb where they will be the first to receive the news of the resurrection.

After the tearing of the Temple veil Mark refers to the confession of the Gentile centurion (15.39) and the presence of the women (15.40–41). The Temple had a series of boundaries separating the Holy of Holies, the court of women and the court of the Gentiles (cf. Philo, *Embassy* 212; Josephus, *Apion* 2.103–4; *Ant.* 15.417–19; *War* 5.193–200). With the tearing of the Temple veil, God's presence moves outwards through the world, crossing these boundaries. Women and Gentiles were two groups excluded from the circle of twelve male disciples. But now representatives from these two marginal groups are the only ones present at the crucifixion, and the Roman centurion's confession (15.39) points forward to the future faith of the Gentiles. In the context of Mark's apocalyptic world-view the death of Jesus is a turning point between the old and the new age. In the new creation the religious and social barriers between Jews and Gentiles, and between men and women are broken. The male disciples, however, are not replaced by the Gentiles and the women. In the next chapter the women will receive the task of passing on to them the news of the resurrection (16.7) so that in the period between the resurrection and the parousia, they may undertake a mission to all nations (13.10). In the new age Mark points forward to an inclusive community which consists of Jews and Gentiles, women and men.

8. *Conclusion*

The women remain loyal to Jesus when the male disciples have fled. In our passage they have the role of witnesses to the crucifixion and burial of Jesus. They are the only followers of Jesus who can testify that Jesus was buried and rose from death, and the proclamation of the gospel depends upon their witness. The women, moreover, are the only witnesses of the events of the Passion Narrative who have also been present during Jesus' mission in Galilee and on his journey to Jerusalem. At the crucifixion the women stand at a distance, afraid to intervene, but their act of keeping watch is itself a sign of resistance to the power of evil. They are the disciples who have been with Jesus and who remain faithful to him even when his mission appears to have failed.

72. M. Grey, *Redeeming the Dream: Feminism, Redemption and Christian Tradition* (London: SPCK, 1989), 100–101.

Chapter 11

THE WOMEN AT THE TOMB (16.1–8)

1. Introduction

Early in the morning, three of the women who have followed Jesus from Galilee to Jerusalem go to his tomb to anoint his body. Their names, Mary Magdalene, Mary the mother of James, and Salome (16.1), remind us that the same women are listed among the witnesses of the crucifixion (15.40), and two of them have been present at the burial of Jesus (15.47). These women have been portrayed as witnesses of the events of the Passion Narrative, and in our passage this role continues with their visit to the tomb. When the women reach the tomb, however, they find that Jesus' body is missing. In Mark there is no reunion of Jesus with his followers.[1] There is only an empty tomb and a stranger's message. Jesus has gone ahead of his disciples into Galilee as he told them (14.28; 16.7).

The women are portrayed more courageously than the male disciples, since they remain faithful to Jesus at his crucifixion and burial, and they are the first of his followers to hear the news of the resurrection. The favourable portrayal of individual women (5.21–43; 7.24–30; 12.41–44; 14.3–9) and the courage of these women lead us to expect a positive conclusion to their visit to the tomb, but the Gospel ends with their terror and silence. Some commentators, such as Catchpole, interpret the

---

1. For an analysis of the manuscript evidence concerning the endings of Mark, see B.M. Metzger, *A Textual Commentary on the Greek New Testament* (London: United Bible Societies, 1975), 122–26. Metzger notes that the longer ending, 16.9–20, is not present in the two oldest Greek manuscripts (ℵ and B), the Old Latin codex Bobiensis (it^k) and the Sinaitic Syriac manuscript. He points out that Clement of Alexandria and Origen have no knowledge of this ending, and Eusebius and Jerome state that the passage is not included in almost all the Greek manuscripts known to them. The longer ending is present in A, C, D, K, W, X, Δ, Θ, Π, *et al.*, and it is attested by Irenaeus and the Diatessaron. Metzger, moreover, observes that the vocabulary and style of 16.9–20 do not appear to be Markan (e.g. ἀπιστέω, βλάπτω, βεβαιόω, ἐπακολουθέω, θεάομαι, μετὰ ταῦτα, πορεύομαι, συνεργέω, ὕστερον), and there is an awkward transition between verse 8 and verse 9, since the women are the subjects of verse 8, whereas Jesus is the subject of verse 9. In addition to Metzger's points, Matthew and Luke appear to follow Mark only as far as verse 8, and the subject matter of 16.8–20 may derive from the other Gospels (e.g. Jesus appears to Mary Magdalene in Jn 20.11–18 and Mk 16.12–13 is reminiscent of the account of the journey to Emmaus in Lk. 24.13–35).

Metzger notes that the additional shorter ending appears in some manuscripts after verse 8 (L, Ψ, 099, 0112 *et al.*). All these manuscripts then continue with 16.9–20 with the exception of one Latin ms (it^k). This ending appears to be a later addition, since it contradicts 16.8 by beginning with a report of the women to Peter and the disciples.

women's fear as religious awe, arguing that their initial fearful response does not prevent them from following Jesus.[2] The women, however, disobey the instructions of the young man; they flee from the tomb, terrified to tell anyone about the resurrection (16.8).

The unexpected conclusion to Mark's Gospel has given rise to contrasting interpretations of Mark's purposes. Weeden argues that the women do not pass on the news of the resurrection to the Twelve.[3] He interprets the ending of the Gospel as part of Mark's intention to discredit the Twelve, whom he associates with the Jerusalem church. Munro develops Weeden's interpretation by proposing that the women are also linked to the leadership of the Jerusalem church.[4] Mark, however, particularly associates the women with Galilee in 15.40–41, and he gives no indication that they are aligned with a Jerusalem faction. He also does not present any alternative group to the Twelve and the women who could continue Jesus' mission.

Mark's ending, moreover, may be interpreted in the context of his apocalyptic world-view. At the end of the Gospel the women are overwhelmed by the news of the resurrection, which points to the mystery and transcendence of God. Their fear and silence is an indication of the gulf between God and humanity. Jesus redeems human beings and inaugurates the new age through his death on the cross. The women, however, remain aligned to the old age, unable to respond to the power of the new age. Mark's community live in the period between the resurrection and the parousia, a time of increasing evil as the old age is finally torn apart. Those who proclaim the gospel will encounter opposition and persecution (13.9–13). Women and men are called to continue Jesus' mission to all the nations (13.10), but they can only do so by following Jesus on the way of the cross.

2. *The Portrayal of the Women*

The three women who visit the tomb are named as Mary Magdalene, Mary the mother of James, and Salome (16.1). All three of these women have been among the witnesses of the crucifixion of Jesus (15.40) and two of them, Mary Magdalene and Mary the mother of James, were present at his burial (15.47). The naming of the women stresses their importance as witnesses of the resurrection. The women are the only followers of Jesus who can testify to his death, burial and resurrection. According to the Old Testament two witnesses are required in order to give a valid testimony (Deut. 19.15). Mary Magdalene and the other Mary are present at each event, and Salome is mentioned at the crucifixion and at the tomb. Women, moreover, are key witnesses of the resurrection in all the Gospel accounts (Mt. 28.1–10; Lk. 24.1–11; Jn 20.11–18). Mary Magdalene has the most prominent role in each Gospel, and her name is always listed first, indicating her significance as a witness of the resurrection (cf. Mt. 28.1; Lk. 24.10; Jn 20.1–18). Some scholars, however,

---

2.   D. Catchpole, 'The Fearful Silence of the Women at the Tomb: A Study in Markan Theology', *JTSA* 18 (1977), 6–10.

3.   T.J. Weeden, *Mark: Traditions in Conflict* (Philadelphia: Fortress Press, 1971), 50.

4.   Munro, 'Women Disciples', 238–39.

such as Swidler, propose that the witness of the women was rejected by the male disciples because the testimony of women was not considered valid.[5] Paul, moreover, records the witness of Peter and the Twelve, but not that of these women (1 Cor. 15.3–5). On the other hand Ilan argues the witness of the women in the Gospels is not portrayed in the context of the courtroom.[6] Ilan also points out that there were occasions in which the witness of women was accepted. Although the extent to which Mishnaic law applied in New Testament times is uncertain, Wegner notes that there are passages in the Mishnah which accept the validity of the testimony of women.[7]

In the Gospels women are presented as witnesses of Jesus' death and resurrection thus bringing continuity to the proclamation of the early church. Setzer, however, argues that the evangelists have an ambivalent attitude to the testimony of women.[8] Mark, for example, ends with the failure of the women to pass on the news of the resurrection (16.8). The doubtful status of the witness of the women is also suggested in Luke, since the message of the women is ignored by some of the men (24.11). Setzer notes that Celsus dismisses the reports of the resurrection because they are based on the witness of a 'hysterical woman' (Origen, *Cels.* 2.55), and she thus proposes that the Gospel writers are also concerned that the witness of women may be disregarded because women were regarded as susceptible to superstition and religious influence (cf. Lucian, *Peregr.* 12.341; Minucius Felix, *Oct.* 8.3–5). MacDonald, however, points out that Celsus' criticism of Mary Magdalene itself indicates the strength of her influence upon early Christianity.[9] Mark, moreover, does not suggest that others doubt the testimony of the women, and the texts referring to the vulnerability of women to religious conversion date from a later period than the Gospels.

---

5.   Swidler, *Biblical Affirmations*, 200–201.

6.   Ilan, (*Jewish Women*, 163–66) notes that Josephus records that women were not qualified as witnesses (*Ant.* 4.219). She observes that the law disqualifying women as witnesses was formulated as a halakhic principle, but there were exceptions such as the testimony of a woman to the death of someone's husband so that a widow might remarry (*m. Yebam.* 16.5; *b. Bek.* 46b). Although there is a Qumran text which refers to the testimony of women (1QSa 1.11), this passage remains ambiguous, since Baumgarten argues that the use of the feminine pronoun is a textual error (J. M Baumgarten, 'On the Testimony of Women in 1QSa', *JBL* 76 [1957], 266–69). Ilan, however, points out that Herod's sister, Salome, acted as judge in the trial of Herod and Mariamme's two sons (Josephus, *J.W.* 1.538), and she also testified against Antipater (Josephus, *Ant.* 17.93).

7.   Wegner (*Chattel or Person?* 120–27) notes that although the Mishnah does not explicitly exclude the testimony of women, the Law listing incompetent witnesses does not include women because it assumes women do not act as witnesses (*m. Sanh.* 3.3–4). The Law concerning an oath of testimony (Lev 5.1), moreover, is applied to men, but not to women (*m. Šebu.* 4.1). Wegner, however, lists exceptions to this rule. A woman could give evidence in cases relating to virginity (*m. Ketub.* 1.6–7; 2.5–6), and a woman could also act as a witness to a man's death (*m. Yebam.* 15.1–2; 16.7). Finally, a woman who had been given charge of another person's property may be required to take an oath of deposit to testify that she has not embezzled any goods (*m. Šebu.* 5.1; 6.1; 7.8).

8.   C. Setzer, 'Excellent Women: Female Witness to the Resurrection', *JBL* 116 (1997), 259–72.

9.   M.Y. MacDonald, *Early Christian Women and Pagan Opinion: The Power of the Hysterical Woman* (Cambridge: Cambridge University Press, 1996), 250.

The women are the last remaining followers of Jesus, and they are the only ones to visit the tomb. The absence of the male disciples at the death of Jesus contrasts with the account of the execution of John the Baptist (6.14–29), since John's disciples request John's body from Herod and they arrange his burial. In Mark, the women visit the tomb with the specific purpose of anointing Jesus (16.1). The women wait until the Sabbath has passed before making their preparations. As the Sabbath ends at sunset, they may buy their spices in the evening and then wait until morning before going to the tomb. The women are depicted as law-observant, and they act in a manner similar to that of Joseph of Arimathea, who was concerned to bury Jesus before the Sabbath began (15.42–43). In chapter 15 Joseph took charge of the arrangements for Jesus' burial, and the women were portrayed as onlookers rather than as active participants. Jesus was not anointed at the time of his burial, and the women may feel that he has not been given a proper leavetaking.

The anointing of the dead is a last act of intimacy, carried out by those closest to the dead person (Ezek. 16.9; 2 Chron. 16.14; Josephus, *Ant.* 16.61). The act of anointing, moreover, is associated with touch, which recalls earlier narratives featuring women. The woman with the flow of blood reveals her faith by reaching out to touch Jesus' garment (5.24–34), and the woman who anoints Jesus expresses her love for him through her costly gift (14.3–9). The literary style of Mark is restrained, and emotions are indicated through the actions of human beings. Gnilka argues that the practice of anointing at death was primarily associated with the preservation of the body, and therefore the intention of the women in our passage is foolish.[10] As Schottroff points out, however, the women may not intend to embalm Jesus, since the use of the verb ἀλείφω could indicate a wish to sprinkle oil on his head or feet.[11] The practice of anointing is intended to give honour to the dead, and has connotations of worship. In Jewish tradition, moreover, angels anoint Adam before his burial (*L.A.E.* 40.2) and Abraham at the time of his death (*T. Ab.* 20.11). It is possible that these traditions may suggest a link between the action of the women in our passage and the description of the angels who serve Jesus in the desert (1.13).

The desire of the women to anoint Jesus recalls the account of the anonymous woman who anointed Jesus in Bethany (14.3–9). The woman who anointed Jesus was portrayed as a prophetic figure, since her action pointed to the identity of Jesus as the Messiah and king. Jesus interpreted her gift as preparation for his burial, and he is revealed as king at his crucifixion. As Lincoln observes, accounts which feature women and anointing frame the Passion Narrative.[12] The two acts of anointing point to the death and resurrection of Jesus. This structure recalls the two accounts of women who serve Jesus, since these narratives are located at the start and the end of Jesus' mission (1.31; 15.41). These two references to the service of the women are linked with Jesus' service in giving his life as a ransom for many (10.45). The service of the women contrasts with the plots of powerful men, who seek to put

10. Gnilka, *Evangelium*, 2.340.
11. Schottroff, *Let the Oppressed*, 181.
12. A. Lincoln, 'The Promise and the Failure – Mark 16.7, 8', *JBL* 108 (1989), 288.

Jesus to death. In the midst of betrayal and violence women bring gifts to Jesus and show their care of him. Through their desire to anoint Jesus, the women seek to align themselves with him, expressing their identification with him in his suffering and death.

The woman who anointed Jesus at the beginning of the Passion Narrative made an extravagant gift ahead of time, whereas the women at the tomb take their gift to Jesus after his death. There is a sense of poignancy because the women who have been part of Jesus' followers have been thwarted in their last leavetaking of him. Instead, an unknown woman has made the gift to Jesus which they wish to make. These women arrive too late, but not because death has won: Jesus has gone on ahead of them heralding the new creation.

3. *Discipleship*

The three women who go to the tomb are followers of Jesus who have served him in Galilee and accompanied him to Jerusalem (15.41). These women, therefore, are part of the group of disciples who have been with him throughout his mission. They have shown courage by their presence at the crucifixion, and they again risk arrest by visiting the tomb to anoint Jesus (16.1). The role of the women as witnesses, moreover, suggests their powerlessness in the midst of the events of the Passion Narrative. The religious leaders and the political authorities who condemn Jesus to death are all male, as are the soldiers who execute him. In chapter 15 Joseph is the one who makes the request for Jesus' body from Pilate, and the women were on-lookers at Jesus' burial (15.47). The powerlessness of the women is further indicated by their inability to move the large stone from the entrance to the tomb (16.3).

In our passage, however, the women emerge as the central figures among Jesus' followers, and they take initiative in going to the tomb. Nevertheless the women do not expect to discover that Jesus has been raised from the dead. Tolbert, therefore, takes a negative view of the women's plan, since she suggests that the women should expect the resurrection of Jesus because they have heard his passion predictions (8.31; 9.31; 10.33–34).[13] Although the women have accompanied Jesus from Galilee to Jerusalem, Mark does not directly record that they have heard the passion predictions. They may be part of the group who hear the first two predictions (8.31; 9.31), but the third and most detailed passion prediction is addressed to the Twelve alone (10.32–34). There is thus no indication that the women are aware of Jesus' predictions of his resurrection. The women are portrayed positively in that they remain loyal to Jesus even after the apparent failure of his mission, and they desire to ensure that he is given a dignified burial.

Mark, moreover, implies that the women are right to go to the tomb, because they discover that the stone has been mysteriously rolled away and that a young man is waiting for them in order to give them the message of Jesus' resurrection. Mark's account contrasts with Matthew's in which the women arrive at the tomb, and only then does the angel appear and open the tomb (Mt. 28.2). In Mark, the young man

---

13. Tolbert, *Sowing*, 294.

appears to expect the arrival of the women, and the women have the role of witnesses. In chapter 15 they have been portrayed in terms of verbs associated with sight (θεωροῦσαι, 15.40; ἐθεώρουν, 15.47). This portrayal continues in our passage in the description of the women (ἀναβλέψασαι θεωροῦσιν, 16.4; εἶδον, 16.5) and in the command of the young man, ἴδε (16.6).

The women, however, do not understand the full significance of the events they have witnessed. The women seek Jesus, but seek him in the wrong place. Lightfoot notes the negative connotations of the verb ζητέω (to seek) in Mark (14.1, 11).[14] This verb is used in association with the plots of Jesus' enemies (ἐζήτει πῶς αὐτὸν εὐκαίρως παραδοῖ, 14.11). It also recalls the conclusion of the first day of Jesus' mission, when Peter tells Jesus that everyone is looking for him (πάντες ζητοῦσίν σε, 1.37). Despite this appeal, the urgency of Jesus' mission compels him to move onwards to neighbouring towns and villages (1.38). In our passage the women also seek Jesus, but he has gone on ahead of them (16.7).

Mark does not describe the resurrection of Jesus but focuses on the women's reaction to the young man's message. The young man acts as a mediatory figure sent from the heavenly realm. The term νεανίσκος (young man, 16.5) could refer to any young man, but also occurs in descriptions of angels (see for example 2 Macc. 3.26, 33 and Josephus *Ant.* 5.277). The supernatural appearance of the man is indicated by the reference to his white clothes (cf. 9.3; Rev 7.9, 13–14). The young man is described as sitting on the right (καθήμενον ἐν τοῖς δεξιοῖς, 16.5). Unlike Jn 20.6–7, Mark does not record the presence of Jesus' grave clothes. Mark's portrayal is puzzling since the tomb is empty; the young man, then, appears to sit on the right of Jesus' missing body. The place on the right is associated with the place of honour, and it recalls the prophecy of Jesus at his trial that the Son of Man will appear sitting on the right hand of power (ἐκ δεξιῶν καθήμενον τῆς δυνάμεως, 14.62). In Mk 16.5, the young man sits to the right of an empty space that is evidence of the power of God, who has raised Jesus from the dead. Jesus has been raised (16.6) and the tomb is empty. Paradoxically, then, absence is a sign of presence.

The women react with amazement and terror to the news of the resurrection. Some scholars view the fear of the women positively; Lane, for example, argues that the fear of the women expresses their religious awe.[15] The response of the women is described as ἐξεθαμβήθησαν (16.5). This verb has strong connotations of amazement and terror. The same verb is used to depict the reaction of the crowd to Jesus when he descends the mountain after the transfiguration (9.15) and to describe the agony of Jesus in Gethsemane as he struggles to follow the will of God (ἤρξατο ἐκθαμβεῖσθαι, 14.33). The women's response of amazement and fear indicates that an occurrence has taken place which is outwith the normal course of life.

The women, however, leave the tomb, trembling and astonished (εἶχεν γὰρ αὐτὰς τρόμος καὶ ἔκστασις, 16.8). As Sabin points out, this construction is

14. R.H. Lightfoot, *The Gospel Message of St. Mark* (Oxford: Clarendon Press, 1950), 23–24.
15. Lane, *Mark*, 591.

reminiscent of the portrayal of the boy who is possessed by a deaf and mute spirit (ἔχοντα πνεῦμα ἄλαλον, 9.17).[16] The women, therefore, appear to be possessed by fear. The term ἔκστασις (amazement), moreover, recalls the description of the amazement of the witnesses at the raising of Jairus' daughter (ἐξέστησαν ἐκστάσει μεγάλῃ, 5.42). The reaction of these witnesses thus points forward to the response of the women to Jesus' resurrection. The description ἔκστασις also has connotations associated with new creation. As Riches notes, this term occurs in the account of the trance of Adam when Eve is created (Gen. 2.21 LXX) and of the trance of Abraham in which he hears of the future slavery and redemption of the Israelites in Egypt (Gen. 15.12 LXX).[17] In these examples the amazement of human beings points to God's creative and redemptive power.

Catchpole, similarly, interprets the fear of the women as a response to the manifestation of God's power.[18] He compares the description of the women to accounts in the Old Testament, later Jewish writings and the New Testament in which human beings experience the revelation of God. He observes that the description φόβος καὶ τρόμος (fear and trembling) is associated with the manifestation of the power of God (Job 4.12–16; Gen. 4.12–16; 28.17; Ps. 2.11; *'Abot R. Nat.* 1; 6; 1 Cor. 2.3; Phil. 2.12). Catchpole thus asserts that fear and silence belong to the structure of epiphany. Other scholars, however, are critical of the fear of the women. Danove, for example, argues that the verb φοβέομαι has negative connotations in Mark and he notes that the fear of the disciples reflects their lack of faith (4.41; 6.50), and the Gerasenes' fear leads them to ask Jesus to leave their district (5.17).[19]

The interpretation of the fear of the women, moreover, depends upon whether or not they communicate the news of Jesus' resurrection. Some scholars, such as Selvidge, compare the women to those who accompany Jesus to Jerusalem despite their fear (οἱ δὲ ἀκολουθοῦντες ἐφοβοῦντο, 10.32), and she argues that their fear does not prevent them from passing on the message.[20] In addition, Catchpole notes that there is a verbal similarity between the ending of Mark which states that the women 'said nothing to anyone' (οὐδενὶ οὐδὲν εἶπαν, 16.8), and the command to the former leper to tell no one of his healing (ὅρα μηδενὶ μηδὲν εἴπῃς, 1.44).[21] He points out that there is an exception to the command to silence to the healed leper, since Jesus must intend the man to speak to a priest in order to bear witness to his cure. In the same way, he argues there is an exception to the silence of the women: they tell no one *apart from* the disciples and Peter.

This interpretation, however, is unconvincing, since at the end of the Gospel Mark states that the women run away from the tomb instead of following Jesus to Galilee (16.8). Although the fear of the women points to the transcendence of God,

16. Sabin, 'Women Transformed', 163.

17. J.K. Riches, *Conflicting Mythologies. Identity Formation in the Gospels of Mark and Matthew* (Edinburgh: T. & T. Clark, 2000), 173.

18. Catchpole, 'Fearful Silence', 7–8.

19. P. Danove, 'The Characterization and Narrative Function of the Women at the Tomb (Mark 15, 40-41. 47; 16, 1-8)', *Bib* 77 (1996), 391–92.

20. Selvidge, 'Those who Followed', 399–400.

21. Catchpole, 'Fearful Silence', 6–7.

Mark places a negative evaluation on their response by adding 16.7, which implies that the fear of the women leads them to disobey a divine command. The Gospel ends abruptly with the phrase 'for they were afraid' (ἐφοβοῦντο γάρ, 16.8). We are told that the women do not pass on the message because they are afraid, but we are not told the reason for their fear.

Some scholars argue that the women are afraid to speak openly because of the social conventions of the time, which prohibited women from public speech. Cotes, for example, interprets the silence of the women in the context of the association of men with public speech and of women with silence in the ancient world.[22] She asserts that the commands to silence are always given to men, for example, the leper (1.44), the blind man (8.26) and the disciples after the transfiguration (9.9), whereas there is no command to silence in the account of the healing of Peter's mother-in-law (1.29–31), the woman with the flow of blood (5.24–34) or the Syro-phoenician woman's daughter (7.24–30). According to Cotes no command to silence is necessary for women, since they were expected to be silent. This distinction, however, does not fully apply to Mark's Gospel. In the account of the raising of Jairus' daughter, there is a command to silence given to those present who include the girl's mother (5.40–43). Furthermore, women are associated with public speech in the account of the healing of the woman with the flow of blood who speaks to Jesus before the crowd (5.33). There is also no indication in our passage that the fear of the women is on account of social conventions. These women, moreover, would have disregarded public conventions in their act of travelling with a group of men.

The commands to silence and to speech may be better examined in the context of the theology of the messianic secret. Throughout the Gospel human beings are commanded to keep silent about Jesus' identity (1.25, 34, 44; 3.12; 5.43; 7.36; 8.26; 9.9). At the end of the Gospel this situation is reversed when the women are asked to pass on the news of the resurrection. It is significant that the turning point in the revelation of Jesus' identity occurs at the resurrection. At the transfiguration Jesus instructs Peter, James and John to tell no one about the event they have just witnessed until the Son of Man has risen from death (9.9). Jesus is revealed as the Son of God at his death (15.39). Through the death and resurrection of Jesus the new age has begun. In our passage, therefore, the women are instructed to speak openly and to continue the proclamation of the gospel.

The women, therefore, disobey the command of the angel and run away terrified to tell anyone the news of the resurrection (ἔφυγον, 16.8). The use of the verb φεύγω (to flee) recalls the flight of those present at the arrest of Jesus (ἔφυγον, 14.50), including the mysterious young man (ἔφυγεν, 14.52). The women's fear is undefined and points to the mystery and transcendence of God. At the end of the Gospel they do not recognize the significance of Jesus' identity as Son of God, nor do they understand that his death and resurrection have inaugurated the new age.

22. M. Cotes, 'Women, Silence and Fear (Mark 16.8)', in G.J. Brooke (ed.), *Women in the Biblical Tradition* (Studies in Women and Religion, 31; Lewiston: Edwin Mellen Press, 1992), 150–66.

The Gospel closes with a sense of loss and compassion both for the women who are afraid to speak and for the male disciples who have not yet heard the news of the resurrection. We are also left with compassion for Jesus. His miracles reveal the abundant life he brings to human beings. He gives his life to redeem humanity (10.45). At the end of the Gospel he gives his life for those who fear to respond to him.

In the apocalyptic context of the Gospel, however, all human beings, both men and women, fail because they are linked to the old age of the world. The fear and silence of the women is an indication of the impassable gulf between God and human beings. This distance is overcome only by the action of God. The miracles of Jesus are thus signs of the kingdom of God breaking into the world. They are proleptic of the new age which comes about through the death and resurrection of Jesus. According to Donahue the experience of fear is a sign of the power of God 'to unsettle and change human existence'.[23] The fear of the women, however, reveals that they are still aligned to the old age. Jesus calls human beings to follow him on the way of the cross (8.35). The male disciples leave everything to follow him, but flee at his arrest (14.50). The women have followed him in Galilee and accompanied him to Jerusalem, but now they also run away (16.8).

The failure of the male and female disciples in the course of the Passion Narrative may be compared to the parable of the absent householder in which the servants are left in charge of the house (13.32–37). The servants are warned that the Lord may return at any time: in the evening, at midnight, at cock crow or in the morning (13.35). Lightfoot relates these times to the events of the Passion Narrative: the Last Supper in the evening, the arrest of Jesus towards midnight, the denial of Peter at cock crow and the morning consultation of the religious authorities to hand over Jesus to the Romans.[24] Although Lightfoot's first three examples describe the failures of the disciples, his last does not. It is possible, therefore, that the reference to morning (πρωΐ, 13.35) corresponds to the time of morning in our passage (πρωΐ, 16.2). In this way the women represent the disciples who flee at the last watch mentioned in the parable.

Jesus has prophesied that his followers will abandon him by predicting that when the shepherd is struck the sheep will be scattered (14.27). Without the presence of Jesus, human beings cannot remain faithful. The young man, however, offers the women and the disciples the opportunity of seeing Jesus again in Galilee (16.7; cf. 14.28). He repeats the promise Jesus made to his disciples that he would go before them into Galilee after he was raised. Jesus acts like a shepherd going before his people just as the angel of the Lord led the Israelites through the wilderness to the promised land (Exod. 14.19). The portrayal of Jesus as a shepherd who goes ahead of his followers, indeed, may be seen thoughout the Gospel: he goes ahead of them on the way to Jerusalem (10.32).

The young man asks the women to pass on the message of the resurrection to the disciples and Peter. Through him Jesus offers the opportunity of reconciliation to

23. J.R. Donahue, 'Jesus as the Parable of God in the Gospel of Mark', *Int* 32 (1978), 381.
24. Lightfoot, *Gospel Message*, 53.

the disciples who have abandoned him (14.50) and especially to Peter who has denied him three times (14.66–72). The women are thus given the role of reconstituting the followers of Jesus. Schottroff points out that the young man includes the women along with the male disciples in the prophecy that they will see Jesus in Galilee.[25] She notes that second person plural verbs are used in the speech of the young man 'go, tell, you will see' (ὑπάγετε, εἴπατε, ὄψεσθε, 16.7). If the women were only intended to pass on the message to the male disciples the message could have been written in indirect speech. It is significant, moreover, that there is no particular reference to the Twelve; the young man, rather, refers to the wider category of disciples (16.7). Judas has betrayed Jesus and his betrayal signifies the breakup of the circle of the Twelve. At the crucifixion of Jesus, moreover, a Gentile centurion (15.39) and the group of women have been the only ones present. The discipleship group is no longer primarily represented by twelve male disciples but is now open to Gentiles and women.

There is some debate amongst scholars as to the meaning of the young man's instruction. According to Lohmeyer, the young man refers to the parousia rather than resurrection appearances of Jesus, when he says 'there you will see him' (ἐκεῖ αὐτὸν ὄψεσθε, 16.7).[26] Lohmeyer argues that the verb ὄψομαι (to see) is used as a technical term referring to witnessing the parousia (13.26; 14.62). This verb, however, is used in connection with resurrection appearances in 1 Cor. 9.1 and Jn 20.18. As Gnilka notes, moreover, the parousia is never associated with the disciples and Peter alone, and in chapter 13 the parousia is not specifically linked to Galilee.[27]

Galilee, moreover, is surrounded by Gentile nations, and is associated with the Gentiles (Isa. 9.1; cf. Mt. 4.15). This location is thus a good starting place for the Gentile mission (13.10). Evans proposes that the verb προάγω (14.28; 16.7) has the meaning 'to lead' (cf. Prov. 4.27; 2 Macc. 10.1; Judith 10.22).[28] The identification of Jesus as a shepherd (14.27; Zech. 13.7) also portrays him in the role of leading his disciples. Jesus, therefore, intends to lead the disciples in the mission to the Gentiles.

There is, however, considerable tension between Galilee and Jerusalem in Mark's Gospel. Freyne associates Jesus' successful mission with Galilee, whereas his opponents, the scribes, are from Jerusalem, and he is put to death in Jerusalem.[29] Likewise the failure of his disciples occurs in Jerusalem, and their place of restoration is Galilee. On the other hand Stemberger points out that the opposition between Galilee and Jerusalem is not as clear-cut as Freyne suggests.[30] Jesus has a triumphant entry into Jerusalem, and he is proclaimed King of the Jews and Son of God in

---

25. Schottroff, *Let the Oppressed*, 186.

26. Lohmeyer, *Evangelium*, 355–56.

27. Gnilka, *Evangelium*, 2.343.

28. C.F. Evans, 'I will go before you into Galilee', *JTS* 5 (1954), 3–18.

29. S. Freyne, *Galilee, Jesus and the Gospels. Literary Approaches and Historical Investigations* (Dublin: Gill & Macmillan, 1988), 33–68.

30. G. Stemberger, 'Appendix IV Galilee – Land of Salvation?' in W.D. Davies, *The Gospel and the Land: Early Christianity and Jewish Territorial Doctrine* (Berkley: University of California Press, 1974), 409–38.

Jerusalem (15.39). There is, moreover, opposition to Jesus in Galilee, since the people of his hometown reject him (6.1–6a).

Freyne's analysis highlights the contrasts between Galilee and Jerusalem, and his study leaves these opposites intact at the end of the narrative. Malbon, however, examines Markan space from a narrative perspective adapted from the structuralist methodology of Levi-Strauss.[31] She interprets Markan space in terms of a series of opposites such as Jewish homeland and foreign lands, Galilee and Judea, and the environs of Jerusalem and Jerusalem proper. At the end of the Gospel, as Malbon argues, there is a residual tension, since these opposites have not been successfully mediated, and Jesus himself is in movement from Jerusalem to Galilee (16.7).[32] Malbon's analysis points to the portrayal of Jesus as someone who is constantly engaged in mission (1.38; 4.35; 7.24; 7.31; 10.32). Jesus crosses boundaries, going ahead of his followers. At the end of the Gospel the mission of Jesus continues, and will do so until the parousia.

The disciples are instructed to go back to Galilee to take up Jesus' mission again. Galilee is associated with the starting place of Jesus' mission (1.14). The male disciples were called in Galilee (1.16–20), and the Twelve were appointed there (3.13–19). The women, moreover, are described as following and serving in Galilee (15.41). Galilee was the base of Jesus' mission, since he repeatedly returned there after his journeys to Gentile lands (5.21; 8.22; 9.30). In this way the instruction to return to Galilee is a call to return to the beginning of the mission and to set out on it again.

The disciples, then, will only understand the true significance of Jesus' identity by resuming their mission and following him to Galilee. The verb ὄψομαι 'to see', moreover, has the deeper meaning of 'to understand' (4.10–12). The death and resurrection of Jesus may only be understood by those who follow the way of the cross (8.34). Mark emphasizes that following Jesus involves facing persecution and death, and only those willing to lose their lives will save them (8.35). The reference to the cross is not depicted as voluntary suffering, but as the suffering which comes about as a result of those who oppose the gospel. Women and men are both called to return to Galilee to continue Jesus' mission. The followers of Jesus will be persecuted and some will even be handed over to death (13.9–13). The conclusion of Mark's Gospel takes seriously the dangers which the community face in the period before the parousia.

Throughout the Gospel Mark focuses on the twelve male disciples. They are chosen to be with Jesus in order to be with him, to be sent out to proclaim the gospel and to cast out demons (3.13–19). They are continually present with Jesus and they carry out their own successful mission (6.6b–13). When threatened with persecution on account of their allegiance to Jesus, they run away (14.50) and Peter, the leading disciple, denies Jesus (14.66–72). In contrast to the Twelve, the women are not sent out by Jesus on a mission. Unlike the male disciples, they remain faithful to Jesus at the time of his suffering. At the tomb, however, they are entrusted with

---

31. Malbon, *Narrative Space*, 2.
32. Malbon, *Narrative Space*, 168.

the task of continuing the proclamation of the gospel. When faced with the prospect of proclaiming the gospel and renewing Jesus' mission they are also terrified
and run away (16.8).

4. *The Ending of Mark*

Scholars have searched for the purpose behind Mark's bleak ending with the terror
and silence of the women. Munro takes a historical approach and argues that the
failure of the women to pass on the news of the resurrection to the disciples reflects
Mark's desire to criticize the Jerusalem church.[33] She believes that the disciples
represent the leaders of the Jerusalem church and the women are also members of
their group. The women, however, have been portrayed positively by their presence
as witnesses of the crucifixion and burial of Jesus, and they fail only at the news of
the resurrection. Feminist commentators, such as Kinukawa, suggest that Mark
downplays the role of the women in order not to offend the men in his audience,
who would not wish to be considered less favourably than the women.[34] Mark,
however, could have included the restoration of the male disciples as Matthew
(28.16–20) and Luke (24.36–53) did.

The women are portrayed more favourably than the male disciples in the Passion
Narrative, but in our passage they fail by running away because of their fear
(ἐφοβοῦντο γάρ, 16.8). Boomershine and Bartholomew note Mark's characteristic
use of γάρ (for, because) to explain unusual events, and they point out that on two
occasions γάρ is employed to raise new questions (6.52; 14.2).[35] Similarly, in our
passage the explanation that the women say nothing to anyone 'for they were
afraid' leaves unanswered questions with Mark's audience. Tolbert argues that
Mark's audience has no positive model of discipleship to follow.[36] She suggests
that the ending of Mark functions as a literary device that encourages the audience
to resume Jesus' mission and follow on the way of the cross. Mark leaves each
reader with a personal decision as to whether or not to tell the message to others.
On the other hand Mitchell interprets the fear of the women as 'religious awe' and
she proposes that Mark intends to lead his audience to the 'threshold of faith'.[37]
She argues that Mark is written at a time when the first generation of eyewitnesses
to the mission of Jesus have died or suffered martyrdom. Mark presents the failures
of the first disciples as a means of encouraging the next generation to take their
places and to continue the proclamation of the gospel.

Mark's ending, however, may reflect his theological purposes. Lindemann notes
that Mark does not include any accounts of the resurrection but the passion predictions, 14.28 and 16.7 indicate that he is aware of the tradition of resurrection

---

33. Munro, 'Women Disciples', 238–39.
34. Kinukawa, *Women*, 121.
35. T.E. Boomershine and G.L. Bartholomew, 'The Narrative Technique of Mark 16.8' (*JBL*
100 [1981], 215) record Mark's frequent use of γάρ as in 1.16, 22; 2.15; 3.21; 5.8, 28, 42; 6.17,
18, 20, 31, 48; 9.6, 34; 10.22; 11.13; 14.2, 40, 56; 15.10; 16.4, 8.
36. Tolbert, *Sowing*, 295–99.
37. Mitchell, *Beyond Fear and Silence*, 96.

appearances.[38] He argues that Mark focuses on Jesus as the suffering Messiah, since the young man at the tomb refers to Jesus as the crucified one (16.6). The resurrection thus does not erase Jesus' suffering and death. In Mark the only evidence of the resurrection is the missing body, and the resurrection is known through the loss and the absence of Jesus. As Drury observes, the lack of resolution at the end of the Gospel points forward to future events which take place outside of the literary context of the narrative.[39] In chapter 13 Jesus prophesies that he will return and the world will come to an end.

The death and resurrection of Jesus signify the beginning of the new creation which will only be fully realized at the parousia. Mark's audience live in the time between the resurrection and the parousia and during this period human beings are called to follow Jesus on the way of the cross. Mark does not downplay the fear that disciples may encounter, since he stresses that Jesus also experiences terror when faced with death. In Gethsemane, the fear of Jesus is emphasized (ἤρξατο ἐκθαμβεῖσθαι), and he prays to avoid suffering and death (14.32–42). Jesus' grief is described in his prayer (Περίλυπός ἐστιν ἡ ψυχή μου ἕως θανάτου, 14.34). The account of the terror of Jesus as he prepares to give his life encourages us to have sympathy towards the fear of the women. Even Jesus, the Son of God, is terrified as he faces the onslaught of evil.

There is evidence within the text, however, which suggests that the news of the resurrection has been communicated by the women to the other disciples. Petersen points out that the prophecies of Jesus in chapter 13 take place before the events of the Passion Narrative. The disciples will continue the mission of Jesus until the parousia and these predictions thus reduce the effects of the disciples' failures.[40] Petersen's analysis, however, downplays the power of Mark's unexpected ending. Lincoln's interpretation is more convincing; he accepts that the Gospel ends with the fear of the women, but he contrasts human failure with the power of God to overcome fear with his promises.[41] Lincoln's interpretation points to God's initiative in seeking to redeem the world.

The power of God to overturn human failure is suggested by the existence of the Gospel account which implies that the women did in the end pass on the message. As Marcus observes, the male and female disciples are the only ones who have been with Jesus, listening to his teaching and witnessing his miracles.[42] They are, therefore, the only people who can communicate the events which we have heard in the Gospel. There are no other individuals who can bring continuity to Jesus' mission in the time between the resurrection and the parousia.

38. A. Lindemann, 'Die Osterbotschaft des Markus. Zur Theologischen Interpretation von Mark 16.1-8', *NTS* 26 (1980), 298–317.

39. J. Drury, 'Mark', in R. Alter and F. Kermode (eds.), *The Literary Guide to the Bible* (Cambridge, MA: Belknap Press of Harvard University Press, 1987), 410–11.

40. N.R. Petersen, 'When is the End not an End? Literary Reflections on the Ending of Mark's Narrative', *Int* 34 (1980), 166.

41. Lincoln, 'Mark 16.7, 8', 293.

42. Marcus, *Mystery*, 146.

Jesus, moreover, has prophesied the course of his disciples' future mission. In chapter 13 Jesus speaks of the events of the end-time, and his words are given the status of authoritative prophecy. The Gospel itself therefore points forward to a future time in which the disciples will be faithful. Jesus describes a period of increased suffering, such as has never been before, from the beginning of creation until the present (13.19). During this time the disciples will be brought to trial before Sanhedrins and governors and kings (13.9), but despite this opposition the purpose of the Markan community will be to continue the proclamation of the gospel throughout the world (13.10). The disciples are not to worry beforehand about what they should say, since the Holy Spirit will be given to them (13.11).

Mark's audience is encouraged to identify with the fear of the women. Their fear stresses the dangers of the mission in the context of a persecuted community. The terror of the women may reflect the fear of Mark's community, who are undergoing persecution on account of their faith (4.17; 10.30). Fander proposes that the lack of faith and the denials of the Twelve are temptations which face Mark's community.[43] Mark's Gospel ends with an account of the fear of the women because it takes seriously the dangers involved in continuing Jesus' mission. As we have seen, women have not been entrusted with the proclamation of the gospel, and they are now afraid because their turn has come to face persecution on account of the word.

The struggle between faith and fear is also seen in the account of the mission of the male disciples. On the first boat journey the disciples are criticized for their lack of faith (4.40), and after Jesus stills the storm they are very afraid (4.41). On the second journey they are described as terrified after Jesus enters the boat (6.50). Their fear is a sign of their inability to understand the miracles they have witnessed which point to Jesus' identity as Son of God. In our passage the fear of the women is also a sign of their misunderstanding of Jesus' identity and their inability to have faith in the power of the new age. The women and men will only understand Jesus by returning to Galilee and following Jesus on the way of the cross (16.7).

At the same time the audience is encouraged to look back over the Gospel to find hope to continue the mission. The women are described as being seized by trembling and astonishment (τρόμος καὶ ἔκστασις, 16.8). This description is reminiscent of the portrayal of the woman with the flow of blood who comes forward to tell Jesus what has happened to her despite her fear (φοβηθεῖσα καὶ τρέμουσα, 5.33). The woman's fear is described after she has been healed, and it is, therefore, a response to her experience of the power of Jesus. This woman gains the power to overcome her fear because she knows that she has been healed by Jesus (εἰδυῖα ὃ γέγονεν, 5.33). She comes forward to reveal what has happened to her, and Jesus praises her on account of her faith, 'Your faith has saved you' (ἡ πίστις σου σέσωκέν σε, 5.34).

The illness of this woman is described in terms which are associated with the way of the cross. As we have noted, the woman is described as having suffered many things (πολλὰ παθοῦσα, 5.26) and Jesus prophesies he will suffer many

---

43. Fander, *Stellung*, 175.

things (πολλὰ παθεῖν, 8.31; 9.12).[44] The woman's encounter with Jesus trans-forms her life, and her cure is associated with the blessing of the new age, as Jesus tells her to go in peace (5.34). The women at the tomb, similarly, are described as being seized by ἔκστασις (amazement, 16.8), and this term is also used in the account of the healing of Jairus' daughter. After the young girl is raised from death those present are described as 'greatly amazed' (ἐξέστησαν ἐκστάσει μεγάλῃ, 5.42). The healing of Jairus' daughter is thus proleptic of Jesus' resurrection.

The struggle between faith and fear, which is shown in the account of the woman and Jairus' daughter, would act as an encouragement to those who faced persecution on account of their faith. These stories depict individuals overcoming disease and death through the healing brought by Jesus. The discipleship commu-nity may be compared to the woman with the flow of blood, who has been afraid to tell the truth. In the case of the woman her knowledge of God's power, which has healed her, gives her courage to come forward (5.33). In the same way the Spirit will come to the disciples, bringing knowledge of what they should say during their trials (13.11). Her story acts to encourage Mark's community to continue their proclamation even in the face of death. The correspondences between the accounts of the women at the tomb and of the woman with the flow of blood suggests that only by following and encountering Jesus will the women receive the power of the new age. The account of the woman and of Jairus' daughter does not ignore the severity of disease and death. The disciples are not protected from suffering and persecution, but through hearing the stories of these women, they know that ulti-mately God will overcome evil.

5. *New Creation*

The visit of the women to the tomb is delayed until the Sabbath has passed (16.1). The women are depicted as law-observant, and they recall the actions of Joseph of Arimathea, who arranges the burial of Jesus before the Sabbath begins. In the passion predictions Jesus has prophesied that he will rise on the third day (8.31; 9.31; 10.32–34). In the context of Mark's Gospel the timing of three days is related to the observance of the Sabbath. The reference to three days, however, may also allude to the account of the offering of Isaac (Gen. 22). Abraham and Isaac set off for Mount Moriah and arrive at the place of sacrifice on the third day. As Levenson points out, Isaac is described as the beloved son (Gen. 22.2, 12, 16), and the voice from heaven proclaims Jesus to be the beloved son at his baptism (1.11).[45] In Gen-esis, however, an angel announces that a ram may be substituted for Isaac, whereas in Mark's Gospel God does not intervene to save Jesus from death.

The timing of the Sabbath recalls the first day of Jesus' mission, which takes place on the Sabbath. Jesus teaches in the synagogue and casts out an unclean spirit from a man (1.21–28). He later raises Simon's mother-in-law from her fever, and

44. Selvidge, 'Those who Followed', 398.

45. J.D. Levenson, *The Death and Resurrection of the Beloved Son: The Transformation of Child Sacrifice in Judaism and Christianity* (New Haven: Yale University Press, 1993), 200–219.

she serves Jesus and his companions (1.29–31). These healings depict Jesus over-coming the power of disease, and the healed conditions of the human beings and the celebration of a meal are signs of the Sabbath rest. The mission of Jesus is depicted as a struggle against evil, which culminates with his death on the cross. The struggle against evil permits the new creation to emerge. God acts to liberate humanity from the forces of evil to which they are enslaved. Jesus overcomes evil through his death on the cross, and the Sabbath rest celebrates the new creation. The uniqueness of this day is indicated by the use of the cardinal rather than the ordinal number in the phrase, 'on the first day of the week' (τῇ μιᾷ τῶν σαβ-βάτων (16.2; cf. Acts 20.7; 1 Cor. 16.2). The resurrection takes place on the eighth day, the first day of the new creation (cf. *Barn.* 15.8–9; Justin, *1 Apol.* 67).[46] Now the boundary between the first six days of the week and the Sabbath is broken. Now all time is holy like the Sabbath.

The associations with the new creation are illustrated by the timing of the women's visit to the tomb. The women go to the tomb at daybreak as light emerges from darkness, echoing God's action of creating light out of darkness in Gen. 1.3–4. Throughout the Gospel the increasing evil of the end-time has been conveyed by references to darkness. Darkness is the time at which the storms arise on the boat journeys (ὀψίας γενομένης, 4.35; 6.47). The arrest of Jesus takes place under cover of darkness (14.43–50), and the growing darkness culminates in the three hours of darkness as he dies on the cross (15.33).

In one sense the progression from night to day suggests that life continues despite the crucifixion. The forces of nature appear to follow their normal course. The cataclysmic prophecy of the sun and moon and stars falling from the sky (13.24–25) has not yet been fulfilled. The movement from darkness to light signi-fies the emergence of the new creation from the old creation. Yet on this day the transition from darkness to light also signifies the time of the resurrection. Jesus is not dead, but is going on before his disciples, bringing in the new creation.

The location of the tomb is a marginal setting, signifying the transition from life to death. The tomb, which is associated with impurity and death, becomes the place of revelation. The description of the stone sealing the entrance recalls the stark atmosphere of the account of the Gentile demoniac, who cut himself with stones and lived among the tombs, suffering torment until Jesus came and set him free (5.1–20). The mission of Jesus has led him into an encounter with impurity, violence and death, and in a similar way these women now move out of the city of Jerusalem to the place of death. Jesus has been rejected by the religious authorities and the politi-cal rulers of Jerusalem (12.1–12). Just as the son of the owner of the vineyard is killed by the tenants and thrown out of the vineyard, Jesus is executed at Golgotha, the place of the skull, and buried in a stranger's tomb. Jesus dies as one cursed (Deut. 21.23; Gal. 3.13), and he becomes identified with impurity. Through the power of the resurrection, however, impurity is cast out. The boundary between the

---

46. For an examination of the origins of Sunday, see S.G. Wilson, *Related Strangers. Jews and Christians 70 –170 C.E.* (Minneapolis: Fortress Press, 1995), 230–35.

clean and the unclean is crossed. Jesus dies, giving up the Holy Spirit in order to inaugurate the new creation (ἐξέπνευσεν, 15.39).

The description of the women's visit to the tomb is reminiscent of the accounts of Jesus' baptism (1.9–11) and of his transfiguration (9.2–8). At the baptism of Jesus and at the transfiguration a voice from heaven declares Jesus to be his beloved Son (1.11; 9.7). In our passage an angelic figure tells the women the news of the resurrection. In the first account God addresses Jesus directly, and no human being seems to hear God speak. In the second narrative God addresses Peter, James and John, the inner circle of the Twelve, whereas in our passage the young man speaks to the three women who form the counterpart to the three male disciples. There is, then, a progression in the three accounts, since the revelation moves from Jesus alone to the women who have the task of telling others.

The human reactions in the transfiguration and in our account are similar, since the disciples are described as being afraid (ἔκφοβοι γὰρ ἐγένετο, 9.6) and the women are also afraid (ἐφοβοῦντο γάρ, 16.8). At the transfiguration, moreover, Peter does not know what to say (9.6) and in our account the women's fear and silence are indications of their lack of understanding. All the accounts are associated with the death and resurrection of Jesus. The baptism is symbolic of death and resurrection, and the shining clothes of Jesus at his transfiguration (9.3) allude to the resurrection. After the transfiguration Jesus instructs his disciples to say nothing of what they have witnessed until the Son of Man has been raised from the dead (9.9). In our passage Jesus, the crucified one has been raised. The identity of Jesus is no longer to be kept secret and the women are thus instructed to pass on the message to the disciples.

Our account, moreover, contains images of restoration from destruction. The young man at the tomb recalls the young man who ran away naked at the arrest of Jesus (14.51–52). This young man has not been previously mentioned in Mark. His presence is described only after all have fled (14.50). He is portrayed in discipleship terms through the use of the verb συνακολουθέω (to follow, accompany) (συνη-κολούθει αὐτῷ, 14.51). He abandons Jesus (ἔφυγεν, 14.52), however, just as the other disciples flee (ἔφυγον, 14.50). The young man is described as wearing a garment around his body (περιβεβλημένος σινδόνα, 14.51), but he leaves it behind at his arrest. There is a verbal similarity with the description of the young man at the tomb, who is now wearing shining clothes (περιβεβλημένον στολὴν λευκήν, 16.5). The two accounts suggest that the young man who fled has now been mysteriously restored.

Scroggs and Groff relate the passage to a baptism account of a new member of the Christian community.[47] In early Christian writings, moreover, those who are baptized receive white clothes.[48] The reception of white clothes also has associations

---

47. R. Scroggs and K.I. Groff, 'Baptism in Mark: Dying and Rising with Christ', *JBL* 92 (1973), 531–48.

48. Scroggs and Groff ('Baptism in Mark', 536–39) cite New Testament references to baptism as dying and rising with Christ in Mk 10.38–39; Rom. 6; Col. 2.11–12; Eph. 2.5–6 and possibly 1 Pet. 3.18–22. Scroggs and Groff find no first-century evidence for the connection between baptism and a change of garments, but they do list early texts which refer to the removal of clothes such as

with martyrdom, as in the descriptions of those who have died for their faith in Rev. 7.9; 13–14. Fleddermann disagrees with this interpretation, since he regards the flight of the young man as incompatible with the portrayal of someone who is about to be baptized.[49] For him, the account of the arrest of the young man may rather be an indication of the persecution the followers of Jesus will face. Scrogg's and Groff's analysis, however, is supported by the symbolic associations of baptism with death and resurrection. The young man represents someone who has mysteriously passed through death. He foreshadows the disciples who are restored by the power of God and not by human means.

The purpose of the presence of the young man is to give the message of the resurrection to the women. Hooker notes that the use of the aorist passive ἠγέρθη (16.6) emphasizes that God is the one who has raised Jesus from the dead.[50] The young man's message is the gospel, the εὐαγγέλιον (1.1), the announcement of God's battle victory over evil. In Genesis, God speaks, and his word separates creation from chaos. In the same way the word of Jesus has the power to cast out demons (1.25; 9.25), to heal (2.11; 3.5; 10.52) and to calm storms (4.39). The word has a power of its own once it is uttered. When the leper who has been healed speaks about his cure, the word breaks boundaries, immediately spreading over a wide area (1.45). In the account of the Syrophoenician woman, the word she speaks brings healing to her daughter (7.29). In the parable of the sower the word of God brings an abundant harvest (4.20), and the words of Jesus will also bear fruit. Heaven and earth will pass away; only the words of Jesus will remain (13.30–31). Jesus' words are the only constant connecting the old age with the new one, for in Jesus' speech itself the new creation breaks into the old.[51] If the women pass on the news of the resurrection, they speak the word of the gospel which is God's battle victory over evil. In the parable of the sower the word attracts acceptance, but also opposition (4.17). The women may, therefore, find themselves at risk of persecution on account of the word.

In our passage, however, the women react with fear and silence to the word. The silence of the women is reminiscent of the primeval silence at the beginning of creation before God speaks and separates creation from chaos. In apocalyptic texts the silence before creation is repeated at the end of creation (*4 Ezra* 6.39–40; 7.30; *2 Bar.* 3.7).[52] After the death of the Messiah there is silence before the new creation. When the message is spoken, God's power breaks into the world. This message is the gospel itself, which begins with the sentence, 'The beginning of the gospel of Jesus Christ' (᾽Αρχὴ τοῦ εὐαγγελίου ᾽Ιησοῦ Χριστοῦ, 1.1) that recalls the

---

Gos. Phil. 123.21–25; Gos. Thom. 37; Acts Thom. 121, 133, 157; Hippolytus, *Trad. ap.* 21.3, 20; *Acts of Xanthippe* 21; *Didascalia Apostolorum* 16. As Scroggs and Groff point out, there are also metaphors of dressing and undressing in Gal. 3.27 and Col. 2.11–13.

49. H. Fleddermann, 'The Flight of a Naked Young Man (Mark 14.51-52)', *CBQ* 41 (1979), 417.

50. Hooker, *St. Mark*, 385.

51. Marcus, *Mystery*, 219–20.

52. See M. Stone, *Fourth Ezra* (Minneapolis: Fortress Press, 1990), 184. Stone compares *4 Ezra* 6.39 and 7.30 with *L.A.B.* 60.2 in which darkness and silence are described before the beginning of creation.

opening of Genesis 'In the beginning' ('Εν ἀρχῇ, 1.1 LXX). In the time between the resurrection and the parousia the disciples are commanded to continue the proclamation of the gospel to the whole world (13.10). The women are the first to receive the news of the resurrection, and they are the first human beings to be instructed to continue Jesus' mission. Mark, however, does not end with speech, but with silence, and the Gospel concludes with the failure of the women.

6. *Conclusion*

The women are the last remaining followers of Jesus who remain faithful despite the apparent failure of his mission. The women desire to anoint Jesus and give honour to him, but he has already been anointed in preparation of his burial by an unknown woman. Their wish to anoint him, however, leads them to the empty tomb. The women were present at his crucifixion and burial, and now they become the first witnesses of the resurrection. The presence of the women thus gives continuity to the proclamation of the gospel. The women, however, respond in fear to the news of the resurrection and run away too terrified to tell anyone, and Mark ends his Gospel on a note of human failure. At the end of the Gospel the silence of the women points to the gulf between the power of God and the powerlessness of human beings, but Mark's Gospel itself is testimony that the women's silence will not hinder the proclamation of the new creation.

Chapter 12

Conclusion

1. *The Portrayal of Women in Mark's Gospel*

In the conclusion to our analysis of women in Mark, we may discern three distinctive ways in which Mark portrays women. Women are presented as the only characters who serve Jesus, they anoint Jesus and they are the key witnesses to Jesus' death and resurrection. The description of the service of Simon's mother-in-law (1.31) and that of the women disciples (15.41) frames Jesus' mission. The account of the woman who anoints Jesus (14.3–9) and the women who go to the tomb to anoint him (16.1–8) surrounds the Passion Narrative, and finally there are two references to the witness of women which frame the account of Jesus' burial (15.40–41; 15.47).

Women and Service
One of the key characteristics of Mark's portrayal of women is their association with the verb διακονέω (to serve). Simon's mother-in-law serves a meal to Jesus and his companions after she has been healed (1.31), and the women disciples of Jesus serve him while he is in Galilee (15.41). The verb διακονέω is used only of the women, Jesus and the angels. The angels serve Jesus during his testing by Satan, and women serve him throughout his mission. The primary meaning of διακονέω is to serve food, and the service of the angels may involve bringing food to Jesus in the desert. Similarly, the women may also have prepared meals for Jesus. The verb διακονέω, however, is also a discipleship term. Jesus teaches the Twelve that they should take on the role of a servant (9.35; 10.43), and he interprets his own mission as service in that he gives his life to ransom many others (10.45). This verb points to the distinctive role of women, since it is not used of the male disciples.

In Mark, the angels serve Jesus during his testing by Satan, helping him in his struggle against evil. Similarly, women also sustain and protect Jesus in the course of his mission. Jesus calls his disciples 'to be with him' (3.14), and he asks his disciples to keep watch in Gethsemane (14.34, 38). Whereas the male disciples flee at Jesus' arrest, the women are present at the crucifixion. Jesus desires relationships with his disciples, and the willingness of the women to remain with him serves to sustain him during his conflict with evil.

The term ἄγγελος, moreover, may be translated as 'angel' but also means 'messenger'. Angels are traditionally depicted as messengers of God, and they transcend the separation between the heavenly and earthly spheres. In apocalyptic texts angels act as mediators bringing revelation of the events of the end-time to chosen recipients (cf. *1 Enoch*, *4 Ezra*). In Mark's Gospel women often take the role of messengers. Jesus heals the woman with the flow of blood, but he does not know whom he has healed until the woman comes forward to tell him πᾶσαν τὴν ἀλήθειαν (the whole truth, 5.33). The Syrophoenician woman also announces that the time has arrived to carry out the Gentile mission (7.28–29). The woman who anoints Jesus makes a costly gift, and her action identifies Jesus as the Messiah (14.3–9). At the end of the Gospel the women who go to the tomb are the first to receive the news of the resurrection, and they are entrusted with the message of the gospel (16.7).

In the apocalyptic context of the Gospel these women appear as figures mysteriously sent by God, but Jesus is the one who interprets the significance of their actions. Jesus commends the act of the woman with the flow of blood who touches his clothes, and he accepts the end of the purity laws (5.34). He praises the word of the Syrophoenician woman, which convinces him that it is time to begin the mission to the Gentiles (7.29). Jesus also interprets the act of anointing as preparation of his body for burial, and he prophesies that her action will be remembered wherever the gospel is proclaimed (14.8–9).

The women disciples are present throughout Jesus' mission following him and serving him in Galilee. They are the last remaining followers of Jesus who are present at his death. Mark, however, delays any reference to the service of the group of women disciples until the crucifixion of Jesus (15.40–41). In Mark's apocalyptic world-view the death of Jesus is a time of revelation. Jesus overcomes evil through his death on the cross and he inaugurates the new age. Throughout the Gospel Jesus' identity is concealed from human beings until his death when the Roman centurion is the first person to recognize him as the Son of God (15.39). Similarly, the hidden service of the women is mentioned only at the crucifixion of Jesus. The values of God are revealed through Jesus' death on the cross. Jesus dies as the suffering Messiah who gives his life for others. The service of the women is described for the first time at the crucifixion of Jesus because the true nature of discipleship can only be understood in the context of his service of giving his life to redeem humanity (10.45).

Mark, moreover, draws a distinction between the service of the women and the actions of the Twelve. Whereas the Twelve seek status and authority, the women unobtrusively serve Jesus. The male disciples' desire for status and power is linked to their wish for a powerful Messiah. Each passion prediction is followed by an account of the failures of the Twelve. Peter attempts to dissuade Jesus from his mission (8.32). The Twelve argue about which one of them is the greatest (9.33–34), and James and John seek the positions of glory next to Jesus (10.35–40). In response Jesus teaches that those who wish to be first must make themselves last and servants of all (9.35; 10.44). On the other hand, the women's lack of status and power within the discipleship group enables them to identify with the powerlessness of Jesus at the crucifixion. The women are present at the crucifixion (15.40–41) and the burial of Jesus (15.47). They discover alternative ways of acting without seeking to preserve their own lives. In this way they do not avoid Jesus' suffering but desire to remain faithful to him despite the apparent failure of his mission.

The Twelve, however, have a symbolic role representing the twelve tribes and they foreshadow the restoration of Israel (3.13–19; *1 En.* 57.1; *4 Ezra* 13.32–50; *2 Bar.* 78.1–7). In the Passion Narrative the focus on the Twelve is broken since Judas, one of the Twelve (14.10, 20, 43), betrays Jesus. At the crucifixion, no member of the Twelve is present. In contrast the Gentile Roman centurion recognizes Jesus as the Son of God (15.39) and the female disciples are mentioned watching from a distance (15.40–41). Through the death of Jesus the religious and social boundaries between Jew and Gentile, and between male and female are broken. Mark does not replace the male disciples, since the women are instructed to pass on the news to the disciples and Peter (16.7). The new discipleship group consists of Jews and Gentiles, men and women.

Mark has perhaps linked women with service because traditionally women are associated with serving food. In Mark's Gospel, however, the accounts of serving of food have theological significance, and healing is associated with eating. Simon's mother-in-law serves a meal after she has been healed (1.31). Jesus raises Jairus' daughter to life, and he instructs those present to give the girl something to eat (5.43). The Syrophoenician woman asks Jesus to heal her daughter, and Jesus interprets her request as a desire for bread (7.27). The pattern of exorcism and healing followed by a meal forms the structure of Mark's narrative. The first day of Jesus' mission consists of an exorcism followed by a healing account and a meal (1.21–28, 29–31). Similarly, the Jewish cycle of the Gospel includes accounts of healings followed by the feeding of the five thousand (5.21–6.44), and the Gentile cycle also includes an exorcism and the feeding of the four thousand (7.24–30; 8.1–9). These meals foreshadow the messianic feast (Isa. 25.6–8; *1 En.* 62.12–14; *2 Bar.* 29.5–8). Jesus is the Messiah who overcomes evil and celebrates his victory with a banquet in the new age.

Jesus is not depicted as a powerful Messiah who acts with force against others. The serving of food is related to the service of Jesus in giving his life to bring life to others (10.45). At times the pressure of the crowds prevents Jesus from eating (3.20; 6.31). His mission is associated with serving food, since at the Last Supper he identifies the bread as his body and the wine as his blood (14.22–24). This meal has an eschatological focus because Jesus predicts that he will not drink wine until he drinks it anew in the kingdom of God (14.25). At the crucifixion, moreover, Jesus refuses to drink the wine he is offered (15.23, 33). The service of the women is over, and is, therefore, described in the past tense (διηκόνουν, 15.41). In the period between the resurrection of Jesus and the parousia, however, Jesus becomes present to his followers in the celebration of the eucharist. This may be seen in the feeding narratives in which Jesus takes bread, breaks it, and gives the bread to his disciples to distribute. Allusions to the eucharist are also apparent in the account of the exorcism of the Syrophoenician woman's daughter in which the woman recognizes that one loaf may feed both the Jewish and the Gentile children (7.28). Throughout Mark's Gospel women have the role of serving food, which suggests that they are also invloved in distributing the eucharist.

The Association of Women with Anointing

Two accounts which feature women and anointing frame the Passion Narrative
(14.3–9; 16.1–8). The gifts of women contrast with the plots of the male religious
and political authorities who wish to arrest and execute Jesus. An anonymous woman
who is not described as being one of Jesus' followers anoints him at the beginning
of the Passion Narrative, and three of his female disciples visit his tomb with the
intention of anointing him at the end of the Gospel. The account of the action of an
individual woman followed by a similar description of a group of women is reminiscent of the two references to the service of women at the beginning (1.31) and
the end of Jesus' mission (15.41).

The first woman who anoints Jesus is portrayed as a prophetic figure, since her
action foreshadows his identity as Messiah and Son of God which is only revealed
at the time of his death on the cross (15.39). Her action is prophetic because it is to
be connected with the proclamation of the gospel throughout the world (14.9). The
woman takes the role of a prophet or priest who recognizes the significance of
Jesus. The anointing of kings, moreover, is associated with the bestowal of power.
The woman anoints Jesus with costly perfume inaugurating the events of the Passion
Narrative. The wish of the women at the tomb to anoint Jesus is also associated with
Jesus' death and resurrection, since they are unable to anoint him because he has
been raised.

The anointing of Jesus takes place in the setting of a meal, and this portrayal
looks forward to the presence of Jesus, the Messiah, at the messianic feast. The act
of anointing is associated with the boundary of life and death. Jesus interprets the
action of the woman who anoints him as the preparation of his body for burial
(14.8). At the end of the Gospel women seek to anoint him at the time of his death.
The association of women with the boundary between life and death may also be
seen in Jesus' prophecies of the end-time in which the advent of the new age is
described in terms of a woman's birth pangs (13.8).

The gender of the woman who anoints Jesus contributes to the association of
Mark's Gospel with the subversion of worldly values. In Mark's Gospel women do
not have the same opportunity to speak in public, since they are excluded from the
formal structures of power within society. Nevertheless, this woman finds an alternative way of expressing her faith, and she is thus aligned with those who use symbolic actions because they have no access to words. Similarly, the woman with the
flow of blood seeks healing by touching Jesus' clothes (5.27), and the dance of
Herodias' daughter before Herod, enables her to gain power over him (6.14–29).

The desire of the group of women to anoint Jesus is also associated with Jesus'
death and resurrection, since they discover his resurrection through their visit to the
tomb to anoint his body (16.1–8). Their wish to anoint Jesus opposes the futility of
death because they continue to follow Jesus beyond the time of his death. The plots
of the religious and political authorities to put Jesus to death dominate the Passion
Narrative. The women's wish to anoint Jesus, however, surrounds the events of the
Passion Narrative and bears witness to the future positive response of both women
and men to Jesus. Their desire is eschatological in that they affirm the preciousness
of life in the midst of death.

The Role of Women as Witnesses

In the Passion Narrative women have the role of witnesses to Jesus' death, burial and resurrection. These women bring continuity to the mission of the early community, since they have followed and served Jesus in Galilee before accompanying him to Jerusalem. Although the women stand at a distance, they show courage by their very presence at the crucifixion scene. Their act of watching is itself an act of resistance, since it bears witness to a hope for a reality different from the present suffering. The role of women as witnesses also points to the isolation of Jesus in the Passion Narrative. He is handed over into the power of his enemies, who bring him to trial and condemn him to death.

Throughout Mark's Gospel there is an emphasis on sight and hearing as metaphors for understanding. In chapter 4 insiders are those who listen to the parables and approach Jesus for further instruction, and outsiders are described as those who hear and see but do not understand (4.10–12). In the apocalyptic context of the Gospel the crucifixion is the time of revelation. No human being understands Jesus' identity until the Roman centurion recognizes him as the Son of God when he sees how Jesus dies (ἰδών, 15.39).

Mark's Gospel depicts a movement from concealment to sight. Nothing is covered up without the purpose of being revealed (4.21–22). Jesus' identity is concealed throughout his mission so that it may be revealed at his crucifixion. The power of witness is evident in Jesus' prophecy to his disciples that they will see the kingdom of God come in power (ἴδωσιν, 9.1), and at the trial of Jesus when he tells his accusers that they will see the Son of Man coming on the clouds of heaven accompanied by angels (ὄψεσθε, 14.62). The act of witness points to the power of God to bring about the new creation. Human beings are called to bear witness to the actions accomplished by God.

The women at the crucifixion of Jesus are portrayed as witnesses, and they also watch the burial of Jesus. Verbs linked with sight are prominent in the account of the visit of the women to the empty tomb (ἀναβλέψασαι, θεωροῦσιν, 16.4, εἶδον, 16.5, ἴδε, 16.6). The women do not expect to discover the resurrection of Jesus. Mark's use of verbs associated with sight expresses the growing understanding of the women, which is indicated by their fear and awe at their discovery of the resurrection.

The women are portrayed more favourably than the male disciples, but at the end of the Gospel, they also fail in discipleship. They run away from the empty tomb, terrified to pass on the news of the resurrection (16.8). In Mark's apocalyptic world-view all human beings abandon Jesus. This failure, however, is depicted within the purposes of God, since Jesus prophesies that his followers will be scattered, and that he will go ahead of them to Galilee (14.27–28; 16.7). Mark contrasts the powerlessness of human beings with the power of God. He presents the fear of the women as part of an eschatological struggle between the old and the new age. The fear of the women is aligned to the old age, whereas faith is acceptance of the power of the new age.

The women respond with fear to their experience of the power of God to bring life from death, and they are afraid to pass on the news of the resurrection. The message itself is a powerful force which corresponds to the creative word of God. Mark is also aware of the persecution which will arise in opposition to the spreading of the gospel. In the time between the resurrection and the parousia the evil age comes to a close with cataclysmic events of wars, earthquakes and famines. The followers of Jesus will be persecuted on account of their faith, and they will face trials before Jewish and Gentile authorities (13.7–9). Jesus instructs the disciples to continue the proclamation of the gospel and to strive to endure until the end of the world (13.10–13). Mark concludes with a focus on the women, which emphasizes their role as witnesses to the events of the Passion Narrative. The future mission depends on the testimony of the women, since they are the only witnesses to Jesus' death, burial and resurrection. Mark's audience is aware that their own discipleship depends on the women's proclamation of the gospel.

Women are thus portrayed as those who serve, anoint and bear witness to Jesus. Mark aligns his presentation of women with Jesus' suffering and death. The women do not reject Jesus' suffering, nor do they attempt to evade their care of him after his death. The women's actions, however, may also be interpreted as signs of the new creation. The service of the women looks forward to the worship of Jesus by the angels in the new creation (cf. 1.13). The act of anointing is associated with God's act of raising Jesus from the dead, and the witness of the women is a protest against those who seek to destroy Jesus. The message of the Gospel is that the force of death is overcome, and that paradoxically God has the power to bring life out of death.

2. *Discipleship*

Our analysis has indicated that women are often depicted at the extremities of life through their suffering (1.29–31; 5.24–34) and that of their children (7.24–30). The illness of the woman with the flow of blood renders her ritually unclean (5.24–34; cf. Lev. 15.25–30). The Syrophoenician woman is an outsider on account of her race as a Gentile (7.24–30), and the poor widow lives on the margins of society because of her poverty (12.41–44). These women, however, display more faith than the religious and political authorities who oppose Jesus. The faith of the women who live at the margins of society also contrasts with the cruelty of the Herodian women (6.14–29). The Herodian women have high social status and wealth, since they are members of Herod's family. John the Baptist threatens Herodias' position at court by his criticism of her marriage, and Herodias and her daughter conspire to bring about his execution. Mark illustrates the corrupting influences of wealth and the cares of the world (cf. 4.19) through his portrayal of these women.

The suffering of the individual women brings them to the boundary between life and death. The women in the healing narratives risk everything they have to seek help from Jesus (5.24–34; 7.24–30). The widow gives away her last two coins placing her trust in God (12.41–44) and the woman who anoints Jesus breaks the jar open pouring out the expensive perfume (14.3–9). Similarly, those who follow Jesus will also encounter the boundary between life and death, since Jesus calls women and men to follow him on the way of the cross (8.34–35). The proclamation of the gospel will attract persecution and his disciples will meet opposition to their message (13.11–13). The greatest human power is the power to kill, but those who murder others cannot escape their own deaths. Mark depicts the power of Satan as an oppressive force, which seeks to torture and destroy human beings. Jesus renounces the power of oppression, but teaches the significance of self-giving in serving others. Through his death on the cross Jesus overcomes evil by giving his life for others. Mark contrasts the human desire to avoid death with the power of God to bring life out of death.

At the end of the Gospel the women at the tomb have the task of communicating the news of the resurrection. The women, however, run away, terrified from the empty tomb (16.8). The conclusion of the Gospel draws Mark's audience back to the beginning, and the earlier narratives act as an encouragement to Mark's audience. These stories portray the power of Jesus to heal and to raise women to life (1.29–31; 5.21–43; 7.24–30). The Gospel ends with the terror of the female disciples (16.1–8), but we have witnessed an account of a woman who overcomes her fear to confess her faith (5.33). The woman with the flow of blood is presented as following the way of the cross and finding life though her meeting with Jesus. Jesus prophesies that the action of the woman who anoints him will be remembered wherever the gospel is proclaimed (14.9). The narratives act as parables and Mark draws out the implications of the actions of those who are hidden from the world. He records the accounts of women who live their lives in such a way that the kingdom of God is revealed in the earthly context.

3. *New Creation*

Our analysis of women in Mark has shown that narratives featuring women have an integral part within Mark's understanding of the new creation. Jesus casts out evil and overcomes disease, and the accounts of the healing of women are proleptic of the new creation in which no evil or disease will remain. The accounts of the healing of the woman with the flow of blood and of the raising of Jairus' daughter, moreover, illustrate the abandonment of the purity regulations in the new age (5.21–43). Through his death and resurrection Jesus liberates human beings from evil and inaugurates the new age. In the new age evil and death are conquered and there is no need for purity regulations. Similarly, the Syrophoenician woman's request for healing illustrates the breaking of the barriers between Jews and Gentiles (7.24–30). In both accounts these women have a key role in the teaching of the nature of the new creation.

Women are also included among those who do the will of God by listening to the teaching of Jesus (3.35). Women and men have equal status within this group as God alone is portrayed as their father. In Mark's Gospel the anti-hierarchical teaching of Jesus subverts patriarchy. The child, who has the lowest status in the patriarchal family is first in the kingdom of God (9.35–37; 10.13–16).[1] Jesus teaches that whoever receives a child receives him, and also the one who has sent

1. Schüssler Fiorenza, *In Memory*, 148.

Jesus (9.37). In this way Jesus and God are depicted as those who are aligned with the least in society. In the apocalyptic context of the Gospel worldly rulers only appear to rule (10.45).[2] Worldly power is depicted as self-serving, whereas the power of God is seen as self-giving. Jesus, moreover, teaches his disciples that they should take the role of servants (9.35) and that of slaves of others (10.44). Those who are among the last become first in the kingdom of God (cf.10.31). These sayings thus contrast the kingdom of God with the hierarchical structures within patriarchal society. The power of earthly rulers, however, is only a façade, since the new age has begun and will be fully realized at the parousia.

Women do not have religious and political authority, and they are not members of the inner circle of the Twelve. They are, therefore, excluded from the centres of power within the Gospel. The twelve male disciples, however, succumb to the same temptations as the earthly authorities who lord it over their subjects (10.42). The male disciples compete with one another for the key places next to Jesus in the kingdom of God (10.35–45). On the other hand the women stand as a group at the crucifixion (15.40–41). In Mark's Gospel women are excluded from positions of authority, but this situation enables them to develop relationships based on mutuality and reciprocity. These relationships contrast with the focus on status and power in the old age, and they illustrate the self-giving which characterizes the new creation. The women demonstrate the true nature of power in their ability to remain faithful to Jesus at the time of his death. Their actions point forward to the future restoration of the relationship between God and humanity in the new age.

4. *Feminist Interpretation of Mark's Gospel*

In the introduction we noted that there is a wide range of feminist perspectives on Mark's Gospel. Mark is the first Gospel to be written, and Schüssler Fiorenza aims to show that it bears witness to the egalitarian nature of the early Christian community.[3] Schüssler Fiorenza thus argues that the female disciples are portrayed with 'apostolic and ministerial leadership'.[4] On the other hand Kinukawa proposes that the interactions between women and Jesus are positive, but that Mark has downplayed the role of women, since Mark's community is in the midst of repartriarchalization.[5] Dewey, moreover, aims to draw attention to the androcentrism of Mark, and to highlight the 'liberating egalitarian vision of the gospel'.[6] She believes that Mark's portrayal of women does not support this teaching, since he mentions women only as models of discipleship or when they are necessary to the plot.[7]

The differing approaches of feminist scholars may be illustrated by their interpretations of Mark's first reference to the group of female disciples at the crucifixion of Jesus (15.40–41). Schüssler Fiorenza interprets these women as the true

---

2. Marcus, 'Epistemology', 558.
3. Schüssler Fiorenza, *In Memory*, 316.
4. Schüssler Fiorenza, *In Memory*, 334.
5. Kinukawa, *Women*, 138–42.
6. Dewey, 'Mark', 470.
7. Dewey, 'Mark', 508.

disciples who are portrayed favourably in comparison to the Twelve.[8] On the other hand Munro argues that Mark has deliberately concealed the presence of female disciples because he is embarrassed by their prominence in the early church.[9] Similarly, Dewey proposes that Mark's Gospel is androcentric because of the central role of the twelve male disciples.[10] She believes that the group of the Twelve is not historical, but has been developed by men in an attempt to assert their authority. According to Dewey's analysis the reference to the women at the crucifixion arrives at too late a stage in the text, and thus does not overturn the general impression of the invisibility of female disciples throughout the Gospel.

Feminist critics also give varied interpretations of Mark's portrayal of the women who run away from the tomb, terrified to pass on the news of the resurrection (16.1–8). The desire of Schüssler Fiorenza to portray the women as apostolic witnesses leads her to argue that the women do not disobey the young man's instruction and that they do tell the disciples and Peter.[11] She follows Catchpole's interpretation that the silence of the women applies to the 'public at large' and not to the disciples.[12] Her interest in the history behind the text prohibits her from analysing the end of the Gospel within the context of Mark's theological purposes, and her interpretation disregards the power of Mark's ending. On the other hand Kinukawa proposes that Mark concludes with the failure of the women because he does not wish to upset the male members of his audience by portraying women more favourably than men.[13]

Other feminist scholars do not differentiate between the female and male disciples. Fander suggests the Mark's ending indicates that women are not portrayed as the better disciples on account of their gender alone.[14] Malbon also argues that Mark's Gospel depicts both women and men as 'fallible followers'.[15] As she observes, not all women are followers, since Herodias and her daughter plot against John the Baptist, and some men are faithful such as Bartimaeus and Joseph of Arimathea. She suggests, therefore, that the significance of the discipleship of women is not defined by their gender, but by their response to Jesus. Malbon's analysis, however, downplays Mark's distinction between the presence of the women at the crucifixion of Jesus and the absence of the male disciples.

In the introduction we raised the issue of the relationship between a feminist interpretation and a theological analysis of the Gospel. A feminist approach examines the New Testament texts critically seeking to discern the ways in which they are liberating or restrictive to women. Some feminist scholars distance themselves from the texts with the purpose of assessing the writings in terms of feminist ideologies. On the other hand a theological approach aims to place God at the centre

8. Schüssler Fiorenza, *In Memory*, 316–23.
9. Munro, 'Women Disciples', 234–35.
10. Dewey, 'Mark', 470.
11. Schüssler Fiorenza, *In Memory*, 322.
12. Catchpole, 'Fearful Silence', 6–7.
13. Kinukawa, *Women*, 142.
14. Fander, *Stellung*, 383.
15. Malbon, 'Fallible Followers', 46.

of the interpretation. A theological reading gives priority to faith and the understanding of God, which is able to influence our concept of humanity. This study focuses on the role of women, and aims to assess the distinctive contribution of women to Mark's understanding of discipleship. It raises feminist questions in that it seeks to analyse the extent to which Mark's view of discipleship is inclusive. It differs, however, from some feminist scholars' extreme suspicion of male authors and their agendas, since it proposes that Mark's concept of new creation is liberating for both women and men. It thus combines feminist concerns with a theological approach in that it aims to interpret Mark's portrayal of women within the context of his understanding of humanity thrown into the new age by Jesus' death and resurrection.

Feminist scholars have highlighted the late reference to the female disciples and their failure to pass on the news of the resurrection. These issues, however, may be understood in relation to Mark's theological purposes. We have noted that Mark has distinctively associated the verb διακονέω only with women (1.31; 15.41) and Jesus (10.45), and it is not used of the male disciples. The use of this verb suggests that Mark intends to portray women in a different way from his presentation of men. Mark's theology, moreover, is expressed through his narrative, and he has placed the first reference to the service of the female disciples at the crucifixion of Jesus. In the context of Mark's apocalyptic world-view, the late reference to these women is interpreted as a literary device intended to highlight rather than to downplay the role of women. The crucifixion of Jesus is a turning point in which he serves by giving his life a ransom for many (10.45) and the service of the women is thus aligned with his mission. Mark emphasizes that the true nature of discipleship can be understood only in relation to the crucifixion of Jesus. Mark's concept of discipleship is thus illustrated by the service of the group of female disciples.

The relationship between the women and the Twelve may also be interpreted in the context of Mark's theology. Although Munro and Dewey correctly note that the first section of Mark centres on Jesus and the Twelve, they have not examined the role of the Twelve within Mark's apocalyptic world-view. The Twelve represent the twelve tribes of Israel and point forward to the future restoration of Israel. At the crucifixion no member of the Twelve is present, whereas a Gentile centurion, not a Jew, is the first human being to recognize Jesus as the Son of God (15.39), and the women are mentioned standing at a distance. Mark depicts the death of Jesus as the turning point between the old and the new age. In the new creation the barriers between men and women, and between Jews and Gentiles are broken. The male disciples, however, are not condemned, since the women are instructed to pass on the news of the resurrection to the disciples and Peter (16.7). In the new creation Mark points forward to an inclusive community which consists of Jews and Gentiles, women and men.

The failure of the women at the tomb may be understood in relation to Mark's apocalyptic world-view. Mark's Gospel describes the mission of Jesus in Galilee, and his journey to Jerusalem where he is arrested and sentenced to death. Jesus' disciples are called to follow the way of the cross, and his journey becomes the path they are to follow. Throughout the Gospel Mark depicts the struggle of human beings between faith and fear (4.40–41; 5.34, 36; 6.50), which culminates in the terror of the women at the tomb (16.8). Mark ends with the silence of the women in order to stress his theology of the cross. He does not conclude with the resurrection appearances of Jesus, since only women and men who are willing to follow the way of the cross will see him.

Our analysis of Mark's portrayal of women expresses an inclusive understanding of discipleship. At the crucifixion of Jesus, moreover, the religious and social boundaries between Jews and Gentiles, and women and men are broken, and Mark points forward to a new egalitarian community. In these ways the interpretation of the role of women in the context of Mark's theology is not in tension with the questions raised by feminist scholars. Mark, moreover, subverts the hierarchical values of the patriarchal society of the first century. The female disciples of Jesus have moved from the patriarchal family to join a new eschatological community in which God alone is father (3.35). As Schüssler Fiorenza points out, the portrayal of God as father (11.25; 14.36) undermines the authority of human fathers in the patriarchal context of the Greco-Roman world.[16] Worldly concepts of oppressive power are overturned, and those who are at the margins of society come first including the child and the slave (9.35–37; 10.15; 10.42–45).

Mark's positive portrayal of women raises the question of whether or not the women in his audience would find his presentation of the gospel liberating. As Fander points out, the narratives featuring women do not have the purpose of providing examples of traditional portrayals of good wives and mothers for Christian women to follow.[17] She observes that these accounts are connected to Mark's presentation of discipleship. In Mark the female disciples break social norms by leaving the stable social structure of the household to live an itinerant existence by following Jesus. The conflict between Jesus and his family acts as a model for disciples who experience tensions with their families (3.20–35). In this account Jesus' birth family is contrasted with his new family who do the will of God by listening to his teaching. Women are included among those who are present in the passage, which may imply that women also experience tensions by leaving their families to become Christians. Tolbert, moreover, argues that the accounts which feature women breaking boundaries (5.24–34; 7.24–30; 14.3–9) may be particularly applicable to female members of Mark's community who have disregarded conventional behaviour to become Christians.[18]

The favourable presentation of female disciples in Mark's Gospel has been interpreted by some scholars as evidence of the leadership roles of women in Mark's community. Schüssler Fiorenza argues that Mark records evidence of the 'apostolic leadership of women'.[19] On the other hand Kinukawa doubts if an 'egalitarian discipleship' was ever achieved in Jesus' lifetime.[20] Mark's association of the verb διακονέω with women, however, indicates that women are leaders because the cognate noun διάκονος is used of leaders in the early church (cf. 1 Cor. 3.5; 2 Cor.

16. Schüssler Fiorenza, *In Memory*, 147–48.
17. Fander, *Stellung*, 178.
18. Tolbert, 'Mark', 352.
19. Schüssler Fiorenza, *In Memory*, 334.
20. Kinukawa, *Women*, 144.

3.6; Rom. 16.1; Col. 4.7). The verb διακονέω is also associated with the serving of the eucharist (cf. *Did.* 14.1–3; 15.1; *1 Clem.* 42.4),[21] which implies that women are involved in serving the eucharist in the Markan community. Mark also portrays the women as the only witnesses to Jesus' death, burial and resurrection. Their testimony, therefore, is foundational for the proclamation of the gospel, which suggests that women are involved in the continuation of Jesus' mission.

This study has focused on the development of Mark's theology through his narrative. Mark does not present a systematic doctrine, but describes the way of the cross. In Jesus' mission the new creation is glimpsed through the healing and exorcisms of human beings, the feeding of the hungry crowds and the quelling of storms. Mark's Gospel depicts the kingdom of God breaking into a world in which there is evil and death but it points forward to a reality in which these powers have been overcome. In Mark, the women who live on the periphery of life show determination to find healing from Jesus, and they act as an empowerment to Mark's audience in their time of persecution. Similarly, the women who remain faithful to Jesus at the crucifixion oppose evil and death by their very presence. In the course of the Gospel women who are depicted at the extremities of life move to the centre of the narrative. The female disciples, who are aligned with Jesus' death and suffering, are the only witnesses who can continue Jesus' mission immediately after the end of the Gospel. Mark ends with their silence but also with the knowledge that the renewal of the discipleship group is dependent upon their witness and discipleship.

21. Collins, *Diakonia*, 238.

BIBLIOGRAPHY

Primary Sources

All ancient sources are from the Loeb Classical Library except:

Charlesworth, J.H. (ed.), *The Old Testament Pseudepigrapha* (2 vols.; Garden City, NY: Doubleday, 1983).

Cross, F.L. (ed.), *Lectures on the Christian sacraments: the Procatechesis and the Five Mystagogical Catechesis* (London: SPCK, 1951).

Danby, H., *The Mishnah: Translated from the Hebrew with Introduction and Brief Explanatory Notes* (Oxford: Oxford University Press, 1933).

Easton, B.S. (ed.), *The Apostolic Tradition of Hippolytus* (Cambridge: Cambridge University Press, 1934).

Elliott, J.K. (ed.), *The Apocryphal New Testament: A Collection of Apocryphal Christian Literature in an English Translation* (Oxford: Clarendon Press, 1993).

Freedman, H., and M. Simon (eds.), *The Midrash Rabbah* (5 vols.; London: Soncino, 1939).

Harkins, P.W. (ed.), *Baptismal Instructions: John Chrysostom* (London: Longmans, Green, 1963).

Hennecke, E., *New Testament Apocrypha* (2 vols.; ed. W. Scheemelcher; London: SCM Press, 1963–65).

Langdon, S., *Enuma elish. The Babylonian epic of creation restored from the recently recovered tablets of Assur* (Oxford: Clarendon Press, 1923).

Lauterbach, J., *Mekilta de-Rabbi Ishmael* (3 vols.; Philadelphia: Jewish Publication Society, 1961 [1933–35]).

Martínez, F.G., and E.J.C. Tigchelar (eds.), *The Dead Sea Scrolls Study Edition* (Leiden: E.J. Brill, 1997–98).

Petrie, A. (ed.), *The Speech against Leocrates* (Cambridge: Cambridge University Press, 1922).

Roberts, A., and J. Donaldson (eds.), *Ante-Nicene Church Library* (Translations of the Writings of the Fathers Down to A.D. 325; Edinburgh: T. & T. Clark, 1869).

Saldarini, A.J., *The Fathers according to Rabbi Nathan: A Translation and Commentary* (Leiden: E.J. Brill, 1975).

Townshead, J.T., *Midrash Tanḥuma: Translated into English with Indices and Brief Notes (S. Buber Recension). II. Exodus and Leviticus* (Hobeken, NJ: Ktav Publishing House, 1997).

Travers Herford, R., *Pirke Aboth* (New York: The Jewish Institute Press, 1925).

Voobus, A. (ed.), *The Didascalia Apostolorum in Syriac* (Louvain: Secrétariat du Corpus SCO, 1979).

Other Works

Allison, D.C., 'Elijah Must Come First', *JBL* 103 (1984), 256–58.

—*The End of the Ages Has Come: An Early Interpretation of the Passion and Resurrection of Jesus* (Philadelphia: Fortress Press, 1985).

—'Psalm 23 (22) in Early Christianity: A Suggestion', *IBS* 5 (1983), 132–37.

Anderson, H., *The Gospel of Mark* (NCB; London: Oliphants, 1976).

Anderson, J.C., 'Feminist Criticism: The Dancing Daughter', in J.C. Anderson and S.D. Moore (eds.), *Mark and Method: New Approaches in Biblical Studies* (Minneapolis: Fortress Press, 1992), 103–34.

Archer, L.J., *Her Price is Beyond Rubies: The Jewish Woman in Greco-Roman Palestine* (*JSOT*Sup, 60; Sheffield: Sheffield Academic Press, 1990).

Aus, R., *Water into Wine and the Beheading of John the Baptist* (BJS, 150; Atlanta: Scholars Press, 1988).

Bach, A., *Women, Seduction and Betrayal in Biblical Narrative* (Cambridge: Cambridge University Press, 1997).

Balz, H., and G. Schneider (eds.), *Exegetical Dictionary of the New Testament* (3 vols.; Grand Rapids: Eerdmans, 1990–93).

Barclay, J.M.G., *Jews in the Mediterranean Diaspora from Alexander to Trajan (323 B.C.E.-117 C.E.)* (Edinburgh: T. & T. Clark, 1996).

Barrett, C. K., *The Holy Spirit and the Gospel Tradition* (London: SPCK, 1947).

—'The Background of Mark 10:45', in A.J.B. Higgins (ed.), *New Testament Essays: Studies in Memory of T. W. Manson* (Manchester: Manchester University Press, 1959), 1–18.

Barton, S.C., *Discipleship and Family Ties in Mark and Matthew* (Cambridge: Cambridge University Press, 1994).

—'Mark as Narrative: The Story of the Anointing Woman (Mark 14:3-9)', *ExpTim* 102 (1991), 230–34.

—*People of the Passion* (London: SPCK, 1994).

—*The Spirituality of the Gospels* (London: SPCK, 1992).

Bauckham, R., 'The Brothers and Sisters of Jesus: An Epiphanian Response to John P. Meier', *CBQ* 56 (1994), 686–700.

—'For Whom Were Gospels Written?', in R. Bauckham (ed.), *The Gospels for All Christians: Rethinking the Gospel Audiences* (Edinburgh: T. & T. Clark, 1997), 9–48.

Bauer, W., *et al.*, *A Greek-English Lexicon of the New Testament and Other Early Christian Literature* (Chicago: University of Chicago Press, 2nd edn, 1979).

Baumgarten, J.M., 'On the Testimony of Women in 1 QSa', *JBL* 76 (1957), 266–69.

Beavis, M.A., 'Women as Models of Faith', *BTB* 18 (1988), 3–9.

Be'er, I., 'Blood Discharge: On Female Im/Purity in the Priestly Code and in Biblical Literature', in A. Brenner (ed.), *A Feminist Companion to Exodus-Deuteronomy* (Sheffield: Sheffield Academic Press, 1994), 154–64.

Best, E., 'Mark III.20, 21, 31-35', *NTS* 22 (1976), 309–19.

—*Disciples and Discipleship* (Edinburgh: T. & T. Clark, 1986).

—'Mark's Readers: A Profile', in F. Van Segbroeck *et al.* (eds.), *The Four Gospels 1992: Festschrift Frans Neirynck* (BETL, 100; Leuven: Leuven University Press, 1992), II, 839–58.

—'Mark's Use of the Twelve', *ZNW* 69 (1978), 11–35.

—'The Role of the Disciples in Mark', *NTS* 23 (1977), 377–401.

—*The Temptation and the Passion: The Markan Soteriology* (SNTSMS, 2; Cambridge: Cambridge University Press, 2nd edn, 1980 [1965]).

Bird, P., K.D. Sakenfeld and S.H. Ringe (eds.), *Reading the Bible as Women: Perspectives from Africa, Asia and Latin America* (*Semeia* 78; Atlanta: Scholars Press, 1997).

Boobyer, G.H., 'The Eucharistic Interpretation of the Miracles of the Loaves in St. Mark's Gospel', *JTS* 3 (1952), 161–71.

Boomershine, T.E., and G.L. Bartholomew, 'The Narrative Technique of Mark 16:8', *JBL* 100 (1981), 213–23.

Boswell, J., *The Kindness of Strangers: The Abandonment of Children in Western Europe from Late Antiquity to the Renaissance* (London: Allen Lane, The Penguin Press, 1989).

Botterweck, G.J., and H. Ringren, *Theological Dictionary of the Old Testament* (8 vols.; Grand Rapids: Eerdmans, 1977–94).

Brock, R.N., *Journeys by Heart: a Christology of Erotic Power* (New York: Crossroad, 1988).

Brooten, B., *Women Leaders in the Ancient Synagogue: Inscriptional Evidence and Background Issues* (BJS, 36; Chico, CA: Scholars Press, 1982).

Brown, R.E., 'The Burial of Jesus (Mark 15:42-47)', *CBQ* 50 (1988), 233–45.

—*The Death of the Messiah: From Gethsemane to the Grave. A Commentary on the Passion Narratives in the Four Gospels* (ABRL; New York: Doubleday, 1994).

—*The Gospel according to John* (AB 29 and 29A; Garden City, NY: Doubleday, 1966–70).

—'Not Jewish Christianity and Gentile Christianity But Types of Jewish/Gentile Christianity', *CBQ* 45 (1983), 74–79.

Brown, R.E., *et al.*, *Mary in the New Testament: A Collaborative Assessment by Protestant and Roman Catholic Scholars* (London: Chapman, 1978).

Bultmann, R., 'Is Exegesis Without Presuppositions Possible?', in *New Testament and Mythology and Other Basic Writings* (London: SCM Press, 1985), 145–53.

Burkill, T.A., 'The Historical Development of the Story of the Syrophoenician Woman (Mark vii:24-31)', *NovT* 9 (1967), 161–78.

—'The Syrophoenician Woman: The Congruence of Mark 7,24-31', *ZNW* 57 (1966), 23–37.

Buttrick, G.A. (ed.), *The Interpreter's Dictionary of the Bible: An Illustrated Encyclopedia* (4 vols.; Nashville: Abingdon Press, 1962).

Cantarella, E., *Pandora's Daughters: the Role and Status of Women in Greek and Roman Antiquity* (trans. M.B. Fant; Baltimore: Johns Hopkins University Press, 1987).

Carrington, P., *According to Mark* (Cambridge: Cambridge University Press, 1960).

Catchpole, D., 'The Fearful Silence of the Women at the Tomb: A Study in Markan Theology', *Journal of Theology for South Africa* 18 (1977), 3–10.

Clark, G., *Women in the Ancient World* (Oxford: Oxford University Press, 1989).

Cohen, S.J.D., 'Menstruants and the Sacred in Judaism and Christianity', in S.B. Pomeroy (ed.), *Women's History and Ancient History* (Chapel Hill: University of North Carolina Press, 1991), 273–99.

Collins, J.J., *The Apocalyptic Imagination: An Introduction to the Jewish Matrix of Christianity* (New York: Crossroad, 1984).

Collins, J.N., *Diakonia: Re-interpreting the Ancient Sources* (Oxford: Oxford University Press, 1990).

Corley, K.E., *Private Women, Public Meals. Social Conflict in the Synoptic Tradition* (Peabody, MA: Hendrickson, 1993).

—'Slaves, Servants and Prostitutes: Gender and Social Class in Mark', in A.-J. Levine (ed.), *A Feminist Companion to Mark* (Sheffield: Sheffield Academic Press, 2001), 191–221.

Cotes, M., 'Women, Silence and Fear (Mark 16:8)' in G.J. Brooke (ed.), *Women in the Biblical Tradition* (Studies in Women and Religion, 31; Lewiston: Edwin Mullen, 1992), 150–66.

Cranfield, C.E.B. (rev. and ed.), *The Gospel according to Saint Mark* (CGTC; Cambridge: Cambridge University Press, 1974).

Crim, K. (ed.), *The Interpreter's Dictionary of the Bible, Supplementary Volume* (Nashville: Abingdon Press, 1976).

Crossan, J.D., 'Mark and the Relatives of Jesus', *NovT* 15 (1973), 81–113.

Dahl, N.A., 'The Purpose of Mark's Gospel', in C.M. Tuckett (ed.), *The Messianic Secret* (Philadelphia: Fortress Press, 1983).

D'Angelo, M.R., '(Re)Presentations of Women in the Gospels: John and Mark', in R.S. Kraemer and M.R. D'Angelo (eds.), *Women and Christian Origins* (Oxford: Oxford University Press, 1999), 129–49.

Danker, F.W., 'The Demonic Secret in Mark: A Reexamination of the Cry of Dereliction (15:34)', *ZNW* 51 (1970), 48–69.

—'The Literary Unity of Mark 14, 1-25', *JBL* 85 (1966), 467–72.

—'Mark 8:3', *JBL* 82 (1963), 215–16.

Danove, P., 'The Characterisation and Narrative Function of the Women at the Tomb (Mark 15,40-41. 47; 16,1-8)', *Bib* 77 (1996), 375–97.

Daube, D., *The New Testament and Rabbinic Judaism* (London: Athlone Press, 1956).

Davies, W.D., and D.C. Allison, *A Critical and Exegetical Commentary on the Gospel according to Saint Matthew* (3 vols.; Edinburgh: T. & T. Clark, 1988–97).

De Lacey, D.R., 'In Search of a Pharisee', *TynBul* 43 (1992), 353–72.

Delorme, J., 'John The Baptist's Head—The Word Perverted: A Reading of a Narrative (Mark 6:14-29)', *Semeia* 81 (1998), 115–29.

Derrett, J.D.M., ' "Eating up the Houses of Widows": Jesus' Comment on Lawyers?', *NovT* 14 (1972), 1–9.

—'Herod's Oath and the Baptist's Head', *BZ* (1965), 49–59; 233–46.

—'Law in the New Testament: The Syro-Phoenician Woman and the Centurion of Capernaum', *NovT* 15 (1973), 161–86.

Dewey, J., 'The Gospel of Mark', in E. Schüssler Fiorenza (ed.), *Searching the Scriptures* (New York: Crossroad, 1994), II, 470–509.

—' "Let Them Renounce Themselves and Take Up Their Cross": A Feminist Reading of Mark 8.34 in Mark's Social and Narrative World', in A.-J. Levine (ed.), *A Feminist Companion to Mark* (Sheffield: Sheffield Academic Press, 2001), 23–36.

—'Mark as Interwoven Tapestry: Forecasts and Echoes for a Listening Audience', *CBQ* 53 (1991), 221–36.

Dewey, K., 'Peter's Curse and Cursed Peter (Mark 14:53-54, 66-72)', in W.H. Kelber (ed.), *The Passion in Mark: Studies on Mark 14-16* (Philadelphia: Fortress Press, 1976), 96–114.

Donahue, J.R., 'Jesus as the Parable of God in the Gospel of Mark', *Int* 32 (1978), 369–86.

Douglas, M., *Purity and Danger: An Analysis of the Concepts of Pollution and Taboo* (London: Routledge, 1966).

Downing, F.G., 'The Woman from Syrophoenicia and her Doggedness: Mark 7:24-31 (Matthew 15:21-28)', in G.J. Brooke (ed.), *Women in the Biblical Tradition* (Studies in Women and Religion, 31; Lewiston: Edwin Mellen, 1992), 129–49.

Drury, J., 'Mark', in R. Alter and F. Kermode (eds.), *The Literary Guide to the Bible* (Cambridge, MA: Belknap Press of Harvard University Press, 1987), 402–17.

—'Mark 1.15: An Interpretation', in A.E. Harvey (ed.), *Alternative Approaches to New Testament Study* (London: SPCK, 1985).

—*The Parables in the Gospels: History and Allegory* (London: SPCK, 1985).

Dufton, F., 'The Syro-Phoenician Woman and her Dogs', *ExpTim* 100 (1989), 417.

Edwards, J.R., 'Markan Sandwiches. The Significance of Interpolations in Markan Narratives', *NovT* 31 (1989), 193–216.

Elliott, J.K., 'The Anointing of Jesus', *ExpTim* 85 (1974), 105–107.

Encyclopaedia Judaica (16 vols.; Jerusalem: Keter, 1971–72).

Engels, D., 'The Problem of Female Infanticide in the Greco-Roman World', *CP* 75 (1980), 112–20.

Evans, C.F., 'I will go before you into Galilee', *JTS* 5 (1954), 3–18.

Fander, M., *Die Stellung der Frau im Markusevangelium. Unter besonderer Berücksichtigung kultur- und religionsgeschichtlicher Hintergründe* (Münsteraner Theologische Abhandlungen, 8; Altenberge: Telos, 1989).

Farrer, A., 'Loaves and Thousands', *JTS* 4 (1953), 1–14.

—*A Study in St. Mark* (Oxford: Oxford University Press, 1952).

Ferguson, E., *Encyclopaedia of Early Christianity* (New York: Garland Publishing, 2nd edn, 1990).

Fleddermann, H., 'The Flight of a Naked Young Man (Mark 14:51-52)', *CBQ* 41 (1979), 412–18.

—'A Warning about the Scribes (Mark 12:37b-40)', *CBQ* 44 (1982), 52–67.

Focant, C., 'Mc 7,24-31 par. Mt 15, 21-29. Critique des Sources et / ou Étude Narrative', in C. Focant (ed.), *The Synoptic Gospels: Source Criticism and the New Literary Criticism* (BETL, 110; Leuven: Leuven University Press, 1993), 39–75.

Fonrobert, C., 'The Woman with a Blood-Flow (Mark 5.24-34) Revisited: Menstrual Laws and Jewish Culture in Christian Feminist Hermeneutics', in C.A. Evans and J.A. Sanders (eds.), *Early Christian Interpretation of the Scriptures of Israel* (Sheffield: Sheffield Academic Press, 1997), 121–40.

Forsyth, N., *The Old Enemy: Satan and the Combat Myth* (Princeton: Princeton University Press, 1987).

Freyne, S., *Galilee, Jesus and the Gospels: Literary Approaches and Historical Investigations* (Dublin: Gill & Macmillan, 1988).

—'The Disciples in Mark and the *Maskilim* in Daniel. A Comparison', *JSNT* 16 (1982), 7–23.

Friedmann, M.A., 'Babatha's *Ketubba*: Some Preliminary Observations', *IEJ* 46 (1996), 55–76.

Gibson, J.B., 'Jesus' Wilderness Temptation according to Mark', *JSNT* 53 (1994), 3–34.

—'The Rebuke of the Disciples in Mark 8:14-21', *JSNT* 27 (1986), 31–47.

Gill, A., 'Women Ministers in the Gospel of Mark', *ABR* 35 (1987), 14–21.

Girard, R., 'Scandal and the Dance. Salome in the Gospel of Mark', *New Literary History* 15 (1984), 311–24.

Glancy, J., 'Unveiling Masculinity: The Construction of Gender in Mark 6:17-29', *BibInt* 2 (1994), 34–50.

Gnilka, J., *Das Evangelium nach Markus* (2 vols.; EKKNT, 2; Zurich: Benziger, 1978–79).

—'Das Martyrium Johannes' des Taufers (Mk 6.17-29)', in P. Hoffmann, N. Brox and W. Pesch (eds.), *Orientierung an Jesus: Zur Theologie der Synoptiker. Für Josef Schmid* (Freiburg: Herder, 1973), 78–92.

Golden, M., 'Demography and the Exposure of Girls at Athens', *Phoenix* 35 (1981), 316–31.

Goodblatt, D., 'The Beruriah Traditions', *JJS* 26 (1975), 68–85.

Graham, H.R., 'A Passion Prediction for Mark's Community: Mark 13:9-13', *BTB* (1986), 18–22.

Graham, S.L., 'Silent Voices: Women in the Gospel of Mark', *Semeia* 54 (1991), 145–58.

Grey, M., *Redeeming the Dream: Feminism, Redemption and Christian Tradition* (London: SPCK, 1989).

Guelich, R.A., *Mark 1-8:26* (WBC, 34; Dallas: Word Books, 1989).

Gundry, R.H., *Mark: A Commentary on His Apology for the Cross* (Grand Rapids: Eerdmans, 1993).

Heine, S., *Women and Early Christianity*, (London: SCM Press, 1987).

Hengel, M., *Studies in the Gospel of Mark* (Philadelphia: Fortress Press, 1985).

—*The Cross of the Son of God* (trans. J. Bowden; London: SCM Press, 1986).

Heschel, A.J., *The Sabbath: Its Meaning for Modern Man* (New York: Noonday Press, Farrar, Straus & Young, 1975 [1951]).

Holst, R., 'The One Anointing of Jesus: Another Application of the Form-Critical Method', *JBL* 95 (1976), 435–46.

Hooker, M.D., *A Commentary on the Gospel according to St Mark* (Black's New Testament Commentaries; London: A. & C. Black, 1991).

Hopkins, J.M., *Towards a Feminist Christology* (London: SPCK, 1995).

Ilan, T., *Jewish Women in Greco-Roman Palestine* (Peabody, MA: Hendrickson, 1996).

—' "Man Born of Woman…" ' (Job 14:1): The Phenomenon of Men Bearing Matronymes at the Time of Jesus', *NovT* 34 (1992), 23–45.

—'Notes on the Distribution of Women's Names in Palestine in the Second Temple and Mishnaic Periods', *JJS* 40 (1989), 186–200.

Jeremias, J., *The Eucharistic Words of Jesus* (Philadelphia: Fortress Press, 1966).

—*Jesus' Promise to the Nations* (London: SCM Press, 1958).

Johnson, E.S., *A Commentary on the Gospel according to St. Mark* (Black's New Testament Commentaries; London: A. & C. Black, 1991).

Juel, D.H., *A Master of Surprise: Mark Interpreted* (Minneapolis: Fortress Press, 1994).

—*Messiah and Temple: The Trial of Jesus in the Gospel of Mark* (SBLDS, 31; Missoula, MT: Scholars Press, 1973).

Kee, H.C., *Community of the New Age* (London: SCM Press, 1977).

—'The Terminology of Mark's Exorcism Stories', *NTS* 14 (1967), 232–46.

Kermode, F., *The Genesis of Secrecy: On the Interpretation of Narrative* (Cambridge, MA: Harvard University Press, 1979).

Kinukawa, H., 'The Story of the Hemorrhaging Woman (Mark 5:25-34) Read from a Japanese Feminist Context', *BibInt* 2 (1994), 283–93.

—*Women and Jesus in Mark: a Japanese Feminist Perspective* (Maryknoll, NY: Orbis Books, 1994).

—'Women Disciples of Jesus (15:40-41; 15:47; 16:1)', in A.-J. Levine (ed.), *A Feminist Companion to Mark* (Sheffield: Sheffield Academic Press, 2001), 171–90.

Kitzberger, I.R., ' "How Can This Be?" (John 3:9): A Feminist Theological Re-Reading of the Gospel of John', in F.F. Segovia (ed.), *'What is John?'* (Atlanta: Scholars Press, 1998), II, 19–41.

Kopas, J., 'Jesus and Women in Mark's Gospel', *Review for Religious* 44 (1985), 912–20.

Kraemer, R.S., *Her Share of the Blessings: Women's Religions Among Pagans, Jews and Christians in the Greco-Roman World* (Oxford: Oxford University Press, 1992).

Krause, D., 'Simon Peter's Mother-in-Law—Disciple or Domestic Servant? Feminist Biblical Hermeneutics and the Interpretation of Mark 1.29-31', in A.-J. Levine (ed.), *A Feminist Companion to Mark* (Sheffield: Sheffield Academic Press, 2001), 37–53.

Lambrecht, J., 'The Relatives of Jesus in Mark', *NovT* 16 (1974), 241–58.

Lane, W.L., *The Gospel of Mark* (NICNT; Grand Rapids: Eerdmans, 1974).

Lee-Pollard, D.A., 'Powerlessness as Power: A Key Emphasis in the Gospel of Mark', *SJOT* 40 (1987), 173–88.

Lefkowitz, M.R., *Heroines and Hysterics* (London: Duckworth, 1981).

Lefkowitz, M.R., and M.B. Fant, *Women's Life in Greece and Rome* (London: Duckworth, 1982).

Legault, A., 'An Application of the Form-Critique Method to the Anointings in Galilee and Bethany', *CBQ* 16 (1954), 131–45.

Levenson, J.D., *Creation and the Persistence of Evil* (San Francisco: Harper & Row, 1988).

—*The Death and Resurrection of the Beloved Son: The Transformation of Child Sacrifice in Judaism and Christianity* (New Haven: Yale University Press, 1993).

—*Sinai and Zion. An Entry into the Jewish Bible* (Minneapolis: Winston, 1985).

Levine, A.-J., 'Second Temple Judaism, Jesus, and Women: Yeast of Eden', *BibInt* 2 (1994), 8–33.

Levine, A.-J. (ed.), *'Women Like This': New Perspectives on Jewish Women in the Greco-Roman World* (Atlanta: Scholars Press, 1991).

Liddell, H.G., R. Scott, and S. Jones, *A Greek-English Lexicon with a Supplement* (Oxford: Clarendon, 1968).

Lightfoot, R.H., *The Gospel Message of St. Mark* (Oxford: Clarendon Press, 1950).

Lincoln, A., 'The Promise and the Failure—Mark 16:7, 8', *JBL* 108 (1989), 283–300.

Lindemann, A., 'Die Osterbotschaft des Markus. Zur Theologischen Interpretation von Mark 16. 1-8', *NTS* 26 (1980), 298–317.

Loader, W., 'Challenged at the Boundaries: A Conservative Jesus in Mark's Tradition', *JSNT* 63 (1996), 45–61.

Lohmeyer, E., *Das Evangelium des Markus* (Göttingen: Vandenhoeck & Ruprecht, 1967).

MacDonald, M.Y., *Early Christian Women and Pagan Opinion: The Power of the Hysterical Woman* (Cambridge: Cambridge University Press, 1996).

Malbon, E.S. 'Disciples/ Crowds/ Whoever: Markan Characters and Readers', *NovT* 28 (1986), 104–30.

—'Fallible Followers: Women and Men in the Gospel of Mark', *Semeia* 28 (1983), 29–48.

—*Narrative Space and Mythic Meaning in Mark* (Sheffield: JSOT Press, 1991).

—'The Poor Widow in Mark and Her Poor Rich Readers', *CBQ* 53 (1991), 589–604.

—'TH OIKIA AYTOY: Mark 2:15 in Context', *NTS* 31 (1985), 282–92.

Manek, J., 'Mark VIII, 14-21', *NovT* 7 (1964), 10–14.

Marcus, J., 'The Jewish War and the *Sitz im Leben* of Mark', *JBL* 111 (1992), 441–62.

—*Mark 1-8. A New Translation with Introduction and Commentary* (AB, 27; New York: Doubleday, 2000).

—'Mark 4:10-12 and Marcan Epistemology', *JBL* 103 (1984), 557–74.

—*The Mystery of the Kingdom of God* (SBLDS, 90; Atlanta: Scholars Press, 1986).

—'Scripture and Tradition in Mark 7', in C.M. Tuckett (ed.), *The Scriptures in the Gospels* (BETL, 131; Leuven: Leuven University Press, 1997), 145–63.

—*The Way of the Lord. Christological Exegesis of the Old Testament in the Gospel of Mark* (Edinburgh: T. & T. Clark, 1992).

Marshall, C.D., *Faith as a Theme in Mark's Narrative* (SNTSMS, 64; Cambridge: Cambridge University Press, 1989).

Matera, F.J., ' "He Saved Others; He Cannot Save Himself", A Literary-Critical Perspective on the Markan Miracles', *Int* 47 (1993), 15–26.

—'The Incomprehension of the Disciples and Peter's Confession (Mark 6, 14—8, 30)', *Bib* 70 (1989), 153–72.

—*The Kingship of Jesus: Composition and Theology in Mark 15* (SBLDS, 66; Chico, CA: Scholars Press, 1982).

—'The Prologue as the Interpretative Key to Mark's Gospel', *JSNT* 34 (1988), 3–20.

May, D.M., 'Mark 3.20-35 From the Perspective of Shame / Honor', *BTB* 17 (1987), 83–87.

Meier, J.P., 'The Circle of the Twelve: Did it exist during Jesus' Public Ministry?', *JBL* 116 (1997), 635–72.

Meltzer, F., 'A Response to Rene Girard's Reading of Salome', *New Literary History* 15 (1984), 325–31.

Metzger, B.M., *A Textual Commentary on the Greek New Testament* (London: United Bible Societies, 1975).

Meye, R.P., *Jesus and the Twelve* (Grand Rapids: Eerdmans, 1968).

Mitchell, J.L., *Beyond Fear and Silence. A Feminist-Literary Reading of Mark* (London: Continuum, 2001).

Motyer, S., 'The Rending of the Veil: A Markan Pentecost?', *NTS* 33 (1987), 155–57.

Munro, W., 'The Anointing of Mark 14.3-9 and John 12.1-8' (SBLSP 1; ed. P.J. Achtemeier; Missoula, MT: Scholars Press, 1979).

—'Women Disciples in Mark?', *CBQ* 44 (1982), 225–41.

Myers, C., *Binding the Strong Man: A Political Reading of Mark's Story of Jesus* (Maryknoll, NY: Orbis Books, 1988).

Nineham, D.E., *Saint Mark* (Pelican New Testament Commentaries; Middlesex: Penguin Books, 1963).

Osborne, B.A.E., 'Peter: Stumbling-Block and Satan', *NovT* 15 (1973), 187–90.

Painter, J., *Mark's Gospel: Worlds in Conflict* (London: Routledge, 1996).

—'When is a House not Home? Disciples and Family in Mark 3:13-35', *NTS* 45 (1999), 498–513.

Perkinson, J., 'A Canaanite Word in the Logos of Christ; or The Difference the Syrophoenician Woman Makes to Jesus', *Semeia* 75 (1996), 61–85.

Pesch, R., *Das Markusevangelium* (2 vols.; HTKNT, 2; Freiburg: Herder, 1976).

Petersen, N.R., 'When is the End not an End? Literary Reflections on the Ending of Mark's Narrative', *Int* 34 (1980), 151–66.

Plaskow, J., 'Anti-Judaism in Feminist Christian Interpretation', in E. Schüssler Fiorenza (ed.), *Searching the Scriptures* (New York: Crossroad, 1993), I, 117–29.

—*Standing at Sinai: Judaism from a Feminist Perspective* (San Francisco: Harpers, 1991).

Pokorny, P., 'From a Puppy to a Child: Some Problems of Contemporary Biblical Exegesis Demonstrated from Mark 7.24-30/ Matt 15.21-8', *NTS* 41 (1995), 321–37.

Pomeroy, S.B., *Goddesses, Whores, Wives and Slaves: Women in Classical Antiquity* (London: Halle, 1976).

Räisänen, H., 'Jesus and the Food Laws: Reflections on Mark 7:15', *JSNT* 16 (1982), 79–100.

Reploh, K.G., *Markus, Lehrer der Gemeinde* (SBM, 9; Stuttgart: Katholisches Bibelwerk, 1969).

Rhoads, D.M., 'Jesus and the Syrophoenician Woman in Mark: A Narrative-Critical Study', *JAAR* 62 (1994), 343–75.

—'Losing Life for Others in the Face of Death. Mark's Standards of Judgement', *Int* 47 (1993), 358–69.

Rhoads, D.M., and D. Michie, *Mark as Story: An Introduction to the Narrative of a Gospel* (Philadelphia: Fortress Press, 1982).

Ricci, C., *Mary Magdalene and Many Others* (Kent: Burns & Oates, 1994).

Riches, J.K., *Conflicting Mythologies. Identity Formation in the Gospels of Mark and Matthew* (Edinburgh: T. & T. Clark, 2000).

—*Jesus and the Transformation of Judaism* (London: Darton, Longman & Todd, 1980).

Ringe, S.H., 'A Gentile Woman's Story', in A. Loades (ed.), *Feminist Theology: A Reader* (London: SCM Press, 1985), 49–57.

—'A Gentile Woman's Story Revisited: Rereading Mark 7.24-31', in A.J. Levine (ed.), *A Feminist Companion to Mark* (Sheffield: Sheffield Academic Press, 2001).

Robinson, J.M., *The Problem of History in Mark* (London: SCM Press, 1957).

Rouselle, A., *Porneia: On Desire and the Body in Antiquity* (Oxford: Basil Blackwell, 1988).

Rowland, C., *The Open Heaven: A Study of Apocalyptic in Judaism and Early Christianity* (New York: Crossroad, 1982).

Russell, D.S., *The Method and Message of Jewish Apocalyptic 200 B.C-A.D. 100* (London: SCM Press, 1964).

Sabin, M., 'Women Transformed: The Ending of Mark is the Beginning of Wisdom', *CrosCurr* 48 (1998), 149–68.

Sanders, E.P., *The Historical Figure of Jesus* (London: Penguin Books, 1993).

—*Jesus and Judaism* (London: SCM Press, 1985).
—*Judaism: Practice and Belief 63 B.C.E.-66 C.E.* (London: SCM Press, 1992).
Schierling, M.J., 'Women as Leaders in the Marcan Communities', *Listening* 15 (1980), 250–56.
Schmitt, J.J., 'Women in Mark's Gospel: An Early Christian View of Woman's Role', *BT* 19 (1981), 228–33.
Schottroff, L., *Let the Oppressed Go Free: Feminist Perspectives on the New Testament*. (trans. A.S. Kider; Louisville: Westminster John Knox Press, 1993).
—*Lydia's Impatient Sisters: A Feminist Social History of Early Christianity* (Louisville: Westminster John Knox Press, 1995).
—'Women as Followers of Jesus in New Testament Times: An Exercise in Socio-Historical Exegesis of the Bible', in N.K. Gottwald (ed.), *The Bible and Liberation* (Maryknoll, NY: Orbis Books, 1983), 418–27.
Schüssler Fiorenza, E., *Bread not Stone: the Challenge of Feminist Biblical Interpretation* (Boston: Beacon Press, 1984).
—'Defending the Center, Trivialising the Margins', H. Räisänen (ed.), *Reading the Bible in the Global Village* (Atlanta: Scholars Press, 2000).
—'The Ethics of Biblical Interpretation: Decentering Biblical Scholarship', *JBL* 107 (1988), 3–17.
—*In Memory of Her: A Feminist Theological Reconstruction of Christian Origins* (New York: Crossroad, 1985).
Schwank, B., 'Neue Funde in Nabatäerstädten und ihre Bedeutung für die neutestamentliche Exegese', *NTS* 29 (1983), 429–35.
Schweitzer, A., *The Mystery of the Kingdom of God: the Secret of Jesus' Messiahship and Passion* (London: A. & C. Black, 1925).
Schweizer, E., *The Good News according to Mark* (trans. D.H. Madvig; London: SPCK, 1971).
Scroggs, R., and K.I. Groff, 'Baptism in Mark: Dying and Rising with Christ', *JBL* 92 (1973), 531–48.
Selvidge, M.J., '"And Those Who Followed Feared" (Mark 10:32)', *CBQ* 45 (1983), 396–400.
—'Mark 5:25-34 and Leviticus 15:19-20: A Reaction to Restrictive Purity Regulations', *JBL* 103 (1984), 619–23.
Setzer, C., 'Excellent Women: Female Witness to the Resurrection', *JBL* 116 (1997), 259–72.
Sherwood, Y., 'Feminist Scholarship', in *The Oxford Illustrated History of the Bible* (Oxford: Oxford University Press, 2001), 296–315.
Smith, M., *Jesus the Magician* (New York: Harper & Row, 1978).
Standaert, B., *L'Évangile selon Marc. Composition et Genre Littéraire* (Nijmegen: Stichting Studentenpers, 1978).
Starobinski, J., 'An Essay in Literary Analysis-Mark 5:1-20', *EcumRev* 23 (1971), 377–97.
Stemberger, G., 'Appendix IV Galilee—Land of Salvation?', in W.D. Davies, *The Gospel and the Land: Early Christianity and Jewish Territorial Doctrine* (Berkley: University of California Press, 1974), 409–38.
Stock, K., *Boten aus dem Mit-Ihm-Sein. Das Verhältnis zwischen Jesus und den Zwölf nach Markus* (AnBib, 70; Rome: Pontifical Biblical Institute, 1975).
Stone, M.E., *Fourth Ezra* (Minneapolis: Fortress Press, 1990).
Sugirtharajah, R.S., ' "For You Always Have the Poor With You": An Example of Hermeneutics of Suspicion', *AJT* 4 (1990), 102–107.
—'The Syrophoenician Woman', *ExpTim* 98 (1986), 13–15.
—'The Widow's Mites Revalued', *ExpTim* 103 (1991), 42–43.
Swartley, W.M., 'The Role of Women in Mark's Gospel: A Narrative Analysis', *BTB* 27 (1997), 16–22.

Swidler, L., *Biblical Affirmations of Woman* (Philadelphia: Westminister Press, 1979).
Tannehill, R.C., 'The Disciples in Mark: The Function of a Narrative Role', *JR* 57 (1977), 386–405.
Taylor, V., *The Gospel according to Saint Mark* (London: Macmillan, 1952).
Telford, W.R., *The Barren Temple and the Withered Tree: A Redaction-Critical Analysis of the Cursing of the Fig-tree Pericope in Mark's Gospel and its Relation to the Cleansing of the Temple Tradition* (JSNTSup, 1; Sheffield: JSOT Press, 1980).
Theissen, G., *The First Followers of Jesus: a Sociological Analysis of the Earliest Christianity* (London: SCM Press, 1978).
—*The Gospels in Context: Social and Political History in the Synoptic Tradition* (Minneapolis: Fortress Press, 1991).
—*The Miracle Stories of the Early Christian Tradition* (SNTW; Edinburgh: T. & T. Clark, 1983).
—*Social Reality and the Early Christians. Theology, Ethics, and the World of the New Testament* (Edinburgh: T. & T. Clark, 1993).
—*Sociology of Early Palestinian Christianity* (Philadelphia: Fortress Press, 1978).
Thrall, M.E., 'Elijah and Moses in Mark's Account of the Transfiguration', *NTS* 16 (1970), 305–17.
Tolbert, M.A., 'Mark', in C.A. Newsom and S.H. Ringe (eds.), *The Women's Bible Commentary* (London: SPCK, 1992), 263–74.
—*Sowing the Gospel: Mark's World in Literary-Historical Perspective* (Minneapolis: Fortress Press, 1989).
Toorn, K., B. Becking, and P.W. van der Horst (eds.), *Dictionary of Deities and Demons in the Bible* (Leiden: E.J. Brill, 1995).
Tyson, J.B., 'The Blindness of the Disciples in Mark', *JBL* 80 (1961), 261–68.
Van Iersel, B.M.F., 'The Gospel according to St. Mark—Written for a Persecuted Community?', *NedTT* 34 (1980), 15–36.
—*Mark: A Reader-Response Commentary* (trans. W.H. Bisscheroux; JSNTSup, 164; Sheffield: Sheffield Academic Press, 1998).
Wainwright, E., *Towards a Feminist Critical Reading of the Gospel according to Matthew* (Berlin: Walter de Gruyter, 1991).
Watts, R.E., 'Jesus' Death, Isaiah 53, and Mark 10:45; A Crux Revisited', in W.H. Bellinger, Jr and W.R. Farmer (eds.), *Jesus and the Suffering Servant, Isaiah 53 and Christian Origins* (Harrisburg: Trinity Press, 1998), 125–51.
Weeden, T.J., 'The Heresy That Necessitated Mark's Gospel', *ZNW* 59 (1968), 145–58.
—*Mark: Traditions in Conflict* (Philadelphia: Fortress Press, 1971).
Wegner, J.R., *Chattel or Person? The Status of Women in the Mishnah* (Oxford: Oxford University Press, 1988).
Wilson, S.G., *Related Strangers. Jews and Christians 70-170 C.E.* (Minneapolis: Fortress Press, 1995).
Witherington, B., *Women in the Ministry of Jesus: a Study of Jesus' Attitudes to Women and their Roles as Reflected in his Earthly Life* (Cambridge: Cambridge University Press, 1984).
Wrede, W., *The Messianic Secret* (trans. J.C. Greig; Cambridge: J. Clarke, 1971 [1901]).
Wright, A.G., 'The Widow's Mite: Praise or Lament?—A Matter of Context', *CBQ* 44 (1982), 256–65.
Yadin, Y., J.C. Greenfield, and A. Yardeni, 'Babatha's *Ketubba*', *IEJ* 44 (1994), 75–101.

INDEXES

INDEX OF REFERENCES

BIBLE

Index of Authors